Charles Bernard Gibson

Historical Portraits of Irish Chieftains and Anglo-Norman Knights

Charles Bernard Gibson

Historical Portraits of Irish Chieftains and Anglo-Norman Knights

ISBN/EAN: 9783337294588

Printed in Europe, USA, Canada, Australia, Japan

Cover: Foto ©ninafisch / pixelio.de

More available books at **www.hansebooks.com**

HISTORICAL PORTRAITS

OF

IRISH CHIEFTAINS

AND

ANGLO-NORMAN KNIGHTS.

BY THE

Rev. CHARLES B. GIBSON, M.R.I.A.,

AUTHOR OF THE HISTORY OF THE COUNTY AND CITY OF CORK;
LAST EARL OF DESMOND; PRINCESS OF BREFNEY; BEYOND THE ORANGE RIVER;
LIFE AMONGST CONVICTS, &C.

"Lives of great men, all remind us,
We can make our lives sublime;
And departing, leave behind us,
Footprints on the sands of Time."
LONGFELLOW.

LONDON:
LONGMANS, GREEN, AND CO.
———
1871.

TO THE MOST NOBLE
THE MARQUIS OF KILDARE, M.R.I.A.

My Lord Marquis,

Of all the Anglo-Norman Knights that invaded Ireland, your ancestors rank amongst the bravest and most chivalrous; I therefore think it fitting to dedicate a work which treats of the Irish Invasion, to your lordship, a noble representative of the Geraldine race.

But you have other claims, besides that of noble descent. You have fairly won your spurs in the field of Irish literature. Your *Earls of Kildare* will always rank as a valuable and interesting contribution to Irish History. I should have been glad, had this volume of Historical Portraits of Irish Chieftains and Anglo-Norman Knights, been more worthy of your lordship's acceptance.

With the sincere desire and prayer that the Kildare Branch of the Geraldine tree, may be ever green and fruitful,

    I have the honour to remain,
        My Lord Marquis,
            Your most obedient Servant,
                CHARLES BERNARD GIBSON.

London, June, 1871.

PREFACE.

An attempt to write History in the attractive form of HISTORICAL PORTRAITS, will, of course, be discountenanced by the "*Dry-as-Dust*" School; but we know of no other mode of dealing with periods of Ancient History, intended for the public, and not for the learned, exclusively. This is true of early Grecian and Roman History, in the production of which the imagination has had some share.

No man, without some kind of imagination, should attempt to write ancient history, for its materials present a dark chaos, from which such a mind alone can produce light and order. There are periods of history which can be read by the light or illumination of romance, only. Mr. Hallam, speaking of the Visigoths, says, "I hold the annals of barbarians so unworthy of remembrance, that I will not detain the reader by naming one Sovereign of that obscure race."

But let Mr. Hallam select a Goth, who may be thought, fairly, to represent the nation, or tribe, and let him tell us all he knows of his personal history, with all the old traditional gossip he can pick up respecting him, and the reader will thank him for the portrait. Attila the Hun, with his large head, imperious will, and dragon-like love of beautiful women, makes an interesting portrait, in the hands of Gibbon, the Historian; but Mr. Hallam's taste, or power, did not lie in this department.

We confess it requires the magic power of the Wizard of the North, to call up and impart individuality to the heroes of the eleventh, twelfth, thirteenth, and fourteenth centuries, and the rapid and careful pen of a Bulwer, to sketch the features of those warlike kings and chieftains, as they pass swiftly through the pages of history, or lie stiff and shrouded in the annals of their age, for they are all alike fierce in aspect, and blood-begrimed. The marks of brutality which would cause any one of those heroes to stand out prominently on the pages of modern history, were too common, in their own time, to create surprise, or give distinction. It was the high and calm brow of an Alfred, the statesman-like bearing of a Harold, and the mild face of a Confessor, that appeared singular at this epoch, and made the principal figure on the canvas.

It must be borne in mind, that during the rude and fierce period to which we refer, the history of the time was little more than the history of the reigning sovereign or chieftain; that it was, in fact, little more than a history of his own making, and could not fail to reflect the principal lineaments of his character; so that to bring out or develope his individuality, is to lighten or illuminate the dark age in which he lived, and ruled. Holding this to be the case, I have attempted to write the history of the Anglo-Norman Invasion of Ireland, in the form of HISTORICAL PORTRAITS.

HISTORICAL PORTRAITS

OF

IRISH CHIEFTAINS AND ANGLO-NORMAN KNIGHTS.

CHAPTER I.

NORMAN INVASION—CIVIL STATE OF IRELAND, COMPARED WITH ENGLAND—MALACHY—BRIAN BORU—THE DANES—THE DEATH OF TURGESIUS.

THE Anglo-Norman invasion of Ireland during the reign of Henry II., did not take place till more than a hundred years after the conquest of England, by William I. Whether it was, that Irish "iniquities were not full"—England, in some things, is a century in advance of Ireland,—or that the latter country was unworthy of a Norman lord or ruler at that time, will depend altogether on the views taken of the political and social effects of the invasion, which some writers have erroneously styled "the conquest of Ireland."

Some seem to doubt whether Ireland has as yet been conquered; and we are not surprised at these doubts. Sir John Davis, the Irish Attorney-General of James the First, wrote a work, which was published in 1613—that is about 440 years after the Anglo-Norman invasion—entitled *A Discoverie of the True Causes why Ireland was never entirely Subdued*. We have no hesitation in pronouncing this book one of the ablest, if not the ablest, work ever penned on Irish affairs.

"The first attempt to conquer this kingdom," writes Sir John, "was but an adventure of a few private gentlemen. Fitz-Stephen and Fitz-Gerald first broke the ice, with a party of 390 men. The Earl Strongbow followed with 112 more, whose good success upon the sea-coasts of Leinster and Munster drew over the king in person the next year, *cum quingentis militibus*, as Giraldus Cambrensis reporteth; which, if they were but 500 soldiers, seemeth too small a train for so great a prince.

"But admit they were 500 knights, yet because in those days every knight was not a commander of a regiment or company, but most of them served as private men—sometimes 100 knights under a spear, as appeareth by the lists of the ancient armies,—we cannot conjecture his army to have been so great, as might suffice to conquer all Ireland, being divided into so many principalities, and having so many hydreas heads, as it had at that time."

These hydra heads displayed the capacity, for the space of four or five hundred years, of growing up as fast as they were chopped off; so that it really was not till near the death of Queen Elizabeth that the conquest *seemed* complete; it was not till then that Sir George Carew was enabled to write his *Pacata Hibernia*—a name that seemed intended as a motto for Ireland's tomb,—but from that time, to the present, one rebellion, or attempt at rebellion, has continued to spring so rapidly and phœnix-like from the ashes of that which preceded it, that we almost hesitate, in this year of Grace 1871, to assert that Ireland is even yet *subjected;* not, at least, in the sense of all its inhabitants being loyal *subjects.*

"The defects," writes Sir John Davis, "which hindred the perfection of the conquest of Ireland were of two kinds, and consisted, first, in the faint prosecution of the warre, and next, in the looseness of the civill Government."

He mentions a third impediment to the conquest. "A barbarous country," he says, "is not so easily conquered as a civil; whereof Cæsar had experience in his wars against the Gauls, Germans, and Britains, who were subdued to the Roman empire with far greater difficulty than the rich"—and, he might have added, settled and civilised—"kingdoms of Asia."

Camden, in his *Itinerary*, describes the English Conqueror William I. as standing on the high cliffs of Wales, which command the Wicklow mountains, in Ireland, and saying, with something of the profane boasting of Artaxerxes, "I will have the ships of my kingdom brought hither, wherewith I will make a bridge to invade this land." When Murchardt, king of Leinster, heard this boast, he asked, "Hath the king, in his great threatening, inserted the words, *If it please God?*" "No," was the reply. "Then, said Murchardt, seeing this king putteth his trust only in man, and not in God, I fear not his coming." When this was told to William, he frowned, and bit his thumb.

Sir John Davis, in showing the necessity of the strong arm of the warrior, such as William the Conqueror, in preparing the field for the legislator and civil ruler, says:—"The husbandman must first break the land before it can be made capable of good seede; when it is thoroughly broken and manured, if he do not, forthwith, cast good seede into it, it will grow wilde againe, and beare nothing but weeds. So a barbarous country must be first broken by a warre, before it will be capable of good government; and when it is fully subdued and conquered, if it be not well planted and governed, after the conquest, it will, eft-soones, return to the former barbarisme."

It cannot be said, as it respects the Norman Conquest of England, that there was any "faint prosecution of the war." William of Malmesbury seems to view the English Conquest as the work of a Mightier arm than that of the Conqueror; to esteem it " an extraordinary work of Providence, that the English should have given up all for lost, after the battle of Hastings, where only a small, though brave army, had perished." Henry of Huntingdon speaks even more emphatically :—"In the year of Grace 1060, the Divine Ruler accomplished what he had before purposed respecting the English nation. He gave them up to the Normans, a cruel and wise people, to be exterminated."*

"God sees the wretched people," says the Saxon chronicler, "most unjustly oppressed; first they are despoiled of their possessions, and then butchered. Whoever had any property, lost it by heavy taxes and unjust decrees." Again, "It is not easy to relate the miseries sustained, at this time, by England, from royal exactions."—*Chro. Saxon*, p. 228.

The English nobles and clergy were as bad as the king. "The nobles and bishops built castles, and filled them with devilish and wicked men; and oppressed the people cruelly, torturing them for their money. They

* "Millesimo et sexagesimo sexto anno gratiæ, perfecit dominator Deus de gente Anglorum quod diu cogitaverat. Genti namque Normanorum asperæ et callidæ traditit eos ad exterminandum."

imposed taxes on towns, and when they had exhausted them of everything they set them on fire. You might travel a day, and not find a man living in a town. If two or three men [Normans] were seen riding up to a town, all its inhabitants left it, taking them for plunderers. And this lasted, growing worse and worse, through Stephen's reign. Men said, openly, that Christ and his saints were asleep."—*Chro. Saxon*, p. 239.

A more complete proof of this state of things results from the comparative condition of English towns in the reign of the Confessor, and at the compilation of Doomsday Book.* At the former period, there were, in York, 1,607 inhabited houses, at the latter, 967; at the former period, in Oxford, 727, at the latter, 243. Of 172 houses of Dorchester, 100 were destroyed; of 243 in Derby, 103; of 487 in Chester, 205. Some towns suffered less, but all presented a decreased and decaying population.

The weight and severity of the Norman yoke was greatly relieved in the time of Henry II., whom Hallam styles "the best of these monarchs;" and the reign of his son John—who perhaps was the worst—is distinguished by the granting of the MAGNA CHARTA. It is worthy of remark that the noble knights who invaded Ireland were the same class of men, and some of them the same men, who afterwards wrested the sword of oppression from the hands of this cowardly prince, and taught him to respect the liberties of the people.

If the unsettled state of England in 1064, demanded the strong and stern rule of a conqueror, like William

---

* *The Compilation of Doomsday Book* was commenced in 1080, and finished in 1086. Edward the Confessor reigned from 1041 to 1066.

of Normandy, the necessity was even greater in Ireland in 1170. "Since the death of Malachy," observes O'Conor, "this nation has been falling into a state of political reprobation. Each province set up for itself, the monarchy grew indifferent, and the monarch hateful to the majority of the chieftains. *When Roderick mounted the throne, the measure of their iniquity was full.*"

I have pored over Irish Annals for years to discover when and why it was that Ireland attained the high appellation of "*the Island of Saints.*" Had there been real saints in the land before the introduction of Christianity, we should say it gained the high appellation during the reign of Gedhe Ollghothach, in Anno Mundi 3960, for "observers of antiquity affirm of him that the conversation of his subjects in general, in his time, *was as sweet a harmony to one another as any musick,* because they lived together in such concord, amity, and atonement among themselves, that there was no discord or strife heard to grow between them, for any cause whatsoever.

An Irish poet gives us a glowing description of the condition of Ireland during the reign of the monarch Cathaeir Mor of the Wine-red hand :—

>"I walked entranced through a land of morn ;
>   The sun, with wondrous excess of light,
>Shone down, and glanced over seas of corn,
>   And lustrous gardens aleft and right.
>Even in the clime of resplendent Spain
>   Beams no such sun upon such a land ;
>But it was the time, 'twas in the reign
>   Of Cathaeir Mor of the Wine-red hand.
>
>"Anon stood nigh by my side, a man
>   Of princely aspect, and port sublime.

Here, queried I, 'Oh! my Lord and Khan,
   What clime is this, and what golden time?'
When he—' The clime is a clime to praise,
   The clime is Erin's, the green and bland ;
And it is the time, these be the days
   Of Cathaeir Mor of the Wine-red hand.'

"Then I saw thrones, and circling fires,
   And a dome rose near me, as by a spell,
Whence flowed the tones of silver lyres
   And many voices, in wreathed swell ;
And their thrilling chime fell on mine ears,
   As the heavenly hymn of an angel band—
It's now the time, these be the years
   Of Cathaeir Mor of the Wine-red hand."

But this happy state of things did not continue. Cathaeir Mor, or Cathaeir the Great, of the Wine-red hand, was slain in battle, in A.D. 122, long before any Christian saint had set foot in Ireland. His death is thus noticed in Irish Annals: "Age of Christ, 122, Cathaeir Mor, after having been three years King over Ireland, was slain by Conn"—that is "Conn of the Hundred Battles," who succeeded to the chief kingship. The effect of Cathaeir Mor's death on the state of Ireland is thus eloquently expressed, in the latter part of the poem, from which I have quoted :—

"I sought the hall, and, behold, a change
   From light to darkness, from joy to woe!
Kings, nobles, all, looked aghast and strange ;
   The minstrel group sat in dumbest show !
Had some great crime wrought this dread amaze,
   This terror ? None seemed to understand!
'Twas then the time, we were in the days
   Of Cathaeir Mor of the Wine-red hand.

"I again walked forth ; but lo ! the sky
   Showed fleckt with blood, and an alien sun

> Glared from the north, and there stood on high,
>   Amid his shorn beams—a skeleton!
> It was by the stream of the castled Maine,
>   One autumn eve, in the Teuton's land,
> That I dreamed this dream of the time and reign,
>   Of Cathaeir Mor of the Wine-red hand."

Feeling some hesitation in deciding for myself against the claims of Ireland to be called the "*Island of Saints,*" I wrote to Doctor O'Donovan, of the Four Masters, and the following is his reply:—"I have been long under the impression that this appellation was given by some foreign writer, in consequence of the number of missionaries which Ireland sent abroad from the sixth to the ninth centuries. I do not believe that the name was applied to Ireland on account of the peace and tranquillity which, at any period, reigned among the laity. If Ireland ever deserved the appellation of which the bards boast, 'Erin, pure Island of Saints,' it must have been during the seventh and eighth centuries. I am a bad believer in saints, or ancient civilisations, for which I must suffer some thousands of years in purgatory. I hope you will weigh this subject well, which is of great importance." Doctor O'Donovan gives the correct clue to the difficulty, where he says, "the appellation was given in consequence of the *number of missionaries* sent abroad." In the first ages of the Christian Church the term "saint" was applied to *all believers*. In course of time it was confined to *churchmen*. It is so employed in the *Annals of Ireland*. [See *Age of Christ*, 664.] The term might be correctly rendered *Island of Monks*, for Ireland was as much the Land of Monks in the eighth and ninth centuries, as are Italy, Spain, and Portugal in the nineteenth.

But every country under heaven has had its golden age. We are told that Rollo, the great ancestor of the Conqueror, suspended a valuable bracelet from an oak, in a forest near the Seine, and that it remained there for three years. Bede says of the kingdom of Northumberland, in the reign of Edwin, that "a woman with a new-born child might travel over the whole island without fear of insult." And it is recorded in the Four Masters, under date A.D. 1167, that "women used to travel Ireland alone." The poet Moore has presented us with one memorable example.

> "Rich and rare were the gems she wore,
> And a bright gold ring on her wand she bore;
> But oh! her beauty was far beyond
> Her sparking gems or snow-white wand.
>
> "Lady! dost thou not fear to stray,
> So lone and lovely, through this bleak way?
> Are Erin's sons so good or so cold,
> As not to be tempted by woman or gold?
>
> "Sir Knight! I feel not the least alarm,
> No son of Erin will offer me harm,
> For though they love women and golden store,
> Sir Knight, they love honour and virtue more!
>
> "On she went, and her maiden smile,
> In safety lighted her round the green isle;
> And blest for ever is she who relied
> Upon Erin's honour and Erin's pride!"

If the women who "travelled alone," in the twelfth century, were anything like this vision of beauty, God must have had them in His special keeping.

MALACHY AND BRIAN BOROIMHE.

The reigns of Malachy and Brian Boroimhe are considered exceptions to the general system of misrule, anarchy, and bloodshed, which devastated the kingdom. These *Grande Monarchs* are looked upon as the very *beau ideal* of Irish kings and heroes; and their names are so associated with the poetry of the country, that we almost hesitate to break the spell; but the interests of truth sometimes demand the sacrifice of poetical fiction.

The Abbé Macgeoghegan says that O'Melaghlin, or Malachy, King of Meath, the same who

> "Wore the collar of gold,
> Which he took from the proud invader,"

"gave himself up to pleasure, and neglected the welfare of the nation." It was, therefore, decreed that he should be dethroned, and the sceptre transferred to Brian Boru, King of Munster.

"The collar of Tomar," says Moore, in his History of Ireland, was a golden torque, which the monarch Malachy took from the neck of a Danish chieftain, whom he had conquered. Dr. O'Donovan—a far higher authority than Mr. Moore—says that "*there was no Tomar in Malachy's time.*" The Danish chieftain, who wore this famous golden torc, or collar, was slain near Castledermot, in A.D. 846, that is about 150 years before the monarch Malachy flourished. This Tomar was the ancestor of the Danish kings of Dublin. Tomar's golden collar was preserved by the Danes of Dublin, and worn, perhaps, by the chief magistrates of that city to the year A.D. 994, when it was carried off by Malachy, who appears to have plundered the Danish corporation chest, from which he took both collar and sword. The Four Masters, under date 994, say, "The ring of Tomar, and the sword of Carlus, were carried away by force, by Malachy, from the Foreigners of Ath-cliath, *i.e.*, the Danes of Dublin. Eight years after this, in A.D. 1002, Brian Boroimhe, or Boru, the son of Kennedy, King of Limerick, assumed the chief sovereignty of Ireland, deposing the legitimate monarch, Malachy. The *Annals of Ireland* say that Brian Boru was seventy-five years old at this time. This probably is a mistake. If it be correct, he must have been twenty-four years older than Malachy, whom he deposed.

Brian Boroimhe, after a reign of eleven or twelve years of anarchy and bloodshed, fell at the famous battle of Clontarf, near Dublin. Malachy, who, on the death of Brian, became reinstated as chief monarch of Ireland, is reported, by Keating, to have witnessed the battle, and to have acted a cowardly and treacherous part. But some of the annalists assert there was no treachery on the part of the dethroned monarch, although it was his interest to support the Danes.

We believe the decree, or law, deposing Malachy, was that of *lamh lathar*, or of the "strong hand." It will surprise, and even shock, some Irish readers, to learn, that when Brian Boroimhe, the very Robert Bruce of Irish history, had conceived the ambitious design of deposing the chief monarch, Malachy, *he joined with the Danes against him*. The intimate connexion existing between the Irish chieftains and Danes, or Scandinavians, may be gathered from the fact that Malachy II., monarch of Ireland, married the daughter of Olaf, the Danish king of Dublin; and that on the death of Olaf, Brian Boru married his widow. The daughter of Brian was married to Sitric III., " of the

Silken Beard," the Danish king who fought against his own father-in-law, Baron Boru, at the battle of Clontarf, on Palm Sunday A.D. 1014.

Sitric reigned for forty years, as Danish king of Dublin, and died on a pilgrimage to Rome. Many of his coins are still extant, an evidence that these Norsemen were no barbarians.

Brian's wrath against the Danes was first aroused by a domestic, or family injury; by the treachery of Ivor, king of the Danes of Limerick, who abetted and aided an Irish chieftain, named Molloy, in the murder of Mahon, Brian's brother, at a feast at Bruree, in the county Limerick. We have a curious account of this murder, and its effects on Brian's mind, in an old Irish book, called *The War of the Gaels, with the Danes.*

Donovan and Molloy, chiefs of Desmond, perceiving the increasing power of the O'Briens, and fearing that if it were not checked, the crown of Munster would remain in the family for ever, united with Ivor, king of the Danes of Limerick, to destroy Mahon, who was then king of Thomond and Ormond. Ivor suggested that Donovon should invite Mahon to a banquet at his house at Bruree. Although Mahon suspected the loyalty of his host, he accepted the invitation, for "his safety had been guaranteed by Columb MacKiergan, successor of St. Barry, bishop of Cork, and other of the clergy of Munster," in other words, by solemn oaths, in which the names of these pious men were invoked. He therefore attended the feast, where he was seized and delivered into the hands of his ruthless foes, Molloy and Ivor, who were waiting for him in a neighbouring wood, with a body of Irish and Danish troops. Molloy ordered his people instantly to despatch him. His order was obeyed. "A bright and sharp sword" was plunged into his heart, and his blood stained St. Barry's Gospel,* which he held in his hand, to protect him by its sanctity. Two of the clergy of St. Barry witnessed the transaction from a hillock. It is said that when Mahon received the stroke, he cast the gospel from his hand, with so much force, that it struck the breast of one of the priests of Cork. "What hast thou done?" demanded the priest of Molloy. "Cure that man if he come to thee," was the sneering reply. The priest, in his wrath, cursed Molloy bitterly, predicting that his grave would be dug near the side of the hill where they stood, and that the sun would never shine upon it. The story goes that Molloy lost his eye-sight, was slain in a hut, constructed of alder trees, and buried on the north side of a hill, in a spot where the sun never shines. We learn from the Dublin copy of the Annals of Innisfallen, that Molloy was slain by Morough, son of Brian Boru.

Brian Boru is said to have given expression to his sorrowful revenge for his brother's death, in an elegy, which we have taken the liberty of paraphrasing, with something *more* than a poet's licence.

> "My heart within this breast had burst,
> If vengeance I had longer nursed:
> A king and brother! deed accursed!
> Oh! Mahon, generous and brave,
> I little thought this early grave,
> Would hide thy manly frame;

* "*St. Barry's Gospel.*"—There is no such manuscript or book now in existence. Doctors Todd and O'Donovan, of Trinity College, agree with me in thinking it must have been a copy of the Four Gospels, written by the priests of Saint Finn Barr's of Cork.

> Wouldst thou hadst fallen behind thy shield,
> A victor in some bloody field,
> And poets sang thy fame!
> Mahon, confiding in a knave,
> Saw foeman's face in the clear wave,
> That gave his own.
> The Church her safety pledged in vain;
> What power divine could bind a Dane,
> With breast of stone.
> The blood that warmed thy tender heart,
> Of Barry's Gospel stained a part—
> Ochone! Ochone!
> *Their* blood shall flow for this vile deed;
> I'll crush these vipers and their seed!
> Now, Ivor, you or I shall bleed."

There is an old harp in the museum of Trinity College, Dublin, called "Brian Boru's harp." Doctor Petrie says it belongs to a later period; but I believe there can be no doubt that this Irish monarch, like Richard Cœur de Lion, used the harp, or ceannaircruit, as well as the sword and battle-axe. The tradition of the harp is that it was sent to Rome after the death of Brian, who fell at Clontarf, where it remained more than five centuries, and was then presented by one of the Popes to Henry VIII., by whom it was returned to Ireland, "to be figured on his coins, in compliment to the musical taste of the Irish." The harp, when perfect, had thirty strings.

Brian proved himself as powerless in the subjugation of the Danes, as in the restoration of order among the Irish chieftains. The battle of Clontarf was not a decisive event, like Bannockburn, or Waterloo. We very much doubt that it was a decided victory. The Danes held Dublin after the battle. From it we may date the fall of the Brian Boru dynasty.

An old Norse, or Danish saga, says that the day before the battle, Odin, the god of war, descended from the clouds on a grey horse, and held council with the King, the Queen-mother, Earl Sigurd and Brodin, a deacon, who had denied the faith, and turned sorcerer. Another seer saw twelve witches, entering a thicket or wood, mounted on twelve broomsticks, or black horses —I forget which. On peering through the trees, he saw them hard at work at a loom with the thread of man's existence, employing a number of devilish and foul incantations, too horrible to describe. These were the Fates, or Odin's "corse-choosers," weaving the destinies of those who were to take part in the coming battle. As they wove they chaunted their death-songs thus :—

> "Weave the crimson web of war;
> Here we go, and here we fly;
> Where our friends the conflict share,
> Where they triumph, where they die.
>
> "Low the dauntless here are laid,
> Gored with many a gaping wound,
> Fate demands a nobler head,
> Soon a king shall bite the ground.
>
> "Long his loss shall Erin weep,
> Ne'er again his likeness see;
> Long her strains in sorrow steep,
> Strains of immortality.
>
> "Horror covers all the earth,
> Clouds of carnage blot the sun;
> Sisters weave the web of death,
> Sisters cease—*the work is done.*"

Which last line means that Brian Boru had been "done for."

There is something very exciting and warlike in the affix of Boroimhe, or Borumha, or Boru. It sounds so like Aboo! Brian Aboo! would be a real battle-cry. But Brian Boru means simply "Brian of the Tribute," or Brian the Cow-Tax Gatherer. He was so styled for imposing an additional cow-tribute on Leinster, which had refused to join him against the Danes. The additional tribute consisted of 300 cows, with brass yokes; 300 steeds, 300 gold-hilted swords, and 300 purple cloaks; besides the usual tribute of 300 bullocks, 300 hogs, and 300 loads of iron. Brian imposed a tribute of 150 pipes of wine on the Danes of Dublin, and 365 pipes of red wine on the Danes of Limerick, over whom he had more immediate sway.

THE DANES OR OSTMEN.

Those who wish to understand the real state of Ireland, at the time of the Anglo-Norman invasion, must bear in mind that at that period, and for 300 years before, Ireland was possessed by two nations, namely, the Ostmen, or Danes and Norwegians, who were in possession of all the principal seaports, and the Celtic Irish, who held the interior of the country. Neither can it be stated that the contentions between the Celts and the Ostmen were more frequent or blood-thirsty than those which prevailed amongst the Celts themselves. The native Irish chieftains found the Ostmen useful traders, on whom they had to depend for foreign wines, dress, and other foreign luxuries imported into the country.

Giraldus Cambrensis states the case very clearly: "The Ostmen* did not come in ships armed for war, but in guise of peace, and under the pretext of being merchant adventurers; so that having first established themselves in the seaports of Ireland, at length, with the consent of the lords of the territory, they built several cities in these places. For as the inherent sloth of the Irish race prevented them, as we have before observed, from making any efforts to explore the seas or engage in commerce, it was deemed advisable, in a general council of the whole kingdom, that some people should be admitted into parts of the kingdom, by whose commercial industry the product of other lands might be brought into the country, in order to supply them with such articles as their own land did not furnish."

To have conquered or driven out the Danes, or Ostmen, which Brian Boru did not accomplish, would have been to destroy the only carriers or merchants of the country. But it must be borne in mind that it was only against the "Danes of Dublin," or one of the ports of Ireland, that "Brian of the Tribute" made war, whilst the Anglo-Normans, as we shall see by and by, did their best to destroy the trade of the whole kingdom. These Norman knights had but little sympathy with merchants or shop-keepers, and therefore treated them, after taking their walled towns, with the most barbarous cruelty. The Irish chieftain was more in their line. So between the Celt and the Anglo-

---

* "They are called Ostmen, in their own tongue, from a word corrupted in the Saxon language, which means *Eastern men*." They came from the North coast of Europe.— *Gir. Cam. Top. of Ireland*, chap. 43.

Norman, the best and most peaceable portion of the inhabitants of Ireland went to the wall.

This may appear to some a new view of the Irish conquest, but it is the true view. Here we have the first blow of England—not unaided by the Celt— against the trade and commerce of every port in Ireland.

Both Keating and Campion speak of a Dane or Norwegian named Turgesius who had ships on all the great lakes in Ireland. He is said to have erected a large number of those circular mounds called Danish raths. Keating says that his troops were quartered through the country, which they plundered with impunity; that they imposed on the head of every family or house a yearly tribute of an ounce of gold, and that those who did not pay had their noses split; hence the name of the tax "nose money"—in Irish, *airgiod srona*. But the oppression of this Norwegian did not end here. He had the audacity to propose that Malachy, king of Meath, should let him have his daughter as a concubine. The story is well told by Campion, from whom we conclude that the girl was a brunette. Her father, Malachy, having wit, and watching his opportunity, said, "Saving your fancy, my lord, there are divers ladies of my blood that would make sweeter wives for a king than that *brown girl*. He then began to enumerate a number of nieces and cousins "endowed with angel-like beauty, whom he painted so lively that the tyrant already doated upon them." But Turgesius is to judge for himself. "I will send you my daughter," says Malachy, "with twelve or sixteen gentlewomen, the meanest of whom is fit for an empress. When they are brought you, make your game.

She is presented, accompanied by sixteen noble youths in female apparel. Turgesius approaches to make his selection, when the young men draw their skeins and kill the tyrant and his friends on the spot. This bold deed, we are told, was followed by a general rising of the Irish against the Danes.

There is another account of this transaction which says that Turgesius was seized by the Irish and drowned in Lough Uair in 846.

This is all interesting enough, but is it true? We turn now to the real romance of Irish history, or the love of Diarmaid, King of Leinster, for Dervorgilla, Princess of Brefney.

CHAPTER II.

DIARMAID AND DERVORGILLA.

THE first great cause of the Norman Conquest of Ireland is laid to the score of woman. Ireland had its Helen and Paris, as well as Troy:—

> "The fruit of this forbidden tree
> Brought death into the world, and all our woe,
> With loss of" *Erin.*

Giraldus Cambrensis, speaking of Dervorgilla,[*] the Princess of Brefney, who eloped with Diarmaid, king of Leinster, says:—" Such is the variable and fickle nature of women, by whom all mischiefs in the world (for the most part) do happen and come, as may appear by Marcus Antonius, and the destruction of Troy."

If we are to believe some of our chroniclers, Dervorgilla was not fickle, but only too true to her first love. Macgeoghegan says she was married, against her will, to Teighernan[†] O'Rourke, Prince of Brefney, and adds, " This princess indulged a secret passion for Dermot,[‡] king of Leinster, who paid his addresses to her before her marriage." The Four Masters say that Diarmaid carried her away, "according to the advice of her brother, Melaghlin, king of Meath," and the Annals of

---

[*] *Dervorgilla,* or Dearforgil, from dear, "a daughter," and forgil, "very fair."

[†] *Teighernan,* or Tiarnan, derived from tiarna " a lord."

[‡] *Dermot,* or Diarmaid, appears to be derived from Dia, in Irish, "a god," and armaid, the genitive plural of arms, "the god of arms." Homer calls one of his heroes διὰ κρατίστος, "the godlike fighting" Diomede. Dermot, by the Irish, "is now, almost invariably, rendered " Jeremiah."—*Dr. O'Donovan.*

Clonmacnoise, that "she was procured, and induced thereunto, by her unadvised brother, Melaghlin, for some abuses of her husband, done to her before."

The death, by poison, of this young Irish king is thus described in Annals of Ireland:—"Melaghlin, son of O'Melaghlin, king of Meath, and of the greater part of Leinster, died in the 30th year of his age, of a poisonous drink, in the flood of his prosperity and reign, on the night of the festival of Brighit, after the victory of penance. The death of this man was like swine fattening by hot fruit, like a branch cut down before its blossoming."—*Four Masters*, A.D. 1155.

The "Song of O'Rourke," by our poet Moore, does cruel injustice to our Irish Helen, whom he styles "the falsest of women":—

> " While now—oh, degenerate daughter
> Of Erin, how fall'n is thy fame!
> And thro' ages of bondage and slaughter,
> Our country shall bleed for thy shame.
>
> " Already the curse is upon her,
> And strangers her valleys profane,
> They come to divide to dishonour,
> And tyrants they long will remain."

The Annals of the Four Masters, and the Annals of Clonmacnoise, place the abduction of Dervorgilla, in A.D. 1152; but we think this is a mistake. It is probable that the Four Masters took the date of this transaction from the Annals of Clonmacnoise, the earlier production.*

The dates on the margin of a *Fragment of the History*

---

* *The earlier production.*—The Annals of Clonmacnoise were compiled in 1627, and those of the Four Masters between the years 1632 and 1636.

of Ireland, attributed to Maurice Regan, secretary of Diarmaid, king of Leinster, place the abduction of Dervorgilla, "a fair and lovely lady, entirely beloved of Diarmaid," in 1167; and Diarmaid's expulsion and flight, in 1168. Here the closeness of events produces the impression that his punishment and flight were the result of his crime. This is denied by Doctors O'Conor, Leland, and O'Donovan, on the authority of Irish Annals; but we do not see how we can go outside Giraldus Cambrensis, or the *Fragment of Irish History* in Harris's *Hibernica,* of which Sir George Carew says, "This history was written by Maurice Regan, who was servant and interpreter to Dermot MacMurrough, king of Leinster; and put into French metre, by one of his familiar acquaintance; for thus he writeth in the beginning of the poem:—

> "Parsoen demande Latinner
> L'moi conta de sim Historie
> Dunt far ici la Memorie,
> Morice Regan iret celui
> Buche a buche par la alui
> Ri cest gest endita."

We shall now give Maurice Regan's account of this love affair. "Diarmaid, by letters and messengers, pursued her love with so much energy as in the end she [Dervorgilla] sent him word that she was ready to obey, and yield to his will, and appointed him a time and place where he should find her, praying him to come so strongly armed as that he might, by force, take her away with him. Diarmaid presently assembled his forces, and marched into the country of Leitrim. At Trimbruen, he found this lady, and took her away with him."

A writer of Irish romance has given the following account of the abduction; and as there is nothing improbable about it, we offer it to the reader for what it is worth. We believe it was from the *Caislean na Nua,* or the "Green Castle," on an islet of Lough Ree, the Princess of Brefney was carried away. If we can rely on the romance—which we conclude is just about as probable as the "Song of O'Rourke," by the poet Thomas Moore—Nedha, Dervorgilla's favourite maid, was in the confidence of Diarmaid, and aided him in gaining access to the princess:—

Dearforgil, the Princess of Brefney, the daughter and sister of a king (of the royal house of O'Melaghlin), sat in a deep embrasure of a window, in a small square apartment, of the *Caislean na Nua,* on the islet of Lough Ree. The evening sun was shining on her golden hair. She raised her dark eyes from her tapestry frame, looked beyond the waters of the lake, which surrounded her dwelling like a silver zone, and said, "Nedha, come hither."

Nedha approached hastily, for she had narrowly marked the princess's steady gaze across the lake.

"See you that *cairbh?*"*

"Where, lady?" inquired Nedha.

"There, beneath the trees. See, two men approach! They enter."

"I see," said Nedha; "they are, no doubt, fishers."

"I think not, Nedha. I saw the sun glinting from the helmet of the tallest. May the Virgin protect us, I hope it is not O'Rourke."

"The saints forefend! I will go to the battlements,"

* *Cairbh,* "Boat," or small ship.

replied the maid, hastening from the apartment, "and let your highness know."

The boat was pushing out from the shade of the trees, as Nedha gained the summit of the castle, from which she waved a red flag, at the appearance of which it quickly returned to the covert of the shore.

"Well, Nedha, what do you make of it? You seem to have frightened it back again."

"I cannot, as yet, say; but hope it is not O'Rourke."

"The Holy Virgin forbid!"

"It might be some of the people of O'Conor, O'Loughlin, or, *the King of Leinster*," said Nedha, emphasising the last name, and watching its effect on the countenance of Dearforgil.

"True: this part of O'Rourke's principality again forms a portion of my father's kingdom."

"Then you are no longer prisoner, and should, while the opportunity offers, make good your escape from that savage prince."

"Nedha, remember the Prince of Brefney is my husband."

"That is the reason I hate him."

"Hush, thou *caireog:** the servants may overhear thee; and I cannot trust them all. Come closer, Nedha."

Nedha approached; went on her knees; placed her arms in her mistress's lap, and gazed into her face, with an expression of mingled pertness and affection.

"Thou art a ⸺." The princess hesitated, smoothing the hair on her fair maid's forehead.

"*Cairin cais*,† thou wouldest say."

* *Cairoeg*, "Prating wench." † *Cairin cais*, "Pretty darling."

"Out with thee!" slapping her cheek.

Nedha caught her hands, held them firmly between her own, and looked up earnestly and anxiously in her face; and as she did so, two large tears started from her dark eye-balls, ran quickly over her cheeks, and fell, like pearls, upon the princess's hands.

"What ails thee, girl?" inquired Dearforgil, in surprise.

Nedha laid her face in her mistress's lap, and sobbed as if her heart would break.

"Thou art a strange girl! For what dost thou weep?"

"Nothing," said Nedha, laughing, as she flung up her head.

"Thou can'st not deceive me, Nedha: what is it?"

"I was thinking," said Nedha, looking deeply into her mistress's eyes, "if"——she weeps again.

"Well, child, 'if' what?"

"If thou wert carried hence—I should die—for I could not live without thee;" and a third time she laid down her head, and wept aloud.

"But why should'st thou think so, silly girl? and if I were, thou should'st accompany me; for there is no one living, who loves, or cares for me, like thee; or whom I love like thee"—kissing her.

"*No one?*" inquired Nedha, looking long and curiously into her mistress's face. "Think again."

The princess blushed slightly, but still replied, "*No one.*"

"I thought there was *one*," said Nedha, timidly, but slyly; "one who loved, and *still* loves thee, truly."

"Of whom do you speak?" asked the princess, with a deeper flush upon her brow.

E

"Need I mention the name of *Diarmaid, King of Leinster?*"

"What of him, child?"

"You saw a boat on yonder shore, before the sun went down?"

"Yes, what of it?"—trembling.

"The sun, you say, glinted from the helmet of the tallest of the two men?"

"Yes, who was he? Speak!"—terribly excited.

"*The King of Leinster!* He is now on the island. I saw him land. He now waits below, to see thee, and bear thee hence."

Dearforgil fainted.

CHAPTER III.

DIARMAID LEAVES IRELAND TO SEEK THE PROTECTION OF HENRY II., AGAINST O'ROURKE AND RODERICK O'CONOR, KING OF CONNAUGHT.

BUT let us now turn to the disconsolate husband, and see how he bears his sad fate, and to what quarter he looks for redress. O'Rourke, the Prince of Brefney and the husband of the "False One," full of grief and rage, addressed himself to the King of Connaught, complaining of the wrong and scorn done him by the King of Leinster, entreating his aid, in revenge of so great an outrage. Roderick O'Conor, who had assumed the title of chief monarch of Ireland,* promises the required aid, and sends messengers to Melaghlin, King of Meath, to Torkil, King of the Danes of Dublin, and other princes and potentates, to join his standard. Diarmaid, feeling his inability to contend against such numbers, seeks sanctuary in the Abbey of Fernes,† where he has a palace. From this he despatches a monk to one of his chieftains, named Murrough O'Byrne. The king follows

---

* *Assumed the title of chief monarch of Ireland.*—O'Loughlin had also assumed this title, and was supported by Diarmaid. Leland says, and, no doubt, with truth, " It was the *partisan* of O'Loughlin, who was pronounced unworthy to fill the throne of Leinster, and not the *Ravisher* of Dervorgilla.

† *Abbey of Fernes.*—Diarmaid seems all through this contest, and during the Norman invasion, to have stood well, both with Irish and English Churchmen. In the Abbey of Fernes he found a safe retreat, in the Bishop of St. David a fast friend. Leland says, " His munificence to his clergy had everywhere made him a favourite to the order."

the monk, and from the side of a wood, sees him deliver the letter. O'Byrne recognised the king, and imperiously warned him to depart. O'Byrne suffered for this, afterwards, as we shall see.

"The distressed king," continues Maurice Regan, "almost distracted with grief and anger, returned to Fernes,* [which he burned to the ground] and fearing to be betrayed there, and delivered, by his people, to the King of Connaught, resolved to abandon his country, and instantly, without delay, went to Horkeran, where he embarked for England, having, in his company, no less a man of mark than Auliffe O'Kinade, and about sixty persons.

MacGorman, who had been the King's tutor, and who was then Bishop of Kildare, is reported to have mourned his departure, in the following religious strain: —"O Virgin Mary, sad is the deed done in Erin, on this day of the calends of August. Dermot, the son of Donagh MacMurrough, King of Leinster, and of the Norsemen, has been banished over the seas by the men of Erin. Alas! alas! O Lord, what shall we do?"

Diarmaid was not exactly *banished*. He *fled* to England for protection, aid, and vengeance. With a prosperous gale, he arrived at Bristol, and was lodged, with all his company, in the house of Robert [Fitz] Harding at St. Augustine's, where, after some stay, he set out on his journey towards France, to speak with King Henry, who then had war, in that kingdom, with the French king.

* *Fernes.* "A.D. 1166. Fearna was burned by MacMurrough, for fear that the Connaught men would burn his castle and his house."— *Four Masters.*

Giraldus Cambrensis says, "The King was far away at Aquitaine."

When he came to the presence of King Henry, he related, at large, the cause of his coming, telling him, that his vassals had forsaken him, that he was forced to run into exile, beseeching him to give him aid, whereby he might be restored to his inheritance, which, if it should please him, in his goodness, to grant, he would acknowledge him to be his lord, and faithfully serve him, during his life.

"This pitiful reaction of the distressed king so much moved King Henry to compassion, as that he promised him aid, and willed him to return to Bristol, there to remain until he heard further from him ; and withall he wrote to Robert FitzHarding, requiring him to receive King Dermot and his followers, and to treat them with all the courtesy and humanity he could. Wherein Robert failed in nothing."

There is an old saying that history repeats itself. About 700 years before this, an Irish provincial king, in somewhat similar circumstances to those of Dermot, King of Leinster, went to the Roman general, then commanding in Britain, to invite him to undertake the conquest of Ireland. The circumstance is thus recorded by Tacitus :*

"Agricola had received one of the petty kings of that nation, who had been expelled for some domestic sedition.

---

* "Agricola expulsum seditione domestica unum ex regulis gentis exceperat, ac specie amicitiæ in occasionem retinebat. Saepe ex eo audivi, legione et modicis auxiliis debellari obtinerique Hiberniam posse. Idque etiam adversus Britanniam profuturum si Romana ubique arma et velut e conspectu libertas tolleretur."—*Tacitus.*

He detained him for some time. I have often heard from him that Ireland might be conquered and retained by one Roman legion and moderate supplies; and that as it regards Britain, it would be an advantage if both Roman arms and liberty were removed from their sight."

CHAPTER IV.

HENRY AND HIS PREVIOUS DESIGNS ON IRELAND—POPE ADRIAN: HIS BULL, AND RING—ABBE MACGEOGHEGAN'S NONSENSE.

NOTWITHSTANDING what is said of Henry being "so much moved," by this "pitiful reaction of the distressed king," there can be no doubt that he had anticipated his Irish ally, in the ambitious design of the conquest, not merely of Leinster, but of the whole of Ireland. But he waited his opportunity. He was too wise, or too cautious, to " outrun Providence," as Oliver Cromwell would have styled it. He waited for God to open the door; or, rather, displayed the forethought of sending John of Salisbury to Rome for the key. England has to thank Pope Adrian, who was himself an Englishman, * for the donation of Ireland.

In "Anno 1155, the king [Henry II.] cast in his mind to conquer Ireland. He saw that it was commodious for him, and considered that they were a rude and savage people. Hereupon, in his ambitious mind, he sent unto Adrian, Bishop of Rome, one John Salisbury, with others, delivering his suit to that effect. Adrian being a man of English birth, heard his ambassadors the more willingly, and considered the matter advisedly, together with his college of cardinals, and granted him his request as follows ":—

* *Adrian*, known as Nicholas Breakspear, was an Englishman, the son of a poor clerk, named Robert Chambers.

"ADRIAN BISHOP, SERVANT OF THE SERVANTS OF GOD, TO HIS DEAREST SON IN CHRIST, THE ILLUSTRIOUS KING OF ENGLAND, GREETING AND APOSTOLIC BENEDICTION:—

"Full laudably, and profitably, hath your magnificence conceived the design of propagating your glorious renown on earth, and completing your reward of eternal happiness in heaven, while, as a Catholic prince, you are intent on enlarging the borders of the Church, teaching the truth of the Christian faith to the ignorant and rude, exterminating the roots of vice, from the field of the Lord, and, for the more convenient execution of this purpose, requiring the counsel and favour of the Apostolic See; in which, the maturer your deliberation, and the greater the discretion of your procedure, by so much the happier, we trust, will be your progress, with the assistance of the Lord, as all things are used to come to a prosperous end and issue, which take their beginning from the ardour of faith and the love of religion.

"There is, indeed, no doubt, but that Ireland, and all the islands on which Christ, the Sun of Righteousness, hath shone, and which have received the doctrines of the Christian faith, do belong to the jurisdiction of St. Peter, and of the Holy Roman Church, as your Excellency also doth acknowledge. And therefore, we are the more solicitous to propagate the righteous plantation of faith, in this land, and the branch acceptable to God, as we have the secret conviction of conscience, that this is more especially our bounden duty.

"You, then, most dear Son in Christ, have signified to us your desire to enter into the island of Ireland, in order to reduce the people to obedience unto laws, and to extirpate the plants of vice; and that you are willing to pay, from each house, a yearly pension of one penny to St. Peter, and that you will preserve the rights of the churches of this land whole and inviolable; we, therefore, with that grace and acceptance, suited to your pious and laudable design, and favourably assenting to your petition, do hold it good and acceptable, that, for extending the borders of the Church, restraining the progress of vice, for the correction of manners, the planting of virtue; and the increase of religion, you enter this island, and execute therein whatever shall pertain to the honour of God, and welfare of the land, and that the people of this land receive you honourably, and reverence you as their Lord, the rights of their churches still remaining sacred and inviolate;

and saving to St. Peter the annual pension of one penny from every house.

"If then you be resolved to carry the design you have conceived into effectual execution, study to form this nation to virtuous manners, and labour, by yourself and others, whom you shall judge meet for this work, in faith, word, and life, that the Church may be there adorned, that the religion of the Christian Faith may be planted and grow up, and that all things pertaining to the honour of God, and the salvation of souls, be so ordered, that you may be entitled to the fulness of eternal reward from God, and obtain a glorious renown on earth, throughout all ages."

With this Bull, was presented to King Henry, a Ring, the token of his investiture, as rightful Sovereign of Ireland. "The better," writes Sir John Davis, "to assure the inconstant sea-nymph, who was so easily wonn, the Pope would needs give her unto him with a ring: Conjugio jungam stabili propriamque dicabo." He then goes on to say, that Adrian had no more authority to give this kingdom to Henry II., than he who offered to Christ all the kingdoms of the earth. But the Bull says, "There is indeed no doubt—non est dubium—that Ireland and all the islands—Hiberniam et omnes insulas—on which the Sun of Righteousness hath shone, and which have received the doctrines of the Christian Faith, belong to the jurisdiction of St. Peter and of the Holy Roman Church." This claim is founded on an alleged ancient grant of the Emperor Constantine to the Roman Church.

The Abbé Macgeoghegan calls this "nonsense," but he cannot deny that Adrian, in this very Bull, refers to the alleged grant, namely, that omnes insulæ de jure antiquo ex donatio Constantine qui cam fundavit dicuntur ad ecclesiam Romanum pertinere. And if this did not stand, we are told, by Keating, that the Irish princes gave the sovereignty of the island to Urban II. in 1092, so that the Church's right to hand over Ireland to the tender missionary zeal of Henry II. will hold good either way. The learned Abbé is pungent and witty at the idea of sending rude Normans to extirpate vice, and reform the morals and manners of the Irish. "Such were the *doctors* whom Henry II. sent to Ireland! They must have acquired politeness by inspiration."

This Abbé styles the Bull, "a decree pronounced against Ireland, by which the rights of nations, and the most sacred laws, are violated under the specious pretext of religion. Could one," he asks, "suspect the vicar of Christ of such gross injustice? Could one believe him capable of issuing a Bull, by which an entire nation was overthrown?" *

* "Un arrêt prononcé contre l'Irlande, par lequel le droit des gens, et les lois, les plus sacrées sont violées, sous le spécieux prétexte de religion, et de réformation des mœurs. Peut-on soupçonner le vicaire de Jesus Christ d'une injustice si criante? Peut-on le croire coupable d'avoir dicté une bulle, qui a bouleversé toute une nation?"

CHAPTER V.

DIARMAID, KING OF LEINSTER, RETURNS TO IRELAND.

DIARMAID, whose conscience had never been much troubled respecting the Pope's power to hand over Ireland to the King of England, returned from France to Bristol with a document which he prized more than the Pope's Bull. It was to the following effect :—

"Henry, King of England, Duke of Normandy and Aquitaine, Earl of Anjou, to all his subjects, English, Norman, Welsh, and Scots, and to all nations and people, being his subjects, greeting :—

"Whereas Dermot, Prince of Leinster, most wrongfully, as he informeth us, banished out of his own country, hathcraved our aid, therefore, for so much as we have received him unto our protection, grace, and favour, whosoever, within our realms, subject to our command, will aid and help him, whom we have embraced as our trusty friend, for recovery of his land, let him be assured of our favour and licence in that behalf."

Diarmaid remained more than a month in Bristol without enlisting a single follower, when he addressed himself to Richard, Earl of Strigel and Chepstow, better known as STRONGBOW, to whom he made the offer of his daughter's hand, and the throne of Leinster, after his death, provided he gave him effectual aid in winning back his inheritance.

This offer was too great to be either accepted or rejected without the most serious consideration. Strongbow knew the jealous character of the King, his master, and hesitated to take a step which might lead to a throne or a dungeon. "The Earl," writes Maurice Regan, "tickled with so fair an offer, made answer that if he could obtain leave of the King, he would not fail to assist him in his person and bring sufficient aid; but, for the present, he desired to be excused." The King of Leinster expressed himself satisfied with this reply, and left Bristol for St. David's, to embark for Ireland.

While waiting for a vessel he was hospitably entertained by David, the bishop of that place, who made him acquainted with his brother, Maurice, as one likely to embark in the Irish enterprise. He also told him of his half-brother Robert Fitzstephen, who was at this time a prisoner in the hands of Rees ap Griffin, that governed South Wales as a feudatory prince under Henry. Rees consented to liberate Fitzstephen, who promised to collect a number of followers for the anticipated invasion.

Giraldus represents the Irish King, while waiting a fit opportunity of returning, as "snuffing from the Welsh coast, the air of Ireland, wafted on the western breezes, and, as it was, inhaling the scent of his beloved country. He had no small consolation feasting his eyes on the sight of his land, though the distance was such that it was difficult to distinguish between the mountains and clouds."

If it were not for the remark about the "*thin* robe," we should imagine that Campbell got his idea of *The Exile of Erin* from this picture of Diarmaid by Giraldus Cambrensis—

> " There came to our shore a poor exile of Erin,
>   The dew on his thin robe was heavy and chill,
> For his country he sighed, while at twilight repairing,
>   To wander alone by the wind-beaten hill."

It is not improbable that Gerald got the idea from Homer, who represents Ulysses looking out for the smoke of Ithaca,—

> "'Ιέ μενος καὶ καπνον ἀποθρώσκοντα νοῆσαι
> 'Ης γαίης."   ODYSS., a. 58.

> " Ulysses happy, might he only see
>   The smoke ascending from his Ithaca."

The exact Grecian must excuse my rendering 'Ης γαίης "His Ithaca." Take another passage from the Odyssey:—

> " Him, pensive on the lonely beach, she found,
>   With streaming eyes, in briny torrents drown'd,
>   And inly pining for his native shore."

Diarmaid returned to Ireland with " one gentleman called Richard Fitz-Godobert, who had many good parts, but so slenderly attended" as to be of small use to the Irish king, who licensed them to depart home.

The Four Masters, under date 1169, called the first set of invaders Flemings. "The fleet of the Flemings came from England in the army of Diarmaid to contest Leinster for him."

These Flemings were Dutch families, established, in 1169, in South Wales, in Derby, and Haverfordwest. "Even at the present day," says Beauford, "the port and countenance of the inhabitants often designate their origin, especially among the females, many of whom, if dressed in the garb of the Netherlands, might be taken for veritable Dutch women."

We are told that "the Irish set nothing by the Flemings"—thought them unworthy of their steel. Could these have been the men who accompanied Fitz-Godobert? But men of better metal were putting on their harness.

CHAPTER VI.

THE ARRIVAL OF THE FIRST BATCH OF NORMAN KNIGHTS, FITZ-STEPHEN,
FITZ-HENRY, FITZ-DAVID, MOUNTMAURICE, AND MAURICE PRENDERGAST.
THEY TAKE WEXFORD BY ASSAULT.

WHEN Diarmaid returned to Ireland he despatched his trusty servant and interpreter, Maurice Regan, with letters to Wales, making large offers of land to all who would come over and help him.

Robert Fitz-Stephen, who had been a prisoner in the hands of Rees ap Griffin, was the first to respond to this call. He landed at Bannow, near Wexford, in the May of 1170. He was accompanied by Milo Fitz-Henry, Milo Fitz-David, and Henry Mountmaurice, or Mountmarisco, whom Giraldus calls "a spy rather than a soldier"—a "man of fallen fortune, without money or armour," who came to see the country, and report to his nephew, Richard Strongbow.

Perhaps it is as well to remark here that we must receive a great deal of what Giraldus says of Hervy Mountmaurice, *cum grano salis*, "with a grain of salt," for he was no relative of his, like Fitz-Henry, Fitz-Stephen, or Fitz-David; and Gerald, like a good Welshman, was very partial to his kith and kin.

These knights were accompanied by thirty men-at-arms,* sixty men in half-armour, and about three

---

* *Men-at-arms.* Some translate the original word *milites*, "knights." It is probable they were gentlemen, or esquires, in complete armour.

hundred archers and foot soldiers, who were their tenants and retainers.

"Then," says Gerald, "was fulfilled the prophecy of *Merlin the Wild*—a knight bipartite shall first break the bonds of Ireland."

I suspect we should read *bones* instead of bonds.

"If you wish to understand this mysterious prediction," continues this "rather credulous" Welshman, "you must have respect to the descent of Robert Fitz-Stephen by both his parents. On the father's side he was an Anglo-Norman, on the mother's a Cambro-Briton, being the son of the noble lady Nesta."*

Fitz-Stephen's party was followed the next day by another under the command of a truly noble knight named Maurice Prendergast. He was accompanied by ten men-at-arms and a large body of archers.

Both parties are said to have landed at the "Banne," probably the Bannow, which lies about eighteen or twenty miles south-west of the town of Wexford, between the towns of Wexford and Waterford. The Normans are said to have disembarked on "the Island of the Banne." There is a tradition that they landed at Bagabun,† much nearer Wexford; but as the forces under Fitz-Stephen and Prendergast were small, it is not probable they would land near the large Danish town of Wexford, till they were reinforced by Diarmaid. Fitz-Stephen's party came in three ships,

---

* *The noble lady Nesta.* Gerald should have told the reader that the noble lady Nesta was the daughter of the Welsh prince Rees ap Twyder and the concubine of Henry I.

† *Bagabun.* Some writers assert they landed near a promontory called Bagabun, where they point to "Fitz-Stephen's Stride," and the remains of a fortification.

and that of Prendergast in two. These five ships would not have ventured to contend with the Danish fleet in Wexford harbour. Giraldus Cambrensis says that they found themselves in a position far from secure, "when the news of their landing was spread abroad." This implies that they did not wish it spread abroad. They, therefore sent messengers in hot haste to Dermot, King of Leinster, apprizing him of their arrival. As the Bannow was as secret a place as they could select, and out of the way of ships, it is not improbable that the King of Leinster had marked it out as an excellent place for a rendezvous. When the king heard of their arrival he sent his natural son, Donnell, at the head of 500 men, to join them. Thus reinforced, they marched to the siege of Wexford, " about twelve miles from the Banne." If Giraldus means Irish miles, we must understand the Bannow, and not Bagabun, as Dr. Walsh, Mr. and Mrs. Hall, and Mr. Wright seem to think. The Danish inhabitants of the town, who held Irish troops in utter contempt, hearing that an armed force was approaching Wexford, sallied out to the number of about 2,000 to meet them. But when they saw the men to whom they were opposed, arrayed in a manner which some of them had never before witnessed, with a body of horsemen in bright armour, and another division with helmets and shields, and a third with the English long-bow, they fired the suburbs and retired within the walls.

Fitz-Stephen lost no time in throwing up trenches and making the attack. He lined the trenches with men in full armour, and posted archers, so as to command the advanced towers. An assault was then made; but the Ostmen stood boldly on the defensive, casting down large stones and beams of timber on the heads of their assailants. A large number of the Normans were put *hors de combat*, and amongst the number one Robert Barry, " a young gentleman of dauntless courage," who was the first to scale the walls. He had scarcely gained the top, when he was struck on the head by a large stone, and rolled into the ditch. " Sixteen years afterwards," so his relative, Gerald, says, " all his jaw teeth fell out, and what is still more strange, new teeth grew in their places."

Disappointed in their assault on the town, they go down to the harbour, and fire the ships of those bold sea-kings. A little way out they see a merchant vessel just arrived from England, with a cargo of corn and wine. The Normans loved wine, so a party rowed out in a boat, to capture the vessel. The Danish sailors receive them on board, and then cut the hawsers, and carry them out to sea, the wind blowing from the west.

The Anglo-Normans have had quite enough fighting for one day. But fighting was their profession; so the next morning, after mass—the Anglo-Normans were as pious as the Prussians—they prepare to renew the assault.

But there were priests in the town, as well as in the Anglo-Norman army—for these Danes were neither infidel nor heathen—and "by the mediation of two bishops, who chanced to be in the town," and who no doubt had received their instructions from Rome, "peace was restored, the townsmen opening the gates to the Normans, and submitting to Diarmaid as their rightful sovereign." Diarmaid, to animate the courage of his foreign friends, granted the town, with a cantred of ground, to Fitz-Stephen. Now, we have no hesitation in saying that to put the walled towns of Ireland into the hands of Norman soldiers, was destruction to the trade and commerce of the country. Sir Henry Sydney, writing to Queen Elizabeth, tells her to take care of the walled towns; that "the loss of them would be the loss of the whole kingdom." He says, "They are the only force your Majesty has to trust outside of the English pale of this realm." He styles them, "*high pieces of regard.*" For Henry II. to give up those towns to the Normans to be pillaged, was as injurious to the commerce of England as of Ireland. The English, at this time, sent Ireland corn and wine, for her cattle and hides.

To Hervy Mountmaurice, the uncle of Strongbow, the king of Leinster granted a cantred of ground, lying between the towns of Wexford and Waterford. By a cantred, we understand a hundred manors, of a thousand acres each. The king, therefore, gave these two men 100,000 acres each. We are almost as much surprised at the magnificence as at the injustice and iniquity of these royal grants; but it was in this way that Diarmaid sustained the courage of these foreign adventurers.

It was by the advice of two bishops, *who happened to be in the town*, that the gates of Wexford were thrown open to the enemy. These may have been Danish, and not Celtic bishops.

But the influence of the Irish clergy, and especially of the Irish bishops, in persuading the Irish nation to accept their English or Norman invaders, can be denied by no one conversant with the history of the period; and can only be explained by the fact that Henry II. and his Norman knights were carrying out the Pope's mission of civilising Irish Celts.

CHAPTER VI.

THE PRINCE OF OSSORY, THE PRINCE OF BREFNEY, AND BLIND ENNA.

THE Anglo-Norman and Irish army, having been reinforced by the Ostmen, or Danes of Wexford, or, as Ware calls them, "Easterlings," advanced towards Ferns, the royal residence of the King of Leinster, for the double object of "curing the hurt men," and feasting the English, who rested there for three weeks.

"The city of Ferns," says a modern writer, "consists of a few poor houses, containing little more than five hundred inhabitants. It is built on the side of a hill, at the summit of which stands the ruins of an ancient castle, which formerly ranked amongst the most famous in Ireland, and may be still classed among the more interesting military edifices of the kingdom. It occupies the site of the humble palace of MacMorough, and also, it is said, of a fortress erected by Strongbow."

The united army, now composed of Anglo-Norman, Welsh, Irish, and Danish troops, marched from Ferns against Donald or Donnell Kill-Patrick, Prince of Ossory,[*] who was Diarmaid's most deadly and accomplished foe. Giraldus relates how that Donald Fitz-Patrick held an illegitimate son of Diarmaid captive,

---

[*] Ossory, or Osreigh, at the time of the Anglo-Norman invasion, included most of the county Kilkenny and the Queen's County. The Prince of Ossory resided in the north-westerly part of his principality. Here was an ancient bishop's see. Was the Bishop of Ossory one of the "two bishops" who persuaded the people of Wexford to open their gates to the Normans? If so, he acted in opposition to his prince.

and how he afterwards had him blinded in a fit of jealousy. Hence the wrath of Diarmaid. This blinding was no uncommon practice at this time, and by no means confined to the Irish. We read in the *Annals of Ireland* that "the hostages of Connaught were blinded by the English at Athlone." The principal object in blinding was to disqualify from ruling. "Cormac held his court at Tara till his eyes were destroyed, for it was not lawful for a king with a personal blemish to reside at Tara." —*Dr. Petrie's Round Towers*, p. 100.

The son, who was blinded, was named Enna.* If the reader will allow us to mix up a little bit of romance with this most veritable history of the Irish invasion— just about as much romance as Gerald the Welshman indulges in—for the sake of lightening the monotonous details of war, we shall introduce him to this blind lad, Enna, and to O'Rourke, and Donald Kill-Patrick, who went to Diarmaid's palace of Fernes during his absence, for the purpose of carrying back Derforgilla to Brefney.

It was the third day from the departure of Diarmaid, who had gone in pursuit of the party that had maimed Enna, when Dearforgil issued from the palace, accompanied by her faithful, but inquisitive and enterprising maid, Nedha.

"I have no desire whatever to see the place, Nedha. Indeed, from what you tell me—which I can scarcely believe—I should fear to put my foot within the 'Queen's Bower'—as you call it."

"The *Bloody Bower*, they call it now," replied Nedha,

---

* "Enna MacMorough, royal heir of Leinster, was blinded."— *Irish Annals.* Dr. O'Donovan says, "He was the son of Diarmaid, King of Leinster, and ancestor of the family of Kinsellagh."

who thought the latter appellation far more fascinating. "If I were in your place"—continued Nedha, who used great freedom of speech—"I should not sleep easy without seeing it; and now, especially, as the king is away. No one will be the wiser. The servants say, it was once very beautiful."

Dearforgil, as well as Blue-beard's wife, had something of woman's curiosity, and allowed herself to be persuaded, and drawn on, step by step, to the fatal bower. The branches of the trees were so numerous, and the briars, nettles, and dog-grass, so thick and matted, that they found it difficult to penetrate to the deserted mansion. But Nedha, after scratching both her hands and face, pushed boldly through, followed by the princess.

"O gemini! but this was beautiful once," exclaimed the maid, as the *coup d'œil* of the principal apartment opened on her. It's fit for a fairy. It's a grand thing to be a queen."

"But they say," replied the princess, "she was unhappy."

"Unhappy!" exclaimed Nedha, who thought nothing of that. "They say he murdered her."

"*He!* who?"

"The king."

"Nedha, never dare utter those words again. Who did you hear say so?"

"Every one"—with confidence.—"They say her blood is on the chamber floor."

"I don't believe it. The King of Leinster could murder no one."

"Well, we can see; seeing is believing. This

must be her chamber "—pushing open the door. "Hist! I thought I heard some one. O gemini! there is the blood!"

The mistress turned her eyes to the spot, and there, sure enough, was a dark red mark, like the stain of Rizzio's blood on the floor of the queen's chamber in Holyrood. As Dearforgil's eyes rested on it, her face paled. Hearing a breathing and rustling behind her, she turned quickly round. She stood face to face with her husband, the Prince of Brefney.

"At last!" said O'Rourke, moving over to close the door. Nedha, whose quick eye marked the movement, sped through the opening like a bird. O'Rourke seized her by the skirt. She escaped from him with the scream of a sea-gull—leaving part of its plumage in the hands of the fowler.

"That *dubhsaigh** will destroy all. Come, madam"—turning to the princess, who stood as pale and rigid as a marble statue—"there is no time to lose; your horse is in waiting below. But were I to deal with you as you deserve, I should leave another mark upon that floor."

As Nedha, with wild screams—which rang through the forest—and dishevelled hair, neared the palace, the cavalcade which had gone in pursuit of Kill-Patrick and his companion (at the head of which rode the King of Leinster) drew up.

"What ails the lass?" inquired Diarmaid.

Nedha—wringing her hands in wild despair—"My mistress! my mistress!"

"What of her, girl?" flinging himself from his horse.

* "Black ——."

Nedha :—"O'Rourke! O'Rourke!"—sobbing.
Diarmaid :—"What of O'Rourke? speak!"
Nedha :—"He has found her! he has found her!"
Diarmaid :—"Where?—speak!"
Nedha :—"In the Bloody Bower, in the Bloody Bower!"

O'Rourke, and the captured princess, had left the Bower fully an hour before the King of Leinster and his party gained it. Diarmaid ground his teeth in vengeance, for they did not leave, that he could observe, a track or trace to direct pursuit; and the evening shades were drawing round them. Turning towards his party in despair, his eye fell on Enna, and his dog, Thorkil, in deep consultation, beneath a large tree. The father started with surprise and delight to see him there, and able, notwithstanding his wound, to ride; for he knew, that for a night-march through the forest, he could have no surer guides than Enna and Thorkil.

"Enna, my boy, I am delighted to see you able to ride. How is the leg? Better? Have you found their track?"

"Yes."

"Thank God! Take the lead. I will keep beside you."

After riding six hours, as fast as their horses could go, without drawing rein, Diarmaid asked whether he was sure they had taken the right road.

Enna drew up, called back Thorkil, caused him to stand on his hind legs, took him by the fore paws, brought his nose into close contact with his own, and commenced a palaver, in dumb show; with the result of which both seemed perfectly satisfied.

"Well, Enna," inquired the king, who watched their proceedings with deep interest; "are we on their track?"

"We are; and they are not far before us."

"Thank God! Ride forward."

They had not ridden more than two miles when Thorkil gave tongue.

"You have them, Thorkil, have you?" said Enna.

Thorkil wagged his tail and moved on. After riding another mile, he halted, and looked perplexed, and seemed to be deciding between two courses, whether he should go to the right or left.

"Quick, man," said Enna, addressing him.

Thorkil dashed through a thicket, on his right, with the king at his tail. Within the thicket was an open space, in the centre of which sat a mounted horseman, as quiet as the equestrian statue in College Green. The moon, breaking clearly through a rack of clouds, revealed to Diarmaid's eye the hated form and features of the Prince of Brefney.

A simultaneous exclamation of delight burst from the bosoms of both these mighty warriors. The next instant they rushed upon each other like two thunder-clouds, from which burst the lightning flashes of their armour. The next the Prince of Brefney lay unhorsed upon the plain, with Diarmaid's sword at his throat. "Where is she? Where is Dearforgil? Speak, before you die!"

O'Rourke, who was badly, though not mortally wounded, grinned horribly in reply.

"May it please you, Ard-Righ," said one of the king's men, rushing up, "the dog, and Prince Enna, are on a new scent."

"Where?" cried Diarmaid, his mind directed to even

a more fascinating pursuit than that of cutting O'Rourke's throat. "A golden collar for the man that finds the Princess of Brefney."

The reward put metal in their heels. They swept the forest with the speed and fury of contending whirlwinds.

As O'Rourke lay on his back, perfectly motionless, a horseman, who could not be distinguished—at that hour—from one of Diarmaid's followers, cautiously approached, and whispered in his ear, "Tiernan O'Rourke, are you dead?"

O'Rourke started to his feet, and reeled, as he asked, "Is that you, Kill-Patrick?"

"Yes. Can you mount?"

"I'll try. Where's the princess?"

"Safe enough, where you left her; and where they'll never find her."

The search for Dearforgil, and the contest for the golden collar, was long and intense. After searching in vain for two or three hours, Diarmaid, in despair, hastened back to the spot where he had left O'Rourke, resolving to hold him a prisoner till the princess was restored. What was his amazement and chagrin to find that he had escaped.

The King of Leinster stamped, and tore his princely hair. He had lost the objects both of his love and revenge. "To horse!" he cried, addressing those around him.

At this instant the sweet sounds of Enna's horn saluted his ear.

"He has found the princess! My noble boy has won the golden collar! Would I could leave him my kingdom.—Is the princess found, Enna?" approaching him.

"Yes."

"Where? I do not see her."

"Here," said Enna.

"Where, Enna? I see her not."

"Put your ear to the tree," said the blind lad—taking his father's hand, and leading him to a large elm.

He did so, and replied, "I hear nothing, boy. Thou art deceived."

"Try again," said Enna, smiling.

Diarmaid applied his ear a second time, and caught a feeble sound, which it was difficult to distinguish from the wind moaning among the branches.

"The tree is hollow," remarked the boy; "they have hidden the princess in the cavity of the trunk."

The king sprang from his horse's back to one of the branches, from that to the main trunk, and found his son's assertion verified. There she lay, her hands bound firmly behind her back, and her face muffled.

After removing the bandages, unloosing the cords, and discovering that Dearforgil had received no personal injury, Diarmaid took the golden collar from his own neck, and said—addressing his son—"Now, Enna, for thy reward."

"Not so," replied Enna, "the prize is not mine."

"Whose, then?" asked the king, in surprise.

"It belongs to Thorkil."

"What! To the dog?"

"Yes."

"Then, by Saint Patrick, the noble brute shall wear it"—placing the golden collar round Thorkil's neck.

CHAPTER VII.

A BATTLE WITH THE PRINCE OF OSSORY—DIARMAID'S BLOODTHIRSTY REVENGE—A REMARKABLE PHENOMENON—THE OSSORIANS AGAIN ROUTED.

THERE was no other Irish king or chieftain, who did half so much to repel the invaders as Donald Kill-Patrick, Prince of Ossory. If, as Leland says, these first adventurers conceived that they had nothing more to do than to march through the land, and terrify a whole nation of timid savages, by the glitter of their armour, they must have been early convinced of their mistake. The king of Leinster, who appreciated the courage and ability of this bold prince, warned the Normans to be on their guard, as they passed through his territory. They found him entrenched, with five thousand men, on boggy ground, over which Diarmaid and his Norman friends must march to get at him. The contest was fearful, and endured from morning till night. The arms and discipline of the English at length prevailed; but the slaughter on both sides was great. Kill-Patrick was scarcely driven out of one position before he had seized another. He is assailed by young Kavanagh (the king's son), whose brother Enna he had blinded. The young prince is driven back, and forced for shelter behind the Norman troops. The Normans now advance, and after three hours' hard fighting, oblige—as they imagine—the Irish, under Kill-Patrick, to give ground, and run. It is only a feint, to draw the English—horse and foot—into a bog, on low moorish ground, where Donnell "assured himself to have a fair day upon them." But Kill-Patrick was mistaken. Cool Norman courage, good generalship, and English arms were too much for him, even in the midst of an Irish bog.

"Let us," cried Maurice Prendergast, "withstand our enemies, and free ourselves from this bottom. We are well armed and they are naked. There is no doubt but they are ours. We shall, at least, die with honour. —Take," said he, turning to one Robert Smith, "fifty soldiers, and lie in ambush in yonder thicket, and move not till the Irish pass."

The ambush succeeded, and the Irish were routed with the loss of two hundred men; whose heads were collected, and laid at the feet of Diarmaid.

The king turned them over, one by one, and having found the head of which he was in search, raised it to his mouth, by the ears and long hair, and bit away the nose and lips. Could it have been the head of the man whom Donald Kill-Patrick had employed to blind Enna?

This seems almost too horrible for belief, but an English Knight, Castide, who had been taken prisoner by an Irish chieftain, with whom he lived for several years, told Froissart, the historian, that the Irish "did not consider their enemies dead till they had cut their throats, like sheep, and opened them, and taken away their hearts, which they carry off with them, and which, some say, who are well acquainted with their manners, they devour as delicious morsels."—*Vide Smith's ed. of Froissart, Vol. II., p.* 78.

About this time there occurred one of those remarkable phenomena which are now and then produced by the excessive refraction of the rays of light. "The same night,* there appeared a strange apparition, first discovered by Randolph Fitz-Ralph, captain of the watch; which was, as he conceived, an army of men well armed. Both he and others conceived it to have been the enemy, concluding in their hearts that the men of Wexford † had betrayed them. Randolph ran towards the camp, to give the alarm. The sentinel, seeing him coming from where this conceived army stood, and taking him for an enemy, gave him, with sword, such a sound blow on the back that he was enforced to touch the ground with his knee. Not long after this, the apparition vanished."

This apparition, or phenomenon, had no effect in turning back Diarmaid from his revenge. Two hundred bloody heads did not satisfy him. The morning after the apparition, he marched to "Athlether, seated on a great river." The next morning, they passed the river, and found the men of Ossory encamped, and waiting their approach. The Wexford men, or Danes, in Diarmaid's army, commence the attack, and for three continuous days are bravely repulsed; the English come to the rescue, take the trench, and put the men of Ossory to flight.

* We may probably read "evening" for "night."

† *Men of Wexford.*—We conclude these Wexford men were Danes, who were probably better armed than the Celtic Irish.

CHAPTER VIII.

MAURICE PRENDERGAST IS JEALOUS, AND JOINS KILL-PATRICK — THE OSSORIANS LAY A PLOT FOR THE NORMAN KNIGHTS, WHO EMBARK FOR WALES—KILL-PATRICK OFFERS TO SUBMIT TO FITZ-STEPHEN.

THE King of Leinster had now obtained a position and power which rendered him obnoxious to some of his Norman friends. "Diarmaid being grown proud with his victories, gave discontentment to the English, insomuch that Maurice Prendergast, with two hundred soldiers, went to Wexford with the resolution to embark and pass into Wales." Diarmaid directs the Wexford men to "give impediment." Prendergast, who discovers it, is indignant and enraged, and sends to Kill-Patrick, offering to join his standard. Kill-Patrick is overjoyed, and promises "great entertainment." They meet, draw up a compact, and bind themselves, by heavy oaths, to keep it. They unite their arms, and make war on O'Moore, of Leix. [Diarmaid's wife, the Queen of Leinster, was an O'Moore.] The expedition is crowned with success; so much so, that the men of Ossory become jealous of Maurice Prendergast; and finding themselves his debtor, and the support of his troop expensive, resolve to discharge their obligations by cutting his throat.

To this Kill-Patrick objected.

Maurice, having heard of the meditated treason, and growing weary of the service, asked Donnell to allow him to depart. The Irish chieftain entreats him to stay; but Maurice perseveres in his resolution of embarking for Wales. He takes leave of Kill-Patrick, and commences his march. The men of Ossory, "persevering in their malicious treason," or purpose of cutting him off, laid an ambuscade, to take him by surprise. Prendergast hears of the danger, and sends a messenger to Donnell, offering to remain for six months longer. The Prince of Ossory is delighted. The Ossorians, hearing of the new treaty, abandon the ambuscade, which Maurice takes advantage of, to march to Waterford, where he embarks for Wales. Donnell Kill-Patrick, feeling it was useless to continue the struggle, after the departure of Prendergast, is represented by Hanmer as making the following tender of submission, in a letter to Fitz-Stephen :—

"Sir Knight, of noble race, renowned for martial prowess, Donald, Prince of Ossory, sendeth greeting. Dermod, that damnable adulterer, in his own person, with the King of Meath's wife, [*recte*, Prince of Brefney's wife] and in his son's * person, with my wife, has drawn thee and those gallants (most worthy knights) upon this poor country and naked people. I will yield myself— it is for the good of my poor followers—into thy hands. Peace I crave, and peace let me have." Spoken like a brave man.

Fitz-Stephen consulted with the King of Leinster, who granted a partial peace, on Donald's acknowledgment of Diarmaid as his lawful sovereign. Ossory is in the province of Leinster.

* *And his son's person with my wife.*—The son, we conclude, was Enna, whom Kill-Patrick had blinded.

CHAPTER IX.

THE BRAVE RODERICK O'CONOR REFUSES TO FIGHT, BUT ATTEMPTS TO TREAT WITH THE NORMANS AGAINST DIARMAID, AND WITH DIARMAID AGAINST THE NORMANS—AT THE ENTREATIES OF THE BISHOPS HE MAKES PEACE.

HOW is it that we find the Prince of Ossory contending single-handed with Diarmaid and his Norman allies? Where is the brave Roderick O'Conor, King of Connaught, who had assumed the title of Monarch of all Ireland? Were we to give our own private opinion of this Irish hero, it would not be very flattering, even on the score of personal courage, in which few Irishmen are deficient. The brave Roderick was skulking behind the broad waters of the Shannon, and it was not till the whole island was aroused, that "he began to deliberate on what was best to be done." He then assembled a large army, and marched into Hig-Kinsellagh.*

Diarmaid and his handful of Norman adventurers, sensible of their inability to cope with the immense multitudes that accompanied O'Conor, adopted the Fabian policy of avoiding a battle, and withdrew into the fastnesses of Ferns, where they "plashed" the spreading branches of the forest trees and underwood, entwining them together in such a way as to render the approach of horse, or even foot, a work of time and difficulty; leaving open, here and there, secret passages for themselves.

* *Hig-Kinsellagh*, a territory extending through the counties of Wexford and Carlow, which took its name from Ennius Kinsellagh, who was King of Leinster about the year of Christ. Many families of the name yet remain.—*Harris's Hibernica.*

This mode of fortification, by plashing trees and underwood, was very common at this time in Ireland; but we doubt that an Irish " plash " would rank as high, in the scale of fortifications, as a modern New Zealand "pah."

O'Conor displayed no disposition to follow them through the forests around Ferns. His forte consisted in writing letters, making warlike speeches, and treating, *privately*, with his enemies. Diarmaid, hearing that some of his friends had gone over to O'Conor, is reported to have addressed Robert Fitz-Stephen in the following style :—

" Fortune is fickle, and the State is in the ague, that cometh by fits. My friends flee away, which argue false hearts. No marvel that I be disquieted. If you stick not to me, I am undone."

Robert Fitz-Stephen is represented to have made the following soldier-like and noble reply:—" We have left behind our dear friends and our native soil. We have fired all our ships, not upon intent to run away. We have already, in arms, engaged our lives. Fall out, as fall out it may, we will live and die together. Be you true to us ; we will not be false to you."

Fitz-Stephen's faith was soon put to the proof. Roderick O'Conor sent him the following message, accompanied by a sum of money:—" The Britons may not, by the laws of war, display their banners and ensigns in foreign possessions, and dispossess the lawful heirs. It is a blemish for the British nation to aid a shameful fact. The lechery of Dermot should not be mantled under British cloaks. Wherefore, depart, and forsake him, who is forsaken of God and man. Receive, by my messenger, what will defray your charges, and transport you to your native soil."

Fitz-Stephen made the following reply :—" Your present I will not accept. The faith and troth I have pawned to my friend, Dermot, I will not break. He forsakes me not, neither will I forsake him. You speak of lechery. What is that among martial men? I hear you have bastards yourself.* To what end is your embassy? If Roderick give counsel, we heed it not. If he prophesy, we credit not his oracle. If he command, as a prince, we obey not his authority. If he threaten, as an enemy, a fig for his threats!"

O'Conor's messenger, we are told, returned with small welcomes; but Roderick swallowed his chagrin, and sent letters to Diarmaid offering peace, on condition of his banishing the Normans; which proposition was indignantly spurned, so that nothing remained for Roderick but an appeal to arms.

Hanmer furnishes us with the speeches addressed by Roderick, Diarmaid, and Fitz-Stephen to their respective troops and followers, which look very like manufactured articles. They are too long for quotation. We give the commencement of O'Conor's and Fitz-Stephen's speeches.

"Roderick," says Giraldus Cambrensis, "perceiving that these proposals were of no avail, and being convinced that he must have recourse to arms, as the last resort, assembled his forces and thus addressed them :—

---

* *You have bastards yourself.*—" The tyrant Roderick hath three wives alive, and eleven bastards, by several women. O villain, to behold a mote in our eye, and see not a beam in his own!"—Diarmaid's Speech to his followers.—See *Hanmer's Chronicle.*

"Right noble and valiant defenders of your country and liberty, let us consider with what nations and for what causes we are now about to wage battle. That enemy of his country, that tyrant of his people, and foe of all men, who was formerly driven out of the land, is now returned with the support of foreign troops, and bent on the general ruin of the State. Envious of his country's welfare, he has brought in a foreign race, that, by the aid of a fierce and detested nation, he may be enabled to inflict upon us the mischief to which his own strength was unequal. Himself an enemy, he has called in our greatest national enemy; a people who have long aimed at being lords over him as well as over all of us, and give out that the dominion of our land justly belongs to them, and is even destined to them by ancient prophecies. Nay, he has so universally diffused his venom, that while all are contaminated with it, he has not even spared himself. Let us, then, following the example of the Franks, and fighting bravely for our country, rush against our enemies; and, as these foreigners have come over few in numbers, let us crush them by a general attack. Fire, while it only sparkles, may be speedily quenched; but when it has burst into a flame, being fed with fresh materials, its power increases with their bulk, and it cannot be easily extinguished. It is always best to meet difficulties half-way, and check the first approaches of disease; for,

"sero medicina paratur,
Cum mala per longas invaluere moras."

Query, was Roderick O'Conor able to quote Latin poetry? If so, would he spout it to his wild Irish Kerne? Cambrensis stole a part of the speech we have quoted, from Geoffrey of Monmouth.

When Diarmaid had made a speech to his Irish followers, Robert Fitz-Stephen turned to the Britons or Welsh troops, and said, "You, my companions in martial affairs, you, lusty young gallants, that have endured with me many perils, still retain your noble and valiant courage; consider whence we came, what we are, and the cause we have in hand. We are lineally descended from Troy, whose fame hath filled the whole earth."

The orator then goes on to describe Diarmaid as "a prince of a bountiful mind," and concludes in the style of a crusading hero, by assuring the Norman soldiers that if they miss their reward here, they are sure of a kingdom, even better than Ireland, in another world.

After all these warlike orations we might reasonably expect one battle. The Abbé Macgeoghegan, King Roderick's panegyrist, says, "he had ordered his officers to send detachments to scour the forests and pursue the rebels, but the bishops of the province, alarmed at the idea of a war breaking out among them, prostrated themselves at his feet. Roderick, moved by the remonstrances of the bishops and clergy of Leinster, ceased hostilities, and entered into negotiations with the king of the province. A treaty of peace was signed, and concluded by both parties." Diarmaid, by this treaty, was restored to his kingdom of Leinster, on his acknowledging the supremacy of O'Conor, King of Connaught. For the faithful performance of the treaty he delivered his favourite, but illegitimate son, Conchobar,* into the hands of the supreme monarch, who promised to give him his daughter in marriage. It was also understood that Diarmaid should take the earliest opportunity of dismissing his Welsh allies.

* *Conchobar*, derived from *cu*, or *con*, "a warrior," and *cobhair*, " aid "—" the helping warrior." This name is anglicised into Conor, and latinised into Cornelius.

CHAPTER X.

THE ARRIVAL OF MAURICE FITZGERALD AT WEXFORD—DIARMAID MARCHES ON DUBLIN, THE DANISH INHABITANTS OF WHICH CITY HAD MURDERED HIS FATHER AND BURIED HIM WITH A DOG—THORKIL, THE KING, SUES FOR PEACE, GIVES HOSTAGES, AND DOES HOMAGE TO DIARMAID.

THE treaty between the King of Leinster and the Monarch, O'Conor, was barely concluded, when Diarmaid heard of the landing of a third batch of Anglo-Normans and Welshmen, under the command of Maurice Fitzgerald. Although the new reinforcement consisted of only two ships, with ten men-at-arms or esquires, thirty mounted retainers, and about a hundred archers and foot soldiers, they were enabled to land at Wexford itself, as that town and port were now in the hands of the Normans, where Fitz-Stephen had erected a fort on a "Rock"—in Irish, *Carrig*. They had no longer any occasion to play "hide and go seek" with the Irish, amongst the windings of the shore at Bannow. They now defied them from their Rock.

Maurice Fitz-Gerald, the leader of this little band of Anglo-Norman robbers, was the half-brother of Robert Fitz-Stephen, on the mother's side. He was the second son of Gerald, of Windsor, by Nesta, the Welsh Princess, who had been formerly the mistress of Henry I. Maurice was the ancestor of the Earls of Kildare and Desmond. He is thus described by his nephew Gerald:—

"This Maurice was a man of dignified aspect and

modest bearing, of a ruddy complexion and good features. He was of the middle height, neither tall nor short. In him, both in person and temper, moderation was the rule; the one was well proportioned, the other equable. Maurice was naturally of an excellent disposition, but he was much more anxious to *be* good than to appear such. He so governed all his conduct that both in morals and courtesy he may be considered the pattern and model of his country and times. He was a man of few words, but his language was polished and there was more sense than sound, more reason than eloquence, in what he said; and when the occasion demanded it, he gave his opinion, though deliberately, with great intelligence. In war he was intrepid, and second to no man in valour; but he did not run headlong into danger, and though prudent in making attacks, was resolute in defence. He was sober, modest, chaste, constant, firm, and faithful; a man not altogether without fault, but not stained by any great and notorious crime."

Diarmaid was delighted to hear of this new arrival, and resolved to take advantage of it to besiege Dublin, which was in the hands of the Ostmen, or Norwegians and Danes.

The Danes of Dublin, at this time, had their own king, and refused to pay either tribute or allegiance to the King of Leinster, who did not approve of this imperium, or independent power, in his imperio, or kingdom. Along with this, he had an old account to settle with this colony of Easterlings. They had treacherously slain Diarmaid's father, and buried his body with that of a dog.

Diarmaid is called MacMurrough—that is, "the son of Murrough." Murrough was King of the Danes of Dublin in A.D. 1136, but the Danes hated him, and would not have him to reign over them, and they therefore treacherously slew him. The story is thus graphically told by Hanmer:—"The King sat merrily in his chair, sporting himself, and reporting some pleasant history, when one suddenly stept up to him and took away his weapon. The rest then came upon him and stabbed him to the death. They were not content with this, but they cast him into a base grave, and in further contempt of his person, they threw a dog upon him, and earth upon them both, the which Dermot, his son, revenged afterwards."

Diarmaid was not the man or monarch to forget so foul an insult. Though perpetrated in 1136, it still rankled in his mind as a deed to be avenged. He, therefore, with his new ally, Maurice Fitzgerald, hastened his march to the devoted city. Asculph MacThorgil, who reigned from 1161 to 1171, hears of their approach, and assembles the principal inhabitants to a council of safety. Dublin trembled at Diarmaid's coming. The citizens send an embassy of peace. Thorkil agrees to do the conqueror homage, and sends hostages to the camp as pledges of submission. Diarmaid receives the ambassadors and accepts the hostage, for he finds the defence of the city of Dublin stronger than he had anticipated. He resolves to await the arrival of Strongbow. His revenge for his father's death and burial will keep. Another time, Master Dane Thorkil. *Au revoir*.

CHAPTER XI.

THE ARRIVAL OF RAYMOND LE GROS AT DUNDRONE—THE NORMANS ATTACKED BY THE IRISH AND DANES—SEVENTY OF THE PRINCIPAL CITIZENS OF WATERFORD SEIZED AND CAST INTO THE SEA—THE SPEECHES OF RAYMOND AND MOUNTMAURICE.

ANOTHER batch of Welshmen are on the sea, under the leadership of the most chivalrous of all these Anglo-Norman brigands—namely, the famous Raymond le Gros. He was the youngest son of William Fitzgerald, and the brother of Maurice. He came as a sort of herald, to prepare the way for Strongbow. The state of affairs is thus described by Cambrensis :—

" Having obtained the king's licence—though it was given in jest, rather than in earnest—Earl Richard [*i.e.*, Strongbow], suffering the winter to elapse, sent forward to Ireland about the calends [*i.e.*, the first] of May, *a young man of his own household, whose name was Raymond*, with ten men-at-arms and seventy archers."

Raymond the Stout, or Fat, or Raymond Fitz-William, is thus described by his relative, Giraldus Cambrensis :—

"Raymond was very stout, and a little above the middle height; his hair was yellow and curly, and he had large, grey, round eyes. His nose was rather prominent, his countenance high-coloured, cheerful, and pleasant; and, although he was somewhat corpulent, he was so lively and active, that the incumbrance was not a blemish or inconvenience. Such was his care of his troops, that he passed whole nights without sleep, going the rounds of the guards himself, and challenging the sentinels, to keep them on the alert. Through this constant watchfulness, he had the good fortune of never, or very seldom, having the troops he commanded taken by surprise, or getting into any difficulties. He was prudent and temperate, not effeminate in either his food or dress. He bore heat and cold equally well. He was not given to anger, and was insensible to fatigue. Thinking more how he could promote the welfare of his men, than of commanding them, he was their servant rather than their master. To sum up his excellencies in a few words, he was a liberal, kind, and circumspect man; and although a daring soldier and consummate general, even in military affairs, prudence was his highest quality."

.Giraldus says, that Raymond and his small party landed at the Rock of Dundunolf, which lies on the sea coast, about four [*recte* eight] miles from Waterford, and to the south of Wexford. Maurice Regan calls the place Dundonnell, or "Donnell's Dun," or fort. Hooker calls it Dundonough; but he gives it an impossible situation, calling it a rock in the county of Waterford, eight miles east, and twelve miles south of Wexford. Ware caps these contradictions by calling the place Dun-devil. The place is probably Dundrone, a promontory on the coast, about, or nearly midway between Waterford and Wexford.

Here Raymond was joined by Hervy Mountmaurice and his party. The Danes of Waterford and the Celts of Offaly, receiving intelligence of this new arrival, hold a council of war, at which they resolve to march against the strangers, for this is the fourth landing. Three batches were bad enough; a fourth was beyond endurance.

Raymond, suspecting mischief from the fact of Celts and Danes uniting in council, throws up a hasty fortification of turf and boughs of trees. But the enemy, numbering about 3,000, is upon them before the little fortification is complete. The band of Welshmen march out to meet them, but are driven back by overpowering numbers. The Normans turn about, and run for the covert of the camp; but the Danes and Irish are on their heels, and some of them enter the camp pellmell, before the barriers can be let down. But the barrier once down, they were caught like rats in a trap.

We are told that in this engagement, "a certain young man, whose name was William Ferrand, exhibited undaunted courage. His body was weak, but his spirit was resolute; for being diseased with leprosy, which threatened his life, he sought to anticipate the natural effects of disease by a glorious death." We conclude he was slain, although Giraldus does not say so.

Amongst the number made prisoners in this unexpected way, were seventy of the principal townsmen of Waterford. The question was—What was to be done with them? Were they to be released on ransom—Giraldus says that "for their ransom they might have obtained the city of Waterford," or were they to be cast from a rock into the sea? The latter course was adopted. Even Giraldus Cambrensis himself, cannot but acknowledge, that "the English abused their good fortune, by evil and detestible councils and inhuman cruelty."

It would appear, from the speeches of Raymond and Mountmaurice, as if the Anglo-Norman leaders left the decision of life and death, in the case of these seventy citizens, in the hands of the soldiers. Raymond pleaded, and pleaded eloquently, to have their lives spared; Mountmaurice, with equal ability, considering the character of his audience, to have them slain. We shall give the two speeches; in the composition of which, we suspect Gerald had something to do. He makes as many speeches for his heroes as Sallust. Raymond and Mountmaurice may have said something like what is here reported:—

RAYMOND'S SPEECH.

"Brave comrades, to enhance whose glory their fortune and courage seem to be enormous, let us now consider what is to be done with our captives. For my part, I see no reason for showing any favour to our enemies; but we must look on these citizens now, not as foes, but as men; they are not resisting, but vanquished, who have suffered adverse fortune while defending their country. Their enterprise was honourable, and they are not to be treated as thieves, insurgents, traitors, or freebooters. They are now in such a position that mercy ought rather to be shown them for example's sake, than cruelty to torture them. It is, indeed, a difficult thing, as was practised in old time, to moderate prosperity, when spirits are apt to be extravagant and unruly, by submission to some disagreeable occurrences. Let our clemency, therefore, procure for us the noble distinction, that we who have conquered others, can conquer our own fury and wrath. It is the part of temperance and moderation to check precipitate resolutions, and soothe angry passions. How worthy is it of a great man, in the midst of his triumphs, to count it for sufficient revenge, that vengeance is in his power! It is the part of a brave man, to consider those as his enemies with whom he is contending for victory, but to consider the vanquished as fellow-men; that while courage brings war to an end, humanity may add to the blessings of peace. Mercy is, therefore, much more worthy of a noble man than victory; the one is a virtue, the other the effect of fortune. It is, indeed, the duty of a soldier, fighting in battle, with the helmet on his head, to thirst for blood, to give no quarter, to think of nothing but cutting down his enemy, and with more than brutal ferocity to be inexorable in all his acts; but when the tumult of battle is ended, and he has put off his armour, his fierceness should also be laid aside, humanity should then take its place, pity actuate a noble mind, and gentle feelings revive."

Hervy Mountmaurice's Speech.

"Raymond has discoursed to us very cleverly concerning mercy, and perhaps has shown us what is passing in his mind, in well-set phrases; as if a foreign land was to be subdued by merciful deeds rather than by fire and sword. Was that the way by which Julius Cæsar and Alexander of Macedon conquered the world? Did the nations voluntarily flock together from all parts to such spectacles of mercy, or were they not rather compelled to submit to the yoke by force of arms and the terrors of cruelty? While people are yet proud and rebellious, they must be subdued by all manner of means, without regard to feelings of pity; but when they have submitted, and are ready to obey, then they may be treated with all kindness, so that due order be taken for their government. We must so employ our victory that the death of these men may strike terror into others, and that, taking warning from their example, a wild and rebellious people may beware of encountering us again. Of two things, we must make choice of one: we must either resolutely accomplish what we have undertaken, and, stifling all emotions of pity, utterly subjugate this rebellious nation by the strong hand and the power of our arms; or yielding to indulging in deeds of mercy, as Raymond proposes, set sail homewards, and leave both the country and patrimony to this miserable people."

Hervy's counsel prevailed; but he "was loaded with weighty and lasting disgrace and infamy; nor could one be found, whom his carnage of the citizens did not disgust." But the author of *Cambrensis Eversus*, for whose judgment we have not the very highest respect, says, "Giraldus has been guilty of a flagitious lie." If a lie, it would be a flagitious one; but we think the bloody deed more becoming the dark and designing nature of Mountmaurice than that of Raymond le Gros.

CHAPTER XII.

THE KING OF LEINSTER'S LETTER TO STRONGBOW, WHO OBTAINS PERMISSION FROM HENRY II. TO DEPART FOR IRELAND—HE LANDS AT WATERFORD—WATERFORD IS TAKEN BY STORM—STRONGBOW MARRIES EVA, THE DAUGHTER OF DIARMAID, KING OF LEINSTER.

A.D. 1170. THE King of Leinster, who had now fully conceived the ambitious design of conquering the whole of Ireland, is said to have addressed the following poetical letter to Strongbow, to hasten his coming:—

"DERMOT MACMURROUGH, PRINCE OF LEINSTER, TO RICHARD, EARL OF CHEPSTOW, SENDETH GREETING:

Tempora si numeres bene quæ numeramus egentes,
Non venit ante suum nostra querela diem.

"Were you, like those who wait your aid, to count the weary days,
You would not wonder that I chide these lingering delays.

"We have watched the storks and swallows; the summer birds have come, and are gone again with the southerly wind; but neither winds from the east nor the west have brought us your much desired and long expected presence. Let your present activity make up for this delay, and prove by your deeds that you have not forgotten your engagements, but only deferred their performance. The whole of Leinster has been already recovered, and if you come in time with a strong force, the other four parts of the kingdom will be easily united to the fifth. You will add to the favour of your coming if it be speedy; it will turn out famous if it be not delayed, and the sooner the better welcome. The wound in our regards, which has been partly caused by neglect, will be healed by your presence; for friendship is secured by good offices, and grows by benefits to greater strength."

Strongbow, who was well pleased with the letter, repaired to Henry, who was in Normandy, to ask permission* to embark. The king's reply is thus rendered by Stanihurst: "Henry, smiling within himself, saith, 'Go, whither and where thou *wilt*, and wander from me: it shall be lawful for thee. Take to thee wings and fly away.'" Campian says, "The king, half in derision, urged him on, in the name of God, as far as his feet could bear him." Strongbow, taking this sarcastic reply as a permission to depart, returned to Wales, and began to collect his friends and followers for the conquest of the island.

Giraldus gives us the following portrait of the great leader, or chief, of the Anglo-Norman Invasion:—

"As to the earl's portrait, his complexion was somewhat ruddy, and his skin freckled; he had grey eyes, feminine features, a weak voice, and short neck. For the rest, he was tall in stature, and a man of great generosity and of courteous manner. What he failed of accomplishing by force, he succeeded in by gentle words. In time of peace he was more disposed to be led by others than to command. Out of the camp he had more the air of an ordinary man-at-arms, than of a general-in-chief; but in action the mere soldier was forgotten in the commander. With the advice of those about him he was ready to dare anything; but he never ordered any attack relying on his own judgment, or rashly presuming on his personal courage. The post he occupied in battle

---

* *Ask permission.*—Henry's letters patent gave permission to his subjects to aid Diarmaid in the "recovery of his lands," not to "*enlarge his bounds,*" for which he now seeks the presence of Strongbow. By a statute of Edward IV., the ministers and nobles were prohibited from leaving the country without the king's permission. It is doubtful whether they might go *coastwise* when passing from one part of the kingdom to another.

was a sure rallying point for his troops. His equanimity and firmness in all the vicissitudes of war were remarkable, being neither driven to despair in adversity nor puffed up by success."

Richard Strongbow arrived in Waterford in August, about three months after Raymond le Gros. The following is Maurice Regan's account:—"While Raymond continued in his abode there [Downdonnell, or Dundrone], Earl Richard arrived at Waterford* with fifteen or sixteen hundred soldiers, and losing no time, presently attempted the winning of the city, which was governed by two chief magistrates, the one called Reginald† and the other Smorth. The success was good, for upon St. Bartholomew's eve the town was taken by force with great slaughter of the citizens. Which done, they sent to king Dermot, praying him, with his English, to come; who, without delay, went to Waterford, and, according to his promise, made in England, gave his daughter, Eva —and only legitimate child—in marriage to the Earl; and with her — after his death — the kingdom of Leinster.

* *Waterford.*—The following story occurs in Hall's *Ireland*, Vol. II., page 149:—"When the ships of Strongbow were entering Waterford Harbour, he perceived on the one shore a tower, and on the other, a church; and on inquiring their names, was answered, "The tower of Hook and the church of Crook."—"Then," said he, "we must enter and take the town, '*by Hook or by Crook.*'" Hence the expression, "By hook, or by crook." Strongbow may have originated the term, but he intended no joke: he was too demure a man for joking; and the taking of Waterford, by Hook, or by Crook, was no joke.

† *Reginald.*—There is a tower in Waterford called Reginald's Tower. Dr. Ryland calls it the oldest castle in Ireland. He says it was erected by Reginald the Dane, in 1003, and possessed by Strongbow in 1171.

The Coming of Strongbow.

"Meanwhile Earl Richard [Strongbow], having prepared all things necessary for so great an enterprise, took his journey to St. David's along the coast of South Wales, adding to his numbers picked youths from the districts through which he passed. When all was ready for the important voyage, he betook himself to the port of Milford, and embarking there with about two hundred men-at-arms, and other troops, to the number of a thousand, sailed over to Waterford with a fair wind, and landed there on the tenth of the calends of September [the 23rd of August], being the eve of the feast of St. Bartholomew. On the morrow of the feast, being Tuesday, they joined their forces to those of Raymond, whose banners were already displayed against the walls of the town, and advanced together to make the assault. But having been twice repulsed by the townsmen, and the rest who had escaped the slaughter at Dundunolf, Raymond, discovering a little house of timber standing upon a post, outside the wall, to which it also hung, loudly called on the assailants from all quarters to renew the assault, and sent men in armour to hew down the post. As soon as it was done, the house fell, and carried with it a great piece of the wall, and the assailants, entering manfully through the breach, rushed into the town, and, slaughtering the citizens in heaps along the streets, gained a very bloody victory. The two Sytaracs being taken in the tower called Reginald's Tower, were put to the sword, but Reginald and Machlachelin of Ophelan, being also taken prisoners in the same place, their lives were spared through the intervention of Dermitius, who just then came up with Maurice and Fitz-Stephen, as well as Raymond. A garrison was placed in the town, and the daughter of Dermitius, called Eva, having been then given to the Earl by her father, and their marriage solemnized according to, and in confirmation of, the treaty before made, the whole army marched towards Dublin, with banners displayed."

It would seem that the marriage between Strongbow and Eva was celebrated immediately after the siege. Diarmaid must have brought the maiden with him from his palace at Ferns. This marriage is the subject of a picture by the late Daniel Maclise, a Cork man, and member of the Royal Academy.

CHAPTER XIII.

DIARMAID MARCHES ON DUBLIN, ACCOMPANIED BY STRONGBOW AND MILO DE COGAN—O'CONOR, KING OF CONNAUGHT, THREATENS OPPOSITION, AND THEN WITHDRAWS—DUBLIN IS TAKEN—SYNOD OF ARMAGH—IRISH TRAFFIC IN ENGLISH SLAVES.

THE period had at length arrived for the siege of Dublin, and for Diarmaid's revenge for his father's death; so without much loss of time the King of Leinster sets out on his march for the capital, with Strongbow at his back, whose wooing and honeymoon must have been of the shortest duration.

Roderick O'Conor, King of Connaught, feeling assured that if Diarmaid and his Norman allies took Dublin, nothing could withstand them, collected an army to impede their progress; but the chronicler goes on to say that when he witnessed the order of Diarmaid's troops, and saw English and Irish marching together, his heart failed him.

Giraldus Cambrensis says, that Diarmaid having received intelligence, that the citizens of Dublin had summoned people from all parts, to oppose the progress of the invading army, was careful to avoid his father's mischance,* and to lead his followers by the ridges

---

* *His father's mischance.*—We do not know to what "mischance" Giraldus refers. By approaching Dublin, through Wexford and Wicklow, and the valley of Glendolough, the King of Leinster kept within his own territory, and outflanked the men of Ossory and Meath, who might have disputed his passage through the woods and bogs that lay in the direct road, where his father, on some previous occasion, may have come to grief.

of the mountains of Glyndelachan [Glendalough, *i.e.*, Glen of the Lough], and conducted them in safety to the walls of Dublin.

Miles or Milo de Cogan, "a gentleman of great worth and valour, marched in the van, with a regiment seven hundred strong, accompanied by Donnell Kavanagh, Diarmaid's son, and his Irish troops. Next Raymond le Gros—of whose praise and worthiness enough cannot be said—led the battle with his regiment of eight hundred English, and with him the King of Leinster, with a thousand of his followers. The rear, with three thousand English, was commanded by the Earl [Strongbow], and in the rear of him a regiment of Irish. When they came near the enemy [O'Conor's followers] their orderly march appalled them so much, that they gave way, so that the army passed by the way of the mountain [through Wicklow] without any interruption till they came to Dublin, when the King of Connaught, by the advice of his council, dissolved his army and returned to his own country."

A greater poltroon than this Roderick O'Conor never drew a sword or bore Irish battleaxe. War does not appear to have been his taste. Would, we could also say, nor the shedding of innocent blood! But we shall not anticipate.

Some think we are more indebted for a correct account of the Norman Irish conquest, to the "Fragment" of the history of Ireland, written by Maurice Regan, the King of Leinster's secretary, or *ollav* in penmanship, than to the more voluminous work of Giraldus Cambrensis. We prefer the Irishman's description of the taking of Dublin. Indeed, he was employed by

Diarmaid and Strongbow to summon the place to surrender, and should, therefore, know all about it. "Hesculph MacThorkil, to withstand his enemies, drew all the forces he could make or procure into the city of Dublin, whereof he was lord.* The Earl and Dermot quartered a pretty distance from the town; but Miles de Cogan lodged close to the walls. Maurice Regan was sent from the Earl and Dermot to summon the city to yield, and for the better assurance to demand thirty pledges. The citizens disagreed in the choice of hostages, the time assigned was spent, of which Miles de Cogan taking advantage, without direction from Dermot or the Earl, gave an assault, and entered the town, with great slaughter of the citizens, and made himself master. MacThorkil and most of the townsmen saved themselves by the strand of the sea.† The soldiers got good spoil, for the citizens were rich. The same day, which was the day of St. Matthew the Apostle, Dermot and the Earl made their entry, and found in the town great abundance of victuals."

We learn from Ware, Hanmer, and Cambrensis that Laurence O'Toole, Archbishop of Dublin, was one of the messengers sent to treat for peace, and that he "had foretold the destruction of the city." We doubt that this patriotic, and noble-minded Churchman was ever inspired to make such a prediction.

Cambrensis says that "Diarmaid now became so

* *Whereof he was lord.*—He is called "Hasculphus Dublineansium principalis," by Cambrensis, in his *Hib. Expug.*

† *Strand of the sea.*—"Asculphus and many of the citizens, in little ships and boats that then lay in the harbour, with the best of their goods, made their escape to the Orcades."—*Ware's Annals of Ireland*, p. 4. For "Orcades" read "Orkneys."

terrible, that the clergy, who were assembled at Armagh, did, with one accord, protest that, for all their sins, and especially for the Turkish kind of tyranny they had used of buying and selling, and with oppressing the bodies of the English, whom their pirates* took, their land was likely to be translated to that nation whose captives they handled so cruelly."

For every calamity, personal as well as national, it is supposed, by some, there must be a special cause. A synod of the Irish clergy was assembled at Armagh, to discover how it was, that Ireland generally, and the City of Dublin in particular, had been handed over to the tender mercies of the Normans. The unanimous decision, as it regards the cause of the invasion, will surprise the reader :—

THE TRAFFIC OF IRISH IN ENGLISH SLAVES.

"After these events, a synod of all the clergy of Ireland was convoked at Armagh, in which the arrival of the foreigners in the island was the subject of long debates and much deliberation. At length it was unanimously resolved, that it appeared to the synod that the Divine vengeance had brought upon them this severe judgment for the sins of the people, and especially for this, that they had long been wont to purchase natives of England, as well from traders as from robbers and pirates, and reduce them to slavery; and that now they also, by reciprocal justice, were reduced to servitude by that very nation. For it was the common practice of the Anglo-Saxon people, while their kingdom was entire, to sell their children, and they used to send their own sons and kinsmen for sale in Ireland, at a time when they were not suffering from poverty or famine. Hence it might well be believed, that by so enormous a sin, the buyers had justly merited to undergo the yoke of servitude, as the sellers had done in former times. It was therefore decreed by the before-mentioned

* *Their pirates.*—We conclude that these pirates who caught the English, whom they either kept in bondage or sold to the Irish, were Danes. The Danes were in possession, at that time, of nearly all the Irish seaports.

synod, and proclaimed publicly by universal accord, that all Englishmen, throughout the island, who were in a state of bondage, should be restored to freedom."

This passage is not only interesting, as portraying the operation of the national conscience, and also as showing some of the commodities in which the Ostmen traded, but also, as evincing the low social condition of the Saxon population of England. We can scarcely realize the idea of parents selling their own children into slavery; but Giraldus says it was a common practice. The Irish Ostmen appear to have been the *buyers*, and not the sellers, in the English slave markets. We learn from William of Malmsbury (Book II., c. 1.) that Bristol was a great mart for this trade, from which the slaves could readily be shipped to Ireland. Wulstan, the bishop of Worcester, who died in 1095, made great efforts to put it down. We are all familiar with the interesting story of Gregory the Great, inquiring respecting the nationality of some beautiful children, whom he saw exposed for sale in the slave market of Rome. He was informed they were Angli, *i.e.*, "English.—"Non Angli," he replied, "sed angeli;" "not English, but angels." There is a tradition that St. Patrick was first carried to Ireland, when about thirteen years of age, as a slave.

CHAPTER XIV.

DUBLIN BESIEGED BY THE DANES AND NORWEGIANS—THEIR DEFEAT.

THE Danes and Norwegians of Dublin were not the men to give up their city without striking a blow for its recovery.

It was Whitsuntide when Hasculf, their King, sailed up the Liffy with sixty ships full of Norwegians and men of the Isles, and burning with revenge for his former discomfiture. Landing from their ships, in all haste, they sat down before the east gate of the city, prepared to assault it. They were under the command of John the Woode, or John the Mad, for such is the signification of the word, and were all warriors, armed in the Danish fashion, some having long breast-plates, and others shirts of mail; their shields were round, and coloured red, and were bound about with iron. They were iron-hearted as well as iron-armed men.

"Milo de Cogan, who was then governor of the city, with his natural intrepidity, boldly dared to march out to attack them, though his force was unequal to theirs. But not being able, with inferior numbers, to withstand the enemy's attack, he was compelled to retreat inside the gate, after losing some of his men, one of whom had his leg cut off, by a single stroke of a battleaxe, though it was cased in iron armour on both sides.

"At length, Richard de Cogan, Milo's brother, sallying unobserved from the east postern, at the head of a small body of troops, fell on the enemy's rear with loud shouts; by which unexpected and sudden attack they were thrown into confusion, having to face their assailants both behind and before; and, such is the doubtful fortune of war, were quickly routed and took to flight.

"They were nearly all put to the sword, and among them John the Mad, who was captured and slain by the aid of Walter de Ridenesford and some others."

Hasculf fell into their hands, while seeking to make his escape over the strand, to his ships. To do more honour to the victory, he was brought back in triumph to the city, of which he had been the ruler not long before. He had been reserved for ransom; but being brought before Milo de Cogan, was imprudent enough to vent his indignation, before the crowded court, in these words: "We are come now," he said, "with a small band, but this is only the commencement of our enterprise; and if life be spared me, it will soon be followed by much more formidable attempts."

Upon hearing this, Milo ordered him to be beheaded; for "on the tongue rested life and death, and God humbleth the proud. It is an ill remedy for trouble, to vent grief in such a manner as to aggravate it. Thus, Hasculf, whose life had been pardoned, lost it for an arrogant speech."

CHAPTER XV.

DIARMAID RAVAGES THE DOMINIONS OF O'CONOR AND O'ROURKE—O'CONOR RETALIATES BY PUTTING CONCHOBAR, DIARMAID'S SON, TO DEATH—DIARMAID RETIRES TO FERNS, WHERE HE DIES—HIS CHARACTER—DERVORGILLA DIES AT MELLIFONT.

DUBLIN was committed to the guardianship of De Cogan, while Strongbow returned to the south, and Diarmaid went to the north, in pursuit of his old enemies O'Conor, and O'Rourke, Prince of Brefney, whose wife, Dervorgilla, he had carried off. It is hard to forgive those whom we have seriously injured.

The conqueror's progress through Meath, was marked by fire and sword. O'Conor, whose dominions bordered those of O'Rourke, heard of his approach, and sent ambassadors complaining of breach of contract. Diarmaid treated the ambassadors with contempt. O'Conor revenged himself by putting Conchobar,[*] Diarmaid's son, who had been left in his hands as a hostage, to death. The Abbé Macgeoghegan, O'Conor (the translator of Keating), and O'Brien (of the Round Towers) have attempted to throw doubt on this cowardly, cruel, and bloodthirsty deed; but there is no historical fact of the period better established. Doctor O'Donovan, indignant at such a perversion of truth, styles those who practise it, "Modern Irish Antiquists." Antiquirks, he might have said; for,

---

[*] *Conchobar.*—"The Irish Annalists speak in such terms of this hostage—the noblest and most amiable youth in Leinster—as plainly show their detestation of this brutal cruelty of Roderick."—*Leland.*

as Shakspeare expresses it, their twists and turns and perversions of history, "excel the quirks of blazoning pens."

But Diarmaid, King of Leinster, did not long survive the conquest of Dublin. A few months after, he retired to his palace at Ferns, and died. Whether the cruel murder of his favourite son, Conchobar, may have hastened his death, we cannot say. It is probable that it did. It was madness, with such a hostage in O'Conor's hand, to provoke him to retaliate, for cowards are almost invariably vindictive and bloodthirsty.

The death of the King of Leinster is recorded by the Four Masters in the following manner:

"A.D. 1171. Diarmod MacMurrough, King of Leinster, who had spread terror throughout Ireland, after putting the English in possession of the country, committing excessive evils against the Irish people, and plundering and burning many churches, among which were Kells, Clonard, and others, died this year of an intolerable and uncommon disease. He became putrid, while living, by the miracle of God, through the intervention of Colum-Kille, Finnen, and other saints of Ireland, for having violated and burned their churches. He died at Ferns, without making a will, without penance, without the eucharist, and without extreme unction,* as his evil deeds deserved."

We should like to know where these Four Masters got their circumstantial account of Diarmaid's death. Not

---

* *Without penance, without the eucharist, and without extreme unction.*—In a catalogue of the kings of Leinster, in Trinity College, Dublin, it is stated that he died at Ferns, "*after the victory of unction and penance.*"

from his secretary, Michael Regan, who merely says, "Diarmaid, King of Leinster, died at Ferns." A man may be sick both in body and mind, without the intervention or malediction of Columkille.

The Abbé Macgeoghegan is as severe in his denunciations of the memory of this Irish prince, as the Four Masters themselves. He styles him "a monster, whose memory must be abhorred by all true Irishmen; who sacrificed his country to his revenge, and caused her to submit to a yoke, which she has never since been able to shake off."

This is the language of "the Chaplain of the Irish Brigade in the service of France;" the language of the friend and historian of James II. I pray you, my good Abbé, not to forget the circumstances under which the Irish Brigade was called into existence, *to compensate the French monarch for the troops he sent into Ireland, to replace James II. upon his throne.* The friend of the dethroned James ought to have some sympathy for the dethroned Diarmaid. Diarmaid did no more than what James tried to do, namely to regain his kingdom, by the aid of foreign troops. But against whom did the King of Leinster and his Normans fight?

Against the Danes and Norwegians of Waterford, of Cork, and of Dublin. He did what Brian Boroimhe failed to do, but what he got so much credit for doing; he drove the Danish kings and rulers from Dublin, Wexford, and Waterford.

He is thus described by Giraldus Cambrensis. We give the original: Erat autem Dermicius vir statura grandis et corpore peramp80. Vir bellicosus et audax in gente sua. Nobilium oppressor humilium erector.

Infestus suis, exosus alienis. Manus omnium contra
upsum, et ipse contrarius omni."

This seems the proper time to conclude the history of
Dervorgilla.

"What became of the *harlot*," writes Hanmer, "I
cannot learn. Belike, she hanged herself, when she
had set all the country in an uproar."

Hanmer is mistaken in his uncharitable surmise. She
left her lover, and the palace of Ferns, for the monastery
of Mellifont, where she died, at a good old age, in the
odour of piety. "A.D. 1193, Dervorgilla, the wife of
Tiernan O'Rourke, daughter of Murrough O'Melaghlin,
[King of Meath] died in the monastery of Drogheda."
Mellifont is near Drogheda. "The church of the Nuns
of Clonmacnois was finished by Dervorgilla."—*Annals of
Clonmacnois*. To build, or re-edify a church, in those
days, was supposed to cover a multitude of sins.

CHAPTER XVI.

DUBLIN BESIEGED BY RODERICK O'CONOR AND OTHER IRISH CHIEFTAINS.

THE jealousy of Henry II., at this time, very nearly resulted, not merely in the loss of Dublin, Wexford, and Waterford, but also in the total ejection of the Anglo-Normans from Ireland. A report having got abroad, and having reached Henry's itching ears, that Strongbow had become master, not merely of Leinster, but of all Ireland, the king issued a proclamation, stating that no ship, sailing from any part of his dominions, should carry stores or merchandise to Ireland; and that any of his subjects residing there, should return before Easter, on pain of forfeiting their lands, and of being banished from the kingdom for ever.

The effect of such a proclamation was to close the ports against Strongbow, who was now in Dublin, straightened for provisions.

As one misfortune seldom comes alone, Donnell, the son of Diarmaid, and brother-in-law and faithful friend of Strongbow, arrived from the south with the intelligence that the men of Wexford had arisen against Fitz-Stephen (the first Norman knight who had set foot on Irish soil), and that they had him closely shut up in his camp at Carrig.

All this was apples and nuts to Roderick O'Conor, who assembled a great army to besiege and blockade the city of Dublin by land. There was a report that he was moved to take this step, by the patriotic zeal of Laurence

O'Toole,* Archbishop of Dublin, who joined with Roderick in sending letters to Godfred, Prince of Man, and to other Lords of the Isles, inviting them to blockade the city on the sea side.

No wonder that Strongbow should lose heart. He had now been confined within the walls of the city for two months, and it seemed, as if the Kings of England and Ireland had resolved on starving him out.

O'Conor assembled an army of sixty thousand men to besiege Dublin. The forces of Ulster were quartered at Clontarf; those of Munster, at Kilmainham; the men of Kinsellagh lay at Dalkey, while the ships of Godfred, King of the Isle of Man, were in the bay, and only waited the word of command to sail up the Liffey.

Maurice Regan says, "These things exceedingly troubled the Earl, yet he seemed to make light of it." He called a council of war, which he thus addressed:— "You see with what forces our enemies besiege us. We have not provision for more than fifteen days; a measure of wheat is now sold for a mark; of barley, for half a mark; therefore, I think it best to send to the King of Connaught, and tell him that if he will raise the siege, I will submit myself to him, and to his men, and hold Leinster of him. And I am of opinion that Laurence, Archbishop of Dublin, is the meetest man to negotiate this business."

This pusillanimous counsel was adopted, and the Archbishop had an interview with O'Conor at Finglas. The

* *Laurence O'Toole.*—This distinguished churchman and patriot was at this time lord of the tribe and territory of Hy Muireadhaigh, comprising the southern half of the present county of Kildare. It extended along the Barrow northward, as far as the Hill of Allen.— Dr. *O'Donovan's Four Masters*, Vol. II., pp. 51—53.

"proud king," whose bravery rose as that of his adversaries sank, replied, "Unless the Earl immediately surrender into my hands, the cities of Dublin, Waterford, and Wexford, with all forts and castles, and at a day assigned, return to England, with all his English forces, I will, without further delay, make an assault upon the city; when I have no doubt of carrying it by force."

When Laurence O'Toole returned, with the king's reply, Miles de Cogan* broke silence, and said :—"We are here a good number of good men; our best remedy is to make a sally, which is least expected by the enemy, and I hope, in the goodness of God, that we shall have the victory; or, at least, die with honour. And my desire is, that I may be the first man to give on their quarter."

Giraldus Cambrensis represents his relative, Maurice Fitzgerald, as having made the following eloquent speech, but he says nothing of the speech of de Cogan :—

"We did not come to this *remote part of the world*" —judging of distance, and time, Ireland must have appeared in the 12th century as far from England, as America now appears from Ireland—"for our pleasure, and to enjoy repose, but to try our fortunes and prove our valour at the risk of our lives. For awhile we were in the ascendant, but now the wheel is turned, and we are in a low state. Such is the mutability of human affairs, that prosperity is always chequered by adverse circumstances. After the day, comes night; and when

---

* *Miles de Cogan.*—Cambrensis, who is fond of glorifying his own relatives, gives the honour of this proposition to Maurice Fitzgerald, but we feel more disposed to credit Regan's account, for de Cogan was soon after appointed Governor of Dublin.

the night is spent the day returns again. We, whose triumphs had gained us such abundance of everything that a successful fortune could bestow, are now beleaguered by the enemy on all sides, both by sea and land, and our provisions have failed. We get no supplies by sea, which is commanded by the enemy's fleet. Fitz-Stephen, likewise, whose valour and noble enterprise opened to us the way into this island, is shut up in a sorry fortress, which is strictly watched by a hostile people. What, then, do we look for? Is it succour from our own country that we expect? Nay, such is our lot, that what the Irish are to the English, we too, being now considered as Irish, are the same. The one island does not hold us in greater detestation than the other. Away, then, with hesitation and cowardice, and let us boldly attack the enemy, while our short stock of provisions yet supplies us with sufficient strength. Fortune helps the brave, and a well-armed though scanty force, inured to war, and animated by the recollection of former triumphs, may yet crush this rude and disorderly rabble."

Talia voce refert, curisque ingentibus æger,
Spem simulat vultu, premit alto corde dolorem.

Maurice having finished his speech, Raymond, who shared his anxiety and distress, delivered his opinion to the same effect; and all joined in approving it. He also added, that they ought first to attack the King of Connaught, as the chief and greatest of their enemies; for having defeated him, they would have little difficulty in dealing with the other armies.

De Cogan's speech met with general applause and approval; so the vanguard, consisting of two hundred men, was assigned to him. He was followed by Raymond le Gros, with two hundred men. The Earl, with two hundred brought up the rear. "In this enterprise," writes Maurice Regan, "so full of peril, they used not the aid of their Irish soldiers; for neither in their fidelity, nor in their valour, reposed they confidence, save only Donnell Kavanagh, MacGely, and Awliffe O'Carney." They marched to Finglas, and as they approached the Irish camp, "In the name of God," said de Cogan, "let us try our valour on these savages, or die like men." "In the name of St. David," said Raymond le Gros, as he and his troops "broke furiously" upon their enemies. Over a hundred and fifty of the Irish were slain. The king, who was bathing in the Liffey,* barely escaped. His camp, which contained great quantities of corn, meal, and pork, "with store of baggage," was broken up and plundered. The English had but "one footman hurt." It is unnecessary to add, that this unexpected assault caused Roderick O'Conor to raise the siege of Dublin, to which he had brought provisions "for a whole year."

* *Bathing in the Liffey.*—" Roderick took his ease and pleasure, and was bathing himself; but when the alarm was up, and he saw his men, on every side, fall to the ground, he never tarried, or called for man or page, to array him, but took his mantle, and ran away, all naked." *Hanmer's Chronicle*, p. 261.

CHAPTER XVII.

STRONGBOW MARCHES TO THE SOUTH—DONNELL O'BRIEN AND DONNELL KILL-PATRICK GO TO WAR—THE MEDIATION OF STRONGBOW—THE NOBLE CONDUCT OF PRENDERGAST.

SOON after the siege had been raised, Strongbow directed his steps to the South. In passing through Carlow he had a skirmish with the chieftain O'Regan, who unhorsed Milo Fitz-Henry, by the blow of a stone; but "Nichol, the monk," who was on the English side, revenged the disgrace, by killing O'Regan, "with the shot of an arrow; at whose fall the Irish broke, leaving the field to the English."

The Earl advanced from Carlow to Wexford, which had risen against Fitz-Stephen. The inhabitants, hearing of his approach, abandoned the town and burned it to the ground, fleeing for safety to an island, called Beg-Erin,* lying off the port of Wexford.

About the same time, Donnell O'Brien, King of Limerick, who had married one of Diarmaid's daughters, and who had so lately joined with O'Conor in besieging Strongbow, in Dublin, sends to the Earl for assistance, against Kill-Patrick of Ossory. Strongbow readily responds, and unites his forces with those of O'Brien. Truly these warriors did not bear malice long. Kill-Patrick, hearing of their approach, sends to the Earl for a safe conduct, and promises to come in person, and give him satisfaction. His request is granted, and Maurice

* *Beg-Erin—i.e.,* "Little Erin."

Prendergast is deputed to ensure his safety, on "the words of the Earl and O'Brien, and the oaths of all the chieftains of the army." He comes, and is charged with treason against the King of Leinster, deceased. O'Brien and his captains recommend the Earl to hang him, notwithstanding his safe conduct. The Earl hesitates; when Prendergast, indignant at the dishonourable proposal, vaults to the back of his horse, and commands his company to mount. "My Lords," he then exclaims, "what do you mean?" Then turning to the captains, he told them that they had dishonoured themselves, and falsified their faith. "But by the cross of my sword, no man here, this day, shall dare lay a hand on the Prince of Ossory.

"Whereupon Strongbow, having sense of his honour, deliverred Donnell to Maurice Prendergast, commanding him to see him safely conveyed to his own men."

They met, on their return, a number of O'Brien's kerne, laden with the spoil of Ossory. Prendergast, who did nothing by halves, charged the freebooters, and slew nine or ten of them. He lodged that night in the woods with his friend, Donnell, and returned the next morning to Strongbow. We all the more admire this conduct, when we bear in mind the resolve, or attempt of the men of Ossory, to cut Prendergast's throat, and cut off his men.

It was about this time that Murrough O'Byrne (who had treated Diarmaid, his legitimate prince, with so much indignity and harshness) was apprehended and brought before Strongbow, who had him beheaded, and his body given to the dogs.

"With him," we are told by Maurice Regan, "the

son of Donnell Kavanagh* was executed." This seems extraordinary, inasmuch as the father, Donnell Kavanagh, was not only the son of Diarmaid, but the brother-in-law to Strongbow, to whom he had always faithfully adhered. "The Earl," continues Maurice, "not being unmindful to reward those who had deserved well, gave to Donald Kavanagh the plains of Leinster." He is called, in old Norman French, " the most valiant son of Dermot." La Regne de Leinster, à Donald Kavanagh,† le Pleis vallant le fils Dermot.

* *The son of Donnell Kavanagh.*—The young Prince Conchobar was executed, along with his uncle, by O'Conor: "The hostages of Diarmaid MacMurrough were put to death by Roderick O'Conor, King of Ireland, at Ath-Luain [Athlone], namely, Conchobar, son of Diarmaid, heir apparent of Leinster, and Diarmaid's grandson—*i.e.*, the son of Donnelly Caemhanach, and the son of his foster-brother, *i.e.*, O'Caellaighe"—anglicised, O'Kelly.—*Four Masters*, A.D. 1170.

† *Donnell Kavanagh.*—The present Arthur Kavanagh, Esq., M.P., of Borris, a lineal descendant of this Donnell, inherits a portion of the princely property of his progenitors.

CHAPTER XVIII.

HENRY II. SENDS FOR STRONGBOW TO ENGLAND—HENRY'S ARRIVAL IN IRELAND—A DESCRIPTION OF HIS PERSON—HE RECEIVES THE SUBMISSION OF IRISH CHIEFTAINS.

HENRY II. left Strongbow just long enough in Ireland to run down the game for him; but when he saw him sitting down to enjoy it, he sent him an express command, on his duty, all excuses set apart, presently to repair to him. The king, whom, Maurice Regan says, was at Pembroke, gave the Earl a gracious welcome; "yet was his heart full of rancour, bred by the ill information of such as maligned his prosperity." Cambrensis says, that Strongbow met Henry at Newham, or Newnham, near Gloucester; and that after much altercation they were reconciled, through the intervention of Henry Mountmaurice, or Mount Marisco. The Earl calmed the anger of the jealous king, by laying all his newly-acquired possessions at his feet, submitting them to his disposal. Strongbow had previously sent a letter to Henry, by Raymond Le Gros, in which he said, "My Lord and King, it was with your licence, as I understood, I came over to Ireland, for the purpose of aiding your faithful vassal, Dermitius, in the recovery of his territories. Whatever lands, therefore, I have had the good fortune to acquire in this country, either in right of his patrimony, or from any other person, I consider to be owing to your gracious favour, and I shall hold them at your free disposal." Ware says, "He made over to him, in writing, under his hand, whatever he had acquired in Ireland, either in right of his wife, or by the sword."

Henry was, at last, propitiated, and made over Leinster on the Earl, reserving Dublin, and some cantreds of ground around it, to himself. There is no copy of the deed, ensuring this grant to Strongbow, extant, that we are aware of; but Ware says he saw a copy of the Confirmation Charter, granted by King John to William Marshall, Earl of Pembroke, who married Isabel the daughter and heir of Earl Richard and Eva. He says, " It is now in the roll of charters, Anno 4 of King John, in the hands of the keeper of the records, in the Tower of London."

The time had now arrived for the king to take formal possession of his new kingdom, which he claimed by the double right of conquest and the gift of the Pope.

He landed at Waterford on the 18th of October, 1171, with four hundred large ships, heavily laden with men and horses, five hundred knights or men-at-arms, or men in complete armour, and four thousand archers and horsemen. This was a strong force in those days; but the success of Henry's expedition was more the result of able statesmanship, and wise conciliation, than of force of arms. He had difficult and opposing elements to deal with, in Celts, Danes and Normans, and he managed to conciliate all parties.

The following graphic description of this most astute of all our English monarchs, who won, during his stay in Ireland, as many Irish hearts as George IV., is from the pen of his secretary and chaplain, Peter de Blois :—
" In praising David, the King [of Israel], it is said that

he was ruddy; but you must understand that my lord, the king, is sub-rufus, or pale-red. His harness hath somewhat changed his colour. Of middle stature. His head is round, in token of great wit. His een pykeled [eye fine] and clear, as to colour, while he is of pleased well; but through disturbance of heart, sparkling fire, or lightning, with hastiness. His head of curly hair. When clipped square on the forehead, sheweth a lion-like visage. The nostrils, even, and comely, according to all the other features. High-vaulted feet, legs able in riding, broad bust, and long champion arms, which telleth him to be strong, light, and handy."

It would seem from the next quotation, that he was negligent of his person,—" In a toe of his foot, the nail groweth into his flesh. His hands, through their large size, sheweth negligence, for he utterly leaveth the keeping of them. Never, but when he beareth hawks, weareth he gloves." Some of the old chroniclers called him "Henry-Curt-Mantle," from his wearing the short Anjou cloak.

His active energy and nervousness are thus pourtrayed:—" Each day, at mass and council, and other open needs of the realm, throughout the whole morning, he standeth on foot, and when he eateth, he never sitteth down. In one day, if need be, he will ride two or three days' journey, and thus hath he often circumvented the plots of his enemies. Not, as other kings, lieth he in his palace, but travelling about in his provinces, espieth he the doings of all men. No man more wise in council, nor more dreadful in prosperity, nor steadfast in adversity. When once he loveth, scarcely will he ever hate, and when once he hateth, scarcely ever receiveth he into grace."

A futile attempt was made to interfere with Henry's landing, by stretching three iron chains across the harbour. This is said to have been done by an Irish chieftain, named Reginald Gillmory, who was hanged by the Norman invaders.

Henry, when landing on the Irish shore, might say with Julius Cæsar, "Veni, vidi, vici." Diarmaid MacCarthy, King of Desmond, or Cork, was one of the first—if not *the* first Irish prince, who went to Henry, to Waterford, and swore fealty. The affair is thus graphically described in *Hanmer's Chronicle*:—"Dermot MacCarthy, Prince of Cork, became tributary, swore faith, truth, and loyalty to the King of England. The king, *thereupon*, gave Cork to Fitz-Stephen and Miles de Cogan."

Hanmer must have read *Giraldus Combrensis* very carelessly, to say that he made this grant "thereupon," for Henry did not grant the kingdom of Cork to Fitz-Stephen and De Cogan till five or six years after. To take the kingdom of Cork, at once, from MacCarthy and give it to a Norman, would have been an unwise return for this Irish king's early submission.

Hanmer forgets all about the seizure of Fitz-Stephen, by the men of Wexford, and the clever policy of Henry, who desired to stand well with those Danes and Norwegians, that were in possession of the principal seaports of the kingdom.

Fitz-Stephen had been constituted Lord of Wexford, by Diarmaid; but it is probable the Ostmen liked their Celtic monarch, who dwelt at Ferns, far better than Fitz-Stephen, who lorded it over them, within the walls. Those Norman knights, armed *cap-a-pie*, would, in a trading town, be almost as dangerous or destructive as a bull in a china-shop; so the people of Wexford laid violent hands on their Norman lord, and carried him in chains before Henry, on his arrival at Waterford.

"While the king was resting a few days at Waterford, the men of Wexford, to court his favour, brought to him, in fetters, their prisoner Fitz-Stephen, excusing themselves because he had been the first to invade Ireland without the royal licence, and had set others a bad example. The king having loudly rated him, and threatened him with his indignation for his rash enterprise, at last sent him back loaded with fetters, and chained to another prisoner, to be kept in safe custody in Reginald's Tower."

In this portion of his history of the Anglo-Norman Invasion, Giraldus tells the following anecdote of King Henry and his hawking:—

"It occurred at this time that while the King was amusing himself in the country, with the sport of hawking, he chanced to espy a noble falcon perched upon a rock." Was this noble falcon, Fitz-Stephen, in his strong fort at Carrig, which signifies "the rock," and from which the Ostmen of Wexford brought him down?

"So he let loose upon it a large high-bred *Norway* hawk which he carried on his wrist.

"The falcon, though its flight was at the first slower than the other bird, having at last mounted above it, became in turn the assailant, and pouncing from aloft with great fury on the Norway hawk, and striking it on the breast with its talons, laid it dead at the King's feet."

It was thus that Henry played off Norwegians

against Normans, and Normans against Norwegians. Although he loudly rated poor Fitz-Stephen, and sent him back to Reginald's Tower, he afterwards liberated and endowed him with half the kingdom of Cork, for there were Norway hawks, that had not yet been struck to the ground. These Norman falcons, in destroying the Norwegian hawks, destroyed the best and most useful portion of the inhabitants of Ireland. Had Irishmen been wise, they would have risen as one man, and united with the Danes in resisting these Norman invaders; but the Celts, in those days, as in the present, thought more of the visit of an English king than they did of the whole trade of Ireland.

Donnell O'Brien, King of Limerick, and son-in-law of Diarmaid, was the next to swear allegiance, and was treated in the same style.* Then came the warlike Kill-Patrick, Prince of Ossory, and made his submission. He was followed by O'Phelan, Lord of Desie, and other principal chieftains of Munster. Stanihurst says, "Henry II. received Kill-Patrick and O'Phelan with great honour. He promised not only to take care of their safety, but to advance them in dignity, and loaded them, besides, with magnificent presents."—*Stan.* de Reb. in Hib. Gest. 125.

Leaving Waterford to the government and care of Robert Fitz-Bernard, Henry proceeded towards Dublin. A number of Irish chieftains met him in the way and swore allegiance. Roderick O'Conor advanced as far as

---

* *The same style.*—" Not far from the Shure came to him, Donnell O'Brien, Prince of Limerick, who submitted himself, became tributary, and swore fealty; whereupon the king, as he had formerly done with Cork, appointed a governor for Limerick."—*Hanmer's Chronicle.*

the river Shannon, where he submitted,* and gave hostages to Henry's Ambassadors, Hugh de Lacy and William Fitz-Adelm. Mac Geoghegan says, "They spent the time in paying mutual compliments." "Thus," says Hanmer, "was all Ireland, saving Ulster, brought under subjection."

The following is Sir John Davis's, a lawyer's, view of the sort of subjection to which Ireland had submitted:—" As for King Henry II., he was far from obtaining that royal and true sovereignty which his Majesty [James I.] hath over the Irish, for the Irish lords did only promise to become tributaries to Henry II. And such as pay tribute, only, though they be placed by Bodin in the first degree of subjection, are not properly subjects, but sovereigns; for though they be less and inferior to the prince, to whom they pay tribute, yet they hold all other points of sovereignty."

Roger Hovenden, who is a very high authority, and whose History was consulted by Edward I., to adjust the knotty point of the amount of homage due from the Crown of Scotland to that of England, gives us the form of a Concorde, made between Henry II. and Roderick, in which the latter is styled liege-man, homo suus, et rex sub eo, to the former:—"Hic est finis et concordia inter Dominum Regem, Angliæ, Henricum Filium Imperatricis et Radoricum, Regem Conactæ, scilicet, quod Rex Angliæ concessit praedict Roderico Ligeo homino suo, ut sit rex sub eo paratus ad servitium

---

* *Submitted.*—" He subtilly alledged that he submitted Connaught, but not the command of all Ireland, which he reserved for the 'monarch' and his successors."—*Hanmer's Chronicle.*

suum, ut homo suus," &c. Sir John Davis speaks of "pipe rols" in Birmingham Tower, Dublin Castle, and of other documents in the Tower of London, where the O'Briens of Thomond, and the O'Neills of Ulster are designated "rex" and "regulus." A deed containing a grant made to the King of Thomond commences thus: "Rex, Regi Tosmond Salutem." But we doubt if these kinglings, even in their own country, ranked higher than an English earl. If we do not mistake, the term was sometimes applied to the great Irish Anglo-Norman lords; it was sometimes applied to Garrett, the great Earl of Desmond, who lorded it over "the kingdom of Cork and Kerry," and parts of Limerick and Waterford.

Henry was not only a great king, but a wise man, who understood the Irish character, and knew the power of rich gifts, dainty dishes, magnificent feasts, and raree-shows, in swaying it.

"Christmas drew on, which the King kept in Dublin,* where he feasted all the princes of the land, and gave them rich and beautiful gifts. They repaired thither, out of all parts of the land, and wonderful it was to the rude people to behold the majesty of so puissant a prince.

"The pastime, the sport, the mirth, and the continual music, the masking, mumming, and strange shows, the gold, the silver and plate, the precious ornaments, the dainty dishes, furnished with all sorts of fish and flesh,

* *Dublin.*—"Here he caused to be erected a royal palace, framed artificially of wattles, near St. Andrew's Church, without the town."
—*Hovenden.*

the wines, the spices, the delicate and sumptuous banquets, the orderly service, the comely march and seemly array of all the servants, the gentlemen, the esquires, the knights, and the lords in their rich attire, —with rugged mantles and Irish trosses they were unacquainted—the running at tilt, in complete harness, the staves, shivered, and flying in splinters; and the barbed horses, safer to sit upon than an Irish pillion, which plays cross and pile, or fast and loose, with the rider; all these things caused the plaine, honest people to admire, and no marvaile."

Giraldus Cambrensis does not say so much about this royal entertainment. "The feast of Christmas drawing near, very many of the princes of the land repaired to Dublin to visit the King's Court, and were much astonished at the sumptuousness of his entertainment and the splendour of his household. Having places assigned them at the tables, in the hall, by the King's command, they learnt to eat cranes, a food which they before loathed."

Maurice Regan says, "In thys tyme of the Kyng's beinge in Ireland, all sorts of victualles were at excessive rates."

We may form some idea of the prices prevailing at this time from the following role of disbursements for Henry's expedition to Ireland:—For adorning and gilding the Kings swords, £1 6s. 2d.; for 1,000 lbs. of wax, £12 10s.; for 569 of almonds, sent to Ireland, £5 18s. 7d.; for five carts bringing the clothes of the King's household from Stafford to Chester, 15s. 11d.; for spices and electuaries for Josephus Medicus, his Majesty's doctor, £10 7s.; for a ship carrying the armour and horses of Robert Poer, £4 ; for wine bought at Waterford, £29 0s. 2d.; for carrying the King's treasure from Oxford to Winton, 9s. 8d.; to John Marshal to carry over the King to Ireland, £333 6s. 8d.; to the King's Chamberlain, to bring to his Majesty on his return, £200.

CHAPTER XIX.

THE SYNOD OF CASHEL - A.D. 1172.

HENRY II. knew too well that the effect of such grand displays of royal bounty and magnificence, would be evanescent and ineffectual, in the establishment of his power, without the more abiding influence of religion. He, therefore, "turned himselfe to reforme the State ecclesiasticall, and the misdemeanours of holy church." The following is Cambrensis' account of this affair:—

"In the year of Christ's incarnation 1172, and in the first year of Henry, the most noble king's conquest of Ireland, Christianus, Bishop of Lismore and Legate of the Apostolic See, Donatus, Archbishop of Cashel, Lawrence, Archbishop of Dublin, and Catholicus, Archbishop of Thomond, with their suffragans, and fellow-bishops, abbots, friars, deans, and archdeacons, and many other prelates of the Church of Ireland, by command of the king, assembled themselves in synod, at Cashel. In this council, there appeared, on behalf of the king, Ralph, Abbot of Buildewas; Ralph, Archdeacon of Llandaff: Nicholas, the king's chaplain, and a number of clerks. Gelasius, the Primate, was unable, on account of his weakness and imperfect sight—the result of his great age—to attend. His stomache failed him, so that, when he travelled, he had with him, always, a white cow, that gave him milk, which was his only sustenance." The editor of *Cambrensis Eversus* thinks it probable enough, for many reasons, that Gelasius would be slow to follow the example of the other prelates. Some of the princes of Ulster had not acknowledged Henry as their lord or king. Gelasius might not wish to offend those among whom he dwelt. He also may have been dissatisfied with the new arrangement, which relieved Dublin from the authority of Armagh, and placed it under that of Canterbury; he, therefore, stuck to the milk of the white cow. We cannot blame him.

The following are the decrees of this synod, as handed down to us by *Giraldus Cambrensis* :—

"*First*. It is decreed that all the faithful throughout Ireland shall eschew concubinage with their cousins and kinsfolk, and contract and adhere to lawful marriages.

"*Second*. That children be catechised outside the church doors, and infants baptised at the consecrated fonts in the baptisteries of the churches.

"*Third*. That all good Christians do pay the tithes of beasts, corn, and other produce, to the church of the parish in which they live.

"*Fourth*. That all the lands and possessions of the church be entirely free from all exactions of secular men; and especially, that neither the petty kings *(reguli)*, nor earls, or other great men in Ireland, nor their sons, nor any of their household, shall exact provisions and lodgings on any ecclesiastical territories, as the custom is, nor under any pretence presume to extort them by violent means; and that the detestable practice of extorting a loaf four times a year from the vills belonging to the churches, by neighbouring lords, shall henceforth be utterly abolished.

"*Fifth*. That in the case of a homicide committed by laics, when it is compounded for by the adverse parties, none of the clergy, though of kindred to the perpetrators of the crime, shall contribute anything; that, as they were free from the guilt of the homicide, so they shall be also exonerated from any payment in satisfaction for it.

"*Sixth*. That every good Christian, being sick and weak, shall solemnly make his last will and testament, in the presence of his confessor and neighbours, and that, if he have any wife and children, all his moveable goods (his debts and servants' wages being first paid) shall be divided into three parts, one of which he shall bequeath to his children, another to his lawful wife, and the third to such uses as he shall declare. And if it shall happen that there be no lawful child or children, then his goods shall be equally divided between his wife and legatees. And if his wife die before him, then his goods shall be divided into two parts, of which the children shall take one, and his residuary legatees the other.

"*Seventh.* That those who depart this life after a good confession, shall be buried with masses and vigils and all due ceremonies.

"*Finally.* That divine offices shall be henceforth celebrated in every part of Ireland, according to the forms and usages of the Church of England. For it is right and just, that, as by Divine Providence, Ireland has received her lord and king from England, she should also submit to a reformation from the same source. Indeed both the realm and Church of Ireland are indebted to this mighty king, for whatever they enjoy of the blessings of peace and the growth of religion; as before his coming to Ireland all sorts of wickedness had prevailed among this people, for a long series of years, which now, by his authority and care of the administration, are abolished."

Although the primate was not present, "he gave his assent to the royal will in all these matters."

The objects of these decrees were two-fold, to amend the morals of the Irish people, and improve the discipline of the Irish Church, making it conformable to that of England.

The famous bull of Pope Adrian making over Ireland on Henry II. in the year 1155, was publicly produced at this Synod of Cashel, and along with it a confirmatory bull of Alexander III. The effect seems to have been magical. "The island was silent in the presence of the king"—silente insula in conspectu regis—in a state of tranquil and delightful silence—tranquilla pace gaudente.

The Irish bishops who were present, and instrumental in producing this state of things, wrote to Rome, informing the Pope of Henry's success. Alexander replies to

Christian, Bishop of Lismore, and the four archbishops, in a letter, bearing date the 20th of September, 1172 :—" When we learned from your letters, that, by the power of our dear son in Christ, Henry, the illustrious king of the English, who, moved by Divine inspiration, with his combined forces, subjected to his dominions that barbarous nation, we exulted with joy, and we have given great thanks to Him, who has conferred on the aforesaid king, so great a victory and triumph."

Alexander III. addressed the Irish princes in a letter* bearing the same date, the 20th of September, 1172 :— "When it became well known to us, by common report, and certain accounts, that you had taken for your king and lord, our very dear son in Christ, Henry, the Illustrious King of the English, and that you had sworn fealty to him, we felt so much the greater joy in our hearts, as by the power of the same king, there may be, with God's help, greater peace and tranquillity in your country and among the Irish people—which by the enormity and filth of their vices† seemed so very much retrogaded—may be more zealously instructed in the worship of God, and may better receive the discipline of the Christian Faith."

* *A letter.*—For the text of these letters, see *Macariæ Excidium*, p. 504. White's *Apologia pro Hibernia; Lingard*, vol. ii., p. 260, ed. 1837 ; and *Cambrensis Eversus*, vol. ii., pp. 270—272.

† *Enormity and Filth of their Vices.*—" Ut alias enormitates et vitia quibus eadem gens omissa religione Christiana fidei satis irreverenter deservit omittamus . . . noveras suas publice introducunt, et ex eis non erubescunt filios procreare, frater uxore fratris eo vivente abutitur unus se duabus sororibus miscet, et plerique illorum, matre relicta, filias introducunt." St. Anselm says, "Viri ita libere et publice suas uxores uxoribus aliorum commutant, sicut quilibet equum equo."— See *Ussher Syl. Epist.*, 70, 94, 95 ; *St. Bernard in Vit. Mal.* 1932, 1936, 1937 ; *Girald.* 742—3.

"Moreover, for your having, of your own free will, subjected yourselves to so powerful and magnificent a king, and to so devoted a son of the church, we give to your prudence its due meed of praise; as no inconsiderable benefits may thence arise to the church, and the people of that land. We therefore sedulously admonish and command your nobility, that you take care to preserve firm and unshaken, in due submission, the fealty which you have promised to so great a king, with the solemnity of an oath; that in humility and mildness, you prove yourselves so faithful and devoted to him, that you may receive more abundant favours from him, and be thence entitled to our praise."

It was thus, as a modern writer observes, that "the nation was induced to submit to Henry, with a facility, which no other means would have secured to the invader." O'Neill, Chieftain of Ulster, presented in 1330, a memorial to Pope John, in which he says, "During the course of many ages, our sovereigns preserved the independence of their country. Attacked, more than once, by foreign powers, they wanted neither force nor courage to repel the bold invaders, *but that which they dared to do against force, they could not do against the simple decree of one of your predecessors.*"

"Vivian, the Legate," writes Campion the Jesuit, "on the Pope's behalf, doth accurse and excommunicate all those that flit from their obedience to the King of England." "The clergy, twice assembled, once at Cashel, secondly at Armagh, plainly determined the conquest to be lawful; and threatened all people, under pain of God's, and the holy church's indignation, to accept the English kings as their lords;" and, saith the Book of Howth, "Alexander besought the devil to take them all that gainsaid this king's title, Amen."

The historian, calmly considering the condition of Ireland, previous to the Norman invasion, may conclude that the state of "political reprobation"—to use O'Conner's words—was such, that no change could possibly be for the worse; but when even a candid and impartial writer, like Mr. Thomas Moore, lays down the pen of the historian, and takes up that of the poet, to express the feelings and passions which influence the life and action of the nation, he writes of this "Norman Invasion," as an unmitigated evil, to which all the subsequent misfortunes of the country are to be attributed. And there is reason to believe that these opinions and feelings will remain irradicable, for they are founded on facts and incidents which can never be erased from the pages of Irish history.

Whatever may have been the ulterior advantages of the Norman invasion, there can be no denying the fact that its immediate result was to produce a new element of contention and bloodshed. If the land was "filled with violence" before the invasion, there was certainly nothing in the circumstances of the invasion itself to decrease this crying evil. Had Henry II., at the head of a powerful army, really conquered Ireland, as William I. conquered England, a different state of things might have been the result; but he adopted another line of policy, better suited to his astute nature; he gave over the country to an indiscriminate number of Norman knights, or adventurers, to cut and carve it for themselves, and to adopt that, or any line of conduct towards the original inhabitants, and Irish chieftains, which best suited their own views, or squared most fully with their own interests. The nature and results of their " *divide et impera* " policy will be better understood as we proceed with this history.

CHAPTER XX.

HUGH DE LACY, TIERNAN O'ROURKE, MAURICE FITZGERALD, ROBERT FITZ-STEPHEN, AND PHILIP DE BROASE.

A. D. 1172. WHILE Henry II. was in Ireland, his son, Prince Henry, who had been admitted to a partnership in the Crown, rose like another Absalom in rebellion against his father. As a rule, royal households do not, for the most part, constitute happy families. When the clergy strove to reconcile Richard to his father, he refused, and replied, "The custom in our family is that the son shall hate his father. Our destiny is to hate each other. This is our heritage, which we shall never renounce; from the Devil we came, and to the Devil we shall go." But we must not forget King Richard's lament over his father's dead body, and Mrs. Hemans' lines on the subject:—

"He came with haughty look, and eagle glance, and clear,
But his proud heart, thro' his breast-plate, shook, when he stood beside the bier."

About the same time the English monarch received intelligence that Cardinals Albertus and Theodinus had come from Pope Alexander III., and were now waiting in Normandy to "inquire of the death of Thomas a-Becket, Archbishop of Canterbury." Cardinals and Popes' delegates are not to be kept long waiting, and they are now come in the character of Henry's judges, so he hastened his departure,* and took shipping from

* *His departure.*—Walsingham says he took shipping on Easter-day; Hovenden, the day following, that is, April 17th, 1172.

Wexford to Wales, and from that to Normandy, taking Miles, or Milo de Cogan, with him.

Before his departure he constituted Hugh de Lacy, Robert Fitz-Stephen, Maurice Fitzgerald, and, I believe, Philip de Broase, joint governors of Ireland; but De Lacy appears to have been chief ruler, or Viceroy, upon whom Henry made over the whole of the country called Meath, which included East and West Meath, and part of the county of Longford, to be held by the service of fifty knights. A copy of the charter, containing this grant, which was made at Wexford, may be seen in *Ware's Antiquities of Ireland*, chapter xxvii. "To Hugh de Lacy, for his service, the land of Meath, with all its appurtenance, as Murchard O'Melachlin held it, or any other before or after him." De Lacy found this a dangerous, and, in the end, a fatal grant.

We are disposed to think that "Tiernan O'Rourke, Prince of Brefney, and husband of Dearforgil, assumed, at this time, a lordship over part of Meath, the King of which, Diarmaid O'Melaghlin, had lately been slain.

O'Rourke is sometimes styled the King of Meath. It is probable that this grant of Meath to De Lacy had the effect of inducing O'Rourke to lay a trap to destroy this first Irish Governor.

Let us describe the Norman knight, before we tell of his narrow escape. "His eyes," says Holingshed, who gets his description from Cambrensis, "were dark and deep-set, his neck short, his stature small, his body hairy, not fleshy, but sinewy, strong, and compact, a very good soldier, but rather rash and hasty." The real picture of this little hairy man, drawn by Cambrensis, is even less complimentary: "If you inquire the colour or countenance of the man, black, with very small, deep-set, black eyes, snubbed nose, the right side of the face, as far as the chin, horribly (turpiter) scorched with fire, a hairy muscular body. If you inquire of his stature, it is small; of his person, deformed; of his manners, decided, and tempered with Gallican sobriety."

We condense the following account of the interview between him and O'Rourke, from *Hanmer's Chronicle*. Not long after the King's departure, O'Rourke, of Meath—more correctly of Brefney—craved a parley with Hugh de Lacy, pretending reformation of abuses and the establishment of perfect love and unity. Cambrensis calls the place of meeting " O'Rourke's Hill." " I take it," says Hanmer, " to be the Hill of Taragh. It was arranged that few should approach, and that arms should be laid aside; but O'Rourke proved treacherous, and laid an ambush, of which Griffith (the nephew of Robert Fitz-Stephen and Maurice Fitzgerald) had intimation in a dream. He saw in his dream, a great herd of wild hoggs [*i.e.* wild Irishmen] rush upon Hugh de Lacy and his uncle Maurice, and one of them [*i.e.* O'Rourke], being more furious and raging than the rest, had rent them with their tusks, and tore them in pieces, if he had not, with his force, rescued them and killed the boar."

The interpretation, or fulfilment of the dream, is as follows:—The hour of parley came, when O'Rourke and De Lacy met face to face upon the hill. Griffith, remembering his dream, chose " seven tall men of his own kindred, well mounted, with swords, sparthes, and shields." They career round the foot of the hill, in " brave tournaments, under pretence of recreation and pleasant pastime; yet always casting an eye to the hill, to see the end of the parlee." O'Rourke steps aside, gives his men, who are lying in ambush, a sign. The next moment he is in the saddle, with his battle-axe descending on the head of Hugh de Lacy. His interpreter intervenes, and has his arm "cleane cut off, and himself wounded to the death." Maurice Fitzgerald, and Griffith, rush in. The contest is a fierce one. O'Rourke turns to flee, when he and his horse are transfixed by Griffith's lance, and his followers dispersed." Hanmer says his head was cut off, and sent to the king. This is a mistake.

The *Four Masters* give a different account of this transaction; from which it would appear, that the treachery was on the other side—that O'Rourke was betrayed by Donnell O'Rourke, " one of his own tribe." Let the reader judge between the statements:—

" Tiernan O'Rourke, Lord of Brefney and Conmaicne [Longford], a man of great power, was treacherously slain by Hugo de Lacy, and Donnell, son of Annadh O'Rourke, one of their own tribe. He was beheaded by them, and they conveyed his head and body, ignominiously, to Dublin. The head was placed over the gate of the fortress, as a spectacle of intense pity to the Irish, and the body was gibbeted, with the feet upwards, at the northern side of Dublin."—*Annals of Ireland*, A.D. 1172.

So ends the story of O'Rourke, Prince of Brefney, and husband of our Irish Helen, whom Giraldus Cambrensis styles, the "one-eyed King of Meath," and the "one-eyed villain." He may have been a villain, and one-eyed, but he was no King of Meath.

Maurice Fitzgerald, who rushed in to save De Lacy

from O'Rourke's battle-axe, was one of the three, united with De Lacy, in the government of Ireland. He was the son of Gerald of Windsor, who is called by Hanmer "Geraldus, Steward of Pembroke." His mother, Nesta, the daughter of Rhees of Twyder, was, as we have said, mistress to Henry I.; secondly, she married Stephen, Constable of Cardigan; thirdly, Gerald of Windsor, by whom she had issue, William, the father of Raymond, the ancestor of the Geraldines of Kildare and Desmond, Maurice Fitzgerald, of whom we now write, and David, Bishop of St. David's; and a daughter, Augareth, who married Robert de Barry, to whom she bore the famous historian, Giraldus Cambrensis.

Giraldus gives the following beautiful description of his uncle, Maurice Fitzgerald. We quote from Hollingshed:—

" A man, he was [*i.e.*, Maurice Fitzgerald] both honest and wise, and for truth and valour, very noble and famous. A man of his word, of constant mind, and of a certain bashfulness. Well coloured, and of good countenance; of middle stature, and compact in all parts; courteous, gentle, and moderate; a pattern of sobriety and good behaviour, a man of few words; his speeches more full of wit and reason, than of words. More wisdom he had than eloquence. In martial affairs, bold, stout, and valiant, and yet not hasty to run headlong into any adventure; but when an attempt was once taken in hand, he would strictly pursue and follow the same."

The Geraldines trace their descent from the Dukes of Tuscany. Lodge, Nichols, the Marquis of Kildare, and Sir Bernard Burke, say, "from Otho, an Italian baron." The

Earl of Surrey says of his ladye-love, the Fair Geraldine:—

> "From Tuscane came my lady's worthy race;
> Fair Florence, was, some time, their ancient seat.
> Fostered she was with milk of Irish breast:
> Her sire an earl, her dame of princes' blood."

Maurice Fitzgerald died in 1177, and was buried in the Abbey of the Grey-Friars at Wexford. "His death," says the chronicler, "was not without much sorrow to all his friends, and much harm and loss to the English interest in Ireland." "Maurice," says Cambrensis, "was an honourable and modest man, with a face sun-burnt and well-looking, of middle height, well modelled in mind and body."

Of Fitz-Stephen, half-brother to Maurice Fitz-Gerald, who was joined with Hugh de Lacy in the Government of Ireland, we have already spoken. Giraldus Cambrensis, his nephew, describes him as "a man of strong frame, good countenance, a little above the middle height, dashing, free, liberal, and jovial, but too much devoted to wine and other pleasures. He was a man of uniform bravery, but one who had experienced all the vicissitudes of good and evil fortune, both in Ireland and Wales. He compares him in evil fortune to Marius—'O vere Marium secundum Stephanidem.'"

"O excellent man, the true pattern of singular courage, and unparalleled enterprise, whose lot it was to be obnoxious to fickle fortune, and suffer adversity with few intervals of prosperity! O, worthy man, who both in Ireland and in Wales experienced so many changes of fortune, and bore them all with equanimity.

> "Quæ pejor fortuna potest, atque omnibus usum,
> Quæ melior.——

"O, Fitz-Stephen! Thou wert indeed another Marius; for if you consider his prosperity, no one was more fortunate; if you consider his misfortunes, he was of all men most miserable. Robert Fitz-Stephen was stout in person, with a handsome countenance, and in stature somewhat above the middle height; he was bountiful, generous, and pleasant, but too fond of wine and women."

Robert Fitz-Stephen was Governor of Cardigan, under Rhees, who ruled Wales, as a feudatory to the English monarch. Having refused to assist Rees in his disloyalty to the King, he was treacherously seized by his own guards and cast into prison, where he lay for three years, till the arrival of Diarmaid, King of Leinster, when the influence of his half-brother, David, Bishop of St. David, and Maurice Fitzgerald, was brought to bear upon the Welsh prince in his favour.

For his services to the English Crown, he had a grant of one-half of the county or "kingdom of Cork," a grant of the other half having been made, at the same time, to his friend, Miles, or Milo de Cogan. For a copy of the charter by which this grant was made see *Gibson's History of the County and City of Cork*, Vol. I., pp. 20, 21. But these two noble knights derived but short-lived pleasure from their immense inheritance. After a few years, in 1180, we have a record of the death of Amere, or Meredith, Fitz-Stephen's eldest son, "a lusty young gentleman and a towardlie." Two years after, in 1182, we find Dermot MacCarthy renouncing his allegiance to the English monarch, and marching on Cork, which fills Fitz-Stephen with consternation and despair. But his brave friend, Raymond le Gros, who is in Waterford, hears of his distress, marches to his relief, and obliges Mac Carthy to raise the siege.

Three years after, in 1185, he loses his second and only son.

Milo de Cogan and young Fitz-Stephen were invited to Lismore, to a friendly conference, by Mac Tyre, of Castle Martyr, the chieftain of Imokilly, who, stealing suddenly and unawares upon them, treacherously murdered them and five of their servants.

Whether these murders had been previously arranged by Mac Carthy we cannot say, but he took immediate advantage of them to attack Fitz-Stephen, who was shut up in Cork. Fitz-Stephen once more applies to his trusty friend, Raymond, who is at Wexford, and who sets sail with a hundred archers and twenty knights. With this reinforcement Fitz-Stephen makes a sally and routs the Irish at the first onset.

This was one of his last acts. Broken with age and misfortune, he first lost his senses, and not long afterwards his life. This was the end of a man whose inheritance, by royal charter, was more than a million and half of acres.*

Cambrensis has left us a very imperfect account of the distribution of property made by Fitz-Stephen and Milo de Cogan; but the confirmation charter† of King John, granted in the 8th year of his reign, throws some

---

* *A million and half of acres.*—The "kingdom of Cork," which was divided between Robert Fitz-Stephen and Milo de Cogan, contained about three million two hundred thousand acres.

† *Confirmation charter.*—This charter confirmed to William de Barry, the son of Robert, "three cantreds of his land in Cork, O'Leithan, with its appurtenances, and of the other two cantreds, Muscherie, Dunegan, and the cantred of Killeda."

light on the affair. From this we discover that Robert Fitz-Stephen made over his inheritance on Philip de Barry, his sister's son, from whom it descended to William de Barry. Giraldus says that Philip de Barry's father, Robert, was the first that was wounded in Ireland. He had some hard fighting with Donnell, Prince of Ossory. "He was the first that ever manned a hawk in this island," afterwards so famous for its hawks. He was a man rather ambitious to be eminent than to seem so. The descendants of these De Barrys are in possession of a portion of this property still.

There are Cogans or Coggans in Cork, but not, I think, amongst the landed gentry.

Philip de Broase, or Bruise, was united with de Lacy, Fitz-Gerald, and Fitz-Stephen in the government of Ireland. He is called Robert de Bruis in Hare's list of Irish governors. Hanmer says that "Henry II. gave to Philip de Bruse all North Munster, to wit the kingdom of Limerick." Miles de Cogan and Robert Fitz-Stephen conducted him to the walls of Limerick, to take possession of the royal grant, when the citizens set fire to the city before his eyes, declaring that "no Englishman shall roost there." Philip de Broase was so discouraged that he turned on his heel, esteeming it better to lose Limerick than his life, "by dwelling among such a set of Jews that fire their own houses and cut all English throats."

We think Philip de Broase was a sensible and prudent man.

CHAPTER XXI.

RICHARD STRONGBOW AND RAYMOND LE GROS.

THE two most distinguished Anglo-Norman Knights were Richard Strongbow and Raymond le Gros.

Richard de Clare, Earl of Pembroke and Strigul, was called Richard Strongbow, or Richard de Arcu-forte. He was the son of Gilbert, who got the title on account of his great strength in discharging arrows. Hanmer is lavish of titles on his son Richard. He styles him Lord of Totenham, Alverdiston, Wolaston, and Cardigan; Earl of Pembroke and Strigul; Dominus de Chepstow; Earl of Ogie, in Normandy; Earl of Leicester, Earl Marshal of England, Vicegerent of Normandy; Lord Lieutenant of Ireland, and Prince of Leinster, in right of Eva, his wife, sole heir of Dermot Mac Murrough, King of Leinster."

We take up the thread of Strongbow's history, where we dropped it. When Henry left Ireland, for England and Normandy, "the Earl," writes Regan, "returned to Ferns, and gave his daughter—by a former wife, or leman—in marriage, to Robert de Quincy, and with her the inheritance of the Duffren,* and the constableship of Leinster,† with the banner and ensign of the same."

* *Duffren* or Dufferin, in the county of Wexford. Dufferin and Clandeboye give the title of baron to Frederick Temple Blackwood.

† *Constableship of Leinster* meant the civil government; and the Banner and Ensign, the military authority.

The affair is thus expressed by Regan's amanuensis, in old Norman French: —La fille i' ad Marie a Robert de Quincy lad donc iloc esteit le mariage vecent fut le Carnage, a Robert la donat de Quincy et tut le Duffer altressi Le Constable de Leynestre et l' ensigne, et le bannere."

The post of honour in those days was one of danger. Robert de Quincy, with his banner and ensign, marched in the vanguard of the army, when going into battle, and in the rear, when leaving the field. Strongbow, with his son-in-law, made an incursion into Offaly, in the county of Kildare, to punish O'Demsey, who " refused to come to him," or give hostages. They preyed upon, harassed, and burned up the whole country. The Earl, on his return, was stoutly assailed by the enemy, when his son-in-law, Robert de Quincy, charged with all his chivalry; but was borne down and slain; when the Banner of Leinster was lost. For his death, there was "great lamentation," not only in the house of Strongbow, but throughout the whole army of Leinster.

The Earl had a comely sister, named Basilia, of whom Raymond le Gros was deeply enamoured. He prays the Earl to give him this lady in marriage, and with her the Constableship, Banner and Ensign of Leinster, till Quincy's daughter is disposed of in marriage.* The Earl turns a "deafe eare" to his suit, saying he would "think upon it," but at present he was not disposed to grant his request. The Constableship was intended— as we shall see—for the Earl's uncle, Hervy Mount-

* *Disposed of in marriage.*—This lady was afterwards married to Philip, the son of Maurice de Prendergast.—*Harris' Hibernica, p.* 41, Dublin ed. 1770.

maurice. Raymond takes fire at this refusal, and immediately passes into Wales, with his followers, to nurse his sorrow and chagrin, in the lonely castle at Carew.

The appointment of the Earl's uncle to the Constableship turned out most unfortunate, for the country was in a most disturbed state, as the consequence of Strongbow's absence in Normandy; and Mountmaurice was not the man to meet the emergency, or bear the banner of Leinster to victory. The soldiers, who understood this, refused to serve under him, and called loudly for Raymond le Gros; and threatened, if he were not forthcoming, to return to Wales, or engage in the service of Irish chieftains. Strongbow was too wise to resist such a demand, so Raymond was sent for, and appointed General of the English Army in Ireland.

His first move was against Offaly, to punish some petty chieftains for defection. From Offaly he proceeded to Lismore, carrying away with him a large booty. On his return, along the shore* he found a number of vessels at anchor, which he seized for the transport of his plunder. The Irish at Cork, say the chroniclers, became acquainted with the circumstance, and equipped thirty ships to intercept the booty. They fell upon the English —or rather Anglo-Normans and Welsh—before they had weighed anchor. The assault was sudden and unexpected, but it was bravely repulsed. The death of the Irish naval commander, who fell by the hand of a Welshman, decided the victory in favour of the English. Raymond, returning to Waterford, by land, was attacked by Dermot

* *The shore.*—At Youghal, we conclude, where Raymond seems to have left his boots, after his encounter with Mac Carthy. This does not look like "a victory in favour of the English."

Mac Carthy, King of Cork, "who had forsaken his allegiance," but the victory was with the English knight, who entered Waterford, with four thousand head of cattle, and with all the pomp and parade of a conqueror.

This seemed the fit time to renew his suit for the hand of Basilia, and the post of Constable and Standard-bearer of Leinster. He did so, and was again refused; so he passed a second time into Wales,* having "news that his father, William Fitz-Gerald, was dead."

This left the chief command in the hands of Raymond's old rival, Henry Mountmaurice, who seized the opportunity to do something grand and startling: not an unfrequent error with incompetent men. He asked Strongbow's permission, who had returned from Normandy, to march into Thomond, and punish Donnell O'Brien—one of the ablest chieftains in Ireland—for his insubordination.

The Earl, in an evil hour, consented. O'Brien allowed Mountmaurice to advance as far as Thurles, where he encamped, in careless security, from which he was aroused by the wild shouts of the Dalcasians. Four hundred† English, and "four principal commanders," were left on the field. This was a great triumph to the

* *Passed a Second time into Wales.*—We know no other mode of reconciling the statements of Maurice Regan and Giraldus Cambrensis. The former represents him as going into Wales before Strongbow went to Normandy, and the latter after Strongbow's return. *See Harris' Hibernica*, p. 39; *Ware's Annals of Ireland*, A.D. 1173, chap. v.

† *Four hundred.*—The Annals of Ireland, say "seventeen hundred." The Annals of Innisfallen, "about seven hundred." The Abbé Mac-Geoghegan makes "Roderick O'Connor, and not Donald O'Brien, the leader of the Irish." The Abbé, I believe, stands almost alone, in this opinion.—*Histoire d'Irlande*, tome ii., p. 9.

Irish. The whole country rose on hearing it, and Strongbow himself had to flee for shelter to Waterford, where he lay closely besieged.

While here, he learned that the monarch, Roderick O'Connor, was again up and active, endeavouring to unite the Irish chieftains, in one great effort, to throw off the incubus of English tyranny; that even Donnell Kavanagh, who had always proved true to him, was asserting his title to the kingdom of Leinster. The townsmen of Waterford looked dark and suspicious, so much so that Strongbow apprehended something like a mutiny among his own soldiers.

There was but one man living, in whom he had perfect reliance, to release him from his present precarious situation, and that man he had more than once disobliged; but he knew that he need only say one word and Raymond would fly on the wings of the wind to succour him. We here give Maurice Regan's account of the matter:

" Earl Richard, missing the service of Raymond, which he much desired, sent a messenger to him, to pray him to return again to Ireland, and then he would give him his sister, in marriage. Raymond, full of joy, presently furnished three ships, and, accompanied with many friends and followers, passed the seas, and arrived at Wexford. From thence he despatched a messenger to the Earl. The Earl rejoiced much to hear of his return, and sent him word that he would repair to him, at a place assigned. From the place of meeting, they marched to Wexford, where, in the presence of a great assembly, he gave his sister to Raymond, and with solemnity the marriage was performed; and as he had promised, he gave to Raymond the Constableship of Leinster, with the Ensign and Banner, to hold the same till the daughter of Robert de Quincy should be out of her minority."

It was therefore the fair hand of Basilia which sustained the English rule of Ireland, in the hour of its greatest extremity; for if we can believe Cambrensis, nothing could have been more desperate than Strongbow's position, or seasonable than Raymond's arrival. Indeed, Strongbow had scarcely left Waterford, for Wexford, before the citizens rose, and murdered all the English they found outside the walls of Reginald's Tower. Purcell, the commander of this fort, who was crossing the Suir in a boat, was cut off, with all on board. It was nothing but a strong hand, like that of Raymond le Gros, which could hold such men in a state of submission to a foreign power. Davies justly observes, that "Henry, in departing from Ireland, did not leave one more true subject behind him, than he found on his arrival."

Raymond had but a short honeymoon. Some writers say he was married in full armour; others that he put it on "the morning after the celebration of his nuptials." Intelligence had arrived that Roderick O'Connor was in the field, had crossed the Shannon, and entered Meath at the head of a large army. Hugh de Lacy was absent in England, having left Meath to the care of his lieutenant, Hugh Tyrrell, who fled before the Irish monarch. Strongbow and Raymond made a rapid march, with the hope of crossing swords with O'Connor, but the brave Roderick, as usual, declined the honour, and turned on his heel, after devastating Meath, and destroying all De Lacy's forts and castles.* But Raymond managed to fall upon his rear, and kill a hundred and fifty of his men. It was about this time that Donnell Kavanagh was slain, in an engagement with a party of his own countrymen, who had enlisted in the English service.

This appears to have been Roderick O'Connor's last effort to free the country of English invaders. He soon after this sent three deputies to Henry, at Windsor; Catholicus Archbishop of Tuam, the Abbot of St. Brandon, and Master Laurence, Chancellor to the King of Connaught, as he was then styled; to arrange the terms of submission. The treaty† stipulated that he was to hold his title of monarch, and his possessions in Connaught and elsewhere, in as ample a manner as he had done before the arrival of the English; and that his vassals should hold under him, provided they paid tribute and proved faithful to the King of England. The annual tribute was every tenth merchantable hide. "The greatest profit," says Sir John Davis, "did arise by the cocket [tax] on hides. For wooll and wooll-fells were ever of little value in this kingdom." O'Connor's vassals were also required to furnish hawks and hounds to the King of England.

The only man of note, now, in actual rebellion, was

* *Forts and Castles.*—Regan says, "Hugh Tyrrell, seeing the enemy at hand, and finding himself too weak to make resistance against their multitudes, abandoned the Castle [of Meath], and burned it." He returned to Meath after "to re-edifie the same, before Hugh de Lacy's return out of England."

† *The treaty.*—We learn from Roger Hovenden that this treaty was made in 1175, and ratified at a council of temporal barons and prelates. We find Laurence Archbishop of Dublin, as one of the subscribing witnesses. For a copy of this treaty see *Hanmer's Chronicle,* anno. 1177, pp. 287-9.

Donnell O'Brien, of Limerick, the son-in-law of Diarmaid, late King of Leinster. Against him Raymond prepares to march. We give Hanmer's graphic account of this affair, with very little curtailment :

"Donnell O'Brien, having sworn faith and fealty to Henry II., is again revolted and turned to his vomit. Raymond maketh preparation and mustereth his men, twenty-six gallants, three hundred horsemen, three hundred archers and foot. He comes to Limerick, where he finds the bridges drawn and the rivers swift and impassable. The armed townsmen are on the walls. David Walsh, a lusty gentleman, without more ado, puts spurs to his horse, and with good guiding crosses the river and calls to his company to follow, that he had found a ford. Two only obey, Jeffrey Walsh and Milo Fitz-Henry. Raymond exclaims, 'We must not allow this worthy gentleman to perish,' and plunges into the broad stream of the Shannon. He is followed by his whole company, each striving who will be foremost. As God would, they all passed over safe, except two common soldiers and a gentleman named Gwydo. The enemy fled before them. In the chase they slew a number and entered the town, where they got great spoil and riches, but greater honour and fame. Raymond left a garrison in the place, under Miles of St. David, and returned to the borders of Leinster."

Such victories created for Raymond as many enemies as he slew. Envy keeps no holiday, and seldom sleeps. Hervy, of Mountmarice, though now allied to Raymond by marriage, endeavoured to ruin him with the King, to whom he sent secret letters, saying that Raymond aspired to the independent sovereignty of Ireland.

Let us here, in a parenthetical sentence, finish up what we have to say of Henry Mountmaurice, or Mountmarisco, who became a monk, and founded the Monastery of Dunbrody, on the river Barrow, in the county of Wexford. "Would to God," writes Geraldus Cambrensis, "that with the monk's cowl, he had put on real piety, and that he had laid aside malignity with his military harness." He died at the age of seventy-five, at Dunbrody, where a tomb of Kilkenny marble was erected to his memory. There he lies, or did lie, in black marble, with a chalice in his right hand and a marshal's *baton* in his left. Here we conclude his "envy keeps holiday and sleeps."

Henry II., who was, by nature, both jealous and suspicious, sends four commissioners to Ireland, Robert de Poer, Osbert of Hereford, William Bendegar, and Adam of Germany, two of whom were to conduct Raymond to the king, and the other two to remain in Ireland, as a watch on Strongbow's conduct.

The commissioners were received with great respect, and Raymond expressed his willingness to obey the pleasure of his liege lord, and prepared for his departure. But while waiting for a favourable wind, intelligence arrived that Donnell O'Brien was again in arms, besieging the English garrison of Limerick, which was straitened for provisions. What is to be done? Strongbow is ailing—laid up with a sore foot—and the soldiers are clamorous for their favourite captain, Raymond: they refuse to march on Limerick without him. There is a consultation between Earl Richard and the commissioners. It is decided that Raymond must delay his visit to England, and go to Limerick. But Raymond feels, or feigns, the utmost dislike for the enterprise. His last victory, in that neighbourhood, gained him enemies, and lost him the confidence of the king. Strongbow and the commissioners entreat him, and he is, in the end, persuaded, and departs, at the head of eighty knights, two hundred horsemen, and three hundred archers, with a good force of Irish auxiliaries, from Kinsellagh and Ossory. He learns, on his march, that O'Brien has raised the siege of Limerick, and is moving east, to meet him at Cashel.

Donnell Kill-Patrick, who is now loyal, and at the head of his Ossorians, addresses Raymond le Gros in the following soldierlike style:—"You are this day about to make an assault upon your enemies. If you do it after your usual manner, I have no doubt of your success. But, if, on the contrary, you be overthrown— which may God forbid—be assured that we shall leave you, and join your foes. Therefore, be courageous, and look well to yourselves. Fort or refuge is far off, and the way dangerous. Trust *us* not, to aid you. We shall be on the jackets of those that flee, and stick to those that have the victory."

We have no doubt that these words truly expressed the minds of his men; and it was well the English should know in time. One of Raymond's generals, Milerius, was "moved and warmed by them, as with the blast of the trumpet." He was one of the first to assail the fortification which Donnell O'Brien had erected on their line of march. The English gained a complete victory. From this they marched to Limerick, and "set things in order."

While resting here, messengers came from Dermot

Mac Carthy, King of Cork, humbly craving Raymond's aid, against his son Cormac, who had risen in rebellion against him. Although Raymond had but lately crossed swords with the father, he did not lose a moment in marching to chastise his rebellious son—who had seized the old man, and cast him into prison. For this he paid the forfeit of his life. He was seized and delivered into the hands of his infuriated parent, who cast him into a dungeon, where he was beheaded. The *Annals of Ireland* say, he was "treacherously slain by his own people." That is, by his father's people. *Hanmer's Chronicle* has it, "The son dissembled with the father, and clapt him into prison. The father requited the son with like. He got him under colour of peace, clapt him into prison, and cut off his head." If we are to believe Stanihurst, the son was a very bad man,—"Cormachas in perfidia instinctus furore perseverans credulum patrem cepit atque in carcerum conjecet." This son is styled "Illustris Filius,"* in an old charter, or grant of land, made by the father, a few years before this, to a church in Cork.

Dermot Mac·Carthy expressed his gratitude to the Norman knight, by bestowing on him a princely inheritance in Kerry, which then formed part of the kingdom of Cork. Raymond afterwards made over this inheritance on his eldest son, Maurice, the descendants of whom became powerful chieftains in Munster, under the name of Fitz-Maurice, and Barons of Lixnaw.

* *Illustris Filius.*—This term occurs in a charter or grant made by Dermot Mac Carthy, king of Cork, to the church of St. John in Cork. We are indebted to the Researches of Daniel Mac Carthy, Esq., [Glas,] of Hants, for a copy of this interesting document. The Latin copy is marked B. M. Addit. MSS. 4793, fol. 65, in the British Museum.

"Not long after this," writes Giraldus Cambrensis, "the men of Cork, at a parley, not far from the town, slew their prince, Dermot Mac Carthy, and most of his company." This short sentence contains two false statements. First, Mac Carthy was not slain by the men of Cork—*i.e.*, his own people, as is here implied—but by the English of Cork, under Theobald Fitz-Walter, the founder of the house of Ormond; and it *was* "long after"—ten years after—the death of his son, and Raymond's visit, that he was slain. The affair is thus stated in the *Annals of Ireland*, A.D. 1185:—"Dermot Mac Carthy, Lord of Desmond, was slain by the English of Cork."

Raymond left Cork for Limerick. It was while he remained in Limerick that he heard his brother-in-law, Richard Strongbow, had died in Dublin. He received the intelligence, secretly, from his wife, Basilia, the Earl's sister. It was the object of Mountmaurice, and all who were jealous of Raymond's talents, success, and influence with the army, to keep him ignorant of Strongbow's death, till a new governor was appointed; but a woman's wit upset all their plans and efforts at concealment. Basilia knew her letters to her husband would be opened, and therefore avoided the forbidden subject, but added in one of her epistles, after speaking of her own sickness, "My master-tooth has fallen out." This was no compliment to Strongbow. She forwarded the tooth "tipped with golde, which Raymond wist well to be none of hers; and therefore quickly smelled the construction, lingered not for letters patent, but stepped over presently, and made his packe;" and was elected by the king's agents, Lord Protector of Ireland, till the king's pleasure was further known.*

Hanmer should have stated that Raymond, on quitting Limerick, committed the city to the care of Donnell O'Brien, who swore allegiance, and said he was "the gladdest man that could be"; but the English were no sooner at one end of the bridge, than Donnell broke down the other, and set fire to the four quarters of the town, saying "There shall no English roost here any longer."

Richard de Clare, Earl of Strigal, better known as Richard Strongbow, died of mortification of the foot. Matthew Paris and the Annals of Ireland say in 1176, which date is adopted by Ware.† The Four Masters record the matter thus:—

"A.D. 1176. The English Earl, that is Richard, died in Dublin, of an ulcer, which had broken out in his foot, through the miracles of St. Bridget and Columbkille, and of all the other saints, whose churches had been destroyed by him. He saw, as he thought, St. Bridget in the act of killing him."

In the Dublin copy of the Annals of Innisfallen, Strongbow is called "the greatest destroyer of the clergy and laity that came to Ireland, since the time of Turgesius."

* It was enacted by a "Statute of Henry Fitz-Empress," that, in the event of the Viceroy, or Chief Governor of Ireland, vacating office, the principal Anglo-Normans should be empowered to elect a successor, to exercise vice-regal power, till the King's wishes should be known.

† *Adopted by Ware.*—Ware cannot always be confidently relied on. In his *Chronological Table of Chief Governors of Ireland,* he gives 1175, and in his *Annals* 1176 as the date of Strongbow's death. Pembridge says about the 1st May, 1177.

"Earl Strongbow," writes Dr. Hanmer, "lyeth buried in the church of the Blessed Trinity [Christ Church], in Dublin, over against the pulpit, in the body of the church, whose obsequies Laurence O'Toole, Archbishop of Dublin, did solemnize." Strongbow's tomb or monument may be seen in Christ Church, at the present day. Beside the stone figure of the knight is a second figure, probably intended to represent his wife, Eva. The smaller figure is broken, as if cut in two in the middle. There is an old tradition that Strongbow had a son, whom he cut in two, with a blow of his sword, for cowardice. The broken monument gives strength to the old tradition. But the inscription, which we have read, proves the contrary:—

"This avncvnt monvment of Rychard Strangbowe, called Comes Strangblensis, lord of Chepsto and Ogny, the fyrst and pryncipall invader of Irland, 1169, qui obiit 1177. The monoment was brocken by the fall of the roff, and body of Christe's Churche, in Ano 1567, and set op agayne, at the chargys of the Right Honorable Syr Henri Sydney, Knyght, of the noble order, President of Wailes L. Deputy of Irland, 1570."

We quote the following passage from Hanmer, to show what little reliance we can place on some of our best chroniclers. Had Hanmer ever seen the tomb, in Christ-church, he could not have had the audacity to refer to it, in order to establish the trumped-up story of the son's death. He even furnishes a Latin epitaph!

"This Richard [Strongbow] had issue, by his first wife, a sonne, a fine youth, and a gallant stripling, who following his father, in some charge in battaile array, as he passed by Idrone, in Leinster—to relieve Robert Fitz-

Stephen in Wexford—upon the sight and cry of the Irishmen, when his father was in cruel fight, gave back, with his company, to the great discouragement of the host; yet the Earle got the victory, and commanded, with teares in his cheekes, that his son should be cut in the middle, with a sword, for his cowardice in battle. He was buried in the church of the Blessed Trinitie, in Dublin, where now his father resteth by his side, and caused the cause of his death, for an epitaph, to be set over him :—

> Nate ingrate mehi pugnanti terga dedisti
> Non mehi sed genti et regno quoque terga dedisti.

How the son pleaded with his father, and how the father answered, Stanihurst hath many circumstances thereof; that his own father in his fury, and in the face of the enemy, cut him off, and marvaileth* that Cambrensis would conceale it; and in the end taketh it as a matter of truth, both by the testimony of the tomb in Christ Church, as also by the industry of Sir Henry Sidney, knight, a great favourer of antiquities, in preserving the same to the knowledge of posterity."

Strongbow's princely inheritance in Leinster, descended to his, and Eva's daughter, Isabel, who was married to William Marshal, Earl of Pembroke, who became governor of Ireland, of whom we shall speak more fully by and bye.

Raymond le Gros, who was appointed Chief Governor, by the four commissioners, "until the king's pleasure

---

* *Marvaileth that Cambrensis would conceale it.*—We learn from Cambrensis, that in the affair of Idrone, in Leinster, the Earl [*i.e.*, Strongbow] regained the plain in safety "*with the loss of only one young man.*" The fate of this young man, may have given rise to the story.

should be known," was superseded by William Fitz-Adelm. We do not find Raymond after this, taking an active part in public affairs. He died about 1185-6, and was buried in the Abbey of Molana, or Dair-Inis,* on the river Blackwater, about three miles from Youghal.

This Raymond le Gros, or Raymond Fitz-William, for he was the eldest son of William Fitzgerald, was perhaps the noblest and bravest of all these Norman knights. He was called le Gros, on account of his great size and strength. He is thus described by Giraldus Cambrensis :—" Raymond was large bodied and broadset, of more than middle stature, his hair yellow and curled, his eyes large, grey, and round, his nose somewhat high, and his countenance well-coloured. He was pleasant and merry, and though heavy in body, yet active. He had special care of his men, and watched many whole nights, ranging and walking abroad in the camp. He was wise, moderate, and wary. Nothing delicate of his fare, nor curious of his apparel. Could bear all weathers, hot and cold, and endure any toil. He was patient and self-commanding as a governor; both wise and circumspect; and albeit a very valiant captain and a noble soldier." It is added that the detachment or troop which he commanded, never, or very rarely—nunquam, vel raris sine—failed, through either rashness or negligence.

* *Molana, or Dair-Inis.*—In the Carew MSS., at Lambeth, we find the following entry, "A.D. 1186, Raymond, surnamed Le Gros, bu: in the Abbay of Molan, nere unto Youghall." This abbey, with its possessions, was granted to Sir Walter Raleigh, in 1585-6, and afterwards passed to the first Earl of Cork. See Lord Cork's MSS. at Lismore Castle. This Dair-Inis, or "Isle of Oaks," may, at one time, have been sacred to Druid worship.

We have already stated that Maurice, the eldest son of Raymond le Gros, the ancestor of the Fitzmaurices, inherited the large property in Kerry, which his father received, from Dermot Mac Carthy. Raymond had a second son, called by some William, and by others Hamon le Gros. His descendants took the name of Le Gras, which was afterwards changed into Grace. Hamon got large grants of lands in Ossory, now the County Kilkenny. "Grace's Country," which comprises the greater part of the barony of Cronagh, took its name from his descendants. Sir John Grace was Custos of the County of Kilkenny, in 1410. The Graces were barons of Courtstown, in the parish of Tullarvan, County of Kilkenny, where the ruins of a fine castle still remain. In the cathedral of Kilkenny, there is a monument to John Grace, baron of Courtstown, who died in 1568. The Graces lost their hereditary estates in the wars of the Revolution. John Grace, the last baron of Courtstown, forfeited thirty thousand acres in the County of Kilkenny, for his adherence to James II. There was a Richard Grace, Colonel in James' army. A number of the Graces entered the Austrian service. The chief representatives of this noble family are the Graces of the Queen's County, and the Graces of Mantua, in the County Roscommon. See *Phelan's* and *Ledwich's Antiquities of Kilkenny*, and *Lodge's Peerage*.

.I am indebted to the kindness and politeness of the Rev. Mr. Drew, Rector of Youghal (from whom I have received many a valuable hint) for the opportunity of inspecting an interesting pedigree of the Grace Family, printed on vellum, now in the possession of Captain Sheffield Grace, of the 68th Regiment. From this we learn that the great ancestor of our "Fat Friend," or favourite Norman knight, Raymond, was Otho or Other, an Italian baron, who was descended from the Lords of Tuscany. He passed from Florence into Normandy, and thence into England, about the time of King Canute's marriage with Emma, daughter of Richard Second Duke of Normandy, and widow of King Ethelred, who died 1016. Other Fitz-Other, the son of Other, appears by Doomsday Book to have been a baron of England in 1058, in 16th of Edward the Confessor. His son, Walter, was the Governor of Windsor, during the reign of William the Conqueror, and was therefore called Walter de Windsor. His son, Gerald, surnamed Carew, or de Carew, was Governor of Carew Castle, in Pembroke. Gerald's son, William, was the father of our hero, Raymond; hence Raymond was called Fitz-William, or the son of William. Raymond's father accompanied his son to Ireland, but afterwards returned to Wales, and died at Carew Castle in 1173. This agrees with the pedigree given by the Marquis of Kildare in his interesting and valuable work, *The Earls of Kildare.*

So much for the ancestors on the father's and mother's side of Raymond le Gros. His descendants, judging from the vellum pedigree, are innumerable. I may here mention that the Rev. Mr. Drew, who forwarded the document for my inspection, is descended from some of the most distinguished of our Norman knights and Irish chieftains—from Strongbow, De Lacy, De La Poer, Earl Marshal, Diarmaid, King of Leinster, O'Brien, Prince of Thomond, and Mac Carthy, King of Cork.

The following interesting anecdote, illustrative of the state of the times, and of the abduction of Nesta, the Welsh Helen, by her cousin Owen, is recorded by the Marquis of Kildare.

It was Christmas in 1108, when Cadwgan, Prince of Cardigan, had invited a number of guests to his castle. It was stated in the course of conversation that Nesta, at this time the wife of Gerald, was the most beautiful woman in Wales. This statement and the description of Nesta's charms excited the curiosity and passion of Owen, the Prince's son, who resolved to see his fair cousin and judge for himself; so he managed with some of his friends, or wild companions, to obtain admission into Pembroke Castle, which he fired in the middle of the night. Nesta, suspecting the object—if not an accomplice—persuaded her husband Gerald to escape by the aid of a rope, after which her chamber was forced open by Owen, and she was carried away. Some time after this, Owen was slain by Gerald and his party, in a wood, when taking a prey of cattle; the arrow of Gerald, or one of his party, having pierced Owen's heart.

This Gerald, as I have before stated, had three sons by Nesta—namely, Maurice, William, and David. Maurice, the ancestor of the Geraldines; William, the father of Raymond, the ancestor of the Fitz Maurices, Carews, and Graces; and David, the Bishop of St. David, who died in 1176.

CHAPTER XXII.

WILLIAM FITZ-ADELM AND JOHN DE COURCY—SYNOD AT WATERFORD—SIR TRISTRAM ARMORICUS—HOWTH HARBOUR.

A.D. 1177-78. ON hearing of the death of Strongbow, Henry writes from Normandy, "I send you William Fitz-Adelm, my seneschal, to whom I have entrusted the management of affairs, as my Viceroy, and enjoin and command that you shall attend to him as to myself; that you obey all his commands on my behalf, as you value my good will, or the allegiance which you owe me. I shall confirm his proceedings, as if executed by myself, and all your transactions with him shall be ratified by me."

William Fitz-Adelm, the new governor, arrived in Wexford, where Raymond had gone to receive him with the reverence due to his commission. He is reported to have looked with a malignant eye upon the numbers and gallant bearing of Raymond's train, and to have said to one of his followers, "I shall soon find means to quell their pride."

The relative,* cup-bearer, and friend of Henry II. could afford to treat the Norman knights, then in possession of the land, with lofty pride, and the native

* *The relative.*—"Arlotta, mother of the Conqueror, was married to Harlowen de Burgo, by whom she had Robert Earl of Cornwall, whose sons were Adelm and John. Adelm had issue, this William Fitz-Adelm. John was the father of Hubert de Burgo, chief Justiciary of England."—*Cox.*

chieftains with courtesy and kindness. Herein consisted his principal offence in the eyes of Giraldus Cambrensis. "I omit," says Ware, "the language which Giraldus Cambrensis used of Fitz-Adelm, for it is sufficiently known how favourable Cambrensis was to his own relations—which truly were not a few of the chief men—and how severe to others." "The English lords," says Leland (who appears to have adopted some of the prejudices of Cambrensis) " had left their native lands, with the hopes of valuable settlements and acquisitions in Ireland; and they who had not yet received their rewards, were particularly displeased with Fitz-Adelm, and impatient of administration *unfriendly to the spirit of adventure.*"

We put these words in italics, as worthy of note, for it was in "the spirit of adventure" the invasion was made. Ireland was the hunting ground or wild prairie for Norman knights. But we have no doubt that Fitz-Adelm, in checking the spirit of adventure and conciliating Irish chieftains, adopted the instructions which he had received from the English monarch. His manner of receiving the native Irish that "crowded eagerly to court," contrasts favourably with the rudeness of Prince John, that drove the chieftains into rebellion. But Fitz-Adelm is accused of indifference, or apathy, in suppressing even *actual* rebellion. Richard Fleming, an Englishman, who commanded in Slane Castle,* had, by his frequent depredations, provoked the men of Meath to rise *en masse*, to slaughter him and his men, and chase the garrisons in

---

* *Slane Castle.*—Baile Slaine is a village near the Boyne, in the county Meath. The site of Fleming's castle is now occupied by the seat of the Marquis of Conyngham.

the castles of Kelly-Galtrim and Derrypatrick, to the very gates of Dublin. But Fitz-Adelm, like a second Gallio, "cared for none of these things."

Fitz-Adelm was accompanied by Vivian,* the Pope's Legate, Nicholas Wallingford, John de Courcy, Robert Fitz-Stephen, and Milo de Cogan. Vivian convened a synod of the Irish clergy at Waterford, where the bulls or decrees of Adrian and Alexander, granting Ireland to Henry II., were publicly read, and denunciations pronounced on all who should deny or resist that monarch's right to the lordship of Ireland.

Dr. Hanmer and Giraldus say, that John de Courcy was joined in the commission† with Fitz-Adelm. But this is, we suspect, a mistake, although we find both their names united in Ware's list of Irish governors. Leland, who says "the commission is still extant," gives the following as a copy from an old parchment roll in possession of the Earl of Meath:—

"Henry, by the grace of God, King of England, Lord of Ireland, Duke of Normandy and Acquitain, and Earl of Anjou. To the archbishops, bishops, kings, rulers, earls, barons, and all his faithful subjects of Ireland, health. Know ye, that by the grace of God I am safe and in good health, and that my affairs go on pros-

---

* *Vivian.*—"A.D. 1177 Cardinal Vivianus arrived in Ireland. A synod of the clergy of Ireland, both bishops and abbots, was convened by this cardinal, on the first Sunday in Lent; and they enacted many ordinances, not now observed."—*Annals of Ireland.* "Vivian, the legate on the Pope's behalf, doth accurse and excommunicate all those that flitte from the obeysance of the King of England."—*Campion*, lib. 2, cap. 2, p. 105.

† *Joined in the commission.*—"The king sent into Ireland William Fitz-Adelme to be his lieutenant, and joined with him in the commission, John de Courcy."—*Hanmer's Chronicle*, Dublin ed., p. 291.

perously and with honour, and that, as soon as possible, I will attend to my great affairs in Ireland. That at present I send you William Fitz-Adelm, my cup-bearer, to whom I have committed the management and transaction of all my affairs in my stead, and as my vice-regent. Wherefore I command and firmly ordain that you pay him the same attention as to me, in transacting business. And that you perform whatever he shall order in my name, as you tender my regard, and by the allegiance you owe me. I also ratify and confirm whatever he may hereafter do, as if I myself had done the same, and hold valid whatever you shall do for him."

It is probable that John de Courcy held the office of Lieutenant under the Viceroy, Fitz-Adelm. It required an armed band to keep the Irish chieftains in subjection.

But John de Courcy ambitioned more than this. Disgusted, we are told, by the inactivity of Fitz-Adelm, he set out for the north, in open defiance of the Viceroy's prohibition. He attempted to do in Ulster what Raymond le Gros had done in Munster. He was a man peculiarly fitted for such an enterprise. He is described by Giraldus Cambrensis, as fair and tall, with great bones and muscles, immense strength, of singular courage and audacity, and like Goliah of Gath, a man of war from his youth. Campion calls him a warrior of noble courage, and in pitch of body like a giant." "Any one," says Cambrensis, "who had seen John de Courcy wield his sword, chopping off heads and arms, might well commend the might of this warrior."

Hanmer styles him "as worthy a knight, for martial prowess, as ever trode on Irish ground." His *Chronicle* goes on to say that Cambrensis "lightly overskipped him, partly upon private grudge, for not allowing him to be Secretary of State and Vicar-General of Ireland, and partly to please Hugh de Lacy, who envied De Courcy's honour and renown." This is not correct, for Cambrensis has not "lightly overskipped" De Courcy.

Hanmer does his best to make amends to his favourite hero for all the imagined omissions of the Welshman, but we must receive a great deal of what both Hanmer and Campion say with a grain or two of salt.

The latter informs us that "the certainty of his exploits"—some of which read like a romance—has been preserved in Latin, and committed to paper by a friar in the north, that the book was brought by O'Neill to Armagh, and translated into English, in 1551, by the Primate, George Dowdall.

John de Courcy, by his father's side was a Norman, by his mother's a Welshman. "He was a gentleman descended, as seemeth by his coate, of an ancient house, of whom the Irishmen hold that Merlin of Caermarthen prophesied,* when he wrote, "A white knight sitting on a white horse, bearing birds in his shield, shall be the first, with force of arms, to enter and subdue Ulster."

While serving in the French wars, under Henry II., he met with a "worthy knight," called Sir Armoricus Tristram. Armoricus married De Courcy's sister, and "the two knights became sworn brethren." They vowed, in the church of our Lady, at Rouen, to serve

---

* *Merlin of Caermerthen prophesied.*—The prophecy, which is said to have been delivered in the fifth century, runs thus:—"Miles albus, albo residens equo, aves in clypeo gerens, Ultoniam hostili invasione, primus intrabit."

together, to live and die together, and equally to divide whatever they won by the sword, or received, as the reward of their services.

The two friends arrive together, in the little harbour of Howth. John de Courcy is too sick to land. The duty of disembarking the troops devolves on Armoricus. They are assailed by the Irish. There is "a cruel fight by the side of a bridge." Sir Armoricus behaves himself "most worthily," and gets the victory; but many are slain on both sides, and among the number seven of his own blood; in consideration of which, and his great valour, he gets the lordship of the place, which now gives title to his descendants, the St. Lawrences,* or the Lords of Howth.

We strongly suspect, that, in this Sir Tristram Armoricus, we have the true type, or original, of King Arthur's famous knight, Sir Tristram, described in the romance of the "Round Table." Armorica is the source from which Geoffrey of Monmouth derived the materials of his histories or stories. We take Sir Tristram Armoricus, simply, to mean, Sir Tristram, the Armorican. These famous knights are represented as doing battle, not only in England, Wales, and Scotland, but also in Ireland.

Sir Tristram is represented as having vanquished an Irish chieftain, somewhere in Cornwall or Wales, who bore the name and title of "*Le Morhout d'Irlande.*" The chieftain turns out to be the Prince or King of Dublin. Now Dermot Mac Murrough (or Le Morhout) claimed,

* *St. Lawrence.*—It is supposed that this name was assumed by the third baron of Howth, Almaric, in fulfilment of a vow made previous to a battle, fought on the festival of Saint Lawrence.

as King of Leinster, to be also "King of the Danes of Dublin." His father also held the same title. Dermot Mac Murrough visited Wales, and was there some time, as we have shown.

Sir Tristram, according to the romance, was driven by bad weather into the port of Dublin, or perhaps Howth, which was the general landing place. Here he assumed the name of Tramtris. Being skilled in playing on the harp, he attracted the notice of the queen, and her beautiful daughter, Isolde. Shortly after this, he slew a dragon which had long been the terror of Dublin. For Dragon, read Dane. Sir Tristram is wounded, and tended in his sickness by the fair Isolde, who, in her turn, imparts and receives a far deeper wound; in simple words, the knight and the Irish princess become deeply enamoured of each other. But Isolde is betrothed to some Welsh or Cornish king. It is the story of Dearforgil, Eva, and Strongbow, jumbled up together. To make a long story short, Tristram dies, with the name of Isolde on his lips; and Isolde, not to be outdone in affection, expires of a broken heart on her lover's bier.

Some amount of probability is given to this, our interpretation of the romance, from the fact, that at one time there existed near Dublin, a tower called "Isolde's Tower," and a spring, or well, called "Isolde's Fount," and there still exists, at no great distance from the same place, the well-known village of Chapel-Isode, now spelt Chapel Izod.

CHAPTER XXIII.

JOHN DE COURCY'S EXPEDITION TO THE NORTH—THE PROPHECY CONCERNING HIM—TAKES DOWN-PATRICK—HIS FORTUNES AND MISFORTUNES.

A.D. 1178-79. FITZ-ADELM is unpopular with the Norman knights. He cares for nothing "but his back and belly," or, as Hanmer renders it, his kindred and his children. He has no sympathy with the soldiers of fortune, with men of enterprise, like John de Courcy, Armoricus Tristram, or Robert de la Poer, who have their own inheritances to carve out. These three men, with a small company* of the boldest and most adventurous of the English, resolve to push their conquests into the north, which had hitherto preserved its independence. They set out from Dublin, headed by De Courcy, on his prophetic white horse. There was another prophecy, ascribed to St. Columbkille, which does not contain so complimentary a description of the party who was to conquer Ulster. He is represented as " a certain pauper and beggar"—quendam pauperem et mendicum—" and a fugitive from other lands"—et quasi de aliis terris fugacem.

Stanihurst asserts that De Courcy was desirous of making his conduct in Ulster, square, as near as possible, with the prediction of the Welsh seer; and that, with this view, he provided himself, in starting on his Ulster expedition, with a white horse, and a shield, upon which

* *Small company.*—Giraldus says it consisted of twenty knights, and three hundred common soldiers. Hanmer says, "seven hundred."

birds were painted. This is supposed to be a poetical enlargement of Stanihurst. Giraldus says, that "De Courcy happened, by mere chance,"—*forte*—" to ride upon a white horse on that occasion ; and had little birds," —*aviculas*—" painted on his shield, evidently the cognizance of his family." But Giraldus says that De Courcy always carried about with him, the prophecies of Saint Columbkille. Stanihurst says, that in going to bed, he placed the book under his pillow,—ad doriendam proficiscens eundem sub cubicularis lecti pulvino collocaret. It seems remarkable that De Courcy should prefer the prophecy which represents the conqueror of Ulster as a pauper and a fugitive, although he assumed the appearance of the knight on the white horse. But the fact is, that Stanihurst had no authority whatever for his embellishments.

On the fourth day after leaving Dublin, De Courcy and his followers arrive at Downpatrick, which they take by surprise, the Irish chieftain Dunlevi or Donslevy making a precipitate retreat. Hanmer's description of the taking of the town is graphic, though overdrawn :— " The trumpets sounded, the armour rattled, the women clapt [or wrung] their hands, and the children cried. The leaders entered, the soldiers rifled, and the town, upon a sudden, was ransacked. Doors, windows, cupboards, chests, flew open. The army, after long march and sore travail, being in great want and weakness, had their housing, firing, diet, and fare of the best, bedding, clothing, gold, silver, plate, and rich booties, without check or controlment; and respite for certain days, to breathe, and *recreate* themselves."

They were in this happy state of recreation, when the

"wind blew" in Vivianus or Vivian, the cardinal. Hanmer says, "He came out of Scotland. He had been in the Isle of Man, on Christmas Day, 1176. He landed at Downpatrick, after the Epiphany, in 1177, and proceeding to Dublin, was met and taken prisoner by De Courcy; and notwithstanding this bad treatment, on his arrival, he convened a synod, in which he enjoined the Irish, on pain of excommunication, to submit to Henry as their lord, in conformity to the letter of Alexander III.— *Cambrensis Eversus,* editor's note, v. ii., p. 554.

The Cardinal at the same time represented to De Courcy, the injustice and cruelty of his enterprise, reminded him of the treaty which Henry II. had concluded with the Irish nation, in the person of its monarch, Roderick O'Conor, and said that the men of Ulster were ready to pay their quota of the stipulated treaty.

To all this De Courcy turned a deaf ear. He had not set out on this enterprise, as Henry's tax-gatherer, or from any spirit of loyalty, but simply to win broad lands in Ulster; and what he had won by the sword he would keep by the sword; so he set himself to fortify Downpatrick and erect other castles and forts in the district.

The Irish consult the Cardinal, who advises them to defend their persons and property by arms. Herein he followed the example of the patriotic Archbishop of Dublin, St. Lawrence O'Toole. So to war they go.

Donslevy, the chieftain of Downpatrick, "no base or mean commander," collected a force of nearly ten thousand men. Sir John De Courcy, with his seven hundred followers, thought it best to give battle outside the town. He divided his men into three companies. "Seven score horsemen" (behind each of whom sits an archer) are committed to the leading of Sir Armoricus St. Lawrence, who occupies the left; Sir Roger de la Poer,* who has married his niece, commands the right. De Courcy takes a central position by the side of a bog. The Irish commander assails the English horse under Armoricus, whose bowmen ply them with arrows, till their quivers are empty, and then draw their swords and endeavour to hough the Irish horses. The battle grows warm, for the Irish fight fiercely. Armoricus calls on De Courcy and De la Poer to bring up the foot. The Irish assail these with darts, stones, and galloglass axes; the English reply with swords and spears. "The splints of broken stones fly about their ears." The blows of the Irish battleaxes sound like sledge hammers on the English helmets. "Both sides," says Hanmer, "deserved honour and singular commendations."

The slaughter on both sides was great; perhaps the English suffered most, for the Irish determined to make an end of them that day. The English occupied a narrow space of ground, protected by a bog on one side, and a ditch on the other. The entrance to this narrow space was literally filled with the bodies of the slain and

* *Roger de la Poer.*—Giraldus Cambrensis speaks of Roger de la Poer as "the youngest, bravest, and handsomest" of all the Anglo-Norman knights. The De la Poers settled in Waterford, and became barons of Donisle and Curraghmore, on the "Great-Plain," now the name of the principal residence of the Marquises of Waterford. The Beresfords, by intermarriage with the De la Poers, became Earls of Tyrone, and Marquises of Waterford. The Powers of Waterford—and they are very numerous throughout the county—are descendants of the De la Poers.

dead horses. The way to the living was blocked up by the dead, whose bodies formed a rampart, which the Irish found it impossible to surmount. So they "break up their battle array, and disperse upon the plain."

They were ignorant of the enemy with whom they contended. Sir Armoricus, watching his opportunity, called on his nephew, Geoffrey Montgomery, to advance his standard, and wheel about upon the foe. Montgomery replied, "Your stomach surpasses your strength. We have won honour enough. Shall we now lose it? Of seven score we have but forty horses left." "Give me the standard," says his uncle, "I will bear it myself." "If that be your pleasure," replied Montgomery, "you shall not charge me with cowardice. Under this standard I have got honour, and under this standard—if God so please—I will die." With this they wheel about and overtake the Irish, who are "laden with arms, and weary with fight." The contest is renewed with obstinate courage. Armoricus is twice unhorsed, and twice lifted into the saddle. He is unhorsed a third time, and his horse slain in the middle of a "filthy ford." He is in imminent danger, but his men stand by him and keep the ford till John de Courcy comes up to the rescue, when the Irish give way, and leave the English masters of the field.

Hanmer, whose account of this battle we have condensed, says the English lost many a brave man, especially Lionel St. Lawrence, nephew to Armoricus, whose death was greatly lamented. When they had buried their dead and gathered their arms, they returned to Dun or Downpatrick.

John de Courcy fought another battle, the next summer, near the walls of Downpatrick, and overthrew—if we can believe Stanihurst—fifteen thousand men. "After that field," quoth the Book of Howth, "Ulstermen had small stomach to give onset on Englishmen."

The field was bloody on both sides. Armoricus, sore wounded, lay under a hedge, eating honeysuckles, to assuage his thirst. Sir Nicholas St. Lawrence was also badly wounded.

De Courcy now began to build castles, to guard the lands which he had won. If we can believe Hanmer's account, he erected two castles at Ferney—correctly, Firlce—on the Bawn, in the country Antrim, which he gave in charge to an Irish chieftain, named Mac Mahon, who had "given De Courcy many gifts, and made him gossip."* Within a month MacMahon had levelled the castle to the ground. When De Courcy sent to know the cause, he replied, "I did not promise to hold stone walls, but land. It is not my nature to crouch myself within stones, the woods being nigh, where I am warmer." De Courcy, annoyed at his reply, leads a party to prey upon his land, which swept away the whole of his cattle. The English with their prey are divided into three companies. In passing over some boggy ground, which is covered with thick bushes, they find themselves in the midst of a powerful force, that lay

---

* *Made him gossip.*—"The parties to be coupled in league, meete at church, become *God-Septes*, or allies, beare each other on his backe, certaine paces, in a ring, kiss together holy reliques, take blessing of the bishop, offer, each to other, a droppe of his owne bloode, and drink it up betweene them."—*Campion's Historie of Ireland*, lib. i., cap. vi., p. 23.

in ambush to intercept them. The Irish rush in between the English companies, and raise a shout which makes the woods ring again. "The cowes ranne like divils, upon the drivers," and overthrew horse and men. More were trodden down in the mire, by the cows, than were slain by the sword.

There were several skirmishes during the retreat; in one of which the Irish leader, Mac Mahon, was slain. But the Irish continued the pursuit to the walls of an old fort, where De Courcy sought protection for the night. Sir Armoricus "after a short nap" arose "to espie the enemies' campe." He soon returns, and awakes De Courcy, whom he thus addresses:—"I have scouted abroad, and spared you in your heavy sleep. I have viewed the enemy, whom I take to be five thousand strong. We are but five hundred fighting men, wearied with fight and long travail, and somewhat discouraged with hard fortune. If the enemy assail us to-morrow, and we are unable to withstand them, our case will be desperate. Let us up, and set upon them now, while some are sleeping, and others feasting."

The advice is adopted, and a night attack made, in which the English slaughter nearly the whole of the five thousand Irish.

Hanmer concludes, "There are some, out of envy, to disgrace Courcy, report the story otherwise; that he was driven, with eleven persons in arms, to travel on foot,* for thirty miles, for the space of two days; the

* *On foot.*—It appears, even from Hanmer's own account, that the Irish had possession of De Courcy's "white horse" and Sir Armoricus' blacke gelding.—*Hanmer's Chronicle*, Dublin Edition, p. 308.

enemy still pursuing; fasting, and without relief, till they came to an old castle."

The Four Masters give a very different version of the story:—

A.D. 1178. John de Courcy soon after proceeded to plunder Dalaradia, and Hy-Tuirtre; and Firlee gave battle to him and his foreigners, and defeated them, with great slaughter, through the miracles of Patrick, Columbkille, and Brendan, John [de Courcy] himself escaped with difficulty, being severely wounded, and fled to Dublin."

Hanmer calls the Irish leader, to whom De Courcy gave charge of two castles, Mac Mahon. Now we learn from Spenser, who was a contemporary with Hanmer, that these Mac Mahons were of English descent, and that the first of them, an Englishman, named Fitz-Ursula, came to Ireland in 1585. Fitz-Ursula and Mac Mahon have the same meaning " the son of a bear." Dr. O'Donovan says that " the Mac Mahons, who are a collateral branch of the O'Connells, were not heard of, as chiefs of Oriel, for some time after De Courcy's disappearance from Irish history, in 1205." Sir John Davis, writing about transactions of the reign of Henry IV., says, " Mac Mahon accepteth a state in the Fernes, for life, rendering ten pound a yeare."

Hanmer gives a long account, taken from the Book of Howth,* of another battle fought by the three friends, De Courcy, Armoricus, and De la Poer, against the Irish, between Drogheda and Dundalk. O'Hanlon had seized one of De Courcy's vessels, and put the sailors to the

* *Book of Howth.*—" A collection of traditional stories written by an Anglo-Irish romancer, in the fifteenth or sixteenth century."—*Dr. O'Donovan.*

sword. "De Courcy, to revenge this injury, rushed alone into the midst of his enemies, and did miracles with his two-handed sword, slashing on both sides like a lion among sheep." The sheep would have overcome the lion, if Armoricus had not come to the rescue of his friend, who was "sore wounded with cruel fight, and in a manner out of breath."

The Annals of Ulster, under date 1178, give a brief account of an inroad made by De Courcy upon the territory Cuailgne; but the Annals of Innisfallen place it under date 1180. De Courcy, on this occasion, took a prey of a thousand cows; but was pursued, had his plunder recaptured, and was driven, for shelter, to the castle of Skeen Columbkille, which he himself had built.

"Not long after this," writes Hanmer, "Sir John de Courcy went into England, where the king, in regard of his good services, made him Lord of Connaught and Earl of Ulster."

CHAPTER XXIV.

HUGH DE LACY, AND HIS TRAGICAL END.

A.D. 1179-1185

HUGH DE LACY, who had been Governor, or Viceroy, in 1172-3, was re-appointed in 1179. Campion calls him "Protector-General." The English complained that the Irish *only* were protected by his predecessor. "Little good did Fitz-Adelm, and less was he like to do, because he delighted to crosse his peeres, and was of them stopped in his course of conduct." Hanmer gives a very different character of Hugh de Lacy:—

"The realme of Ireland, at this time, was singularly well governed by Hugh de Lacy, a good man and a wise magistrate, who, for the good of the land and the people, established many good orders. He made bridges and builded towns, castles, and forts, throughout Leinster, as Sir John de Courcy did in Ulster. The priest kept his church, the soldier his garrison, and the ploughman followed his plough."

But we could not expect a semi-millenial state like this to last for a thousand years. It did not last six months. "Cankred envy quieted not herself, but practised mischiefe against him." De Lacy was charged before the King with an attempt on the Crown of Ireland, and of making himself "absolute lord of the land." Perhaps he gave some cause or colour for these charges by marrying the daughter of Roderick O'Conor, King of Connaught, the acknowledged monarch of Ireland. This appeared a bolder and higher flight than that of Strongbow, who married Eva, the daughter of the King of Leinster. But the latter had no legitimate male heir. Roderick O'Conor had legitimate male heirs.*

The Irish, or Connaught princess, bore the romantic name of *Rose*.† She was De Lacy's second wife. They were married in 1180, but "contrary (says Holingshed) to the wishes of Henry II.," who sent for him to England. There all matters were satisfactorily explained, and De Lacy permitted to return as Chief Governor of Ireland, with Robert of Shrewsbury as his assistant, or deputy. De Lacy's office in Ireland had been filled, during his absence, by John Constable, of Chester and Richard de Pech, Justices.

Hugh de Lacy is celebrated in Irish history for the number of castles which he built. He castellated Meath, from the Shannon to the sea. Without the protection of these stone forts, the English could never have held possession of Ireland. A Norman knight, in his panoply of mail, was a formidable opponent in the field, and hard to bring down. But Norman knights could not always keep the field, or saddle, armed *cap-a-pie;* and without their armour they were as vulnerable as the crab without its shell, and therefore adapted the crab's policy, and sought the protection of some rock or stronghold, for doffing it. The number of Norman castles built in Ireland, during the thirteenth century, was very great.

* *Legitimate male heirs.*—We read in the *Four Masters*, under date 1186, of the roy-damnus, or royal princes of Connaught; of "Conor Moinmoy, the son of Roderick"; and Cathal Carragh, the son of Conor Moinmoy.

† *Romantic name of Rose.*—It appears that this little hairy knight had a penchant for Roses. His first wife was Rosa de Munemone.

Not to mention Hugh de Lacy's castle in Meath,—of which he had received a royal grant—he built the Black Castle, at Leighin, in Idrone, another at Tachmeho, now Timahoe, in Leix; a third at Castle Dermot, in O'Toole's country, a fourth at Tullow, in the county Carlow, a fifth on the Barrow, near Leighlin, another at Kilkee, another at Narragh, in the county Kildare. For a more complete account of De Lacy's castle building, we beg to refer the curious reader to *Hanmer's Chronicle*, Dublin edition, from pages 320 to 322, and the *Hibernia Expugnata*, cap. 19, 21, 22.

Sir Hugh de Lacy lost his life, while building the castle of Durrow, in the King's County, near the boundary of Westmeath. The tragic event is thus recorded in the Annals of Ireland:—

"A.D. 1186. Hugo de Lacy, the profaner and destroyer of many churches, lord of the English of Meath, Breifney, and Oriel—to whom the tribute of Connaught was paid— he who had conquered the greater part of Ireland for the English, and of whose castles, all Meath, from the Shannon to the sea, was full, after having finished the Castle of Durrow, set out, accompanied by three Englishmen, to view it. One of the men of Teffia, a youth named Gilla-gan-inathar O'Meyey, approached him, and drawing an axe, which he had kept concealed, with one blow, severed his head from his body; and both head and trunk fell into the ditch of the castle."

Keating calls the "youth," who did this bold deed, "a young gentleman in disguise." Giraldus says he was the foster-son of an Irish chieftain, called Sinnagh, that is "the Fox." To him we find the young cub running to cover. "He afterwards went to Sinnagh (the Fox) and O'Breen, at whose instigation he had killed the Earl." Sinnagh, or Sinnach, O'Charney, or O'Kearney, the Fox, was the Irish chieftain of Teffia, the territory in which the Castle of Durrow had been built.

Campion's description of the affair has somewhat the appearance of invention. We give an abridged account, in Campion's own words:—" Sundry times came Lacy to quicken his labourers, full glad to see them fall in use with such exercise. He merrily would command his gentlemen to give the labourers example, in taking pains—to take their instruments in hands, and to worke a season—the poore souls looking on and resting. But this ended tragically. While each man was busie, to try his cunning, some lading, some plastering, some heaving, some carving, the generall also himself digging with a pykeaxe, a desperate villain of them, he, whose toole, the generall used weapon,* espying both his hands occupied, and his body with all force, inclining to the blow, watched his stoope, and clove his head with an axe, little esteeming the torments that ensued."— "No torments ensued," exclaims Doctor O'Donovan, "for the murderer, who was as thin as a greyhound, baffled all pursuit"—ran to cover, to his friend, and fosterer, the Fox.

The annals of Ulster say that Hugo, the profaner and destroyer of sanctuaries, was killed in revenge of Columbkille, whose churches he had desecrated. "It

---

* *The generall used weapon.*—" From an ancient and wicked custom, they always carry an axe in their hands, instead of a staff, that they may be ready, promptly, to execute whatever iniquity their minds suggest."—*Giraldus Cambrensis*, cap. xxi. *Top.*

may not be here out of place to remark," observes the learned, wise, and impartial translator and annotator of the Annals of Ireland, "that in our time a somewhat similar disaster occured at Durrow,* for its proprietor, the Earl of Norbury, was assassinated by a hand still unknown, after he had completed a castle on the site of that erected by De Lacy, and, as some would think, after having insulted St. Columbkille by preventing the families under his [Columbkille's] tutelage, from burying their dead in the ancient cemetery of Durrow."

De Lacy's head and body were buried in this cemetery, by his own people, where they remained till 1195, when the Archbishops of Cashel and Dublin had them removed from the Irish territory—"ex Hibernica plaga"—and buried—the body in the Abbey of Bective, in Meath, and the head in St. Thomas a'Becket's new church, in Dublin.

A controversy afterwards arose between the canons of St. Thomas and the monks of Bective respecting the proper place of interment for the body, when it was decided, in 1205, that it should rest with the head, in the tomb of De Lacy's first wife, Rosa de Munemene. If we take into account the size of the body, and that it was only a headless trunk—a *trunk* indeed, for it was covered with hair—we must confess that all due honour was done this little man.

Hugh De Lacy, according to Grace's Annals, left two sons—we are not informed by which wife, but we conclude by Rosa de Munemene—Walter and Hugh. The former is styled, in the Annals of Innisfallen, "King of

* *Durrow.*—*Vide* Book of Durrow, containing the Four Gospels in Latin, in Trinity College, Dublin.

Meath," and the latter "King of Ulster." He also had a son by the king of Connaught's daughter, called William Gorm, from whom descended—according to Duald Mac Firbis—the famous Pierce Lacy, of Bruree, and Bruff, the fast friend of *Sugan Earl of Desmond*. The Lynches of Galway are also descended from this William Gorm, grandson of our last Irish monarch. The race of Walter and Hugh became extinct, in the male line. "Walter," says Doctor O'Donovan, had two daughters—Margaret, who married Lord Theobald Verdon; and Matilda, who married Geoffrey Genevile. Hugh had one daughter, Maud, who married Walter de Burgo, who became, in right of his wife, Earl of Ulster.

CHAPTER XXV.

JOHN COMYN, ARCHBISHOP OF DUBLIN—PHILIP OF WORCESTER AND HUGH TYRRELL, HIS FELLOW-SCRAPER, WHO CARRIED OFF THE BREWING-PAN FROM DOWN-PATRICK — THE ARCHIEPISCOPATE OF DUBLIN BECOMES INDEPENDENT OF ARMAGH.

A.D. 1185. THE Normans have now been in possession of the country for a period of sixteen years, from 1169 to 1185, during which time every man of them* did pretty much what seemed right in his own eyes, when Henry II. resolved to send over a more responsible chief ruler, in the person of his son, John. "King Henry," writes Ware, "designing now to transfer the whole dominion of Ireland to his son John, sent over John Comyn, Archbishop of Dublin, as his forerunner."

Comyn was chosen Archbishop, by the clergy of Dublin, who were called together by Henry, at Evesham, in Worcestershire, on the 6th of September, 1181; but he did not arrive in Dublin till 1184. He succeeded the famous Lawrence O'Toole,† who died November 14th, 1180, in the monastery of Eu, in Normandy. The Four Masters say he "suffered martyrdom in

---

* *Every man of them.*—For a list of the heads or leaders of these Norman invaders, see the list in *Harris's Hibernica*, pp. 46, 47, 48. It occurs as the Appendix to *A Fragment of the History of Ireland*, by Maurice Regan.

† *Lawrence O'Toole*—The O'Tooles were lords of Hy-Muireadhaigh, a more important territory than Imaill. This distinguished Irish bishop is described as "tall and graceful, and of a comely countenance."

England," but this is a figure of speech. He was attacked by a maniac, in Canterbury, in 1175, while celebrating mass, but lived for five years after the attack. He was canonized, in 1226, by Pope Honorius III.

When Giraldus Cambrensis displayed contempt of Irish churchmen—a feeling which marks his class to the present day—the Irish replied by recounting the number of saints which their country had produced. "Saints," exclaimed the Welshman, "Yes, you have saints, but where are your martyrs? I cannot find one Irish martyr in your calendar." "It must be acknowledged," was the able and witty retort, "that as *yet* our people have not acquired the guilt of murdering God's servants; but now that the English have settled in our island, and Henry is our sovereign, we may soon expect martyrs enough."

Ware thinks the man that made this reply was Maurice (and not Matthew O'Henry), archbishop of Cashel from 1182 to 1194. We do not know how this can be, for Cambrensis himself calls this Maurice not only "a learned" but a "*discreet* man."

Ware describes John Comyn, the forerunner of John Lackland, as "an Englishman, learned, eloquent, and grave." When appointed, he was only in deacon's orders. It was during his archiepiscopate that the See of Dublin was made, to a great extent, independent of Armagh. In a bull bearing date the 13th of April, 1182, we read, "In pursuance of the authorities of the sacred canons, we appoint that no archbishop, or bishop, shall, without the assent of the Archbishop of Dublin, presume to hold any convention within the diocess of Dublin; or hold any causes or ecclesiastical matters of that diocess, without being thereunto authorised by the Pope of Rome, or his legate."

The archiepiscopal estates were granted to Comyn, " in barone," so that he and his successors became barons, and were entitled to sit in the great councils, and hold courts.

We learn from Ware that St. Patrick's Cathedral was built by this John Comyn, in 1190, " having demolished the old parish church that was there." Of the conduct of the Lord Deputy, Hannon de Valois, to this archbishop, we shall speak in the proper place. " He died," says Ware, " at Dublin, the 28th of October, 1212, and lies buried in Christchurch, where he has a marble tomb, in the south part of the quire." The tomb is there still.

Philip of Worcester, the ostensible governor, either accompanied, or immediately followed, the Archbishop. Ware styles him Philip de Pergornia, more correctly Wigornia.* The Four Masters call him Philip Unserva. One of the first acts of his government was to restore the royal revenues, which had been alienated by De Lacy, and applied to his own uses. About the beginning of March he went to Armagh, where he stayed for six days, and extorted much money and other things from the clergy. But, on his return, was struck with a sudden pang [" a fit of the gripes "], and hardly escaped. How Hugh Tyrrell, one of his captains, was punished for his extortion, you may read in Giraldus Cambrensis. This mysterious passage is thus explained by Hanmer and Cambrensis :—

* *Wigornia.*—He is called Philip Worcester in the old translation of the *Annals of Ulster*, in the British Museum; and Philippus Wigorniensis by Cambrensis. Some think that Philip de Broase and Philip of Worcester were the same.

"Hugh Tirrell, his fellow-scraper, took from the poore priests at Armagh a great brasse panne, or a brewing vessel, which served the whole house. See the just judgment of God. Philip [of Worcester], at the townes end of Armagh, was taken with a sudden pang; and the same so vehement, that it was supposed he should never have recovered it." A monk, standing by, said, "Let him alone; he must have breath, till he go to the devil, who will have him, for all that he extorted from us."

Tyrrell carried the brewing pan as far as Downpatrick; but here a fierce judgment overtook him. The house in which he lodged was burned down, and the two horses, that carried the pan, destroyed; so Tyrrell made a virtue of necessity, and sent back the brewing pan, as he had no horses to carry it away.

CHAPTER XXVI.

JOHN, THE SON OF HENRY II., ARRIVES IN IRELAND—HE AND HIS COURTIERS OFFEND THE IRISH PRINCES, WHO TAKE THEIR REVENGE—JOHN RETURNS TO ENGLAND.

BUT let us turn from Philip of Worcester, and Hugh Tyrrell, his "fellow-scraper," to the king's son, and see how he deported himself as Chief Ruler. It is quite clear that Henry had previously obtained liberty from Pope Alexander III. to erect Ireland into a distinct dominion, and to make one of his sons, king. Hovenden says that it was decreed, at a Parliament held at Oxford in 1177, to confer this high honour on John, Earl of Morton, better known as John Lack-land, or Sans-terre. Eight years after this, when John was preparing to visit Ireland, Lucius III. sent a legate to England, who offered to accompany the new prince to his new kingdom, and crown him there,* with a diadem of peacocks' feathers, or, as Hanmer styles it, "a crowne of peacock's tayles." But Henry declined this honour for his son. He probably thought that a crown of this light material was more than the young man's head could

* *And crown him there.*—So far as English rule or law prevailed, all public acts in Ireland were executed in the name of "John, Lord of Ireland, son of the King of England." The coinage of Ireland bore, on one side, his face, with a diadem of fine pearls, with the inscription, "Johannes Dom." It is not so clear as many imagine, that any other prince or king had, or used, the title of Dominus, or "Lord of Ireland." Palgrave says the title Dominus Angliæ indicates a right to superiority over the soil, to be distinguished from the chieftainship of the people.

carry. But he was knighted by his father, at Windsor, on the last of March, in the nineteenth year of his age.*

He sailed with a fair wind from Milford Haven, on the third day after Easter, "the evening of Easter Wednesday, 1185," and landed safely at Waterford, accompanied, according to some, by three hundred, and by others, four hundred knights, besides horsemen and archers.

Sir John Davis says "the people of this land, both English and Irish, out of a natural pride, did ever love and desire to be governed by great persons." Here is a splendid opportunity. The Irish chieftains, or nobility, flocked to welcome the king's son, as they had done his father; who had received them with attention and respect, and entertained them with a prodigal hospitality. But John did not see the wisdom of walking in the footsteps of his aged sire, or of following the counsel of his ministers. He was influenced, like Jeroboam, the son of Solomon, by the young men of his court; whom Hanmer styles "greene heads."

But this term cannot be applied to all the young men at his court. There was one noble exception, namely Gerald Barry, clerk, better known as *Giraldus Cambrensis*, "a dilligent searcher of the antiquities of Ireland." If we can take *his* testimony on the subject, he was a young man of a most distinguished appearance,—Eram statura procerus, facie quoque fragilique ac momentaneo naturæ bono, formae nitore praeclarus. An old monk, named

---

* *The nineteenth year of his age.*—Sir John Davis says, "The Earle of Morton was very young, about twelve years of age." This is a mistake. John was born in 1166—at the palace of Woodstock—and was, therefore, nineteen, instead of twelve, years of age, in 1185.

Serlo, asked, "Is it possible that so handsome a young man could ever die"?

Though he has died, his works still live, and are likely to live, notwithstanding the very learned, very classical, and very foolishly inflated attempt to upset their authority, in a work by Dr. Lynch, called *Cambrensis Eversus*. Giraldus candidly confesses that one of his motives, for writing, was, that he might live in the memory of mankind. "I may acquire jealousy in life"—*invidiam in vita*—but "glory hereafter"—*gloriam post fatum*. Query, would Giraldus have penned these words, had the fates revealed to him that John Lynch, of Galway, would write a book styled *Cambrensis Eversus*, which may be rendered "The Welshman floored"?

Let us turn to the reception which the " greene heads" of John's court, gave " the chiefest commanders of those parts":—

"They [the Irish chieftains] resorted unto him, in peaceable manner, to salute him, and congratulate his coming. One made curtesie, another kneeled, some took him by the hand, other some offer to *kisse* him. The new gallants and Normans, such as had not beene before acquainted with the country, neither the homlinesse of the people, set them at nought; laughed at their mantles and trosses, and derided their glibbes, and long beards. One takes a sticke, and pats the Irishman on the pate, another hauls the mantle, and prickes him behind with a pinne; some have their glibbes and long beards pulled; and departing, have flappes on the lippes, thumpes on their neckes, and the doores clapt on their heeles, with divers other abuses and undiscreete entertainment."

Campion calls the gallants, that gave this rude handling to the Irish nobility, great quaffers, proud, bellyswaines, fed with extortion and bribery. Even Giraldus Cambrensis calls them verbose boasters, enormous liars, and contemptuously proud of their own superiority.

An Irishman can give or take a joke, but does not like his beard pulled. These men—not without cause——were mightily displeased, and shifted themselves out " of the town, and in all haste got them home; and from thence, with their wives and children, and households, departed and went, some to the Prince of Limerick, some to the Prince of Cork, and some to Roderick, Prince of Connaught," and told what they had suffered. They informed their friends that the new Viceroy was a young man, surrounded and guided by a set of "beardlesse boyes," without sobriety or steadfastness; from whom the country could derive neither honour nor security.

Their report was not exaggerated. "They were fine in apparel, delicate mouthed, feeding upon dainties : they could not digest their meat, without spice and wine at every meal. They would not endure service in the marches and borders. They would not remain in remote places. They brooked not the forts, holds, and garrison places. Liberty they liked, so it was in a walled town. A warm chamber, a soft bed, a furred gown, a lady's lap, pleased them well. They would talk and brag of service, sware and stare, stand upon the pantofles of their reputation, disdain others, especially the Irish; but durst not shew their faces in the field."

These carpet knights were not calculated to confirm the impression of chivalrous bravery produced on the Irish mind by Richard Strongbow, Raymond le Gros,

Milo de Cogan, Robert Fitz-Stephen, and John De Courcy. Giraldus Cambrensis, who is desirous of saying the very best of Prince John, has to acknowledge that he was "led away by the fervour of youth, and ensnared by his passions; that he was prone to vice, and rude to his monitors"—that is to Gerald himself. He was "more given to pleasure than to arms; to dalliance than endurance." He employs his time "in evil practices which gallants persue." But notwithstanding all, this clerical tutor, or monitor, hopes that, in the end, he will "soar from the camp of Cupid, to the arts and towers of Pallas;" that although then obeying the "laws of green youth," he will eventually conform to those of mature age.

The same authority says, that both he and his brother, Geoffrey Count of Britany, (who had more of aloes than honey in him, whose tongue was smoother than oil,) were of rather short stature, a little below middle height; and, for their size, well shaped enough.

The Irish princes resolve to absent themselves from John's Court, and make a united effort to drive him and his courtiers out of the country. And they were sustained in this purpose by the first Norman settlers, who had no intention of dividing their large possessions with the new comers.

The Four Masters give a very succinct account of John's visit:—

"A.D. 1185, the son of the King of England, that is John, the son of Henry II., came to Ireland with a fleet of sixty ships, to assume the government of the kingdom. He took possession of Dublin and Leinster, and erected castles at Tipraid, Fachtna, and Ardfinan, out of which he plundered Munster; but his people were defeated with great slaughter by Donnell O'Brien. The son of the King of England then returned to England, to complain to his father of Hugh de Lacy, who was the King of England's deputy in Ireland, and who had prevented the Irish kings from sending either tribute or hostages."

John sailed for England about the end of the year, where he laid charges against De Lacy of disloyalty, of seeking an Irish crown; but De Lacy's head, severed from his body by an Irish battleaxe, had rolled into the moat of Durrow Castle before proper action could be taken in England against him. The "young Irish gentleman" in disguise, called Gilla-ganinather O'Meyey had anticipated the English headsman.

CHAPTER XXVII.

JOHN DE COURCY AND HUGH DE LACY, THE YOUNGER—THE IRISH RISE AGAIN—THE ENGLISH JOIN WITH O'CONOR-DEATH OF ARMORICUS—DEATH OF RODERICK O'CONOR—DEATH OF HENRY II.—THE STATE OF IRELAND.

A.D. 1186-1189. STANIHURST says that Henry II. committed the government of Ireland, on John's departure, to De Broase, De Courcy, Giraldus, and De Lacy. The words are "Bruceo, Courceo, Giraldini et in primis, Hugoni Lacæi Virtuti." As Giraldus Cambrensis, whose name is here introduced, does not mention this, we may conclude that Stanihurst was mistaken. But it would appear that De Lacy the younger was joined with De Courcy in the Irish government. We are informed by Campion that "they continued lovingly together," and did "streight execution upon the rebels." If we are to believe the Four Masters, the rebels, or Irish, who were again in arms, did straight execution upon them:—"A.D. 1187 the Castle of Kildare, which was in the possession of the English, was burned and demolished by Conor Moinmoy and Melaghlin Beg, and not one of the English escaped, but were all suffocated or otherwise destroyed." The Irish slew two horsemen or knights, and carried away their "horses, arms, shields, and coats of mail." A.D. 1188, "The English of the Castle Moy set out upon a predatory excursion into Tyrone, where they seized on some cows. Donnell O'Loughlin pursued them with his retainers, and overtook them at Cavan *na g-craun ard*, that is 'the hollow of the high trees,' where an engagement took place, in which the English were defeated with great slaughter." Donnell, son of Hugh O'Loughlin, called by the Four Masters "presumptive heir to the throne of Ireland," and who was possessed of "personal symmetry, intelligence, and wisdom," fell in the heat of the conflict, thrust through by an English spear."

We learn from the next quotation that the English were not only at war with the O'Loughlins of the north, but also with the O'Conors of the west and O'Briens of the south; in fact, that the whole kingdom, which had never been effectually conquered, was up in arms again :—

"A.D. 1188, John De Courcy and the English of Ireland made an incursion into Connaught, accompanied by Conor O'Dermot, upon which Conor Moinmoy, King of Connaught, assembled all the chieftains of Connaught, who were joined by Donnell O'Brien at the head of some of the men of Munster. The English set fire to some of the churches of the country, as they passed along, but made no delay until they reached Eas-dara (Ballysadare) with the intention of passing into Tir-Connell. Here they were met by the Kinel Connell, and defeated on their retreat across the Curliew mountains."

It was on this occasion that Armoricus is supposed to have met his death. We give the account, as it appears in the Book of Howth, for what it is worth. Sir John De Courcy, when hard pushed by one of the O'Conors—perhaps by Conor Moinmoy, the usurper, or

his son, Cathal Carragh, or his cousin, Cathal Crovderg*
—sends for his brother-in-law Armoricus, who, mindful
of his compact and oath, flies to aid him with thirty
knights and two hundred foot. O'Conor, hearing of
their approach, prepares an ambush, "most secred
wise," and sends out scouts of horse "to cut off all
espials" that might betray it. Armoricus marches
boldly on till he finds himself within the very jaws of
what is called "the Devil's-mouth," which begins to
close around him with its "twenty thousand dragons'
teeth, or fighting men." Armoricus is actually amazed
as he looks about him, and sees this "huge army"
emerging, or, as Hanmer says, "peeping out of their
ambush." A knight named Mountgomery, the nephew
of Armoricus, rides up to St. Lawrence, and says, "Let
us that have horses fly; as for the foot they are beyond
redemption." These dastardly words are overheard by
the brother of Armoricus, who asks, "What means my
noble brother by giving ear to these cowardly horsemen? Will you leave us, like sheep, in the mouths of
these ravening wolves?" Have you forgotten all the
bloody fields in which we supported you? If you
weigh not our estate, regard your own honour and the
house from which you are descended. Will you lose in
an hour the honour you have won through many years?
When you were in a like distress in Uriel, you dismounted, slew your horse, and led the foot to victory.
I am your flesh and blood. Let us who have lived
together, die together. I know the worst, and am
resolved to die, fighting, rather than to be slain fleeing."

* *Cathal Crovderg, i. e.,* "Charles the Red-handed."—"The name
Cathal, which means warlike, and appears to be synonymous with the
Welsh Cadell, is generally Anglicised, Charles."—*Dr. O'Donovan.*

"I have no power to leave my friends," replied the noble St. Lawrence, dismounting and kissing the cross of his sword, with which he pierced his steed, saying, "Thou, who hast so worthily served me, shall never serve against me." Then, turning with a cheerful countenance to "two young gentlemen," he directed them to an adjoining eminence, and told them to mark the fight and carry a true account of it to De Courcy. He then prepared for battle, with a coolness and courage at which their "enemies marvelled." To conclude, Armoricus was slain, and all his brave companions, fighting "back to back." O'Conor lost a thousand men.

The Conor Moinmoy, mentioned here as King of Connaught, was the son of Roderick. He had lately seized his father's throne, having banished the old man into Munster. The son was killed the next year:—
"A.D. 1189, Conor Moinmoy, son of Roderick, King of all Connaught, both the English and the Irish, was killed by a party of his own people and tribe." The transaction is thus recorded in the *Annals of Ulster*. "Conor Moinmoy Mac Roary, arch-king of Connaught, *and to be King of Ireland*, was killed by his minions, by his brother's advice."

"Alas," exclaim the Four Masters, "for the army that plotted this conspiracy against the life of the heir presumptive to the throne of Ireland!" They go on to describe how the Kings of Thomond, Cork, and Tara had "gone to his house," and thus acknowledged his supremacy, and how he had given, to one, a large stipend, to another, rich ornaments, and to O'Brien, King of Limerick, a golden goblet; but not a word do they drop of the unnatural rebellion and Absalom-like conduct of this Irish prince.

Old Roderick was recalled on the death of his son. But he was now too feeble to clamber to his throne. We read of his going to the north and other parts of the country, soliciting aid from the English, as well as the Irish, "to recover his kingdom;" but without success. In the end he had to compromise his claim for a cantred* of land, and to end his days in the monastery of Cong.†

The Four Masters' entry of this transaction, which we give in a note, is rather curt, and not in their usual verbose style.

We are happy to say one good and kind word of this old king, of whom we have been compelled to write some hard things. Roderick O'Conor, King of Connaught, was the friend and patron of literature. In 1169, when the English first landed, he was endowing colleges and religious institutions:—

"A.D. 1169. This was the year in which Roderick O'Conor gave ten cows, every year for himself, and from every king that should succeed him, for ever, to the Lictor of Ard-Macha [Armagh], in honour of [St.] Patrick, to instruct the youths of Ireland and Alba in literature."—*Four Masters*.

---

* *Cantred, i.e.,* 100 manors. See O'Brien's *Irish Dictionary*. Colgan translates it Cantaredus.

† *Monastery of Cong.*—"A.D. 1198. Roderick O'Conor, king of Connaught, and all Ireland, both the Irish and the English, died among the canons at Cong, after exemplary penance, victorious over the world and the devil. His body was conveyed to Clonmacnoise, and interred at the north side of the altar of the great church."—*Four Masters*.

Another authority says it was for "learning to the strollers," or what are now called "poor scholars."*

This transaction—if correctly recorded—of which we have no doubt—brings us to the year of King Henry's death, that occurred on the 6th of July, 1198. The Four Masters give, under the years 1188 and 1189, several accounts of battles and skirmishes, but nothing like the foregoing at which Armoricus fell; but we have given quite enough to convince every reader of Irish history, that Ireland was still unconquered, that the sons of Roderick O'Conor were prepared to contest the lordship of Ireland, not only with the gigantic and warlike De Courcy, but, if need-be, with the heroic Cœur de Lion himself. For Giraldus Cambrensis to call his history of these times *Hibernia Expugnata*, or "Ireland Conquered," is to put a lie on his title page. He might just as well have anticipated Sir George Carew, and written "Pacata Hibernia," or "Ireland Pacified;" a blissful state of affairs which yet remains *in futuro*. The true title of his book would have been *Hibernia Pugnacitas*, or "Ireland alive and kicking;" for it had actually advanced, in the art and practice of war, under the tuition of the Normans. Even Giraldus himself had a sort of presentiment, founded on prophecies, that the English would not obtain possession of the whole of Ireland, till "a short time before the day of judgment," paulo ante diem judicii. "If," says Sir

* *Poor scholars.*—The passage is rendered by Colgan thus:—"A.D. 1169. Rodericus Rex summopere cupiens in Academia Ardmachana studia promovere honoraria annuaque decem boum pensione, stipendiam Archi magistri illius scholæ audivit, et dato diplomati suos successores ad eandum pensionem quotannis solvendam obstriuxit, ea conditione ut studium generale pro scholaribus, tam ex Hibernia undequaque quam ex Albania adventantibus Ardmachae continuareter."—*Triae Thaum*, p. 310.

John Davis, who quotes this passage, "St. Patrick, and the rest [of the prophets, to which Giraldus refers], did not utter this prophecy, Giraldus himself is a prophet, who hath reported it."

Mr. Thomas Moore, speaking of the death of Henry II., says, "Some think that it was unfortunate for Ireland that the pressure of other cares had prevented Henry from devoting more attention to the government of that country, and regret that he was unable to follow up his invasion, by a complete conquest. The world, in that case, would have been spared the anomalous spectacle that has ever since been presented by the two nations; the one subjected, without being subdued; and the other rulers, but not masters; the one doomed to all that is tumultuous in independence, without its freedom; the other endued with every attribute of despotism, except its power." See *History of Ireland*, vol. ii., p. 299.

CHAPTER XXVIII.

RICHARD CŒUR DE LION—WILLIAM, EARL MARSHAL, AND HIS DESCENDANTS.

RICHARD I. took far more interest in fighting for the Holy Sepulchre than for the Island of Saints, in battleaxing the Saracens than in ruling his Irish subjects. But this will not surprise us, when we remember that he left the more important kingdom of England for the honour and glory of leading an army into the Holy Land.

During the first two years of the reign of Richard I. the Irish government of Ireland was in the hands of William Petit, who is styled a warlike baron. Of his short administration we have nothing to recount worthy of particular notice. He was succeeded by a greater man, William, Earl Marshal.

"King Richard, the first year of his raigne, gave the Lady Isabell, sole daughter and heire of Richard, surnamed Strongbow, Earle of Pembroke, to William, Lord Maxfield, Earle Marshal of England, Anno 1189."

"This William's surname," continues Hanmer, "was not Marshal, as Sir John Plunkett's collection hath laid down, but Maxfield." He gives his genealogy thus: "William was the son of John, the son of William, the son of Walter, who came to England with William the Conqueror, and was his Marshal."

The William of whom we now write, was a great favourite, as we may conclude, with Richard I. He bore the sceptre at his coronation, and before Cœur de Lion passed into Normandy, he made William Maxfield, or Marshal, the third governor of the realm. He was also a great favourite with King John. Hume calls him "the man of greatest vigour and capacity in the English Court." He was Marshal of England when King John died, and during the minority of the young prince Henry, was appointed, by a general council of barons, convened at Bristol, Protector of the Realm and guardian of the young king; with whom he used his influence to gain a new confirmatory charter, that granted liberty to the subject to go out of the kingdom, without royal consent; the necessity of which royal consent somewhat checked the frequent appeals of churchmen to Rome.

Of his Irish administration we know positively nothing. Indeed, historians are divided respecting the exact period of his Viceroyship. Leland places it between 1195 and 1197, and makes him succeed Petit, who, according to Ware, was united with him in the government. We are disposed to think he commenced his government soon after his marriage with Isabel, the daughter of Strongbow and Eva; perhaps in 1190 or 1191. Ware gives the latter date.

He was in Normandy, with John, in 1195, when King Richard died, and was sent to England by the new king to prepare for his coronation. Hanmer says, " King John gave him this year his full creation to the Earldom of Pembroke, and girded him with the sword." He was soon after this sent on an embassy to Philip, King of France. He sailed for Ireland in 1200, and was nearly lost at sea; but found safety in Barrow

Bay in the county of Wexford, and in commemoration of his signal deliverance, erected Tintern Abbey, on the banks of the Bannow, for Cistercian monks, whom he brought from Tintern, in Wales. The ruins of the Irish Abbey, which is called "Tintern Minor," remain to the present day. This property, on the dissolution of religious houses, was granted to Sir Anthony Colclough, at the annual rent of twenty-six shillings and four pence. It still remains in the family. A part of the old abbey has been converted into a dwelling-house, which is considered unlucky, for the family were thought to be under "the curse of fire and water."

The following story is told in *Hall's Ireland*, Vol. II. p. 151, which has an air of truth about it. Sir Cæsar Colclough was engaged to a lovely and rich heiress, who promised, like the Princess of Breffney, to have a lamp burning on his return from England. The lamp hung in the Castle of Hook, on the sea coast. Her lover's barque neared the shore, when some malicious fiend or fairy put out, or removed the light to another position. The following morning Sir Cæsar's dead body was washed ashore. He must have been under the curse of fire or water. The disconsolate heiress converted her father's tower into a lighthouse, which remains to the present day.

William, Earl Marshal, returned to Ireland in 1207, when he built Kilkenny, in Irish Cill-Cainnigh (*i.e.* the Church of St. Canice), and gave the town, which was built on the site of the old church, a charter, with privileges, which it enjoys to this day. He founded there the Monastery of the Black-Fryers, "and ended the way of all flesh, in London, in 1220, and lyeth buried in the temple of his lady, Isabel, at Tintern in Wales." Hanmer says in another place, the Earl "ended the way of all flesh, and was buried in the new Temple at London."

These two statements can be reconciled on the supposition that his body was removed from London to Wales. This removal or re-interment of bodies was not unusual. The body of Roderick O'Connor, King of Connaught, was removed from the Abbey of Cong to Clonmacnois.

A curious incident occurred at the Marshal's grave, which strikingly illustrates the state of society in the thirteenth century. He had, before he died, in right of his wife, the daughter of Eva and Strongbow, taken possession of two manors belonging to the Bishop of Fernes, in Leinster. The Bishop remonstrated, but with no effect, so the Earl was excommunicated, and died with the guilt of this sacrilege upon his soul. He left ten children, five sons and five daughters. To the eldest son, William, the Bishop appeals for the sake of his father's soul; but he appeals in vain; the young Earl Marshal has no bowels of compassion for his father's soul. The Bishop, therefore, went to London to the young king, Henry, who accompanied him to the old Earl's grave, where, in a loud voice, the Bishop uttered the following words—" O William that here liest interred, and wrapped in the bonds of excommunication, if the thing which thou hast injuriously taken from my church, be restored by the King, or by the heir, or by some of thy kindred, or friends, with competent satisfaction, I absolve thee—otherwise I do ratify the said sentence, that thou being for ever wrapped up in thy sins, do remain damned in hell."

The King, who was greatly shocked that such a sentence should be ratified against the soul of his old friend and guardian, appealed to young William, who replied, " I do not believe, neither is it to be credited, that my father took these manors injuriously; but in anywise that which is gotten by the sword* may be lawfully enjoyed. If that old doting Bishop hath pronounced a wrong sentence, let the curse light upon his own pate." To these words his four brothers gave hearty concurrence. When the Bishop heard this decision he pronounced the following awful words:— " What I have said, I have said, and what I have written, I have written, never to be blotted out."

Keating, alluding to this affair, says, " Out of five sons not one survived to enjoy the cursed acquisitions of the father, who died childless " The angry historian should speak better sense, and not contradict himself. The father did not die childless, but was succeeded by his five sons, each of whom came to the earldom.

The eldest son, William, who refused to give back the Bishop's lands, married Eleanor, the sister of Henry III., daughter of King John, but had no issue. He died childless in Kilkenny in 1231, and was buried there, in the monastery which his father had founded. His widow was afterwards secretly married to Simon de Montford,† Earl of Leicester, the third son of Simon

---

* *Gotten by the sword.*—The two manors of Fernes were not gotten by the sword, for here the King of Leinster had his principal palace. It is probable he or one of his ancestors may have given their manors to the church.

† *His widow was afterwards secretly married to Simon de Montford.*— This lady had taken the ring, but not the veil of a nun. We learn from Matthew Paris that *there were circumstances* which rendered a hasty marriage necessary. The marriage was performed in St. Stephen's Chapel, Henry giving away his sister.

Count de Montford, the leader of the crusade against the Albigenses.

The second brother, Richard, who succeeded William, was treacherously killed on the Curragh at Kildare, in 1233. We shall speak more at large of his death, on a future occasion.

The third brother, Gilbert, died under royal displeasure. Henry III. kept Christmas at Winchester. Gilbert and his retinue were approaching the gates of the palace, with tipstaves in their hands, and were kept back by the porters and others. He complained to the king of the indignity done him, who gave him an overthwart answer. The Earl, and his brother Walter, being offended, estranged themselves from court, and afterwards went to Scotland, where Gilbert married Lady Margaret, sister of Alexander, King of Scots. He was afterwards killed, by a fall from his horse, at a tournament in Hereford, which the King had especially forbidden. He, also, died childless, in 1241, and was buried in the new Temple Church, in London.

Walter, who arranged the tournament, at which his brother was slain, demanded the office of Earl Marshal, from the King, as his hereditary right. Henry, in a passion, denied his right, telling him that his two brothers were a pair of turbulent traitors, who had presumed to attend a tournament which had been forbidden. Walter applied to Eleanor, the Queen, and through her influence and intercession, obtained the office of Marshal for Walter. He died at Grodrich Castle, Monmouth, in 1245, and was buried in Tintern Abbey.

Anselmn, the last, and youngest brother, married Matilde Maud, the daughter of the Earl of Hereford.

He also obtained the title of Earl Marshal, but died without issue, and was buried at Tintern. "Thus," writes Florig, "all, successively, became earls, as their mother, by a prophetical spirit, had foreshewed; so the noble shield or buckler of the marshals, dreadful to so many and so great enemies of England, vanished away."

We have stated that the great Earl William Marshal, had five daughters, who inherited his vast estate in Leinster. Matilde, or Maud, who had the County of Carlow, for her portion, and who married Hugh Bigod, Earl of Norfolk, was, probably, the eldest; for Norfolk, in right of his wife, had the Marshalship of England. The title "Earls Marshal of England," is borne by the Dukes of Norfolk to the present day.

Johanna, the second daughter, who got the County of Wexford, as her portion, married Warren de Mountchensy. They had one daughter, heiress to their estates, who married William de Valence, son to Isabella of Angouleme, widow of King John, and therefore stepbrother to Henry III. This William was created Earl of Pembroke, in right of his wife.

Isabel, the third daughter, who had the County of Kilkenny,* as her portion, married Gilbert de Clare, Earl of Gloucester and Hereford. She afterwards married Richard, Duke of Cornwall, brother to Henry III. This young Prince had been highly flattered by the attention of Eleanor la Belle, the beautiful daughter of the Count of Provence, who wrote a poem, with a paladin of Cornwall for a hero. As it was out of Cornwall's power to testify his gratitude, by offering the beautiful and poetic Princess his hand, he

* *County of Kilkenny.*—The property afterwards passed by intermarriage to the families of the Butlers and Spencers.

did the next best thing, he recommended her to his brother Henry III., for a Queen, who wooed and won her. Henry had previously made five unsuccessful attempts to enter within the holy pale of matrimony.

Sibelia, the fourth daughter, who got the County of Kildare, as her portion, married William Ferrers and Derby, who become Lord of Kildare; a title which passed, by intermarriage, to the De Veseys, and afterwards to the Fitzgeralds.

Eva the fifth daughter, who married William de Broase, Lord of Gower and Brecknock, in Wales, got Leix and the Manor of Dunamase, or O'Meara's Country, comprising the greater part of the Queen's County, as her portion. De Broase became, in right of his wife, Lord of Leix. They had a daughter, Matilda, who married Roger Mortimer, Lord of Wigmore, in Wales, and Earl of March, in England. A descendant of theirs, Edmund Mortimer, married Philippe, a daughter of Prince Lionel, Duke of Clarence, son of Edward III., and of Elizabeth de Burgh.

From this union of English and Irish royal houses, we can trace the descent of the Stuarts of Scotland. "King James," writes the author of *Cambrensis Eversus* —and we may say Queen Victoria—" is descended from the Kings of Leinster, and other Irish kings in the following line:—Edmund Mortimer, Earl of March, was son of Matilda, daughter of Eva de Broase, daughter of William Marshal, the elder, by Isabel, daughter of Richard, Earl of Strongbow, and Eva, daughter of Diarmaid Mac Murrough, King of Leinster."

Sir John Davis, speaking of the marriage of the five daughters of the first William Marshal, says, "All writers do impute the decay and loss of Leinster, to the absence of these English lords, who married the five daughters of of William Marshall, Earl of Pembroke." He mentions the absence of these great proprietors, as one of the principal reasons why Ireland was never entirely subdued.

CHAPTER XXXI.

PIERRE PIPARD—HAMO DE VALOIS—JOHN COMYN—MILER FITZ-HENRY—
GIRALDUS CAMBRENSIS—CATHAL CROVDERG.

A.D.
1194-99. WILLIAM, Earl Marshal, was succeeded in the Viceroyalty by Pierre Pipard, in 1194. During his administration one William Brun was summoned to Dublin Castle, and whilst standing on the Castle Bridge, was slain by Warren de London, with the blow of an Irish axe, an instrument, with the use of which Englishmen had become familiar. The body of William Brun rolled into the Castle fosse. The interest of this case consists in the fact (which is recorded in a State paper) that the King's Court in England refused to grant an inquiry, by inquest, but declared that the case should be decided by the ordeal of fire and duel. Whether Warren of London stood the fire, or met the avenger of blood in open combat, is not stated. Here we have an example of an appeal from the Irish Government, to the King's Court in England. This may have resulted from the fact of Warren's being a Londoner, or Englishman.

Pierre Pipard was succeeded in the office of Viceroy by Hamo de Valois, or Haman de Valognes, in 1197. He was an Anglo-Norman, from Suffolk, allied both to the Ormonds, or Butlers, and the Fitzgeralds. Hamon commenced his administration by laying violent hands on church property—seizing lands which had been granted to the See of Dublin; an act of violence most odious and offensive, at a time when the rights of ecclesiastics were accounted infinitely more sacred than those of other subjects.

John Comyn was at this time Archbishop of Dublin, an Englishman, learned, eloquent, and grave; but one who thoroughly understood the rights of his order. He first remonstrated and then denounced the vengeance of Heaven on this wicked Hamon; but without effect. He then repaired to the Cathedral Church of St. Patrick (which he had lately built), and, like a confessor, weighed down by persecution, bemoaned the condition of the Church. He caused the altars to be divested of their ornaments, and the crucifixes to be crowned with thorns. The eyes of one of the images of Christ dropped tears; while blood and water is said to have issued from the side of another; but none of those things melted or moved the impenitent Viceroy, who did not confine his sacrilegious depredations to the See of Dublin. When that of Leighlin became vacant, he would not allow the Abbot of Rosseval, who had been elected bishop, by the Church, to be consecrated; but seized the temporalities, and applied them to his own use and that of the State.

John of Dublin, as a *dernier ressort*, left his bishoprick, and went to England; but found his appeals to Prince John and King Richard equally unavailing. He therefore appealed to the Pope, and this produced a monitory epistle from Innocent III. What the monitory epistle produced, we cannot say; but we are told that Hamon granted to the monks of the Abbey of St. Thomas, a tithe of all salmon brought to his, the Viceroy's kitchen. In estimating the value of this tithe, we should require to know the *price of salmon* at that time. Some seventy or eighty years ago, it was not an unusual clause in the indenture of a tradesman's apprentice, that the boy should not be required to eat salmon more than four times a week.

It appears, however, by the register of John Alan, or Allen, who was Archbishop of Dublin in 1528, that Hamo made satisfaction to John Comyn, by giving him twenty carucates of land. But a far greater satisfaction to the Archbishop was the removal of Hamo de Valois from the Government of Ireland. He was also fined in a sum equal to £15,000, which was transferred to the royal treasury, on the death of Richard I.

This heroic monarch, as the reader is aware, died, in 1199, of a wound from an arrow, in the left arm, at the siege of the Castle of Chalons, near Limoges. "Wretch!" said the dying king, to the archer who had wounded him, and who was now a prisoner in his hands, "what have I done that you should seek my life?" "You killed my father and two brothers with your own hand," was the bold reply. The noble-minded Richard ordered the archer to be set at liberty, but—as the story goes— Marcadee had him, privately, flayed alive, and then hanged.

Richard I. never visited Ireland, nor does he appear to have taken much interest in its affairs. He held the conquest of Palestine as a far nobler work. Had he turned his manly face, and strong battle-axe westward we should have had another story to tell.

MILER FITZ-HENRY.

Miler, or Milo Fitz-Henry was appointed Governor or Justiciary of Ireland in the place of Hamo de Valois. This Milo Fitz-Henry was the son of Fitz-Henry, and grandson of Henry I.* by Nesta, whom we have spoken of in another place. Miler Fitz-Henry accompanied his uncle, Robert Fitz-Stephen, to Ireland. He is mentioned by Maurice Regan, among the first batch of Norman adventurers, that landed at a place called Bann, not far from the town of Wexford, in 1169, that is just thirty years before his appointment as Irish Governor, of which we now write. "Men of all sortes, and from divers places, prepared themselves to go into Ireland; especially Robert Fitz-Stephen, a man of good esteeme in Wales, who had been enlarged out of prison, by the mediation of Dermond."

Although but a stripling, we find the name of Miler Fitz-Henry first on the list, after that of the leader of the expedition, his uncle, Robert Fitz-Stephen. And he seems to have been worthy of the first place, for a little farther on, when giving an account of a dangerous passage of arms with that warlike chieftain, Donald, Prince of Ossory, Maurice Regan says, " All of them "—that is the English—" did admirably well, but Miler Fitz-Henry deserved the most honour."

Miler Fitz-Henry was with Strongbow, when besieged in Dublin, by Roderick O'Conor and the Danes; and in the memorable sally from the city, "his valour was admired at by all men." He afterwards accompanied Strongbow from Dublin, and was with him in the dangerous skirmish with O'Regan, King of Hy-Drone, where he was unhorsed by the blow of a stone.

* *Grandson of Henry I. by Nesta.*—Leland calls him the natural son of Henry I.; and Ware, in his chronological table of Chief Governors, Miler Fitz-Henry, King John's sun—a most absurd mistake. Miler's father, Henry, was the natural son of Henry I. by Nesta.

Giraldus Cambrensis thus describes the person of Miler Fitz-Henry : " Of a dark complexion, with black eyes, and a stern, piercing look. Below the middle height, but, for his size, a man of great strength. Broad-chested and corpulent, his arms and other limbs bony and muscular, and not encumbered with fat."

The same writer calls him an " intrepid and adventurous soldier, who never shrank from any enterprise. He was the first in the onset and the last in retreat."

On one occasion, when engaged with Raymond le Gros, in cattle stealing, near Waterford, he was nearly cut off by the Irish, whose 1,000 head of cattle he was driving. The Irish, lurking at the entrance of a wood, drove off some of the cattle. Miler, followed by only one horseman, dashed after the robbers into a deep thicket." Query, *who* were the *robbers?* The Irish rush out, and cut Miler's companion to pieces, with their broad axes, and surround Miler himself; but he manages, somehow, to cut his way through them, chopping off a hand here, and there an arm, hewing through heads and shoulders.

Miler Fitz-Henry lived to a good old age and died, according to Ware, in 1220, and was buried in the Abbey Great Connell, in the County Kildare. The following is his epitaph :—

> Conduntur tumulo Meleri nobilis ossa
> Indomitus domitor totius gentis Hibernæ.
>
> Translated—
> Entombed the bones of him they Noble Miler call ;
> The tameless tamer of the Irish nation all.

GIRALDUS CAMBRENSIS.

Giraldus Cambrensis, or Gerald Barry, Archdeacon of

Menevia in Wales, came to Ireland during Miler's administration, to consult with his relations respecting the bishoprick of Menevia, which was now vacant, and for which he was a candidate. They, like other kind friends and relatives, commended his undertaking, and promised him great assistance. But Gerald lost the bishoprick, although, as he informs us, in his autobiography, he had the voices of the Canons of Menevia with him. There were heavier guns than the canons of Menevia. Hubert, Archbishop of Canterbury, wrote to these canons, commanding them, on the next Sunday after the Assumption of Our Lady, to elect and receive as their bishop, Geoffrey, Prior of Lanthony, and warning them that if they did not so appear, he would have the Prior consecrated and sent to them, *nolens volens*.

CATHAL CROVDERG.

There was fierce war during Miler Fitz-Henry's administration, between Cathal Crovderg and his cousin, Cathal Carragh, Princes of Connaught.

Cathal Crovderg, or "Cathal of the Wine-Red Hand," was the son of Turlough More O'Conor, Monarch of Ireland, and the brother of Roderick O'Conor, the last of the Irish monarchs. According to a traditional story in the neighbourhood of Ballintobber, he was the illegitimate son of King Turlough, by Gearrog My-Moran, a beautiful girl from the territory of Umhall. When the Queen, who was as jealous as Sarah, heard that the King's leman was *enceinte*, she sent for a witch to work her a spell against both child and concubine. The witch gave her a magical string, with three knots, telling her that no child could be born to Gearrog My-Moran while she held the knotted string in her hand; but, unfortunately for her, the child had thrust its right hand into the external world, before the Queen had got full possession of the charm. Here was a predicament!

Cathal of the Red Hand remained *in statu quo* for several days, when a kind but cunning man went to the Queen, and told her, among other scraps of news from the west, that Moran's daughter had been brought to bed of a thumping boy, to the King of Connaught. The Queen, in a fury, cast the magical string into the fire, which allowed Crovderg to make his full entry into life, which he did in the islet of Lough Mask, in Connemara, in the kingdom of Connaught.

The Queen, with all the malignity of a barren woman, continued to persecute both mother and child, till, like Hagar and Ishmael, they had to seek safety in flight.

Years had rolled by, when the poor boy, who was toiling in the field to support himself and his fond mother—who never failed to remind him that he was the son of an Irish king—saw a Connaught *bollscaire*, or newsmonger, approaching. "What's the news?" inquired Crovderg, who was reaping rye. "The King of Connaught is dead, and the people, assembled in council, will have no king but Cathal Crovderg, his son," replied the bollscaire. The heart of Cathal leaped for joy. "Would you know him?" asked the young prince. "Among a thousand," said the Connaught newsmonger, "for his hand is as red as blood, from the wrist out." Cathal drew off the glove or mitten that concealed the wine stain, when the bollscaire fell prostrate at his feet, for he then recognised his great resemblance to the King, his father. Cathal cast the sickle on the ridge, and exclaimed, "*Slan leat a chorrain anois d'on cloidheamh,*" "Farewell to the sickle: now for the sword." Cathal's farewell to the sickle has been a common proverb among the Sil-Murray and their followers ever since.

He returned home, and was solemnly inaugurated King of Connaught, in the presence of twelve chieftains and twelve courts of Sil-Murray; and succeeded, after many reverses, in dethroning his cousin, Cathal Carrah.

Cathal Crovderg died in the habit of a grey friar, in the Abbey of Knockmay, A.D. 1224—"the best Irishman that was from the time of Brian Boru, for gentility and honour." "No wonder," exclaim the Four Masters, "there were ominous signs and distempers among the cows, and inward disease, produced by the milk."

At his death the government of Connaught was assumed by his son, Hugh, who, at his father's death, held the hostages of Connaught in his hand.

SIR JOHN DE COURCY.

Miler Fitz-Henry was succeeded by Hugh de Lacy the younger. It would be more correct to say that he gained the position of Viceroy, by craft and violence. His conduct to John de Courcy was abominable, but as it has helped to develope the character and fortunes of this wonderful Norman knight, we shall let it pass, for the present.

The *Book of Howth* contains the following most romantic account of John de Courcy. He was accused by Hugh de Lacy of publicly stating that King John had murdered his own nephew, Arthur. John heard this, and gave instructions to De Lacy, to have De Courcy arrested, and sent to England. The latter replied by sending his rival, De Lacy, a challenge, which De Lacy refused to accept; but issued a proclamation, offering a large reward to anyone who would deliver John de Courcy, dead or alive, into his hands.

It was Good Friday—*bad* Friday for De Courcy. On that day he bore no arms, and wore no armour, but was wholly given up to divine contemplation. Now pacing, all solitary, round the church of Downpatrick, and anon kneeling before a huge wooden cross; perhaps mentally ejaculating a Salus in cruse, or a Sub hoc signo vinces; or his own motto, Vincet omnia veritas—when he is surprised by a rush of armed men. "The Philistines are upon thee, Sampson." He tears up the cross, before which he has been kneeling, and lays about him with all his Herculean might, laying thirteen of his assailants dead at his feet. But he is, at length, overpowered by numbers, seized, bound, and shipped for England, where he is condemned, by King John, to perpetual imprisonment, in the Tower of London.

> "He lieth low, in a dungeon now,
> Powerless in proud despair;
> For false King John hath cast him in,
> And closely chained him there."

There he lies, and grows gaunt and morose, when a dispute arises between John of England, and Philip Augustus of France, on their respective and clashing claims to some town or city on the borders of Normandy. It was resolved to leave the decision of the quarrel to two champions, instead of to a general engagement. The French champion is chosen, and sends his challenge, but there was no knight in England, Ireland, or Normandy, to accept it, when a courtier whispers to King John, that De Courcy, who now lies in the Tower, is the only man in his wide dominions that is able to meet the French champion. The King sends to De Courcy, who replies, "Not for him. I esteem him unworthy the adventure of my blood. He has rewarded my loyalty to his person and services to the Crown, by imprisoning me, unheard, at the suit of my rival and enemy, Hugh de Lacy." The King becomes a suppliant, and sends a second, and a third time ; when the grim features of De Courcy relax, as he replies, "For the Crown, for the dignity of the realm, in which many an honest man lieth bound against his will, I am contented to hazard my life." The king swallows all this, and a great deal more, with a good grace. De Courcy is released from the Tower, made much of, "cherished and fed wonderfully, and attains great bulk by the sudden change from hard keeping, to so large an allowance of diet."

The day of combat, which is to come off in Normandy, arrives. The trumpets sound, and the champions enter the lists, in the presence of the assembled kings and nobles of England, France, and Scotland, surrounded by the chivalry and beauty of the three kingdoms. De Courcy, armed with a tremendous sword, for which he had sent to Ireland, approaches his adversary, and eyes him with a wonderfully stern countenance, not unmingled with contempt, and then rides by.

That grim look has decided the contest. It froze the Frenchman's blood. When the trumpet sounded for the onset, the Frenchman took to his heels, or more correctly, put spurs to his horse, broke through the lists, and fled into Spain. The men threw up their caps and clapped their hands, the ladies smiled at the Anglo-Norman, and jeered the poltroon Frenchman. The victory was adjudged to De Courcy, and the town in dispute to King John.

Philip of France, wishing to see a specimen of De Courcy's great strength and swordsmanship, the King of England ordered a helmet, of excellent proof, and a shirt of mail to be laid on a block or post. De Courcy, frowning grimly on their highnesses of England and France, raised his sword and cut helmet and shirt of mail asunder, at a blow, striking his weapon so deeply into the timber that he alone could draw it hence.

The Kings of England and France inquired why he had eyed them with so grim a face. " If I had missed my stroke I should have cut off both your heads," was his reply, which was taken in good part. King John restored the champion to his title and estates in Ulster, valued at 25,000 marks per annum, and asked him if there was any other favour he could grant him. The favour he asked was that he and his successors, for all ages, should remain covered in the presence of the King of England and his successors. This request was both willingly and graciously granted:

"So he gave this graceful honor
To the bold De Courcy's race,
That they ever should dare, their helms to wear,
Before the king's own face.
And the sons of that line of heroes
To this day their right assume ;
For when every head is unbonnetted,
They walk in cap and plume."

The account of this contest between the Frenchman and John de Courcy, of which the *Book of Howth* contains a graphic description, is looked upon as a myth, by Dr. Leland, who says, " Before the date of John's safe conduct, granted to De Courcy, Normandy had been lost, and even Rouen, its last remaining city, abandoned by his shameful conduct."

We beg to say, in reply, that King John had other dominions on the Continent besides Normandy. There was the large Province of Poitou still in his possession, and other towns which might have furnished ground for a feat of arms such as we have described.

But, whatever Dr. Leland may say to the contrary, the right or privilege is still claimed by the descendants of John De Courcy of wearing their hats in the royal presence. This fact gives countenance and weight to the story. When William III., Prince of Orange, asked why Almericus, the twenty-third Lord of Kinsale, appeared covered in his presence, this Irish nobleman replied, May it please your Majesty, my name is De Courcy, and I am Lord of Kinsale, in the kingdom of Ireland. The reason of my appearance covered in your Majesty's presence is, to assert the ancient privilege of my family, granted to Sir John de Courcy, Earl of Ulster and his heirs, by John, King of England, and his successors for ever.

The King, we are told, graciously acknowledged the right. This privilege is enjoyed to the present day by Michael Conrad de Courcy, the 30th Lord of Kinsale.*

I may here mention that a grandee of the first class, in Spain, is privileged to remain covered before the

---

* *Kinsale.*—The name of the town from which the title is derived is spelled Kinsale from *Cean-saile* the "Head of the sea." The title of Lord, or Baron of Kinsale, was fraudulently assumed by Sir Dominic Sarsfield, in 1627, who was compelled, on a full hearing of the case, to relinquish it.

sovereign. A grandeeship, or any number of grandeeships, may be inherited, without merger, through males and females. Hence the phrase of a nobleman having so many hats, that is so many rights or privileges to wear his hat in the presence of royalty.

Giraldus Cambrensis says that Sir John De Courcy had no legitimate son, but Cambrensis' historical notices of Irish invaders do not extend beyond the year 1186, and we learn from the Dublin copy of the *Annals of Innisfallen* that De Courcy's wife, Affrica, the daughter of Godfrey, King of the Isle of Man, died in 1193. Campion, who wrote his *Historie of Irelande* in 1571, says, " Courcye, dying without heires of his body, the Earldom of Ulster was bestowed upon Hugh de Lacye, for his good services." But Hanmer says, "King John gave De Courcy gifts, and restored him to his former possessions in Ireland." Dr. Smith, in his *History of Cork*, refers to a record in the Tower of London (Rol. Pat. 6, Johan M. Dors.) to prove that Milo de Courcy, the son of John de Courcy, was a hostage for his father, upon his enlargement from the Tower, to fight the French champion. Dr. O'Donovan says the Patent Roll, referred to by Dr. Smith, mentions a Milo de Curcy juvenis, the son of John de Curcy junior. The great John de Courcy had a brother, Jordanus de Courcy, who was killed by his own people in 1197. Dr. O'Donovan thinks he may be the ancestor of the Mac Patricks of Kinsale and Ringrone. Milo de Courcy was created Baron of Kinsale the 29th of May, 1223. He married a De Cogan, and built a castle near the Old Head of Kinsale, and another at Ringrone, where he and De Cogan slew Reann-Roinn, or Ringrone

Mac Carthy. Milo was succeeded by his grandson, Sir John De Courcy, who built the Castle of Kilbrittain,* of which he was afterwards dispossessed by Mac Carthy Reagh, by whom he was slain in the Island of Inchidonny, in the harbour of Clonakilty, in 1295. There is a pedigree of the Mac Carthys of Corraun Lough, in the Royal Irish Academy, from which it appears that this branch of the Mac Carthys is descended from a daughter of John De Courcy.

Notwithstanding the royal pardon, John de Courcy never regained the earldom and estate of Ulster, which were seized by Hugh de Lacy, whose plea for retaining them was that De Courcy had never returned to Ireland, to have his sentence of outlawry reversed. De Courcy, as the story goes, had fifteen times attempted to cross into Ireland, but was driven back by contrary winds, upon which he altered his course, and went into France, and here we lose sight of him.

* *Kilbrittain.*—There is a story that De Courcy pawned the castle to M'Carthy Reagh, for a white weazle; that the weazle died, and that M'Carthy retained the castle. Young Gerald of Kildare, the brother of Silken Thomas, and the Fair Geraldine, sought refuge here. Kilbrittain Castle is now in the possession of Lieut.-Colonel Alcock Stawell. He and his lady are earnestly engaged in the interesting work of restoring and re-edifying the old building.

CHAPTER XXVI.

KING JOHN PREPARES TO GO TO IRELAND—A CHURCHMAN'S LETTER TO A KING—THE DE LACYS—THE DE BROASE TRAGEDY—ENGLISH LAWS FOR IRELAND.

A.D. 1210. KING JOHN'S eyes are at length opened to the disloyal and ambitious designs of Hugh de Lacy and his brother, so he sends over Philippe of Worcester, Roland Bloet, and Robert of Chichester, to inspect and report on the state of the Irish Government.

What could they say? That the whole country was in a state of confusion and rebellion, and that the greatest rebel of all was the Viceroy, De Lacy, in whom the King had, or professed, so much confidence. There was but one course. John must take the bull by the horns and go to Ireland himself. For want of manly decision he had lost Normandy. Let him have a care or Ireland will slip through his fingers also. He, therefore, resolves to go.

John's resolve to visit Ireland may have been strengthened by a letter, or address, of his old tutor, Gerald Cambrensis, who reminds him of their early relationship of tutor and pupil, and then of the value of the prize won by his father, Henry II., telling him "not to be unmindful of his dominion of Ireland."

"It pleased your excellent and noble father, Henry, some time ago, when I was in attendance on yourself, to send me over to Ireland, in your company"—where he, Giraldus, collected valuable materials, from which he produced a book, whose "worth was more commended than rewarded."

He goes on to remind John, that, through neglect, or rather many occupations, the recollection of not the least of the islands of the West, had faded from his mind.

Much, he says, was done by those who made the beginning, and much by those who followed, but more by Henry II., who gave his whole mind to those expeditions. "Do not undervalue, noble king, what cost your father and yourself so much toil. Do not part with so much glory and honour to strangers, nor for the sake of an island of *silver*, hazard the loss of an island of *gold*."

Does Giraldus really mean to compare Ireland to gold and England to silver? It would seem so. We style Ireland the Emerald Isle.

"One does not exclude the other, but both, together, become doubly valuable. The gold of Arabia and the silver of Achaia enrich the same treasury, though in different heaps."

But other considerations may induce him not to forget, or throw up Ireland.

"It has pleased God to send you several sons, both *natural* and legitimate!"

For shame, Giraldus! And you, a churchman, looking for the bishoprick of St. David's!

"Two of these you may raise to the thrones of two kingdoms; and under them you may amply provide for your followers, by new grants of land; especially in Ireland; a very small part of it being yet occupied and inhabited by our people."

"But, if neither the desire of augmenting your own glory, nor of royally endowing and elevating your own sons"—of a truth, Master Gerald, you put the temptation in as forcible a way, as a certain personage, mentioned in the Gospels, who shall be unnamed,—"if these considerations have no power to move you, you ought, at least, to protect and reinstate, in their rights, those veteran warriors who have served your father and yourself, with so much devoted fidelity; by whose enterprise the land was gained, and by whose valour it is still retained."

He then goes on to tell the king, that he has nothing to fear in the "West" of Ireland; but he must watch his "Eastern districts;" and he hints darkly at the king "fostering hydra-heads, in " his "dominions," "wrapping snakes in the folds of his robe," and "nourishing fire in his bosom, which is ready to burst into a flame."

We suspect the references here are to the younger De Lacys, one of whom was in possession of Meath, in right of his father, and the other, of the large inheritance of the brave John de Courcy, in the North-east of Ireland. It was for the special object of lowering the high crests of these two wily, cruel, and ambitious men, that King John made preparations to visit Ireland a second time.

But before his departure he sends a spy, who was either a son, nephew, or cousin of the famous John de Courcy. Now the younger Hugh de Lacy having seized the whole of the De Courcy property in Ulster, there was a double motive to get *this* De Courcy—who seems to have been the Lord of Rathenny*—out of the way, so they hired manslayers to fall upon him and kill him.

* *Lord of Rathenny.*—Dr. O'Donovan thinks he was the son of Vivian de Courcy, to whom Strongbow had granted Rathenny. Ware thinks he was a natural son of the great John de Courcy. Giraldus Cambrensis says that neither Hervey, Raymonde De Courcy, or Meyler had "lawful issue."

He was slain, we are told, of "special malice and deadly hatred," within five miles of Dublin.

King John, who held the person of his spy—if it be correct to call this De Courcy a spy—as sacred as that of an ambassador, prepares to embark, in order to drive both the De Lacys out of Ireland.

He cast anchor, with a large fleet—the *Annals of Kibronan* say " a prodigious fleet "—at Crook, in the estuary of Waterford, on the 20th of June, 1210. William, Earl of Salisbury, styled Guillaume de Longe Espée, or William of the Long Sword (the half brother of King John, and the son of Henry II. by Fair Rosamond de Clifford) was the Commander-in-Chief of the army, which consisted, for the most part, of Flemish and foreign soldiers. An Irish annalist thus describes the expedition :—

"A.D. 1210. Johanna, the son of Fitz-Empress, King of England, came to Ireland with a prodigious fleet this year. On his arrival he levied a great army of the men of Ireland, to march them to Ulster, to take Hugh de Lacy and Carrickfergus. Hugh departed from Ireland, and those that were guarding Carrickfergus left it and came to the King. The King marched from Dublin into Meath, and dispatched a large fleet northwards to a fortress of the English, called Carlingford, to command the sons of Hugh de Lacy—viz., Walter, Lord of Meath, and Hugh, Earl of Ulster, and then Lord Deputy of Ireland—to appear before him, to answer for the death of the valiant knight, John de Courcy [that is King John's spy] who was treacherously slain by them."

King John was well received by the people of Waterford, where he had founded an hospital, and to whom he had given a charter* of incorporation, conferring some important privileges upon the city. Here he spent a few days at his favourite pursuit of hawking, gathering up his strength and that of his army all the while, to swoop down upon those two kites or cormorants called De Lacy.

John advanced from Waterford through Thomastown, Kilkenny, and Naas, to Dublin, where he arrived on the 28th of June, 1210.

He remained here but two days, and proceeded, without delay, for Trim and Kells, two towns in the territory of Gaultier de Lacy, who fled before him. Here King John was reinforced by O'Brien, of West Munster, and O'Conor, of Connaught, and marched into Ulster, and took possession of the territory of which Hugh de Lacy had despoiled John de Courcy. Hugh de Lacy fled before the enraged monarch, as did his brother of Meath, firing his castles, which he left blazing behind him.

John marched towards Carrickfergus, where Hugh de Lacy's strongest castle stood. Here were many of Hugh's bravest soldiers, but they were unable to withstand the force brought to bear against them. The castle was taken and De Lacy's men were made prisoners.

The De Lacys, as we learn from a pretty story in the *Book of Howth*, fled to France and " obscured themselves " in the Abbey of St. Taurines, " meekly " working as gardeners, for daily wages, for the space of

---

* *A charter*.—In 1603, when the citizens of Waterford closed their gates against the Deputy Mountjoy, pleading the privilege of this charter, Mountjoy replied, that if they did not open their gates, he would " *draw King James' sword, and cut the charter of King John in pieces.*"

two or three years, till the Abbot, who may have got some private information respecting them, smelt their estates from their countenances and behaviour, and demanded their birth and parentage. They told the good man the whole truth, and he undertook to be their suitor to the King, procuring their pardon and getting them restored to their estates, on the payment of fines; Hugh four thousand marks for Ulster, and Walter two thousand five hundred marks for Meath. Nor were they wanting in gratitude to the kind Abbot. They brought his nephew, one Alured, to Ireland, knighted him, and made him Lord of Dengle.

It was during his stay at Carrickfergus that John was informed that the wife of William de Broase and their daughter, Matilda (the wife of Roger Mortimer), their son, William de Broase, his wife, and two children, who had been for some time "fugitives from justice," had been arrested in Galloway. No pleasanter news could have reached the ears of King John. The royal hawk had never struck a richer quarry. It was a full compensation for the escape of the De Lacys.

William de Broase had been at one time in high favour with King John. Indeed, it is stated that he was the man who first delivered Prince Arthur into his hands. Arthur being the son of Geoffrey, an elder son of Henry II., had a better claim to the English throne than his uncle John. His uncle Richard, in setting out for the Holy Land, declared Arthur, Duke of Britanny, his successor.

William de Broase was one of the richest and most powerful barons in England. He had large estates in England, Ireland, Normandy, and Wales. When John quarrelled with the Pope, the kingdom was placed under interdict. Fearing that such a state of things might result in a rising amongst the great lords, he demanded of them hostages, as pledges of their allegiance to his cause and throne. He required William, the son of William de Broase, to deliver up his eldest son, who was to act as a page to Queen Isabella. De Broase's wife refused to comply, stating, to the messenger, Peter de Maluc, who is supposed to have taken part in Prince Arthur's murder, that she did not think her child would be safe in the hands of John, who had murdered his own nephew.

When this reply was made known to the king, he vowed to be revenged. De Broase's wife, repenting her unwise words, strove to avert the king's wrath, by sending a rich present to the queen. With other things she sent a herd of four hundred white cows, with red ears; but no offering could atone for such words, but the blood of the offender. William de Broase fled with his wife and children to Meath, and from Meath to Galloway, where the whole family were arrested, and brought to John, to Carrickfergus. John carried them to England, where he had them starved to death. Miss Strickland says that the husband, wife, and five children were all starved to death. The following account is from the pen of a Fleming, who appears to have been in the king's service :—

"Maud, the wife of William de Breusa, and her son, (the father having some time before escaped to France,) were committed to Corfe Castle, in the Isle of Purbeck, where, by the king's orders, they were confined in a room, with a sheaf of wheat and a piece of raw bacon. On the eleventh day, their prison was opened ; they were both found dead, in a sitting posture, the mother between her son's legs, with her head leaning on his breast. In the last pangs of hunger she had gnawed her son's cheek, probably after his death.

"When William de Broase heard the tragical end of his wife and son, he died in a few days."

Another account says that De Broase, disguised as a beggar, escaped to France, where he soon died, and was buried in the Abbey of St. Victor in Paris, by his son Gilles, Bishop of Hereford. This we take to be the elder William; so that Miss Strickland's statement, that the husband (*i.e.* the younger William), wife, and five children were all starved to death, may be correct.

O'Neill visited King John while he was in the north, in pursuit of Hugh de Lacy, who had burned down his own castles before the king's eyes; but we do not find that this great Irish chieftain gave hostages to the English monarch. "O'Neil *came to the King of England's house*, and departed from it again, without hostages or security." But to go to the King's house was a token of submission. O'Neill must have felt grateful to John, for driving Hugh de Lacy out of Ulster, of which he had assumed the lordship.

Cathal Crovderg O'Conor, King of Connaught, went further than O'Neill, for he went to the King of England's house twice, and gave hostages, as pledges of his obedience. John asked for Cathal's son, but Cathal's wife, who may have heard of John's treachery to his wards, said, "Nay"; so the Irish chieftain tendered Conor-God O'Hara, Lord of Leyny; Dermot, son of Conor O'Mulrowy,

Lord of Moyburg ; Finn of Carmacan ; and Torvenn, son of the King of the Gall-Gaels, whom the king accepted.

King John was a cruel tyrant, but it was during his reign that England obtained the Magna Charta, and the English in Ireland, the privilege of being governed by English laws. "King John," writes Sir John Davis, "in the 12 yeare of his raigne, did establish the English lawes and customes heere, and placed sheriffs and other ministers to rule and govern the people, according to the law of England; and to that end he brought over with him discreet men, skilled in the laws—viros discretos in legis peritos—by whose advice he commanded the laws of England to be observed in Ireland, and left the said laws, in writing, under his seal, in the Exchequer of Dublin." See Patent Rolls in the Tower 11 Henry III, m 3. Tracts and Treatises, p. 637.

We are not to suppose that these laws extended to the whole of Ireland, the most of which was still governed (to the reign of Elizabeth) by its own Brehon laws. "King John," writes Davis, "made 12 shires in Leinster and Mounster, namely Dublin, Kildare, Meath, Uriel, Catherlogh [Carlow], Kilkenny, Wexford, Waterford, Corke, Limerick, Kerrie, and Tipperary ; yet these lawes did stretch no further than the lands of the English colonies did extend. In these ways were the English lawes published and put in execution."

King John having thus provided for the better administration of justice for Ireland, set sail for England, leaving to his deputy, John de Gray, the difficult task of bringing English laws into operation.

CHAPTER XXXI.

JOHN DE GRAY, BISHOP OF NORWICH, AND JOHN DE LOUNDRES, ARCH-
BISHOP OF DUBLIN—MAGNA CHARTA—DEATH OF KING JOHN—
HENRY III.—ENGLISH LAWS.

A.D. 1210-1216. KING JOHN, as well as his father, Henry, seem to have had a partiality for clerical Viceroys. Perhaps he esteemed them, on the whole, more able and astute than laymen; or was it to enable him to carry on the war with Rome that he filched shafts from the Papal quiver?

When leaving Ireland John committed the viceregal government to the hands of John de Gray, who was at this time under the papal ban of excommunication.

The Four Masters, who got hold of the wrong end of the story, say "the English were excommunicated for sending the bishop [John de Gray] to carry on the war in Ireland."

The true state of the case was that England was placed under edict on account of John's opposition to the Pope. John induced the canons of Christchurch to elect John de Gray as Archbishop of Canterbury, in preference to Cardinal Langton, who had been chosen by the Pope, and who was a greater and better man than John de Gray.

But the complication produced by appointing two archbishops for Canterbury was further increased by some of the junior monks of Christchurch meeting clandestinely, and, without *congé d'élire* from the King, choosing Reginald, their sub-prior, to the office; so

R

there were, at this time, three in the field for the chief mitre of England.

John de Gray displayed as much ability in directing the movements of troops in Ireland as he did at the Council board. He not only hired soldiers, but headed them. He led predatory excursions, took castles, carried away cows; and, in fact, did everything which a Christian bishop should not do; we are, therefore, by no means surprised that the Pope should refuse to sanction John's selection of such a man as the Archbishop of Canterbury.

I believe it was during his administration that a calamity occurred to the inhabitants of Dublin, which turned a day of rejoicing into one of sorrow and lamentation, and which caused the anniversary of the day of the calamity to be ever afterwards styled "*Black Monday.*"

It was on a Monday in Easter week, when the inhabitants of Dublin flocked out of the city towards Cullenswood, for a holiday; some for fresh air, and some for pastime; when the O'Byrnes and O'Tooles came down upon them, like two mountain wolves, and slew about 300 men, besides women and children.

The chronicler implies that Dublin was desolated by the calamity, and goes on to say, "The town was soon peopled again by Bristolians, yet that dismal day is yearly remembered and solemnly observed by the mayor, sheriffs, and citizens, with feast, banquet, and pitching up of tents in that place; in most brave sort, daring the enemy upon his peril not to be so hardy as once to approach near their feasting camp."

We learn from Dr. Leland that "the singing boys of

the Cathedral," even in his time, were in the habit, on Black Monday, of going to Cullenswood, daring the O'Byrnes or O'Tooles to show their faces."

But if they *had* but shown their faces, what a run, and "the devil take the hindmost," there would have been!

John de Gray was succeeded in 1213 by John de Loundres, or John of London, who was chosen Archbishop of Dublin in 1212, and was made Viceroy on the 23rd of July, 1213. He had been formerly Archdeacon of Stafford.

He was called by the Irish *Scorch-villain*, or "*Burn-bill.*" *Camden's Annals of Ireland* for 1212 contain an account of the way in which he gained this nickname.

Being installed in the Archbishoprick of Dublin, he summoned his tenant farmers to arrange their rents, telling them to bring their title-deeds with them. "Mistrusting nothing," they placed their papers in his hands, which he, before their faces, cast into the fire. Before they recovered from the shock and amazement, their title-deeds were consumed. It was then the tenants' turn to blaze, or burn: "*Thou*, an archbishop! Nay, thou art a Burn-bill, a Scorch-villain." Another drew his weapon and said, "As good for me to kill him as to be killed, for when my papers are burned and my living taken away, I am killed." The bishop became alarmed, and escaped by a "back door," but his chaplain, his registrar, and bailiffs were well beaten, and some of them "left for dead." They even threatened to fire the palace, and would have done so if their wrath had not been appeased by "fair promises that all should be to their content."

I have a strong suspicion that the farmers whose title-deeds were destroyed, were tenants who held under the see of Glendalough, or the seven churches, which had lately been united to Dublin. We learn from Felix O'Reardan, Archbishop of Tuam, that "Master John Papiron, coming to Ireland, found a bishop living at Dublin who exercised his episcopal functions *only within the walls*," and that he found, at no great distance "another church *in the mountains*, which was called a city, and had its bishop." The legate decided that Dublin should be the metropolis, to which he gave the pall, and divided the diocess of the mountain bishoprick between the Bishop of Glendalough and the Archbishop of Dublin, and ordered, that on the death of the Bishop of Glendalough, the whole should revert to Dublin. William Piro, the last bishop of Glendalough, died about 1214, soon after the appointment of John de Loundres. The union between the two sees might now have been effected " but for the insolence of the Irish," who were " very powerful in the country," and who, we conclude, were then as much opposed to ecclesiastical, as they are now to political unions. It is not, therefore, improbable that the opposition came from the *farmers whose leases may have been rendered null and void by the change;* but of this they would never have been convinced, without the application of fire.

The abolition of this bishoprick rendered the *city* of Glendalough a "a vast and desert solitude." The "holy church in the mountains, which was anciently held in great veneration, for St. Kevin's sake, who had there led a hermit's life, became so wild and desolate, that instead of a church was a den of thieves and robbers. More murders are committed in that valley than in any other place in Ireland." So says the Archbishop of Tuam. Woe to the tythe proctors or bishop's agent who went there for church dues!

In the passage quoted above, it is stated that the church in the mountains, was held in great veneration for St. Kevin's sake, who led a hermit's life there.*

There is a tradition that St. Kevin, in his youth, loved a beautiful maiden, named Kathleen, who adored him in return; for the saint himself had the face and form of a holy angel; but feeling himself divinely called to the service of the church, he fled from the face of his betrothed bride to the wild rocks and lakes of Glendalough. But what can surpass the love of woman? She found him out, though he lay hidden in the cavern of a rock, as difficult of access as an eagle's eirie. One night as he lay watching the moon, shining in her beauty, like the church to which his soul was eternally wedded, he saw what he first imagined to be two stars descending from heaven, above his head. He raised himself, in holy admiration, to see "this great sight," and as he did so, heard a whisper in his ear, and felt a soft hand on his shoulder. It was the hand and voice of Kathleen, whose eyes he mistook for stars. Starting from his bed in terror, he cast her from him, into the lake beneath.

* "S. Coemgenus, *i.e.* St. Kevin, exivit ipse ab eis solus ad superiorem ipsius vallis partem, quasi per unum milliarium â monasterio, et constituit mansiunculam ibi in loco angusto, inter montem et stagnum sibi, ubi erant densæ arbores et clari rivuli, et præcepit Monachis suis, ut nullum ciborum cibi genus darent; et nemo ad eum veniret, nisi pro maxima causa."—*Vita S. Coemgeni Die Tertia Junii,* c. iii.; *Acta Sanctorum,* tom. i., p. 315. *Vide* also Dr. Petrie's *Round Towers,* p. 172.

We learn from Moore's melodies that Kathleen's eyes were of "the most unholy blue." The poet thus describes the cruel conduct of the saint:—

> "Where the cliffs hang high and steep,
> Young St. Kevin stole to sleep.
> 'Here, at least,' he calmly said,
> 'Woman ne'er shall find my bed.'"

He was never more mistaken in his life. At that moment Kathleen was bending over him,—

> "Ah! your saints have cruel hearts.
> Sternly from his bed he starts;
> And with rude, repulsive shock,
> Hurl'd her from the beetling rock!"

Our Irish Viceroy, John of London, the unworthy successor of St. Kevin, or rather the inheritor of half of his diocese and income, was held in high estimation by John Lackland. When this false and pusillanimous monarch resigned the kingdoms of England and Ireland to the See of Rome, and consented to hold them as a fief,* this prelate is named first among the lords who were present at the execution of the deed. It is true that when John bowed down to the ground, and did homage to Pandolph, the Archbishop ventured to express his indignation, at the insolent bearing of the legate.

John de Loundres was present—*but on the King's side*—at Runnymede, when John so unwillingly granted the great charter of English liberty. And we shrewdly suspect that this Irish Viceroy was privately employed by the King, to induce Pope Innocent to annul the charter.

---

* *As a fief.*—"By the service of one thousand marks, to be paid annually; seven hundred for England, and for Ireland, three hundred."—*Leland*, vol. i., p. 200.

The King, we are told, retired to Windsor, after signing it, and gave himself up to chagrin, and tempests of fury, which must have undermined his constitution, and brought him to an early grave. He execrated his birth, and in his paroxysms of passion—like his father—seized sticks and straws, which he bit and gnawed and broke to pieces, thinking all the time of the great charter and the noble barons of Runnymede, who had put a bridle upon him, which he could neither break nor gnaw; so he sent De Loundres to Rome, to have it removed or revoked.

There can be no doubt that John de Loundres went to Rome in 1215, the year the charter was signed, and that he was present at the general council, there, in which the charter was annulled. Pope Innocent III., to whom John had made over his kingdom, and who now stood to the King in the relation of a feudal lord and protector, was incensed at the temerity of the English barons, who had dared, without waiting for his consent, to impose such terms on a prince, that had placed himself under the protection of the papal throne. He therefore, in the plenitude of his apostolic power, issued a bull to annul and abrogate the charter. By this bull the Pope prohibited the barons from exacting the observance of the charter, and the king from regarding it, as of any binding power, and pronounced a general sentence of excommunication against every and any one, who should persevere in maintaining such treasonable and iniquitous pretensions. Langton, the Primate of England, who was a different man from John of London, refused to publish the excommunication, and was cited to the general council at Rome, at which our Viceroy was present; and suspended for disobedience. A new sentence of excommunication was then pronounced against England. Encouraged by such high and sacred authority, King John renews the war, and takes the field, at the head of foreign troops, reducing his subjects to the desperate extremity of offering the throne of England to Lewis, the eldest son of Philip, King of France. This soon brought matters to extremities and King John to grief. His nobles deserted his standard, his castles fell, one by one, into the hands of the barons, and when passing from Lynn to Lincolnshire, where he expected to take his enemy by surprise, he was himself overtaken, like Pharaoh, King of Egypt, by the sea, which carried away his baggage, carriages, treasures, and regalia. He never recovered this overthrow. God seemed to fight against King John; and the devil, with whom he was in close league, to desert him. The King arrived at Swinshead Abbey, unwell, dispirited, and in a most malignant humour. "I hope," said he, as he sat at meat in the Abbot's refectory, "to make the half-penny loaf cost a shilling before the year is over." That day, if we can believe contemporary writers, he got his death sickness, "from a dish of autumn pears."*

He got his death sickness from spleen, after signing the charter. He was conveyed from the Abbey, in a litter, to Newark, where he died. He was buried in the cathedral of Worcester, close to the grave of St. Wulstan, a Saxon bishop of great sanctity; who had been lately canonized—far too holy a resting-place for one, by whose presence, "hell felt itself defiled;" so, at least, said

---

* *A dish of autumn pears.*—The *Annals of Clonmacnoise* say he died in the Abbey of Swynshead, "being poisoned by drinking a cup of ale, wherein there was a toad, pricked with a broach."

churchmen; for John, though a favourite with the Pope, was no friend to the clergy, at whom he sometimes sneered. "How plump and well-fed is this animal"—said the king of a fat stag, he had just run down—"yet I dare sware, he never went to mass." "This sally of wit"—says that infidel Hume—"upon the usual corpulency of the priests, more than all his enormous crimes and iniquities, made him pass with them for an atheist." John's personal appearance is thus described, when about fifty years of age, by Robert the Clerk. His hair is quite hoary; his figure made for strength, compact, but not tall. His queen—adds the cleric—"hates him, and is hated by him."

John de Loundres, or Burn-bill, or Scorch-villain, outlived his master King John, and was made Legate of Ireland by Pope Honorius, in 1217, and held a Synod in Dublin,* "wherein he ordained many profitable things concerning the church of Ireland." Ware thinks the Archbishop re-assumed the government of Ireland in 1219, which was in the hands of Geoffrey de Maurisco from 1215 to that period; but this is a mistake; for he was sent over, as appears by a letter from the young King Henry III., to aid the Viceroy, Geoffrey de Maurisco.

This prelate gets the credit of " causing the castle of Dublin to be built," or rather completed. He also caused the church of St. Patrick to be erected into a cathedral, and " united it," as John Alan says, " with the cathedral

---

* *Synod in Dublin.*—See *Annals of Mary's Abbey.* The decrees are still extant, in an old register, called "Bride Mihi."—See Ware's *Archbishops of Dublin—John de Gray.*

of Christchurch, under one spouse, saving to the other church, the pre-eminence of dignity."

John de Loundres died in the beginning of July, 1228, and was "buried in a wooden tomb, in the north wall at Christchurch, over against Comin." That is, John Comin, his predecessor. "But at this day," adds Ware, "there is no appearance of his tomb." John of London, nick-named Scorch-villain, was an able and determined Viceroy, and, with all his faults, a zealous churchman. Perhaps it was in the interests of Mother Church that he burned the tenants' leases.

Henry III.—English Laws for Ireland.

Henry III. was but nine years old when he ascended the throne of England. He had a younger brother, Richard, Earl of Cornwall. "The Irish," who, as Sir John Davis says, "have a desire to be governed by great people," petitioned to have the young Earl of Cornwall or the Queen Mother sent to Ireland. The young King Henry, who writes a most gracious letter to his Irish Deputy, Geoffrey de Maurisco, thanking him for faithful services, sends this reply to the petition : "As to the sending our lady the Queen Mother or our brother into Ireland, our answer is, that, taking the advice and assent of our faithful subjects, we shall do that which shall be expedient to our interests, and the interests of our realm."

The letter goes on touchingly to refer to his own "tender age," and concludes, "Our pleasure is that you, our other faithful subjects of Ireland, shall enjoy the same liberties which we have granted to our subjects of

England, and these we will grant and confirm to you."

By the liberties granted to his subjects of England, he means the renewal of the great charter, which was granted at a council convened at Bristol* on the 12th of November, 1216. A copy, or rather duplicate of this new or renewed charter, was sent to Ireland with the following letter:—

"THE KING TO ALL ARCHBISHOPS, BISHOPS, ABBOTS, EARLS, BARONS, KNIGHTS, AND FREE-TENANTS, AND ALL OUR FAITHFUL SUBJECTS SETTLED THROUGHOUT IRELAND GREETING:

"With our hearty commendation of your fidelity in the Lord, which you have ever exhibited to our lord father, and to us in these our days, our pleasure is, that in token of this your famous and notable fidelity, the liberties granted by our father and by us, of our grace and gift, to the realm of England, shall, in our kingdom of Ireland, be enjoyed by you, and by your heirs for ever. Which liberties, distinctly reduced to writing, by the general Council of all our liege subjects, we transmit to you, sealed with the seals of our Lord Gualon, Legate of the Apostolic See, and of our trusty Earl William Marshal, our Governor, and the Governor of our kingdom; *because, as yet, we have no seal*. And the same shall, in process of time, and on fuller counsel, receive the signature of our own seal. Given at Gloucester, the sixth day of February."

It was the sincere desire of the young king, or his governor, William Earl Marshal, that the English colonists in Ireland should be governed by the same laws as the English living in England.

* *Council at Bristol.*—We find the name of "Walter de Lacy, an Irish baron, lately restored to favour," as one who attended this council. The young king addressed a letter to Hugh de Lacy, requesting him to forget all "former animosities."

In the 30th of Henry III. it is thus recorded:

"Quia pro communi utilitate terræ Hiberniœ, ac unitate terrarum, provisum est, quod omnes leges et consuetudines, quæ in regno Angliæ tenentur, in Hiberniæ teneantur; et eadem terra ejusdem legibus subjaceat, ac per easdem regatur, sicut Johannes Rex, cum illuc esset, statuit et firmiter mandavit; ideo volumus quod omnia brevia de communi jure, quæ current in Anglia, similiter currant Hibernia, sub novo sigillo nostro, &c. Teste meipso apud Woodstocke."

"Because for the common interest of the land of Ireland, and the unity of both countries, it is provided that all laws and customs which are observed in the kingdom of England, should be observed in Ireland, and that the said land should be subject to and governed by the same laws as King John, when he was there, ordained and firmly commanded; therefore, we will that all writs at common law which run in England, shall in like manner run in Ireland, under our new seal. In testimony whereof witness myself at Woodstock."

We must again remind the reader that these laws did not extend to the native Irish. They were intended for English colonists. Sir John Davis, the Attorney-General to James I., who is the best authority on such a subject, says "Although King John did establish English laws and customs here, though likewise Henry III. did grant the like charter of liberties to his subjects of Ireland, as himself and father had granted to his subjects of England, notwithstanding it is evident by all the records of this kingdom, that only the English colonies and some few septs of the Irishry, which were enfranchised by special charters, were admitted to the benefit and protection of the laws of England."

CHAPTER XXXII.

RICHARD DE BURGO—HIS GREAT POSSESSIONS AND POWER IN CONNAUGHT.

A.D. 1227-1234. RICHARD DE BURGO succceded to the chief governorship of Ireland, on the 10th of March, 1227. He was the son of William Fitz-Adelm, and was hence called Mac William. His mother was Isabel, a natural daughter of Richard I., and widow of Llewellyn, Prince of Wales.

Richard de Burgo was styled Richard More, the "Great Lord of Connaught," of the whole of which he procured a grant from young King Henry, before the death of Cathal Crovderg. The young king probably acted under the advice of his new governor or guardian, Hubert de Burgo, Justiciary of England; but for Connaught to go without its own Irish King was not to be thought of, so Richard de Burgo elected Hugh O'Conor, the son of Roderick :—"A.D. 1228. Hugh, the son of Roderick O'Conor, assumed the kingdom of Connaught *by the election of the Justiciary* and the chiefs of Connaught, in preference to Turlough O'Conor, his elder brother," whose claims the former Governor, Maurisco, had latterly supported.

Hugh O'Conor commenced his reign in the Turkish fashion, by killing his nearest relations. He began operations on his nephew, O'Melaghlin, the son of his brother and rival, Turlough. "An intolerable famine" was the result of these bloody feuds among the sons and grandsons of Roderick, who plundered churches as well as territories, and "banished clergy and ollaves [wise and learned men] into remote countries."

The conduct of the English in Ireland was so much of a piece that the King wrote to Richard de Burgo commanding the observance of English laws and customs in Ireland. The letter is dated 1228.

Hugh O'Conor, in his madness, turned his arms against his powerful patron, Richard de Burgo, and actually plundered his territory. Richard, or Mac William de Burgo, as he was styled, was not the man to stand much of this sort of work. "The son of William," [*i.e.* Mac William,* or Richard de Burgo,] read the *Annals of Kilronan* for 1229, "mustered the greater part of the English of Ireland, and marched into Connaught, accompanied by Felim, the son of Cathal Crovderg, to give him the kingdom of Connaught, and to expel Hugh, the son of Roderick, and every Connacian who had joined with him and opposed himself." Hugh was expelled in 1230, and Felim, the son of Red-hand, or Crovderg, "proclaimed king, by the son of William," or Richard de Burgo.

But Felim was merely used as a cats-paw to take the kingdom from Hugh. The next year we meet this entry in the *Annals of Ireland*—"A.D. 1231. Felim, the son of Cathal Crovderg, was taken prisoner by the son of William Burke, in Meelick, in violation of the guarantee given by all the English chieftains of Ireland."

Conor, the son of the former King, Hugh, is also in

* *Mac William.*—Mac in Irish is "son." Mac William signifies "the son of William."

bonds as a hostage for his father's good behaviour. He makes his escape; and what is the result? "The kingdom of Connaught was again given to Hugh by the son of William Burke, who made peace with him, after he had taken Felim, the son of Cathal Crovderg, prisoner." Young Conor, whose escape procured his father's re-establishment on the throne, was killed by a man who " carried a white-handled battle-axe;" therefore the people of the Tuathos, among whom he was slain, *"whitened all the handles of their battle-axes."* Lest the murderer should be detected, they adopted the white-handled battle-axe, of which they were, no doubt, proud.

Richard de Burgo was deposed from the Irish Government this year, 1233, and his place filled by Maurice Fitzgerald, of whom we shall speak in the next chapter. Richard Burke owed his fall, as well as his rise, to his relative, Hubert de Burgo, who is styled by Hume, "the ablest and most virtuous minister that Henry ever possessed." But Hubert suddenly lost all favour, and was called "an old traitor" by a prince whose affection for him was at one time so great, as to be attributed to enchantment. Hubert had married the eldest sister of the King of Scots, and acquired numerous castles and demesnes, which, we conclude, excited the envy of his enemies, more especially that of the King's brother, Richard, Earl of Cornwall.

His Irish relative, Richard de Burgo, who fell with him, married Hodierna, daughter of Robert de Gernon, maternal grand-daughter of Cathal Crovderg, King of Connaught. He had by this marriage two sons, Walter and William. Walter married Maud, the daughter and heiress of Hugh de Lacy, junior, and became, in her right, Earl of Ulster. He had by her one son, Richard, commonly called the Red Earl, who was esteemed one of the most powerful subjects in Ireland. Richard de Burgo, the Viceroy, died in January, 1243, when proceeding to France—accompanied by a number of barons and knights—to meet the king, in whose favour, we may conclude, he had been re-established.

The Four Masters record the death of William Burke in 1248,—" William Burke died in England. His body was brought over to Ireland and buried at Athossel," or the " Low-Ford," where William Fitz-Adelm founded a priory for canons of the regular order of St. Augustine.

CHAPTER XXXIII.

MAURICE FITZ-GERALD, ANCESTOR OF THE EARLS OF KILDARE—HIS CONDUCT TO WILLIAM MARSHAL—VISITS WALES WITH FELIM O'CONOR—MORTALLY WOUNDED BY O'DONNELL—BURIED IN YOUGHAL.

A.D. 1234-1246. THIS Maurice Fitz-Gerald was the son of Gerald, as the name signifies, and the grandson of the first Maurice, of whom we speak in a former chapter. - He was the ancestor of the Earls of Kildare. His brother, Thomas More, was the ancestor of the Earls of Desmond. These were the two great branches of the Geraldine tree, which flourished for centuries in Leinster and Munster. The former is still green and fruitful, the latter "*is not*."

By a mandatory letter of Henry III., dated the 26th of November, 1216, Maurice came into possession of Maynooth (where his noble descendants now reside), and all the other lands in Ireland, of which his father, Gerald, died seized. He was also put into possession of the castle of Crom, in the county Limerick, from which the Earls of Kildare are supposed to have got their battle cry of *Crom-a-boo*. In a manuscript entitled Carbriæ Notitia,* we learn that Crom belonged to the O'Donovans, a family of royal extraction among the Irish; that "they built the famous castle of Crom, which, afterwards falling to the Earls of Kildare, gave the motto of Crom-a-boo, still used in their scutcheon."

One of the first acts of Maurice Fitz-Gerald's administra-

* *Carbriæ Notitia* was written in 1686. It was numbered 591 in the sale catalogue of the books and manuscripts of the late Lord Kingsborough.

tion, as Lord Justice of Ireland, added no honour to his shield. Richard, son of William Marshal, Earl of Pembroke, and grandson of Strongbow and Eva, the daughter of Diarmaid, King of Leinster, had incurred the displeasure of Henry III., by joining in a confederacy with the king's brother, the Earl of Cornwall, and other malcontent lords; he was therefore deprived of his high office, and forced to retire to Wales, where he defended his person and castles against the king's troops. He fled from Wales to Ireland, where he had immense possessions. Letters under the King's seal* had been previously addressed to the Viceroy, Maurice Fitz-Gerald, and other lords, to seize his person, with the promise that his forfeited estates should be divided among them. This was an immense bribe. Richard Marshal was a brave and powerful baron, it was therefore resolved to lay a trap to destroy him. Geoffrey de Maurisco, one of the conspirators, met him on his landing, and joined him, with a hundred men, and united with him in recovering some places which the Viceroy Fitz-Maurice had seized. The Irish lords now affected alarm, and proposed a conference. The place of conference was the Curragh of Kildare. Richard Marshal was accompanied to the ground by his false friend, Geoffrey de Maurisco, who at a given signal withdrew with more than eighty of his hundred men, leaving Richard with about fifteen followers, to contend with a foe more than ten times his number. But this young Earl of Pembroke, who has been styled the "Flower of Modern Chivalry," the virtus militiæ, and the

---

* *Letters under the King's seal.*—Matthew Paris speaks of "forged letters," and of secretly fixing, "as it were, by stealth," the King's seal.

protectio patriæ, stood his ground, till unhorsed by overpowering numbers, and stabbed in the back. He was conveyed to one of his own castles, which had just fallen into the hands of the Justiciary, Maurice Fitz-Gerald, where he died, surrounded by enemies, with only one friend to close his eyes. Leland speaks of Pembroke's "young brother," as on the field with him. This, we think, is a mistake. Moore styles his companion "a youth of his own household." Matthew Paris says, "Cum uno tantum juvene de suis inter hostes remansit." The Four Masters, who make a great bungle of this affair, say, the confederate lords killed Richard Marshal, and "made a prisoner of Geoffrey Mareshal, who had stood alone, fighting in the field, after all his people had fled from him." There was no such person as Geoffrey Mareshal.

Geoffrey de Maurisco, who acted so base a part by Richard Marshal, met the reward of a traitor knight. He incurred the displeasure of the King, and was banished and died in exile, having "suffered great miserie." "Thus," writes Hanmer, "the unstable wheele goeth round about."

Matthew Paris says, the King called the lords who conspired against Richard, Earl of Pembroke, traitors and Judases; and Geoffrey de Maurisco, who had the principal share in drawing the noble earl into the net, Ahithophel, the "Brother of Ruin."

Richard de Burgo, the late Viceroy, who was also among the conspirators, was now about to reap the fruits of his mal-administration. Felim, the son of Cathal Crovderg, with a sagacity not unusual in his countrymen, took the earliest opportunity, after the removal of his enemy from office, to write a submissive letter to the King, requesting permission to go to England, to cast himself at Henry's feet, and explain to him the enormous injustice he had suffered at the hands of the late Viceroy. Henry, who was just in the proper mood to hear anything and everything, to the prejudice of a De Burgo, wrote to the new Viceroy in the following style :—

"THE KING TO HIS WELL-BELOVED AND FAITHFUL MAURICE FITZ-GERALD, HIS JUSTICIARY OF IRELAND, HEALTH:

"Whereas our well-beloved and faithful Felim, son of our most dear friend [Cathal Crovderg], King of Connaught, hath proposed unto us to come to England, to see and converse with us, on our and his affairs; and whereas, we have sent him word, that before his arrival, he should advise with you, and endeavour to take the Castle of Melic,* now in the possession of Richard de Burgo, and that when the said castle shall be taken, and given up to us, it is very pleasing to us, and we will that he come to England."

Nothing could please Felim better than to take a castle belonging to the late Viceroy; but to be commissioned by the king to take Meelick Castle, where Richard Burke had made him prisoner, must have been the very height of his ambition and delectation. He therefore loses no time in qualifying himself for his visit to London. We read in the Four Masters, under date 1235, "The Castle of Meelick was demolished by Felim O'Conor." He had previously "demolished the castles which had been erected by the sons of Roderick and the son of William Burke—namely, the Castle of

* *Castle of Melic*, or Meelick.—In the parish of Meelick, on the western bank of the Shannon, near Eyrecourt, in Galway.

Bungalvy,* Castle-Kirk,† Castle-na-Cally,‡ and the
Castle of Dunamon§—and had slain his old rival, Hugh
O'Conor, and his brother, the sons of Roderick."

This Hugh was the last descendant of Roderick
O'Conor who sat on the throne of Connaught. The
Annals of Kilronan state that the Pope offered Roderick
and his issue for ever "the title to the sovereignty, and
six married wives, if he would thenceforward abstain
from the sin of women." The Four Masters say that
"God bestowed upon Cathal Crovderg," the father of
Felim, "the greatest virtues, for he kept himself content
with one married wife."

It was not till 1240 that Felim, who had become
gossip to Fitz-Gerald, or godfather to one of his children,
was allowed to go to England, " on which occasion he
received great honour from the King, and returned safe
home." The *Annals of Clonmacnoise* say, " Felym
O'Conor went into England because the English of
Ireland refused to yield him any justice. The King
granted him five cantreds [of land], which himself had,
and returned in safety."

His visit had the effect of inducing Henry III. to
command Maurice Fitz-Gerald to " pluck up by the root
that fruitless sycamore, De Burgo, which the Earl of

---

* *Bungalvy.*—" In the mouth of the river Galway, from which the
town takes it name."—Dr. O'Donovan.

† *Castle-Kirk.*—Now called the Castle of the Hen, on an island in
Lough Corrib, in Connemara.

‡ *Castle-na-Cally*, or Caislen-na-Caillighe, or the Hag's Castle, on
an islet in Lough Mask, Connemara.

§ *Dunamon.*—On the river Suck, between the counties Galway and
Roscommon.

Kent, in the insolence of his power, had planted in these parts; nor suffer it to bud forth any more."

We find Fitz-Gerald on some former occasions uniting with De Burgo in making raids into Connaught, burning towns and churches, and carrying away cattle; but we must do Fitz-Gerald the credit of saying that "he protected Clarus, the Archdeacon of Elphin, and the canons of Trinity Island, in honour of the Blessed Trinity; and the Lord Justice himself, and the chiefs of the English, went to see that place, and to kneel and pray there." The violence of these murderers, marauders, and cattle-stealers was often turned to profitable account by churchmen:—

"A.D. 1245. The Castle of Sligo was erected by Maurice Fitzgerald, and by the Sil-Murray. Felim, who had been ordered to erect it, at his own expense, attempted to convey the stones, lime, and houses of Trinity Hospital thither, although the Lord Justice had granted that place to Clarus Mac Mailin, in honour of the Holy Trinity."

The next entry in the *Four Masters*, tells of the departure of Fitz-Gerald and Felim to Wales:—

"A.D. 1245. A great army was led by the King of England into Wales. He pitched his camp at the Castle of Gannoc,* and he invited to his aid the Lord Justice [Maurice Fitz-Gerald], the English of Ireland, and Felim, the son of Crovderg O'Conor, and his forces."

This is not the first time that Henry III. sought the aid of Irish troops against his enemies on the other side

---

* *Castle of Gannoc.*—In Caernarvonshire, near the Conway shore. It is called Digauwy by the Welsh.—See *Gough's Camden*, p. 560.

of the water. Rymer furnishes us with a copy of the following letter:—

"THE KING, TO DONALD, KING OF TIRCONNEL, HEALTH.

"Whereas, provoked by the injuries of the King of Scotland, we have now prepared to make war upon him, and for the revenging the many transgressions he has committed against us, unless he does, of his own accord, make amends for the same. Confident of your love, that you will not deny us your assistance, in this our expedition, we order you, that with our Justiciary of Ireland, and other our faithful subjects, who are to come to the nearest ports of Scotland, to harass our enemies, that you furnish such powerful succour by coming, personally, with them, guarded by some brave people, so that in our necessity you may more confidently fly to us, and that we, for the succour granted to our prayer, may be the more willingly bound to grant you any favour you shall demand. Witness the King, at Stampford, the seventh of July."

A sudden accommodation with the King of Scotland did not give time to prove the effect of these honied words. It is evident from the whole tone of the letter that Henry was asking the presence and aid of these Irish chieftains, as a *special favour*. Even the Anglo-Irish Norman barons *claimed exemption from foreign service*. The Four Masters say the King "*invited*" the Lord Justice and Cathal Crovderg O'Conor to go to Wales. The writs issued by Henry III. on this occasion, were accompanied by a declaration that their attendance should not be pleaded as a precedent. See Close Roll, 28 Henry III. The King, on this account, displayed the greater impatience at what he conceived the negligent delay of the Irish troops. Matthew Paris gives a copy of a letter said to have been penned by a nobleman in Henry's camp, which conveys a good idea of the condition of Henry's army :—" The King, with his army, lyeth at Gannocke, fortifying that strong castle, and we live in our tents, thereby watching, fasting, praying, and freezing with cold. We watch for fear of the Welshmen, who are wont to invade and come upon us in the night-time; *we fast for want of meat*, for the half-penny loaf is worth five-pence; we pray to God to send us home speedily; and we starve with cold, wanting our winter garments, having no more than a thin linen cloth between us and the wind." "The King," says Matthew Paris, " looking impatiently for the Irish forces, mused with himself, fretted with himself, the wind serving, and yet said nothing. At length their sails were descried, and Maurice Fitzgerald and the Prince of Connaught presented themselves in battle-array before the King."

Hanmer adds, that the King, having overthrown the Welsh, and re-victualled his castle, returned to England, "winking awhile in policie at the tarriance and slow coming of Maurice Fitz-Gerald," who returned to Ireland, and made some successful forays into Ulster and Connaught; but this was of no avail, for the King, whose displeasure was inexorable, dismissed him from his office, and appointed Geoffrey de Maurisco in his stead.

"John Fitz-Geoffrey came to Ireland, and Maurice Fitz-Gerald was unkinged." So writes the Four Masters, under date 1246. But a Fitz-Gerald "unkinged" was more of an Irish ruler or Viceroy than any Fitz-Geoffrey could possibly be. Take the following example:—" A.D. 1246. Maurice Fitz-Gerald marched with an army into Tirconnell. He gave the half of Tirconnell to Cormac, son of Dermot, and obtained hostage of O'Donnell for the other half." Could anything be more king-like?

Take another example, under date of following year, and let the reader say who was King or Viceroy, Fitz-Geoffrey or Fitz-Gerald:—

"A.D. 1247. A great army was led by Maurice Fitz-Gerald and other chiefs, first to Slygo, and then to Cataract, of Aedh-Roe. Melaghlin O'Donnell, Lord of Tirconnell, Kinel Moen, Inishowen, and Fermanagh, were slain by Maurice Fitz-Gerald."

Fitz-Gerald's last contest with O'Donnell was at Drumcliff, where these brave Norman and Celtic foemen seem to have exchanged death wounds. Maurice died of his wound before the end of 1257, and O'Donnell the year after:—

"A.D. 1258. O'Donnell was lying on his back for a year after the battle, when O'Neill, of Tyrone, marched into Tirconnel, and demanded hostages and submission. When this message was given to the dying chieftain, he ordered his *bier*, in which he was carried to battle. He gained a complete victory. After the battle " the bier on which O'Donnell was carried was laid down in the street of Conghail, *and here his soul departed.*"—*Four Masters*.

Fitz-Maurice, who died the previous year, is styled by old annalists, "The Destroyer of the Irish." Matthew Paris calls him " a valiant knight and a pleasant man." The Franciscan Friary in Youghal, where Maurice Fitz-Gerald died—in the habit of a monk,—and where he was interred, was founded by him in 1224. It was originally designed for a castle. The workmen while digging for a site asked Maurice Fitz-Gerald for money to drink his health, which he directed his eldest son to give. The son gave the men abuse instead of money, "more kicks than halfpence," which so annoyed the father that he changed his plan, and built a friary instead of a castle. Mr. Hayman says, "This is the earliest foundation in Ireland for the order of St. Francis." The building was completed by Thomas Fitzmaurice, the second son of the founder, who died in May, 1260, and who was also interred here. Here lie the remains of some of the Earls of Desmond.

For further information respecting Youghal and its antiquities, I beg to refer the reader to the learned and interesting work of the Rev. Samuel Hayman, formerly of Youghal, now Rector of Doneraile.

CHAPTER XXXIV.

JOHN FITZ-GEOFFREY — THEOBALD BUTLER — IRELAND VESTED IN PRINCE EDWARD.

A.D. 1246-1256. OF John Fitz-Geoffrey, the regularly constituted ruler, we know nothing more, than that he was appointed by the King, in a pet, in 1246, and removed in 1247. He visited Ireland at the command of Queen Eleanor, in 1253, to obtain horses, arms, and trusty soldiers for the protection of Gascony. Matthew Paris speaks of William de Maurisco, a brother of John, and a son of Geoffrey, as "an exiled and banished man"— banished for some "heinous offence." He "kept himself on the Isle of Lundy, not far from Bristol, preying, robbing, and stealing, as a notorious pirate. At length, being apprehended, together with seventeen of his confederacy and by the King's commandment, adjudged to cruel death, he was drawn, at London, with his confederates, at horse tails, to the gibbet, and there hanged and quartered."

John Fitz-Geoffrey was succeeded by Theobald Butler, in 1247. The ancestor of the Butlers came from Normandy, to England, with William the Conqueror. Theobald Fitz-Walter came to Ireland with Henry II. The family, or surname, Butler, was derived from the office of Chief Butler, to the Kings of England. It was the privilege of the Fitz-Walters, or Butlers, to attend the coronation, and present the first cup of wine to the King. The Butlers became Earls of Ormond and Ossory, of Kilkenny, Gowran, Glengall, and Carrick; Viscounts of Galmoy and Mountgarrett; and marquesses and dukes of Ormond.

Theobald Butler, of whom we now treat, led an army into Tyrone against O'Neill, in 1248, on which occasion he built the bridge of the Bann—now called Banbridge and the castle of Druim-Tairsich. "The Justiciary of Ireland went to Coleraine, with an army, and a bridge and castle were built by him, at Druim-Thairsich." See Dublin copy of *Annals of Ulster*, A.D. 1248.

The next year, 1249, we find the Viceroy mustering and marching an army on one side of the Shannon, and Mac-Maurice Fitz-Gerald, the son of the Viceroy, of whom we speak in a former chapter, marshalling an army at the other side; but without coming to blows.

Here we have the first indications of that fierce rivalry between the Butlers and Fitz-Geralds, which deluged the country in blood for three centuries.

As Irishmen do not understand how soldiers could meet "without coming to blows," the grandsons of Roderick, or heirs presumptive of Connaught, marched out to meet the English, and came up with them, at Athenry. As it was Lady-Day, the English asked for a truce, in honour of the virgin, which the roydamnas, or grandsons of Roderick, refused. The consequence we may imagine: The Irish were seized with dismay, and routed, "through the miracles of the Blessed Virgin, on whose festival they had refused to grant a truce."

Among the slain was a remarkable character, Donough Kill-Patrick, the grandson of the Prince of Ossory, who so bravely withstood the first invaders. This Donough is styled "the third greatest plunderer of the

English." The other two were Conor O'Melaghlin, and Conor Mac Coghlan. This Fitz-Patrick was in the habit of going out to reconnoitre, in the market towns of the English, in the guise of a hawker, a pauper, a carpenter, a poet, or a merchant, as the occasion might require :—

> "My darling is a bookman,
> My Donough is a carpenter,
> He sells his wine, he sells his hides
> Where'er he sees a gathering."

The *Irish Annals* from 1250 to 1256 are solely occupied with accounts of battles, taking of preys or prisoners, the deaths of chieftains and priests, and the founding of religious houses. These Norman knights endeavoured to make atonement for all the evil they committed in their lives, by founding monasteries, where their souls would be prayed for after death. Did any of these cut-throat church-builders ever read what God said to King David?—"*Thou shalt not build an house unto my name, because thou hast shed much blood upon the earth.*"—1 Chronicles xxii. 8.

"A.D. 1250. Florence Mac Carthy was slain by the English of Desmond."

"A.D. 1251. A monastery was founded at Kilnamullagh,* in the diocess of Cork, by Barry, who chose a burial place for his family in it."

"A.D. 1252. The Lord Justice of Ireland, came to Armagh with a numerous army."

"A.D. 1253. The Franciscan Monastery of Ardfert, [near Tralee], was founded by Fitz-Maurice of Kerry."

---

* *Kilnamullagh.*—From *cill-na-mullach*, or "church of the hills." Now Buttevant, from Boutez-en-avant, the war cry of the Barrys. The poet Spenser's *Mullagh*, or Aubeg, runs near the town of Buttevant.

"A.D. 1254. Pierce Ristubart [perhaps Rochfort] was slain by Murrough O'Melaghlin, on Lough Ree."

"A.D. 1254. The Green Monastery of Kildare was founded by the Earl of Kildare. There is a superb tomb in the chapel of the Blessed Virgin Mary."

It was about this time—on the occasion of his marriage with the Infanta of Spain—that the whole of Ireland, with the exception of church lands, and the towns of Dublin, Limerick, and Athlone, were vested in the young prince, Edward. For some time after this, Ireland was styled the "Lands of Lord Edward." It was proposed that this able and warlike prince should rule Ireland in person, but the disorders of his father's administration in England, did not warrant his absence from that country. Ireland was therefore left in the hands of Deputies, or Viceroys, of some of whom we have little more than a name to record.

CHAPTER XXXV.

ALAN DE LA ZOUCH—PRINCE EDWARD—THE OLD CHRONICLERS' TRAGICAL ACCOUNT OF DE LA ZOUCH'S DEATH.

A.D. 1256—1258.

A.D. 1256. "A JUSTICIARY arrived in Ireland from the King of England. He and Hugh O'Conor held a conference at Rinn Duin, where a peace was ratified between them, on condition that so long as he should be Justiciary, the territory or lands of O'Conor in Connaught should not be circumscribed."
—*Four Masters*.

His father's—Felim's—inheritance had been already circumscribed to five cantreds, or five hundred thousand acres. The *Annals of Ireland* say, "The King granted Felim O'Conor *a charter* to hold the five cantreds of the King," of England.

Although this Alan de la Zouch was the deputy of Prince Edward, who had been appointed Lord of Ireland, and whose seal was to bear royal authority, all Irish movements were jealously watched by the King, and regulated by those who acted in his name. The deputy was strictly commanded to acknowledge no superior but the King, nor to resign his authority, without the royal mandate.

When Prince Edward was about to remove a Lord Justice, the King, by the advice of the barons of England, sent a precept to the archbishops, bishops, priors, and knights, "that he heard his son designed to make a new Justiciary for Ireland, without his consent, and to put his castles in such hands as might be of great damage to them, not without danger of their disinheriting; therefore he commands them not to be obedient to any such Justiciary, constables, or keepers of castles, made or appointed, without his letters patent, by the assent and advice of his council." He also commanded Alan de la Zouch not to obey, or give authority to any new Justiciary.

"How far," says Moore, "the lot of *that* country might have been ameliorated and brightened, had Prince Edward, as was once intended, gone over thither, as Lord Lieutenant, and assumed personally the administration of affairs, there is now no use in speculating."

Having said so much from an English point of view on this vexed question, the poet and historian turns about to his Irish reader, and adds, "That he [Prince Edward] would have allowed any ordinary scruples, either of justice or humanity, to stand in the way of his stern policy, the course pursued by him afterwards, in Scotland, sufficiently forbids us to suppose. Whether among the Irish chiefs of that day he would have found or called forth a Bruce, a Douglas, or a Randolph, is a question involving too melancholy a contrast between the champions of respective countries."

Did Thomas Moore ever read of a Scottish hero, named *William Wallace*, that he should omit his name, on such an occasion? We might as well omit the name of *Moore*, when speaking of Irish poets.

We learn from Ware, who quotes from the records of Conway, as copied by Owen, that "the Earl of Chester fell to outrage" against King Henry, in 1256, and sent to Ireland for succour; but Prince Edward rigged a navy, which met the Irish fleet, killed their men and sunk their ships; so that a few only returned, "to report their hard success in Ireland."

The old chroniclers say that Alan de la Zouch, who afterwards became Chief Justice of England, met a violent death in Westminster Hall. It would appear from Ware's account that he was claimant, as well as Judge, in the case of certain lands in the possession of Earl Warren,—"The second [controversy] was between this Earl Warren and Allan de la Zouch. This Zouch, being Chief Justice, asked Earl Warren how he held his land. Earl Warren drew forth his sword, and said, 'By this, mine ancestors held the same, and by this I presently hold it,' and with that ran the Chief Justice through in Westminster Hall; and in his flight wounded also his son. Thence he fled to his castle at Risgate, whom Prince Edward, the King's eldest son, pursued with an army, to whom he submitted, and afterwards, with friends, and with money, pacified all."

This account of Zouch's death is taken by Ware from Florilegus, Lloyd, and Stowe. Something like this occurred in 1275, during Edward's reign. A commission sat to inquire into the encroachments on the royal demesne. Earl Warren being asked to show his title, drew his sword, and said, "William, the Bastard, had not conquered the kingdom for himself, alone; my ancestor was a joint adventurer in the enterprise." But there is no account of his running the Chief Justice through with his sword. This is a purely *Florilegious* account of the transaction.

T

CHAPTER XXXVI.

STEPHEN DE LONGSPEE — HIS BATTLE WITH O'NEILL, WHOM HE SLEW IN DOWNPATRICK—DRESS OF THE IRISH.

A.D. 1258-1260. STEPHEN DE LONGSPEE, or Stephen of the Long Skein, or two-handled sword, as Ware has it, succeeded Alan de la Zouch. He is styled by some Earl of Salisbury, and by others Earl of Ulster. It is probable that the latter title was assumed, in right of his wife, who was the widow of Hugh de Lacy, Earl of Ulster. Stephen de Longspee was the son of William de Longspee, Earl of Salisbury, who was the son of Henry II., by the beautiful Rosamond, daughter of Lord Clifford. Leland calls "Stephen Longspee the King's [Henry III.'s] own natural brother," and says, "he was excommunicated, with all his train, by the Archbishop of Dublin, as appears by a close roll of the 36th of his reign." That would be 1252, or six years before he was Viceroy.

This Viceroy, or, as he was styled, Lord Justice, is celebrated for his victory over O'Neill, whom he slew in the streets of Downpatrick, with a large number of his Irish chieftains. The battle of Druim-dearg, or the "Red-hill," is placed by Dr. Hanmer in 1258, by Dr. Cox, in his *Hibernia Anglicana*, in 1259, and by the Four Masters, in the Annals of Ulster, Kilronan, Connaught, and Clonmacnoise, in 1260. The *Annals of Innisfallen* give 1258, and say that the battle was fought on Sunday, and that O'Neill's head was sent to England. Mac. Namee, the bard of the O'Neills, says, "The head of O'Neill, King of Tara, was sent to London, to the King of England." He adds that the Irish, in this battle with Stephen Longsword, fought at a great disadvantage, being dressed in satin shirts only, while the English were protected by shirts of mail:—

> "The Galls from London thither,
> The hosts from Waterford,
> Came in a bright green body,
> In gold and iron armour.
>
> "Unequal they entered the battle,
> The Galls and the Irish of Tara;
> Fair satin shirts on the race of Con,
> The Galls in one mass of iron."

We conclude that the "fair satin shirts" were confined to the Irish chieftains, a large number of whom fell on this occasion. If we can believe ancient chronicles and poets, Irish kings and queens wore mantles of the richest silk, fringed with lace, and fastened at the neck with golden buttons. The chieftains wore shirts of thirty ells of linen, of saffron dye, fastened round the waists with leathern girdles, red cloaks, with hoods and borders of shagged hair, drawn together at the breast, with silver fibulas or buckles, short boots, of untanned skin, and long beards running to a point. When mounted on their wild horses, with their brazen-handled swords and golden-bitted bridles, glistening in the sun, they must have presented a bright array.

"Linen shirts," says Campion, "the rich do wear, for wantonness and bravery, with wide, hanging sleeves, plaited. Thirty yards are little enough for one of them." In another place, "They have now left off their saffron, *and learn to wash their shirts four or five times in the year.*" What unheard-of extravagance!

Stephen of the Long-sword was treacherously murdered, by his own people, in 1260, and was succeeded by Sir William Denn.

CHAPTER XXXVII.

WAR BETWEEN THE MAC CARTHYS AND FITZ-GERALDS—"THE CARTIES PLAYED THE DIVELLS IN DESMOND"—THE GERALDINE MONKEYS.

A.D. 1260-1261. HANMER'S account of the contentions between the Mac Carthys and the Fitz-Geralds, that is the Irish and Anglo-Norman lords of Desmond, or South Munster, is very graphic:

"Anno 1260. William Denn was made Lord Justice, in whose time Green Castle, Arx-Viridis, was destroyed, and the Carties plaied the divells in Desmond, where they burned, spoiled, preyed, and slew many an innocent. They became so strong, and prevailed so mightily, that for the space of twelve years, the Desmonds [the Fitz-Geralds] *durst not put plow in ground, in their owne country!* At length, through the operation of Satan, a bone of discord was thrown between the Carties, the O'Driscolls, O'Donovans, Mac Donochs, Mac Mahons, Mac Swines, and the inhabitants of Muscerry, insomuch that, by their cruel dissentions, they weakened themselves on all sides, that the Desmond, in the end, overcame and overtopped them all. In the beginning of these garboils, I find, that the Carties slew of the Desmonds, John Fitz-Thomas, founder of the monastery and convent of Tralee, together with Maurice, his son, eight barons, fifteen knights, beside infinite numbers, at a place called Callan, where they were buried."—*Hanmer's Chronicle*, Dublin edition of 1809, p. 400.

The Fincen Mac Carthy who won this battle was the

Mac Carthy Reagh. We discover from the *Annals of Innisfallen*, and other authorities, that the Lord Justice, Sir William Denn, with Walter de Burgo, the Earl of Ulster, Walter de Riddlesford, the great Baron of Leinster, and Donnell Roe Mac Carthy, were on the side of the Geraldines. The Irish, on this occasion, had ample vengeance for the victory gained by Stephen de Longspee, the former Viceroy, at Downpatrick. It would be difficult to say which was the more decisive victory, that of Downpatrick, or Callan.

It was during this sudden rising of the Mac Carthys that a curious circumstance is said to have occurred which gave the Fitzgerald coat of arms *apes*, or monkeys, as supporters. Thomas *Na n-ape*, "Thomas of the Ape" was a child of nine months old, when messengers arrived at Tralee, with the news of his father's and grandfather's death, and of the approach of the Mac Carthys. The nurses started up, in fright, and fled, leaving the child behind them, when a large ape caught up the infant and carried it to the battlements of the castle; and when the alarm of the threatened danger had subsided, brought it safely down and quietly laid it in its cradle.

The following is the Marquis of Kildare's account of the origin of the monkey supporters. He removes the scene of the story from the castle of Tralee, to that of Woodstock, near Athy :—" John Fitz-Thomas, afterwards Earl of Kildare, then an infant, was in the castle of Woodstock, near Athy, when there was an alarm of fire. In the confusion the child was forgotten, and when the servants returned to search for him, the room in which he lay was found in ruins. Soon after a strange noise was heard on one of the towers, and on looking up, they saw an ape, which was usually kept chained, carefully holding the child in its arms. The Earl, afterwards, in gratitude, adopted the monkey, as his crest and supporters; and some of his descendants, in memory of it, took the additional motto, *non immemor benificii.*"

We leave the reader to decide which is the more correct version of the story, for both the Kildare and Desmond branches of the Geraldines adopted the apes as supporters.

CHAPTER XXXVIII.

SIR RICHARD DE RUPELLA—TRADITION RESPECTING THE NAME—HE IS SEIZED AND IMPRISONED BY THE FITZGERALDS—THE KING INTERFERES—GENERAL STATE OF IRELAND.

A.D. 1261-1267. SIR WILLIAM DENN, or Denny, who died in 1261, was succeeded by Sir Richard de Rupella, as Lord Deputy of Ireland. The *Annals of Innisfallen* say that he landed at Portnalong, in Ivahagh, in 1262. The name of Adam de Rupe appears—in the Appendix to the *Fragment of History*, ascribed to Maurice Regan—among "the English and Welsh adventurers, who assisted in the reduction of Ireland, during the first sixteen years from the Invasion." He is mentioned, by chroniclers, as a man of "great possessions and power." In Pembrokeshire, who founded Hill Priory, the church of St. Mary Roche, and built Roche Castle, on a barren rock, from which the surname *De Rupe*,* is derived.

He became possessed of Roche's Country, in the county of Cork, in right of his wife. Fleming was the first Norman knight who obtained possession of this district. Fleming had a fair daughter, named Amy, whose heart and hand were won by young Adam de Rupe, who entered the lists, as Fleming's champion,

---

* *De Rupe.*—Some think the present family name of Roche is derived from the *roach* fish. The Roche arms are three fishes. The armorial shield, of the Lords Roche, or Fermoy, in Bridgetown Abbey, in the County Cork, is "charged" with one fish.

against Condon,* whom he slew by a cross shot, in the thigh. With Amy came the inheritance, known afterwards as "Roche's Country." There is a story that Adam de Rupe died of the bite of a viper, and that such a death had been predicted; and that he therefore built a castle on a rock, at a distance from any kind of vegetation which would be likely to harbour such a reptile; but that a viper was introduced in a faggot of wood, which fulfilled the prophecy.

The Lord Justice, Sir Richard de Rupella, accompanied by Mac William Burke, and John de Verdun, led a large army against Felim, the son of Cathal Crovderg O'Conor, who gave them so warm a reception, that they sent messengers to offer peace. After they had concluded this peace, Hugh O'Conor and Mac William Burke, *slept together, in one bed,*† *cheerfully and happily:*

> "And the brave foemen, side by side,
> Lay peaceful down, like brothers tried,
> And slept until the dawning beam
> Purpled the mountain and the stream."

The following extract from the *Four Masters* records the death of Gerald Roche, "the third-best knight of his time." We conclude he was a relative of the Viceroy or Lord Justice:—

"A.D. 1262. An army was led by Mac William Burke and the English of Ireland into Desmond, against

---

* *Condon.*—The Condons, or Cantons, were a Norman family, and had large possessions in the County Cork. The town and parish of Fermoy is in the barony of Condons and Clongibbon.

† *In one bed.*—Sir Anthony St. Leger, writing to Henry VIII., of Lord Roche, and the White Knight, says, "I have laid them both in your castle of Dublin, where they now agree very well together, and *lie bothe in one bedde.*"—*State Papers*, vol. iii., p. 466.

Mac Carthy, and arrived at Mangartagh* of Lough Leane. Here Gerald Roche, who was said to be the third-best knight of his time, in Ireland, was slain by Mac Carthy."

The Mac Carthy here mentioned was the Mac Carthy More, who lived at Pallace, near the Gap of Dunloe. Donnell God Mac Carthy, or the "Stammering Mac Carthy," was slain in this battle. "Both the English and Irish suffered great losses about the Mangartagh [Mangerton] Mountain on that day."

In the annals of the next year we read of Mac William Burke making fierce war on Felim O'Conor and his pleasant bed-fellow, Hugh, who fled before him into the north of Connaught. The Mac William here mentioned was Walter, the son of Richard More, who was the son of William Fitz-Adelm de Burgo. He became Earl of Ulster soon after this, by his marriage with Maud, the daughter of Hugh de Lacy, the younger.

The following extracts from the *Four Masters* give a more graphic picture of the state of society at this period than any we could draw :—

" A.D. 1264. A conference was held this year at Athlone, between the Lord Justice of Ireland, attended by the English, the Earl of Ulster, and Maurice Fitzgerald, with their respective forces, and Felim O'Conor and his son, on the other side. The English were seized with fear and perplexity of mind, when they saw the King of Connaught and his son approaching with a numerous and complete muster of forces, and came to the conclusion of suing for peace. Felim and the chiefs

---

* *Mangartagh.*—Better known to tourists as "Mangerton Mountain" at Killarney. The lake is still known as "Lough Leane."

consented to make peace, and they afterwards separated on amicable terms.

"A war broke out between Mac William Burke, Earl of Ulster, and Maurice Fitz-Gerald, so that the greater part of Ireland was destroyed between them. The Earl took all the castles that Fitz-Gerald possessed in Connaught, burned his monasteries, and plundered his people. The Castle of Lough Mask and the Castle of Ardrahin were taken by Mac William Burke. The Lord Justice, John Goggan,* and Theobald Butler, were taken prisoners by Maurice Fitz-Gerald in a consecrated church."

The seizing and imprisoning the Lord Justice is thus recorded in *Hanmer's Chronicle:*—"At the same time the fury of the Geraldines was so outrageous, in so much so that Maurice Fitzgerald, the second Earl of Desmond,† opposed himself against the sword, and took at Trisledermot, now called Castle Dermocke, Richard de Capella, the Lord Justice, Theobald le Butler, and John, or Millis de Cogan, and committed them to prison in Leix and Donamus; but the year following Henry the Third, not pleased with these commotions and hurly-burlies, by mature advice taken of his council, pacified the variance between them, discharged Denny of his Justiceship, and appointed David Barry Lord Justice in his place."

The "Denny" here mentioned was Sir William Denn, who was Lord Justice in 1260-61. We conclude

---

* *John Goggan.*—In the *Annals of Clonmacnoise* he is called Cowgan. He was probably a descendant of the famous Milo de Cogan, who, with Robert Fitz-Stephen, got a grant of the county of Cork.

† *Maurice Fitz-Gerald, the second Earl of Desmond.*—This is a mistake. Maurice Fitz-Thomas, the First Earl of Desmond, was not so created till 1329.—*Gibson's History of Cork*, Vol. I., p. 44.

that he assumed the duties of the Viceroy on the seizure and imprisonment of Richard de Capella, or Rupella.

Felim O'Conor, the son of Red-Hand, died during De Rupe's administration, or rather incarceration, and his son Hugh, Mac William's cheerful bedfellow, "reigned in his stead." We cannot conclude this chapter without giving the reader the Four Masters' description of both father and son:—

"A.D. 1267. Felim, the son of Cathal Crovderg O'Conor, the defender and supporter of his own province, and of his friends on every side, the expeller and plunderer of his foes, a man full of hospitality and prowess, and renown, the exalter of clerical orders and men of science, a worthy *materies* of a King of Ireland, for his nobility, personal shape, heroism, wisdom, clemency, and truth, died after the victory of extreme unction and penance, in the Monastery of the Dominican Friars at Roscommon,* which he himself had granted to God and that order.

"Hugh O'Conor, his own son, was inaugurated King over the Connacians, as his successor. Hugh committed his regal depredation in Offaly; and on his return to Athlone put out the eyes of Cathal, son of Teige O'Conor, who died in consequence."

* *Monastery of Dominican Friars.*—"Felim was interred in his own Abbey of Roscommon, and his monument, of which Mr. Walker has given a drawing in his *Dress of the Ancient Irish*, is an object of melancholy curiosity to this day."—*Dr. O'Conor's Life and Writings of Charles O'Conor, of Belanagare*, p. 43.

CHAPTER XXXIX.

THE FRIAR STEPHEN FOLEBURNE.

A.D. 1267-1272. SIR RICHARD DE RUPELLA was succeeded by John Fitz-Geoffrey, who became Viceroy for the third time. He was followed by David Barry, Viscount of Buttevant; David Barry, by Robert d'Ufford; Robert d'Ufford by Richard of Exeter; and Richard of Exeter by Jacques D'Audeley, who was slain in Thomond. On the death of D'Audley, the Council elected Maurice Fitz Maurice, Baron of Offaly, to fill his place, who was made prisoner by the O'Conors in the King's County. The imprisoned Viceroy was succeeded by Sir Geoffrey de Joinville, the friend and confidant of Edward I., who administered the affairs of Ireland from 1273 to 1276.

About thirty years after this he resigned his inheritance in Meath to his grand-daughter, the wife of Roger de Mortimer, and ended his days, as a monk, in a Dominican Abbey, which he and his wife had founded in Trim.

De Joinville was succeeded by Sir Robert D'Ufford, for the second time, who had, as his Deputy, the famous Friar Stephen de Foleburne, who was successively Bishop of Waterford and Archbishop of Tuam, and also King's Treasurer for Ireland.

Things were in a very bad state during Friar Foleburne's reign, whose nephew was in the hands of the O'Mores of Leix, while Maurice Fitz-Gerald was in those of the O'Conors. "Les Irreys," said the Friar, in writing to Edward I., who had just ascended the English throne, "ke le tenent en prisone, ne le voillent deliverer pour or ne pour argent, sil ne puissent aver le delivraunce del fiz de lur oncle, e del fiz de lur frere ke sunt en hostage a Duvelin."

Edward I. sent for D'Ufford to explain why such enormities should exist under the Irish Government. D'Ufford told Edward he must not believe all he heard, but at the same time implied that the Government had to wink while one knave cut the throat of another. Take the following specimen:—

"A.D. 1277. The son of the Earl of Clare took Bryen Roe O'Bryen prisoner, very deceitfully, after they had sworn to each other all the oaths of Munster, as bells, relics of saints, bachalls [*i.e.*, croziers], to be true to each other for ever, and not endamage each other; also after they became sworn gossips; and for the confirmation of their indissoluble bond of perpetual friendship, *they drew part of the blood of each of them, which they put in a vessel, and mingled it together*"—and, we conclude, *drank it*. Notwithstanding, the said Earl's son took the said "Bryen and bound him to sterne steeds, and so tortured him to death." It is probable the "Earl, whose son acted so treacherously, was John Geoffrey, to whom the King made a grant in the county of Clare, of a territory of sixty-seven thousand acres. It was then, as now, a *land* question.

The Friar, or Archbishop, had the usual pension or pay of five hundred pounds a year. Besides this he got into arrear, as King's Treasurer, for the Treasurer was a sporting statesman, and kept fifty horses for hunting down Irish or Anglo-Norman rebels. The names of some of his favourite steeds have come down to us, as Lynette, Jordan, Feraunt de Trim, Bancan, Blanchard de Londres, Connetable, Bendour, Scampane, Obin the Black, and Dunning.

Friar Foleburne was succeeded in the government of Ireland by John Saunford, Archbishop of Dublin; and he was succeeded by Sir William de Vescy, who laid claim (in right of his grandmother, the Princess Margaret, daughter of "William the Lion") to the throne of Scotland.

CHAPTER XL.

THE LIMITS OF THE ENGLISH BORDER—THE CHALLENGE BETWEEN DE VESCY AND FITZ-GERALD—JOHN DE WOGAN—PERSECUTION OF THE KNIGHTS TEMPLARS.

A.D. 1272-1307. WHEN Edward I. ascended the English throne in 1272, a hundred years from the first invasion, the English territory and English rule in Ireland had scarcely extended beyond the limits it had reached at the death of Strongbow. The counties of Dublin, Louth, Kildare, Waterford, Tipperary, Cork, Limerick, Kerry, Roscommon, and a part of Connaught, were nominally under Irish rule, and called "*Liberties*," but the subjection was only nominal. To say that Ireland was *ruled* at this period, or for two centuries afterwards, by Irish Viceroys, or their deputies, would be altogether opposed to facts. The representatives of English monarchs were bearded and defied, and, on some occasions, held in custody, not only by Irish chieftains, but by Norman knights, from whom they might have expected more loyal behaviour. Sir William de Vescy, a Yorkshire man, and a great favourite with Edward I., was sent over to Ireland as Lord Justice in 1290.

He had a quarrel with John Fitz-Thomas Fitz-Gerald of Kildare, about some land. This dispute rose so high that De Vescy told Fitz-Gerald to his face that he was a traitor, a rank thief, an upholder of thieves and traitors, and a murderer of the King's subjects.

Fitz-Gerald told him to withdraw his words, telling him he would make him eat them.

"Before I eat these words," was De Vescy's bold reply, "I will make thee eat a piece of my blade." Both parties were summoned before Edward I., when Fitz-Gerald challenged De Vescy to single combat, saying, "To justify that I am a true subject, and that thou, De Vescy, art an arch traitor to God and the King, I here, in the presence of his Highness, and in the hearing of this honourable assembly, challenge thee to combat." The assembly gave a shout of applause.

The challenge was accepted, and the day fixed by the King; but when the hour for the onset arrived the brave De Vescy was *non est inventus*. He had conveyed himself to France, leaving the lands which caused the dispute in the hands of his antagonist.

Holingshed, who often puts speeches into the mouths of his heroes, represents De Vescy as addressing Fitz-Gerald in the presence of King Edward I. and his council thus:—"A gentleman! Thou bold baron, I tell thee that the Vescies were gentlemen before the Geraldines were barons of Ophaly; yea, and before that Welsh bankrupt, thine ancestor, feathered his nest in Leinster." Holingshed goes on to say, "As the day approached for the battle, De Vescy, turning his great boast to small roast, began to cry *creak*,"—that is, craven—"and secretly sailed to France."

Fitz-Gerald was retained in England till the 14th May, 1316, when Edward II., by letters patent, declared that he had granted to John Fitz-Thomas Fitz-Gerald "castrum et villam de Kildare, cum terris, redentibus, et aliis pertinentiis, sub honore et nomine

Comitis de Kildare ipsumque præfecisse in comitem ejusdem loci." See *Lodge's Peerage*, by Archdall—"Kildare."

On the departure or flight of De Vescy, in 1293, his place in Ireland, as Viceroy or Justiciary, was filled by John Wogan, who laboured hard to make peace between the Fitz-Geralds and the De Burgos; the Red Earl, Richard de Burgo, Earl of Ulster, being at this time a prisoner in the hands of the Fitz-Geralds.

But Wogan was soon summoned by Edward to Scotland, and during his absence, his place was filled by William de Ross, Prior of Kilmainham, who held the position till the death of Edward I.

The Viceroy, on his return to Ireland, was employed to seize the persons, properties, and papers of the Knights Templars in Ireland, before they were made aware of similar proceedings instituted against their order in England. Before the papers for their arrests were issued, the clerks in the employment of the Irish Government were bound by an oath, to secrecy. But notwithstanding these precautions, John Wogan did not succeed in enclosing the whole of the Templars, residing in Ireland, in his drag-net, for two years later we find similar orders issued to secure and imprison, in Dublin Castle, the members of this community, still at large. There they were maintained by levies made upon their own lands, goods, and chattels.

This persecution of the Templars was initiated and carried out by the Knights of St. John of Jerusalem, under the direction of the Church. An inquiry into their heterodox practices was conducted in St. Patrick's Cathedral, where Henry Tanet, Grand Preceptor of the order in Ireland, along with thirteen members of the fraternity, were charged with "paying no attention to the reading of the Gospel, with turning their heads aside and gazing on the ground during the elevation of the host, and after the Agnus Dei, with declining the kiss of peace, saying that they were 'soldiers of the Cross, and had nothing to do with peace.'"

These charges against the Knights Templars, having been substantiated to the satisfaction of their judges, the Knights of St. John of Jerusalem (who were considered a far more orthodox fraternity) were allowed to enter upon the inheritance of the suppressed order.

These Templars may bless their stars for escaping with the loss of land and goods only. The treatment of this order of knights was very different in France, where Philip the Fair, on no better information than that of two Knights Templars, who had been condemned by their superiors, for their profligacy, ordered that all the Templars of France should be suddenly arrested and cast into prison. The charges against them were of the darkest hue. They were not only accused of robbery and murder, but of incest and other unnatural crimes. It was asserted that on being received into the order, they renounced Christianity and spat upon the cross; and that, to infidelity, they added the superstition of worshipping some head of gold, which they had secretly stowed away, at one of the houses of their order, at Marseilles.

Many of the principal men among them were put to torture, in order to extract a confession of guilt. About fifty who had been branded as heretics, died in the flames at Paris. The Grand Master, John de Molay, and another great officer, were conducted to the hurdle of wood prepared before the Church of Notre Dame. A complete pardon, on confession and repentance, or death, by fire, was laid before them. They boldly stepped into "the chariot of fire." There was nothing of this kind enacted at Dublin, under the administration of John Wogan.

CHAPTER XLI.

PIERS GAVESTON, THE ROYAL FAVOURITE.

A.D. 1307-1317. EDWARD II. was a weak prince; and one of the characteristics of a weak prince was strongly developed in him, a great love for favourites; towards whom he exercised the virtue of constancy. He was thoroughly loyal in his friendships.

Piers, or Peter Gaveston, the son of a Gascon knight, of some distinction, had procured admission into the household of the Prince of Wales, and managed to ingratiate himself into the favour of young Edward; so that when he became King, under the title of Edward II., the Gascon was placed near the throne. Even before Gaveston arrived at Court, he had been endowed with the Earldom of Cornwall. Along with these broad lands, Edward gave him his niece, the sister of the Earl of Gloucester, in marriage.

Piers Gaveston was handsome, accomplished, and proud; and did not take much trouble to please or conciliate the great barons of England. He was a *Gascon*. Query, has our word *gasconading* received its peculiar significance—that of boasting, or bragging—from the bold and presumptuous audacity of this royal favourite? We feel more disposed to father the term on the individual, than on the whole community of Gascons.

Hume says that nothing pleased Gaveston so much as eclipsing his rivals at Court. He was profuse and rapacious, vain-glorious and giddy; but, notwithstanding, accomplished and clever. At tournaments he took delight in "taking the shine" out of the English nobles, by his address, conversational powers, wit, and raillery; in which departments of polite education, the Norman Knights, as a rule, were rather "slow."

It behoved the King to take a journey to France, to do homage for the duchy of Guienne, and to espouse the Princess Isabella, to whom he had been long affianced. Before his departure, he perpetrated the great folly of making Piers Gaveston guardian of the realm of England, during his absence; bestowing upon him privileges and powers that produced a great deal of jealousy and ill-will amongst the nobles. "Where," they asked themselves, " is all this to stop? Who is to bell the cat, or clip the wings of this young falcon?"

Assistance came from an unexpected quarter. Isabella, the young queen, who was of an intriguing disposition, was not long in discovering, after her arrival in England, that the King was weak-minded, and naturally disposed to be ruled; and feeling that no one has so just a claim to rule a weak-minded man as his wife, determined, with the assistance of Lancaster and his party, to get rid of the favourite; to hew down the tree, which cast its shadow over the Court and Throne.

A parliament having been summoned at Westminster, Lancaster, and a number of other nobles, with their armed retainers, attended, and then and there demanded the banishment of Gaveston; requiring from him a solemn oath, never again to set foot within the kingdom. The King complied; *and appointed Gaveston, Lord-Lieutenant, or Viceroy, of Ireland!*

There can be no doubt, that, at one time, the appointment to the Lord Lieutenancy of Ireland was looked upon as a sort of banishment. It was viewed in this light by Essex. Whether Edward and his favourite took this view, we cannot say.

But justice compels us to say that this young Gascon did not prove an unsuitable or unwise Chief Governor for Ireland. He went there in June, 1308, being accompanied by the King as far as Bristol. He was accompanied to Ireland by his wife, Margaret, the daughter of the Earl of Gloucester. He established himself in Dublin, with great pomp and kingly pretension, which had the effect of exalting his office and reputation in the eyes of the nation at large, who loved grand people to rule over them.

But William Burke, or De Burgh, the Red Earl of Ulster, as he was styled, could not endure the *parvenu*, and, disregarding his royal letters patent, showed his contempt of the new Viceroy by making war, on his own account, marching at the head of armed forces, to the north. Returning to his castle at Trim, he gave sumptuous entertainment, and conferred knighthood on some of his followers, as if he, and not Gaveston, were chief ruler.*

Gaveston wisely turned his face toward the south, and with the aid of his troops and armed colonists, cut passes through the woods, between Castle-Kevin and Glendalough, which were generally infested by armed bandits;

---

* *Chief ruler.*—Sir Richard Cox makes the following remarks on the Red Earl, in his *Hibernia Anglicana*, p. 87 :—" A.D. 1303 : Richard Burke, Earl of Ulster, accompanied with Eustace le Poer, and a good army, went to the aid of the King [Edward I.] in Scotland ; and the Earl made thirty-three knights in the Castle of Dublin, before he set out ; and it is observable, that, in all commissions, and even in the Parliament Rolls, this Earl is always named before the Lord Justice," *i.e.* the Viceroy.

and terminated his expedition by thanksgiving offerings at the altar of St. Kevin. In this way, and by "his liberality, he won"—or bought—"the hearts of both the clergy and the people."

But no success in Ireland could compensate Edward for the loss of his favourite. He must have him back to England, no matter at what cost. As he felt himself utterly incompetent to beard his great lords, he must bribe them; so he conferred the high office of hereditary steward upon Lancaster, and bought off his father-in-law, the Earl of Lincoln, by other concessions. Even Earl Warren was mollified by civilities, grants, and promises, to agree to Gaveston's return; so Edward, having thus paved the way, sent out his mandate to the proud prodigal to come back to the paternal or royal roof. The King went to Chester to meet him, and as he landed, " flew into his arms, with transports of joy."

Gaveston himself, whose year of banishment might have taught the necessity of at least a change of deportment, at once resumed all his original pride, ostentation, and insolence. He carried this to such an extent, that the barons determined to employ sharper and more effectual remedies. They assembled, in what was styled a parliament, and with a numerous host of armed retainers, presented a petition to the King, calling upon him to devolve the whole authority of the Crown upon a junto of twelve, chosen, by themselves, to conduct the whole affairs of the kingdom, from March till Michaelmas. The King, who had neither force of arms nor moral courage to resist, signed the document, constituting the new Commission, which un-kinged him for the space of six months. Amongst the ordinances, or enactments of the Commissioners, was one for the removal of evil counsellors from the King's presence, who were excluded from all offices of power and profit. Piers Gaveston was banished the King's dominions, under the penalty, in case of disobedience, of being declared a public enemy.

Gaveston left the kingdom, for Flanders, to abide the King's time for reversing a decree which he had been most unconstitutionally compelled to sign. As soon as Edward arrived in York, where he felt himself free from the immediate terror of the barons, he reversed the act of banishment, declaring it illegal, and contrary to the laws and customs of the kingdom. So Gaveston returned to England.

The Earl of Lancaster, Guy, Earl of Warwick, Humphrey Bohun, Earl of Hereford, and Aymer de Valence, Earl of Pembroke, were furious. Affairs were approaching a crisis. The question now was, who was to be master or chief ruler, the King or his great barons. Both sides had advanced too far to retreat, so the Earl of Lancaster raised an army and marched to York, where he hoped to get the King into his hands; but Edward, who had intimation of his approach, fled to Newcastle. Thither the Earl pursued him. The King had just time to escape to Timouth, where he embarked, and sailed with his favourite, to Scarborough. Here he left Gaveston, as he thought, in perfect security, while he returned to York, where he hoped to raise an army. But, through some omission or design, the fortress at Scarborough, which was deemed impregnable, had not been provisioned for a siege, so that Gaveston was obliged to capitulate, and surrender himself prisoner. He stipulated that he should remain in Pembroke's hands for two months; that during that time, endeavours should be made for mutual accommodation, and that if the terms proposed by the barons should not be accepted, the castle should be restored to him in the same condition as when he surrendered it. The Earl of Pembroke and Henry Piercy pledged themselves to the fulfilment of these conditions. Gaveston was carried from Scarborough to Deddington, where he was left by Pembroke, on the pretence of business. In his absence Deddington Castle was besieged by Warwick, and taken, and Gaveston carried to Warwick Castle, to which Lancaster, Hereford, and Arundel repaired, and ordered the head of the King's favourite (without regard to law or military capitulation) to be struck from his body.

This was a sad blow to poor, weak-minded Edward; but his own imprisonment and cruel death were far more terrible transactions. It is reported, that, on one occasion, when he asked to be shaved, his keepers brought him dirty water from the ditch, and that, with tears in his eyes, he insisted that " he should be shaved in clean, warm water." Hume speaks of having seen a French manuscript, which, amongst other items of personal expense, mentions "*A crown paid to one for making the king laugh.*" Could anything be more sad?

CHAPTER XLII.

EDWARD BRUCE'S EXPEDITION TO IRELAND—HIS DEATH—IRISH FAMINE, AND CANNIBALISM.

A.D. 1315-1317. IT was during the reign of this weak prince, that Scotland retaliated for the various inroads of the English, by the invasion of Ireland. The battle of Bannockburn, in which Edward was so signally defeated, was fought on the 25th of June, 1314, about seven years after Edward II. had ascended the English throne. The next year, 1315, Robert Bruce sent his brother Edward* to Ireland, with an army of six thousand men. Edward assumed the title of King.† He was followed to Ireland, with more numerous forces, by his heroic brother, Robert, in 1317, and if it had not been for a famine (which resulted more from exterminating warfare than from nature), and which had reduced the Scottish army to great extremities, the Irish nation might have seized the opportunity of changing their masters, for which many Irish chieftains were well disposed.

* "*Edward* Mac Robert Bruce, Earle of Carrick, and brother of King Robert, King of Scotland, landed with a fleet of 300 shipps, in the north of Ulster; at whose coming all the inhabitants of the kingdom, both English and Irish, were stricken with great terror, that it made them shake with fear."—*Annals of Clonmacnoise*, A.D. 1315.

† *Title of King.*—The *Annals of Clonmacnoise*, as translated by Macgeoghegan, say that Edward Bruce made "the Ulstermen consent to acknowledge him as their King," and that "they delivered him the Regalities belonging to the King, and gave him the name of the King of Ireland."

The *Annals of Clonmacnoise* give the following account of the death of Edward Bruce:—"Edward Bruce, a destroyer of all Ireland in general, both English and Irish, was killed by the English in battle, by their valour, at Dundalk, the 14th of October, 1318, together with Mac Rowrie, King of the Islands, and Mac Donnell, Prince of the Irish [*i.e.* Gaels] of Scotland, with many other Scottish men. Edward Bruce, seeing the enemies encamped before his face, and fearing his brother Robert, King of Scotland, would acquire and get the glorie of the victorie, which he made himself believe he would get, without the assistance of his brother, he rashly gave them the assault, and was therein slain himself, as is declared, to the great joye and comfort of the whole kingdom [of Ireland] in general; for there was not a better deed, that redounded more to the good of the kingdom, since the creation of the world, and since the banishment of the Fine Fomores out of this land, done in Ireland, than the killing of Edward Bruce; for there reigned scarcity of victuals, breach of promises, ill-performance of covenants, and the loss of men and women, through the whole kingdom, for the space of three years and a-half, that he bore sway, *insomuch that men did commonly eat one another for want of sustenance during his time.*"

The *Annals of the Four Masters* lend their authority to this account of Irish cannibalism:—"During the three and a-half years that Edward spent in it, [Ireland] famine prevailed to such a degree, that men were wont to devour one another."

Pembridge says, "The people were so pinched with famine, that they dug up the graves in the church-yards, *and after they had boiled the flesh, in the skull of the dead body, ate it up.*"

"But this," observes Dr. O'Donovan, with dry and grim humour, "is evidently an exaggerated account, *for surely the famine had not consumed the pots as well as the food.*"

The battle in which Edward Bruce was slain, was fought near the Hill of Faughard, within two miles of Dundalk. The people of the district still point to the spot where Edward fell. The Anglo-Irish attribute the victory to the desperate bravery of Sir John Maupas, who, feeling convinced that the death of Bruce would ensure the victory to the English, rushed through a host of enemies upon him, and cut him down. When the body of Bruce was discovered, that of Sir John Maupas was found stretched across it. Sir John Bermingham is said to have brought the head of Bruce in a kest, pickled, to the King, and to have received, in return, the Earldom of Louth and the barony of Ardee.

There is a tradition, or legend, that Bermingham, desirous of seeing Bruce, disguised himself as a mendicant friar, and approached him as he was on his knees, at mass, the day before the battle, asking alms. "Give this saucy friar somewhat," said Bruce, "as he disturbs me in my devotion." The friar, having received a gratuity, departed. After mass was over, Bruce asked to see the friar, saying, "My heart has not been quiet since I saw his face. My heart telleth me that this friar is Bermingham."

CHAPTER XLIII.

O'MORE OF LEIX, WHO KEPT A PLENTIFUL HOUSE—THE CIRCUMSCRIBING OF THE ENGLISH DOMINION IN IRELAND—WILLIAM DE BURGH, EARL OF ULSTER — HIS DEATH, BY SIR RICHARD DE MANDEVILLE—SIR WILLIAM BURKE OUGHTER, AND SIR EDMUND BURKE EIGHTER—SIR ANTHONY LUCY AND SIR WILLIAM DE BERMINGHAM—THE BISHOP OF HEREFORD—AN IRISH PARLIAMENT, AT KILKENNY.

A.D. 1327-1341. WHEN Edward III. ascended the throne of England, the English in Ireland had lost about one-third of the land which they had originally acquired. The Norman mailed knight no longer inspired the terror or admiration which his prowess and chivalry, at first, created; nor was his castle any longer looked upon as a strong and impregnable fortress. O'More of Leix is reported to have levelled eight castles in one day. "Never," exclaimed the brave Sir Henry Savage, "shall I, by the grace of God, cumber myself with dead walls : my fort shall be where young bloods are stirring, and where I have room to fight." He said his protection consisted in making friends, by hospitality and kindness ; he therefore resolved to keep a plentiful house, and have a number of retainers about him. On one occasion, before going out to chastise some marauding septs, he treated his men "to a mighty draught of aqua-vitæ, wine, and old ale," and gave orders to have abundant provision prepared for their return. Some of his friends, doubting whether they should ever return, recommended that a portion of the beeves, venison, and fowl, should be poisoned, and the rest secreted. Savage smiled, as he replied, "Tush, ye are too greedy: this world is but an inn, whereunto you have no special claim; you are only tenants, at the Lord's will. If it please Him to command us from it, as it were from our lodging, and set other good fellows, in our room, what hurt shall it be us to leave them some meat for their suppers? Let them win it, and wear it. If they should enter our dwellings, it would be my good manner to bid them welcome. Notwithstanding, I presume so far upon your noble courage, that, verily, my mind giveth me, that we shall return at night, and banquet ourselves with our store."

The story goes on to say, "And so they did, having slain three thousand Irishmen." We suspect that three hundred, would be nearer the truth; or, that if the former figure is to stand, we must reckon the "*Kilt*," or wounded, among the killed.

It is pleasant to see such a spirit amongst marauders, but Edward III. was not a monarch to sit down quietly under such a state of things, in so important a part of his dominions, as Ireland; nominally, under British rule and management, for 160 years. He therefore convened a Parliament in England, in 1331, with special reference to Irish affairs. Enactments were passed, limiting the power of the Viceroy; and ordering that wardships, and other crown perquisites, should be disposed of, by sale; and that payment should be made in money and not in cattle; that sheriffs should account, at least, once a year; that none should keep kern or soldiers, except within their own borders; that the Viceroy should annually inspect the King's castles, and attend to their repairs; that English proprietors, ecclesiastical as well as lay, should dwell on their lands, and provide a sufficient force for their defence; otherwise, the King would seize their estates on the ensuing August of 1331.

It was at this time that William de Burgh, known by the Irish as the Brown Earl, *Dun Surla*, was appointed Lieutenant of Ireland.

William de Burgh, Earl of Ulster, was, from a youth, a favourite of Edward III., as Gaveston had been of Edward's father. He was the young King's junior, by a few months, and at the age of nineteen was appointed to the responsible position of Lieutenant of Ireland. He appears to have been clever and enterprising, but cruel; for he was slain in the 21st year of his age, for having first imprisoned, and then starved, his uncle, Walter Burke, to death. Walter had a sister, named Gisle, who was married to Richard de Mandeville; and she persuaded her husband to avenge the death of her brother, upon her nephew, William de Burgh, before he joined Edward, who was then in Scotland, waiting his arrival.

Mandeville seems to have executed his commission in a treacherous and sacrilegious way. It was on Sunday, the 6th of June, that Mandeville and the DUN EARL, rode forth to mass, to Carrickfergus. They spoke together of the proposed expedition to Scotland, when Mandeville, falling behind, for a moment, drew his weighty sword, and cleft the skull of the young Earl in twain.

The Four Masters, under date 1333, say "William Burke, Earl of Ulster, was killed by the English of Ulster." Lodge says "by Robert Fitz-Richard Mandeville, and others, his servants; near the Fords; at the instigation of Gyle de Burgh, wife of Sir Richard Mandeville."

The Four Masters go on to say, "The Englishmen who committed this deed were put to death in divers ways; some were hanged, others killed, and others torn asunder." Macgeoghegan says, "Hanged, drawn, and quartered." Mandeville, who struck the first blow, appears to have escaped.

The young Earl of Ulster left an only child, Elizabeth, who was married in 1352 to Lionel, Duke of Clarence, the third son of King Edward; who, in right of his wife, became Earl of Ulster and Lord of Connaught. The immense estates of Sir Walter de Burgo, descended, through princes of Royal blood, to Edward IV., and became the special inheritance of the Crown of England. But the Crown's possession of the estates was purely nominal; for immediately after the Earl's death, the minor branches of the family of Burke or De Burgo, seized upon his estates in Connaught. The two most powerful of these were Sir William, or Ulick, the ancestor of the Earls of Clanrickarde, and Sir Edmund Albanagh, the ancestor of the Lords Mayo. These Anglo-Irish chieftains renounced the English dress and language; Sir William, taking the name of Mac William Oughter, or "Upper," or Southern Connaught; and Sir Edmund, or Edmund Eighter, or "Lower" Connaught. The village or town of Oughterard, on the shore of Lough Corrib, derives its name from Mac William Oughter, who was Lord of Galway. The English Crown, no doubt, laid claim to Connaught; but it was too weak to assert its authority. Its arm was not long enough to reach into these Irish wilds; so these immense territories were allowed to descend, in course of tanistry and gavelkind, to the Burkes.

The *Annals of Ireland* have the following notices respecting Edmund Burke :—

"A.D. 1338. The son of the Earl of Ulster was taken prisoner by Edmund Burke, who fastened a stone to his neck, and drowned him in Lough Mask.

"Turlough O'Conor afterwards banished Edmund Mac William Burke out of Connaught.

"A large fleet of ships and barques was, after this, collected by Edmund Burke, and he remained for a long time on the islands of the sea.

"Edmund Mac William Burke was driven, with all his fleet, from the islands of the sea, by Turlough O'Conor, King of Connaught."

Anthony de Lacy, the new Viceroy, arrived in Ireland in June, 1331, and soon after his arrival, personally, and with his soldiers, aided the inhabitants of Dublin in capturing and killing a shoal of whales, cast on the strand of Clontarf. De Lacy, as we shall see, had quite a penchant for capturing and destroying large fish. Suspecting that the Irish were encouraged in their rebellious propensities, by the great English lords, he took the Earl of Desmond, at Limerick, by surprise, and carried him to Dublin, and committed him to the Castle prison. At the same time he seized his friend, Lord William of Bermingham, whom he caught in Clonmel, sick in his bed, and compelled them both to swear on the Gospels, the sacrament, and the relics of saints, to future loyal behaviour. He obliged others to make their peace with the King, or Irish Government, by the payment of heavy fines. The year after he caused William de Bermingham, who was a connexion of his own, to be hanged in Dublin, " to the consternation" of the nobles, among whom he held a foremost place. "Alas the day! Great pity it was, and who that heard it could forbear tears."

De Bermingham was styled Baron Mac Fevrais [*i. e.*, Bermingham] and Lord of Athenry, in the county Galway, once a corporate town, but now an obscure village. Here Richard de Bermingham and Sir William de Burgo gained a great victory over Felim O'Conor, in the year 1316. The King of England on receiving news of the victory, granted to Richard de Bermingham the title of Baron of *Athunree, i. e.*, Regum vadum, or King's ford.

The position of Ireland had now become so desperate, that the King, Edward III., resolved to visit it in person; indeed, nothing short of a Royal visit presented any hope of recovery or amelioration of the condition of the patient. Irish and Anglo-Irish rebels must see the King's face and touch the hem of his Royal garment, or they will continue in their evil courses; so a Parliament was summoned at Westminster in September, 1333, to consider the state of Ireland; and it was there decided that King Edward should proceed thither, in person, and as soon as possible, and that, in the interim, he should strengthen the hands of the Viceroy, by an increased military force.

An order was likewise issued that expert lawyers should be sent to Ireland to see to it, that those who held lands and offices in that country, discharged the duties devolving upon them.

In November, 1331, Edward summoned a council of Anglo-Irish noblemen, to meet him in England, to consider the affairs of Ireland; and in the following

January the King's uncle, the Earl of Norfolk, Marshal of England, and all other absentee proprietors of land in Ireland, were required to meet the King on the 1st of August, 1334, to accompany him to that country, for the salvation of their lands, the reformation of the State, and the repelling of the Irish, who had seized demesnes claimed by the Crown, or by subjects of England.

The "expert lawyers" were sent over to make the claims of the English to Irish lands, plain and easily to be understood by the natives, who had been dispossessed of these lands, for reasons which they did not understand.

On the 12th of July Edward proclaimed, that for certain reasons, he should delay his departure to Ireland, till the 29th of September; but on the 25th of July a royal writ was issued to the Justiciary, directing him to impress all ships in Ireland, or on their voyage thither, and to send them to Holyhead, well furnished with marine gear for the royal visit.

Who could imagine that all this preparation was to end in nothing, that there was to be no royal visit to Ireland after all—for an English Parliament was convened in December, 1332, at which it was decided that "it would be perilous for the King to absent himself from the realm, as the Scots might invade the northern parts of England; and what was the salvation of the whole of Ireland compared to that of even the northern parts of England?"

De Lacy, who had been superseded this year in the Viceroyalty, by Sir John Darcy, went to Scotland, where he captured another large fish, in the person of Sir William Douglas, the Knight of Liddesdale; while Sir

John Darcy went to the north, to hunt up, or hunt down, the murderers of the Earl of Ulster. From Ulster he went to Scotland, where he contributed to the victory of Edward III. at Halidon Hill, and to the placing of Baliol on the Scottish throne.

During Sir John Darcy's employment in Scotland, the administration of affairs in Ireland was committed to Sir Thomas de Burgh, the brother of Mac William Oughter, and Sir Edmund Eighter, who had divided the Connaught estates of the late Earl of Ulster between them. Sir Thomas de Burgh, having proved himself a corrupt ruler, was sharply reproved by Edward, who told him that "princes were appointed by God to punish evil doers and reward good. We expressly command you, to judge equitably all those under the law of England, both small and great, rich and poor, so as to silence those who blame you, and to merit our approbation." There was no law of this kind for the Irish.

Sir Thomas de Burgh was succeeded, in 1337, by Sir John de Cherlton, who held the office of Viceroy but six months, and was succeeded by his brother Thomas, Bishop of Hereford.

The Bishop was a man after Edward's own heart. "He took the largest prey of cattle in Carlow, ever known to be taken by English settlers from the Irish." The King, highly gratified with his conduct, writes him a letter of thanks, commencing, "Venerable Father;" and, in consideration of his cattle-stealing, soldiering, and other abilities, the Treasurer was ordered to pay the Bishop's salary before that of any other officer of the Crown in Ireland.

The Bishop of Hereford returned to England in 1340, leaving the Government to Prior Roger Utlagh, who died the same year; when Edward again appointed Sir John [Darcy, who deputed Sir John Morris, that had been Royal escheator, in his stead; whose chief duties were, to lay claim to, and dispose of, forfeited estates on behalf of the Crown.

Edward, who was hard driven for money, had recourse, at this time, to the extreme measure of declaring void all Royal grants of lands and tenements in Ireland, made from the reign of his father. The execution of this most obnoxious measure devolved on Sir John Morris, who summoned a Parliament in Dublin, in October, 1341, which the Earl of Desmond and other Anglo-Irish nobles, refused to attend; but they convened a sort of parliament or assembly of their own, at Kilkenny, where they denounced the new measure for raising money, and put the following queries to the King, which were evidently aimed at the Viceroy, Sir John Morris:

1st. "How can a country, in a state of war, be managed by a Governor unskilled in military affairs?"

2nd. "How can an official of the King, in so short a time, have acquired so much wealth?"

3rd. "How does it happen that the King has not derived larger revenues from Ireland?"

These queries too plainly intimated that Sir John Morris was no soldier, and that he had managed to feather his own nest, out of the public purse. "Needy men," continue these nobles, "have been sent from England to govern us, without knowledge of the land or its circumstances; men possessing little or no substance of their own, who live and maintain their state by fees—in addition to their salaries—for the practice of extortion."

This spirited remonstrance was laid before the King, who at once revoked the objectionable measure.

CHAPTER XLIV.

THE TYRANNY OF D'UFFORD—BAD WEATHER AT HIS DEATH—SIR JOHN MORRIS—SIR THOMAS ROKEBY, THE GOOD UNCLE AND JUST GOVERNOR —THE ENGLISH COLONISTS TRY TO LEAVE IRELAND—ST. PATRICK'S PURGATORY—THE CAPTIVITY OF CRYSTEDE.

A.D. 1344-1367. SIR JOHN MORRIS, the deputy of Sir John Darcy, in the Viceroyship, was as we have seen, in the last chapter, utterly despised and bearded by the Earl of Desmond, and other great Irish and Anglo-Irish lords; but this feeling gave place to one of fear and trembling, at the appointment of Sir Raoul D'Ufford, in 1344. King Log gave place to a real rattle-snake.

He and his wife, Maud Plantagenet, the widow of the murdered Earl of Ulster, entered Dublin in great pomp in July, 1345, and took up their residence in the Priory of the Hospitallers at Kilmainham, where, we are told, the Countess "lived royally, with her friends about her, like a queen in the island of Ireland."

D'Ufford, on assuming the reins of Government, asserted there should be but "one war, and one peace in the whole of Ireland;" and that one war and one peace, should be made by himself. This was a most presumptuous statement, with respect to a country, whose chieftains, both English and Irish, looked upon the making of peace, or war as their natural and inalienable birthright. Deprive an Irishman of the right of breaking his neighbour's head, or of making a prey of his cattle, when a fair opportunity occurred! Deprive an Irish chieftain of the pastime, to say nothing of the honour and glory, of war! The idea was not to be entertained for one moment.

When a sept in Louth, upon which the Viceroy was disposed to make an inroad, sought admission, to what was styled "The King's peace," D'Ufford ordered the sheriffs to empanel a jury of the settlers of the county, to inquire, upon oath, and report *the precise profit which the Crown and colony would be likely to gain by acceding to the application.* This was most certainly a practical view of the question. The Viceroy felt, that war had its advantages, as well as the King's peace; that, in fact, the King's peace might prove a barrier to the taking of a prey, when a favourable opportunity offered, or when the state of the public treasury required that an inroad should be made upon a clan, well to do in corn and black cattle.

The Viceroy was, by nature, more a man of war than of peace, so he marched an army into Ulster, of which his wife was the nominal Countess; but in passing through a defile, in the county Down, he was fiercely attacked by Mac Artan, the chief of the territory, who slew a number of his soldiers and carried away his money, plate, horse, and clothes; and if it had not been for the assistance of the English settlers of Down, he would not have come alive out of that defile.

Soon after this he summoned a Parliament in Dublin; but the Earl of Desmond, instead of attending, invited his fellow nobles to meet him at Callan. This raised the choler of the Viceroy, who entered the principalities of the great Earl, took his Castle of Iniskisty, and called upon the garrison of the strong fortress of Castle-island, to surrender. It refused to do so, so D'Ufford besieged the castle, and in a fortnight it was in his hands, when he hanged Le Poer and Grant, two of the Earl of Desmond's knights; for the Earl was in the habit of making knights. D'Ufford's next move was against the Earl of Kildare, whom he seized and imprisoned in Dublin Castle. Soon after this he was seized himself, by a malignant disease, and expired on Palm Sunday, 1346, to the great delight of both clergy and laity.

Just before his death, there was a great deal of bad weather, with tempests and flood; but the sky cleared up, as he was placed in his "leaden coffin;" in which, it is reported, his wife had secreted her jewels and other treasures, to be conveyed with the remains of D'Ufford to England.

He was interred in the Nunnery of St. Clare, in Suffolk, with the body of his wife's first husband, William de Burgh, Earl of Ulster.

Roger, the son of Sir John Darcy, was elected by the Irish Council, to fill D'Ufford's place, till the King's pleasure was known. The King appointed Sir John Morris, who at once liberated the Earl of Kildare from his prison, in Dublin Castle. The Earl of Desmond, with his wife and sons, sailed from Youghal to England, and surrendered himself as a prisoner to the King; and while there, obtained an allowance from the Treasury, of twenty shillings a day, for his expenses, until his appeal against the judgment of D'Ufford could be heard and decided on by Edward.

A Parliament was held this year, 1346, in Kilkenny, which voted a tax of two shillings, for every plough-land, and one shilling for property or goods to the value of sixty shillings; in order to provide soldiers against the Irish of Leinster. An attempt was made to levy this tax on Church, as well as other lands; but the Archbishop of Cashel, with the Bishops of Emly, Limerick, and Lismore, claimed exemption, and threatened to eject any clergyman from his living, and to excommunicate any lay tenant, who paid it. The Government stormed, but the bishops and the clergy, who sympathised with the natives, upon whose bodies the money was to be expended, in making war, persevered. The Bishop of Ossory went so far as to excommunicate King Edward's Treasurer, for sending men to collect the tax in his diocese.

As Sir John Morris was unequal to cope with this state of things, and as the Church had decided that Irishmen were not to pay for making war on themselves, or each other, the King withdrew Morris, and appointed Walter Bermingham, Lord of Athenry, to the Viceroyship. Walter Bermingham was the brother of William, who had been hanged by the Viceroy, De Lacy. Walter himself had, at that time, been imprisoned, by De Lacy, in Dublin Castle. The Government gave De Lacy ten additional men-at-arms, in his Viceregal train, at one shilling a day each; and fifty mounted archers, at fourpence a day, each. Bermingham was considered a good Viceroy. He resigned his office to John Carew, in 1349, and died the following year.

Baron Carew was succeeded, the first year of his appointment, by Sir Thomas Rokeby who had been at one time a sheriff in Yorkshire. He was styled "L'Oncle," or "the Uncle," to distinguish him from his nephew. The "Uncle" was an honest, high-minded man, and a right good Irish Viceroy, who commenced his administration by prosecuting the Irish Treasurer, Robert Emeldon, a great favourite of the King, who had been a long time in the royal service. He also punished those government victuallers, who carried away corn, cattle, poultry, and other articles of food, to supply the tables of government officials, at shamefully low prices; fixed by themselves, and sometimes without payment at all. "I would sooner be served," he is reported to have said, "with plain fare, on wooden dishes, and eat from wooden platters, and drink from wooden cups, and pay in gold and silver for what I consume, than to eat and drink from gold and silver, and to pay in wood."

There was an old song, half Latin and half French, composed during the reign of Edward I., which runs thus:—

"Si le roy freyt moun consail
Tunc villem laudare;
D'argent prendre le vessel,
Monetamque parare;
Mieu valdreil de fust manger,
Pro victu nummos dare,
Qe d'argent le cors servyr,
Et lignum pacare,
Est vitii signum
Pro victu solvere lignum."

"If the King would take my advice, I would commend him. Let him take his silver plate and turn it into money. It is better to eat out of wood, and pay for it, than to eat from silver and pay in wood."

To "pay in wood," means not to pay at all, or with the blow of a stick; to give the creditor, to use a common phrase, "more kicks than halfpence."

Such a ruler could scarcely fail to win the warm hearts of the Irish. We find him arranging with Aed, a leader of the O'Tooles of Wicklow, to defend the English border, about Tallaght, with a force of twenty "hobbelers," at fourpence a day each, and with forty foot-soldiers, at twopence a day, with a gift, or douceur, of ten marks, for Aed himself. A similar arrangement was made with Shane, Aed's brother, for defending Imail. We find that Shane's chaplain, who, of course, was an Irish priest, got six-and-eight-pence, for transmitting intelligence to the Irish Viceroy. But most of the border chieftains felt themselves sufficiently independent, to contemn and reject the Viceroy's bribes, for good and loyal behaviour.

Truly the kingdom of Ireland, at this time, was " neither in good plight, nor at peace." The uncertainty of life, and the heavy demands made upon the colonists, to protect their borders, caused numbers of them to quit the country, so that Edward had to issue a proclamation, in 1353, prohibiting any noble, ecclesiastic, or able-bodied man, capable of defending the territories of the Crown, from leaving Ireland. They did so at the penalty of forfeiture; and those whom this penalty could not deter, were seized, with their horses and effects, for attempting to withdraw. The King, at this time wrote to Richard Fitz-Ralph, the Archbishop of Armagh, commanding him to return from Rome, instead of expending his revenues abroad; for which he gave no return. Campion, with his usual quaintness, tells us a story of " Richard Havering, who five years, by dispensation, received the fruits and revenues of Dublin, and long might have done, had he been so disposed; but feeling in sleep a weight upon his stomach, heavier, to his weening, than any mass of metal; whereof to be released, he vowed [dedicated] in his dream, all that ever he could make in this world. So, suddenly, the next morning, he resigned the custodium of the bishoprick, and contented himself with other ecclesiastical cures, incident to his vacation."

The Earl of Desmond, whom the Viceroy D'Ufford had outlawed, in 1349, was restored to his lands, and in 1355, appointed Viceroy. He died in July, 1356, when Sir Thomas Rokeby was appointed. Sir Thomas died the same year, when Baron Almaric, of St. Amand, became chief ruler.

It was during St. Amand's administration that Malatesta Ungara, of Rimini, and Nicolo de Beccario, of Ferrara, performed pilgrimages to the "Purgatory of St. Patrick," in Lough Derg; in testimony of which act of daring devotion, during which Malatesta Ungara experienced "many bodily toils,—having for the space of a day and a night, as is the custom, remained therein enclosed"—the King granted him "letters patent." What ulterior use could be made of Royal "letters patent" bearing testimony to the fact of the bearer having spent a day and a night in any sort of purgatory,* we cannot imagine. The idea probably was, that "a day and a night" spent there, or in or near a locality styled "*Hell or Connaught*," would count for a longer period elsewhere. It would be difficult to say whether the performance of such a pilgrimage was a greater

* *Purgatory.*—" Station Island " lies in Lough Derg, in the county of Donegal. The islet is little more than a bare rock, about half a mile from the shore. The worshipper was carried to this purgatory, in a ferry-boat. The Irish Charon must have found this superstition (which it is only fair to say is now discountenanced by the Roman Catholic clergy) a profitable business. When Mr. Inglis visited the islet, or rock, " there could not have been fewer than 2,000 persons upon the spot."—*Hall's Ireland*, vol. iii., p. 272.

proof of courage or of piety, for Ungara could not say, as Pious Æneas did, of his descent into hell, Facilis descensus Averni; for his pilgrimage to Lough Derg, must have been as dangerous as his remarkable escape from it. "We, therefore," writes the King, "considering the dangers and perils of such a pilgrimage—although the assertion of such a noble knight might suffice—further certify thereof, by letters patent, from our trusty and beloved Almaric de St. Amand, Knight Justiciary of Ireland; and give him our royal authority concerning the same, to the end that there may be no doubt of the premised; and that the truth may more clearly appear, we have deemed proper to grant to him these our letters, under our royal seal."

I doubt if we could quote anything more demonstrative of the violence, anarchy, and disorganisation of the state of society in Ireland, during the reign of the third Edward, than these letters patent.

But, on the other hand, it is only fair to mention, that as late as "the year of Grace" 1834, it was esteemed dangerous and foolhardy to enter the wilds of Connemara, alone. It was called "*Going Back*." The writer attempted this daring enterprise, in the above-mentioned year, and penetrated the district as far as "Joyce's Country"; but as he has no royal letters patent, to verify to the wild and extraordinary adventure that befell him, he will not attempt to record it, lest he should get the credit of telling a traveller's story. All he will venture to say, is that he drew out a clasp-knife, in self-defence, or, more correctly, in bodily fear of being murdered, and thrown into Lough Corrib, like Edmund Burke, with a stone about his neck. There were giants in that land in those days. Take, for example, that red-headed monster, "Big Joyce," in whose "castle" the writer spent a night.

The Baron St. Amand was succeeded in the Irish Government by James Butler, Earl of Ormond, in 1359; and in the July of 1361, Lionel, the King's son, was nominated Viceroy; but his attempts to bring the country into a state of subjection, or order, were just as futile as that of any one of his predecessors. The following interesting story, told by Sir John Froissart, or told to Sir John Froissart, by one Henry Crystede, is so descriptive of the state of society, and of the Irish mode of kidnapping and treating a prisoner, and it displays, at the same time, so much of what was truly amiable in an Irish chieftain, that I cannot resist quoting it.

"I," said Crystede, "know the Irish language as well as I do the French, or English; for, from my youth, I was educated among them.

"The Earl of Ormond, who kept me, from affection, for my good horsemanship, sent me, with three hundred lances, and a thousand archers, to make war on the frontier of the Irish. The Earl had that day mounted me on one of his best and fleetest coursers. I rode by the Earl's side. The Irish having formed an ambuscade, to surprise the English, advanced, and began to throw darts; but were so sharply attacked by the archers, that they soon retreated. The Earl pursued them, and I, being well mounted, kept close to his side. It chanced, that in the pursuit, my horse took fright, and ran with me, in spite of all my efforts, into the midst of the enemy. As I rushed through, one of them, by a great feat of agility, leaped on the back of my horse, and held me tight with both his arms, but did me no harm, with lance or knife. Turning my horse about, he rode, with me, for more than two hours, till he reached a large bush, in a very retired spot, where he found his companions, who had retreated from the English. He seemed much rejoiced to have made me prisoner, and carried me to his house, which was strong, in a village, surrounded with wood palisades and water. The name of the town was Herpelipin, and the gentleman who had taken me was called Brin Costerec. He was a very handsome man.

"He kept me with him seven years, and gave me his daughter, in marriage, by whom I have two girls.

"I will now," continued Crystede, "explain to you how I obtained my liberty. It happened in the seventh year of my captivity, that Art Mac Murrough, King of Leinster, raised an army against Lionel, Duke of Clarence, and both armies met very near the city of Leinster [Dublin]. In the battle many were slain, and many taken prisoners, and among the latter, Brin, my father-in-law. He was mounted on my horse, which was recognised as having belonged to the Earl of Ormond. He then explained that I was alive, and had been honourably entertained in his house, having married one of his daughters. The Duke of Clarence, Sir William Windsor, and all the English party were well pleased to hear this news, and Brin was offered his liberty, if he gave me mine. He refused first, from his love to me, his daughter, and his grandchildren; and when he found no other terms would be accepted he agreed, provided my eldest daughter remained with him.

"So I returned to England," concludes Crystede, "with my Irish wife and youngest daughter, and fixed my abode at Bristol. My two children are now married. The one living in Ireland has three boys and two girls, and her sister four sons and two daughters. The Irish language is as familiar to me as the English, for I have always spoken it with my wife, and I introduce it among my children as much as I can."

CHAPTER XLV.

THE STATUTE OF KILKENNY.

A.D. 1367-1377. AT a Parliament held in Kilkenny, in 1367, and presided over by the young prince, Lionel, was passed the famous "STATUTE OF KILKENNY."

It commences by stating that "many of the English of Ireland, discarding the English tongue, manners, style of riding, laws and usages, lived and governed themselves according to the mode, fashion, and language of the 'Irish enemies,' and also made divers marriages and alliances between themselves and the Irish, whereby the said lands and the liege people thereof, the English language, the allegiance due to their lord the King of England, and the English laws, were put in subjection and decayed, and the Irish enemies exalted and raised up, contrary to reason." It was not only esteemed a wrong, but an *unreasonable* thing, that Irishmen should be exalted and raised up.

The Statute of Kilkenny, amongst other things, forbade—

(1.) Alliance by marriage, gossipred and fostering. The godfathers and godmothers of the same child were gossips. The children nursed by the same mother were fosters. Two boys nursed on the same milk were foster brothers.

(2.) The English were not to sell to "Irish enemies," in times of peace or war (therefore at no time), horses, armour, or victuals.

(3.) The English were forbidden to use the Irish, language,

(4.) Or to adopt the custom of the Irish, of riding without saddles.

(5.) Ecclesiastics who had fallen into the habit of using the Irish language, and riding without saddles, were allowed till the Feast of Saint Michael, to learn the English tongue, and provide themselves with English saddles.

(6.) No Irishman was to be admitted to any cathedral or collegiate church, or benefice whatsoever, nor were religious houses to receive Irishmen into their profession or order. This certainly was not in accordance with the spirit or rules of the *Catholic* Church.

(7.) The English were not to be governed by Brehon Laws,* nor by the mongrel laws in use in the marches, or on the borders.

(8.) The English were forbidden to receive into their houses, or make gifts to, Irish musicians, story-tellers, or rhymers.

(9.) The English dwelling on the borders, were not, without legal permission, to hold parleys or make treaties with any hostile Irish or English.

(10.) The English born in England were to be no longer called English hobbes, or "clowns," nor were the English born in Ireland to be called "Irish dogs."

(11.) The common English were not to practise hurling or quoiting, but to accustom themselves to the gentleman-like sports of drawing the bow and casting the lance.

* *Brehon Laws.*—A Brehon was an Irish judge, who administered justice according to Brehon laws.

The English Archbishops of Dublin, Cashel, and Tuam, and the Bishops of Lismore, Waterford, Killaloe, Leighlin, and Cloyne, were present, and took part in this Parliament; and (at the request of Lionel, the Lord-Lieutenant, the nobles, and commons) these bishops pronounced sentence of excommunication against all who might, in rebellion of heart, oppose the several ordinances of this Statute of Kilkenny.

This Kilkenny Parliament passed one good enactment, that of forbidding Anglo-Irish lords to take "coyne or livery" from the King's subjects, which Baron Finglas, in his *Breviat of Ireland*, says "*would destroy hell if it were used in the same.*" "This extortion of coyne and livery," writes Sir John Davis, "was taken for the maintenance of their men-of-war; Irish exactions, extorted by the chiefs and tanists, by colour of their barbarous seigniory."

Then followed *coshering*, that is, "visitations and progressions, made by the lord and his followers, among his tenants, wherein he did ate them, as the English proverb is, out of house and home, with his kerne, his horses, and his horse boys, his dogges, and his dogge boyes, and the like."

One of the chief impediments to the civil and social advancement of society was the neglect of the English Government to insist that there should be but one law for the English and Irish in Ireland. Sir John Davis says, "The Crown of England did not, from the beginning, give laws to the Irishry; whereas to give laws to a conquered people is the principal mark and effect of a perfect conquest."

It is true that Matthew Paris writes that Henry II.,

before he left Ireland, held a Council or Parliament at Lismore, where Leges Angliæ ab omnibus sunt gratanter receptae, et juratoria cautio praestita confirmatae, and that John, in the twelfth year of his reign, established English laws and customs in Ireland, and that to that end, Ipse duxit secum viros discretos et legis peritos, quorum communi consilio statuit et præceptit leges Anglicanas teneri in Hibernia; but it is not true that these laws, or wise men, were intended for the mere Irish.

Ware says, "The generality of historians have been mistaken in ascribing to King John the introduction of English laws into Ireland, which indisputably had an earlier source; for in the successful expedition, made into that country Anno 1172, by King Henry II., it was reduced to the model and form of the English Government, both in Church *and State*." *Antiquities of Ireland*, chap. xiii., p. 78., Dublin ed., by W. Harris.

This is a very strong, and, we cannot avoid saying, a very unguarded statement of Ware, for which he himself supplies the refutation in the very paragraph, the former part of which we have quoted. The assembly in which he says that Ireland was reduced to the model and form of the English government, both in Church and State, was not a Parliament, but a Synod, the Synod of Cashel; composed altogether of churchmen, as Ware shows:—
"Wherein appeared Christian, Bishop of Lismore, the Pope's Legate; Donat, Archbishop of Cashel; Lawrence, Archbishop of Dublin; and Catholicus, Archbishop of Tuam; with all their suffragan bishops, abbots, archdeacons, priors, deans, and many other prelates of the Church of Ireland. On behalf of the King appeared

Ralph, Abbot of Bildewas; Ralph, Archdeacon of Landaff; Nicholas, the King's chaplain, and divers other good clerks."

"In this Synod," says Ware, "many *ecclesiastical* constitutions were made, and among the rest, that all divine service in the Church of Ireland, should be kept, used, and observed in the like order and manner as it is in the Church of England; for it is meet and right, that as by God's Providence and appointment, Ireland is now become subject to the King of England, so it should take from thence the order, rule, and manner, how to reform themselves and live in better order; for whatsoever good thing has befallen to the Church and realm of Ireland, either concerning religion, or peaceable Government, they are indebted for the same to the King of England, and are to be, therefore, thankful unto him."

Ware lays by his positive mood, in the next paragraph, and says, "Whether this Synod may be considered as *merely ecclesiastical, or as a mixed assembly, convened for civil as well as religious purposes, is not clear from history.*"

In proof that it was a civil, as well as an ecclesiastical assembly, he says that "sundry *good statutes and wholesome laws* "—in italics—" were there devised, which were afterwards subscribed by the King himself and under his authority."

But the King subscribed purely ecclesiastical, as well as civil statutes.

Ware concludes by stating that if it were not in this mixed assembly, or Parliament, at Cashel, it was at *another* Parliament, convened the same year, at another place, namely, at Lismore, that the King granted the laws of England to the people of Ireland; which were joyfully received by them all, and confirmed, by the King having first accepted their oaths for the observance of them.

Lest any one should be so curious or impertinent as to ask for a specimen of English law, intended for a mere Irish subject, Ware informs us that "*whatever laws were enacted at this time, were lost;*" but traces of them remain in the Rolls office; for example, a statute of Henry II., made for the election of a Governor of Ireland, confirmed by a long list of civil officers and lay nobles, all Englishmen; and he thinks it apparent from this, that Henry II. made laws and statutes for Ireland generally.

We cannot quote a higher authority, on such a subject, than Sir John Davis, the Irish Attorney-General of James I., who says, "It is evident, by all the records of this kingdom, that only the English colonists, and some few septs of the Irishry—which were enfranchised, by special charters—were admitted to the benefit and protection of the laws of England. They were not only disabled from bringing any action, but they were so far out of the protection of the law, that it was adjudged no felony to kill a mere Irishman in time of peace."

There was an exception to this rule made in the case of any one of Irish royal descent; that is, descended from any of the *five* Kings, or *bloods*; that is, of Ulster, Munster, Leinster, Connaught, and Meath. Simon Neal brought an action against William Newlagh, of the County Dublin, for trespass. The defendant pleaded that the plaintiff was an Irishman, Hibernicus, et non de Quinque Sanguinibus, "and not of the five bloods." The plaintiff proved that he was one of the "five bloods;" that he was a descendant of the O'Neills of Ulster, and therefore gained the suit. Thomas Butler brought an action against Robert Almain, for certain goods. Almain replied that the plaintiff was *Hibernicus*, and not of English blood. Butler swore on the sacrament, that he was a true-blooded Englishman, *Anglicus et de libero sanguine*, and therefore he got the value of his goods.

An Englishman in this and other ways was able to take advantage of the double code of laws which prevailed in Ireland. In the case of murder he might, for himself, prefer the Brehon Law, and the Irish award, of paying *eric*, or a fine, of from £1 to £100, according to the estimation made of the person slain; but in the case of an Irish enemy, convicted of murder, he might prefer the sentence of hanging, pronounced by an English judge.

The Prince Lionel left Ireland in 1367, soon after the passing of the Statute of Kilkenny, when the Viceroyship was committed to Gerald, or Garrett, the fourth Earl of Desmond, who was styled "The Poet." Notwithstanding the Statute of Kilkenny, forbidding fosterage, we find this Earl seeking and obtaining the King's permission to send his son, James, to be fostered, and brought up among the O'Briens of Thomond. This Viceroy was held in high veneration by the Irish, for his poetry, learning, and general Irish propensities. He was a nobleman of "marvellous bounty and mirth, witty, cheerful in conversation, a learned chronicler, and an ingenious composer of Gallic, or Irish poetry." He died about the year 1397. Doctor O'Donovan says that "tradition still vividly remembers Garrett; and it is said his spirit appears once in seven years on Lough Gur, in the County Limerick, where he had a castle." If by "*his spirit*," we may venture to interpret Doctor O'Donovan to mean his love of Irish learning and poetry, and his Irish geniality of mind, we should say that much of this spirit has lately died out in Ireland with Doctor O'Donovan himself, and with another distinguished labourer in the vineyard of Irish literature, namely, the accomplished Dr. Petrie. They were none of your old Irish dry-as-dust school, "books in breeches," but men full of sap and greenness, and Irish humour, and love of country. I fear we shall never see their like again. I esteem it a great honour to have known them both well, and to have had the pleasure of reckoning them among my friends and correspondents.

Notwithstanding the Statute of Kilkenny—perhaps it would be more correct to say, in *defiance* of it—the "Irish enemy" rode over the country "in hostile array," slaying all who opposed them, despoiling and burning English towns, castles, monasteries, and even churches; their only regret being that the English priests were not inside. Things were in such a state that "the land was like to be totally lost." So a new Viceroy, in the person of Sir William Windsor, was appointed in 1369. He was a brave and vigorous soldier. As he claimed considerable property in Ireland, in Inchiquin, Youghal, and Kinsale, he marched to the south, coercing the English colonists to vote subsidies to cover the expense of the war. The colonists complained that he had summoned a Parliament at Ballydoyle, near Dublin, where there was no building but a chapel, and that he kept the "honourable members" there for two or three days in the cold, till he had extorted from them a grant of £2,000. He was also accused of unfair dealing in the commissary or food department.

Windsor returned to England in 1371, when Sir Richard Pembridge was appointed in his stead; but Pembridge, feeling convinced that neither gain nor honour, but rather loss and disgrace, were likely to result from the appointment, declined to accept the office; whereupon Edward, in a most arbitrary manner, stripped him of the lands and offices which he held from the Crown, on the plea that they had been granted "in consideration of *future*, as well as of past services." Pembridge laid the case before the English nobles, who were all interested in the matter, and they decided that the King could not legally oblige Pembridge to go to Ireland, or imprison him for refusing to go; as, according to Magna Charta, "no free man could be forced to abandon the realm of England, unless by sentence of Parliament, or in case of felony or abjuration."

Edward had to bow to this decision of his great lords, and appointed Maurice Fitz-Thomas, fourth Earl of Kildare, to the Viceroyship, leaving the management of Munster and the mustering of forces there, to Stephen de Valle, Bishop of Meath; the Government being ordered to supply him with money, to pay the wages of his soldiers.

The last Irish Viceroy, appointed by Edward III., was James Butler, Earl of Ormond. He was appointed in August, 1376. The King seems to have learnt, in the last year of his reign and life, that a milder discipline might possibly suit Ireland better than that which had been in vogue with some of his predecessors; that it was sometimes better to use the whip of small cords than the lash of scorpions; so Ormond was authorised to receive *Irish*, as well as English rebels, into the

"*King's peace*," to grant general as well as special pardons, to receive fines and ransoms, or, as the Irish would say, *eric*, for Irish as well as English crimes and offences, to displace unjust and incompetent officers, and supply their places by honest and competent men.

These measures were all very good, but they had the disadvantage of coming too closely on the heels of the Statute of Kilkenny, which had completely failed of its objects. We get no credit, but rather contempt, for a mild discipline, when it is well understood that a severe one has been tried and proved a failure.

Nothing could be more unfortunate for Ireland, as well as England, than the Irish administration of affairs during the reigns of Edward I. and Edward III., two monarchs of great ability. "It is strange," says Richard Butler, the learned editor of the *Annals of Friar Clynn and Dowling*, "that the reigns of the worst and the weakest of English kings, should have been times of the greatest prosperity of the English in Ireland." During the reigns of John and Henry III., the English authority appeared to be consolidating, the fiery passions evoked by the Norman invasion appeared to have exhausted their force, when a tide of anarchy set in, which quickly dissolved the newly-formed basis of government, and plunged the rulers into an Irish bog, or quagmire, through which they have been floundering from that day up to the present.

It is in the following pithy and able manner that Sir John Davis hits off the conduct of the first three Edwards toward Ireland, and its sad effect:—" Edward I., who was a prince adorned with all the virtues, did, in the management of his affairs, show himself a right good husband; who, being owner of a lordship, ill-husbanded, doth first enclose and *manure his demesnes near his principal house,* before he doth improve *his wasts afarre off.*"

We know what is meant by his " wasts afarre off."

" Therefore he began first to establish the commonwealth of England, by making many excellent laws and institutions, the form of public justice, which remaineth to this day. Next he fully subdued and reduced the dominion of Wales; then, by his power and authority, he settled the kingdom of Scotland; and lastly he sent a royal army into Gascoyne, to recover the duchy of Aquitaine.

" These four great actions did take up all the reign of this great prince; therefore we find not in the record, that this king transmitted any forces into Ireland; but on the other side we find it recorded in the annals, and in the pipe-rolles of this kingdom, that three several armies were raised of the King's subjects in Ireland, and transported, one into Scotland, another into Wales, and the third into Gascoyne; and that several aids were levied here [Ireland] for the setting forth of those armies."

Edward II. is thus hit off. "The sonne and successor of this excellent prince, much against his will, sent one smal armie into Ireland, not with a purpose to finish the conquest, but to guard the person of his minion, Piers Gaveston, who being banished out of England, was made Lieutenant of Ireland, that so his exile might seem more honourable."

During the reign of Edward III. the impediments in the way of his giving any attention to the state of Ireland are so notorious, that he scarcely deems it necessary to mention them; "to wit, the war which the King had with the realms of Scotland and France, but especially with France, for the space of forty years. And, indeed, France was a fairer mark to shoot at than Ireland, and could better reward the conqueror."

CHAPTER XLVI.

RICHARD II.—THE ENGLISH RULERS SUBJECTED TO THE IRISH—MORTIMER, EARL OF MARCH—MORTIMER, THE BOY VICEROY—DE VERE, EARL OF OXFORD—IRELAND A PENAL COLONY—BALSCOT, BISHOP OF MEATH —SIR JOHN STANLEY.

A.D. 1377-1393. WHEN Richard II.* ascended the English throne, the Irish Viceroyship was in the hands of James Butler, Earl of Ormond.

It may be truly said, that, at this time, the Irish rulers, that is, the Irish Viceroy, with his council and subordinates, had been brought under subjection to Irish chieftains. If the payment of tribute be a mark of subjection or subordination, this was the position of King Richard's Viceroy, in Dublin. Diarmaid Mac Murrough, King of Leinster, as well as his father, Murrough, were styled "Kings of the Danes of Dublin," and took tribute from the Danes of that city. A like state of things was brought about again, two hundred and five years after Henry II. had landed on the Irish shores. The only difference is that for Danes we are to read English. On the rolls of the Chancery Court of Dublin, for the year 1377, is a decree, that Art Mac Murrough Cavanagh (a descendant of Donnell Cavanagh, the illegitimate son of Diarmaid) claimed his fee or tax of eighty marks a year, from the King of England ; and continued to make war

---

* *Richard*, the only son of Edward the Black Prince, succeeded to the throne, June 21st, 1377, and was crowned in Westminster the 16th July ; being then only eleven years old.

in the counties of Wexford, Kilkenny, Carlow, and Kildare, till the tribute was paid. And it *was* paid; for the council decided, that to prevent damage and peril, the sum demanded should be paid by the Viceroy, Ormond; so a royal writ was issued to this effect. Who can deny that Art Mac Murrough, at this time, was King of the English of Dublin? He not only demanded tribute, but *eric*, from Geoffrey de Vale, Sheriff of Carlow, for his brother Donnell Cavanagh, who had been killed.* The amount of the *eric*, or blood money, was forty pounds, the half of which was paid by the Treasurer, and the other half was, probably, raised by the sheriff in the County of Carlow. These were not solitary or exceptional cases, for O'Conor, of Offaly, and other Irish chieftains, were in the habit of receiving tribute, or black mail, from the treasury, or of levying it on the English colonists, at the point of the sword.

Take the following as an example of the state of affairs, even in Leinster. A Parliament had been convened at Castle-Dermot, in Kildare, of which the chieftain, Murrough O'Brien, got notice, and hastily crossed the country, with the object, no doubt, of "bagging" the whole Parliament, Lords and Commons. The Parliament was attended by its own guard of soldiery, but they were not able to cope with the "following" of O'Brien

---

* *Donnell Cavanagh, who had been killed.*—We find the following entry in the *Four Masters* :—" Age of Christ 1361, Art Mac Murrough, King of Leinster, and Donnel Reagh, heir apparent to the throne of Leinster, were treacherously made prisoners, by the son of the King of England. They afterwards died in prison." By the son of the King of England, we, of course, understand Lionel, Duke of Clarence, third son of Edward III. "Age of Christ 1375, Donough Cavanagh, King of Leinster, was treacherously slain by the English, among whom he had often before spread desolation."

of Thomond. What did the honourable members do? They agreed to redeem themselves, for one hundred marks; a decidedly modest estimate of their own worth; but they were the best judges. At this time there were only *nine marks* in the Treasury; so the remainder of the redemption money was obtained, in the form of advances, or loans, from the following parties: from the Prior of the Hospitallers of Dublin, sixteen marks; from William Fitz-William, the Master of the Hospitallers of Kilclogan, a horse and cuirass, worth twenty marks; from Robert Lughteburgh, a horse worth twenty marks; from John Moore, a bed, value thirty shillings; from Sir Patrick Freigne, seven marks ten shillings. If this was the way the descendants of Anglo-Norman Knights redeemed themselves from the hands of the Irish, with money, and beds, and war-horses, and cuirasses, without striking a blow, we are not surprised to find the conquered becoming conquerors; the English inhabitants of the walled towns, trembling in their shoes, as the wild Irish hovered around, thundering at the gates, for eric, or annual tribute.

James Butler, Earl of Ormond, after the experience of a single year, resolved to resign the office of Viceroy, which he did contrary to the wishes of all the English in Ireland.

The offer of the Viceroyship was then made to the Earl of Kildare, and declined by him; when the Council elected, as a sort of locum tenens, a churchman, or episcopal chancellor, named Alexander Balscot, Bishop of Ossory, better known as Little Balscot, of Ossory; who was succeeded, in the next year, in November, 1379, by John Bromwich. In the absence of great men, the Council had to choose small ones.

John Bromwich was succeeded in 1380, by a man of real mark, namely, Edmond, Earl of March, the Marshal of England, and head of the great house of Mortimer. The appointment of this nobleman gave great delight to the loyal Anglo-Irish. This Earl of March was the grandson of Roger Mortimer, Viceroy to Edward III. He had married Philippa, Duke Lionel's daughter, through whom he claimed the Earldom of Ulster.

Edmond Mortimer, Earl of March, was able to make his own conditions, in accepting the government of Ireland. He agreed to lord it over the English colonists, and the wild Irish, for the space of three years, on condition of being paid twenty thousand marks, in discharge of all his expenses; a fabulous sum to be expended in Ireland. No wonder the Earl was popular.

He arrived in Dublin in the pleasant month of May, 1380, in great splendour, where he displayed a princely hospitality. The chroniclers tell of the Earl's "gold cup and cover," called "Benison;" his sword, ornamented with gold, which belonged to good King Edward; "his great and his little golden horns;" his "tortoise-shaped cup," and his "little cup," fashioned like a hart, with an eagle's head; his salt-cellar, in the form of a dog; his "great bed," covered with black satin, embroidered with white lions and golden coloured roses, with the arms of Mortimer and Ulster. The arrival of such a Viceroy in Dublin, was esteemed a great day for Old Ireland.

Mortimer's first efforts were to gain possession of the territories which he claimed, in Ulster, in right of his wife, Philippa, the daughter of Lionel. In this effort he was aided by some Irish chieftains, until he lost their favour and confidence, by seizing Magennis and O'Hanlon, two men held in high reputation by them. The seizing of Magennis is thus recorded by the Four Masters:—

"Age of Christ 1380. Mortimer came to Ireland, with great powers, as Lord Justice; whereupon the Irish nobility repaired to pay their court to him, and among others, the Roydamna* of Ireland; *i.e.*, Nial O'Neill, O'Hanlon, O'Farrell, O'Reilly, O'Molloy, Mac Geoghegan, and the *Sinnach*, [*i.e.*, the Fox], with many other nobles. Art Magennis, Lord of Iveagh, in Ulidia [*i.e.*, Ulster], was treacherously taken prisoner in the house of Mortimer. After this the Irish, and many of the English, stood very much in awe of him"—as an Irish sinnach, or "fox," would of an English bull-dog—"and seeing themselves at his mercy, they resolved *not to cultivate any familiarity with him.*"

His utter inability to make way in the North, after losing the confidence of the Irish chieftains, is evinced by the fact that he could not procure timber, from the thick woods of Ulster, to construct a bridge across the River Bann; so that he had to send to his estates, in Wales, for the material. There were abundance of Irish oaks in Ulster, but it was death to an Englishman to enter an Irish forest. The lady is represented as saying to the knight, in Spenser's *Faerie Queene*,

* *Roydamna.*—That is, as Dr. O'Donovan quaintly expresses it, *materies regis*, the matter, or stuff, out of which a King is formed; "one who, from descent, personal form, and valor, might be elected a King."—*Notes on Annals of Ireland*, A.D. 1362.

> " The peril of this place,
> I better wot than you. Though now too late
> To wish you back returne, with foule disgrace,
> Yet wisdom warnes, whilest foot is in the gate,
> To stay the steppe, ere forced to retrate.
> This is the wandering wood, this errors' den,
> A monster vile, whom God and man does hate;
> Therefore, I read, beware. Fly, fly, quoth then
> The fearefull dwarfe, this is no place for living men."

Mortimer, unable to meet the Irish chieftains of Ulster, made war upon the Irish clergy, and seized their cattle, and sent the spoil to the monks of the Augustinian Priory of Wygemore, on the borders of the Welsh Marches; in return, perhaps, for the Welsh timber for building a bridge across the Bann. This was a clear robbing of Peter to pay Paul. But it was for want of a bridge that this Irish Viceroy got his death. Proceeding south, he took cold in crossing a river, probably the Blackwater, which divides the county of Waterford from that of Cork. He died the 26th of December, 1381, in the Dominican Abbey, in Cork.

The Barretts of the county Cork, who were originally English,* took advantage of the death of the Viceroy, and the withdrawal of his soldiery, to rise and pillage their English neighbours around the city of Cork.

In this emergency, the Council that had accompanied the Viceroy to the South, consisting of the Earls of Ormond and Desmond, bishops and other nobles, the Mayor of Cork, and other representatives of that city,

---

* *The Barretts, who were originally English.*—"There came also many of the ruined relics of the ancient English inhabitants of the province, as the Arundels, Rochfords, Barretts, Flemings, Lombards, Terries, &c."— *Gibson's History of the County and City of Cork*, vol. i., p. 229: vol. ii., pp. 161, 162.

and also of the city of Limerick, hastily convened an assembly, or Parliament, in St. Peter's Church, where the Earl of Ormond was requested to take the office of Viceroy. He refused, when the same offer was made to the Earl of Desmond, who also declined. They both alleged that the continual risings on their own borders would prevent their discharging the duties of the office, without leaving their own territories unprotected.

It was then proposed, by a member of the Council, that Sir Thomas Mortimer, brother of the deceased Viceroy, should fill the vacant office, when it was objected that the whole revenue of Ireland would not defray the wages of his archers and men-at-arms.

Little Alexander Balscot, Bishop of Ossory, was next solicited, but declined; when it was resolved that the next person nominated *should*, whether he liked it or not, be the Viceroy; so the lot fell on the Chancellor, who was a churchman, Dean John Colton, who became chief ruler; and succeeded, after a short time, in arresting Richard Barrett, and sending him, by sea, to Waterford; but the whole sept of the Barretts kept up such a continual warfare about the city that the English settlers began to leave it; and to such an extent, that the Viceroy had to issue a royal writ, ordering the arrest of any citizen who should attempt to leave the town.

John Colton was superseded, in January of 1381, by Edmund Mortimer, the eldest son and heir of Roger Mortimer, then a lad in his eleventh year. Can we imagine anything more absurd or wild than such an appointment at such a period? The appointment was made by the young King Richard, who was only three or four years older than his Irish Viceroy, Roger Mortimer.

But the nomination of this lad was not objectionable or displeasing to the English colonists in Ireland. Although young Roger was not a great man himself, he was the son and heir of a great man, and he had plenty of money to spend; so the English in Ireland clustered round him, as Virgil represents a new colony of bees clustering round a young queen, or as the Irish did around a young roydamna, or *materies regis*, who had in him the stuff out of which Irish kings were made.

Sir Thomas Mortimer, of whose extravagant expenditure the Council, assembled at Cork, had displayed such a wholesome dread, was appointed Deputy to his nephew, the young Viceroy, with an allowance of two hundred marks per annum above his own charges.

A writ was issued this year, for summoning a Parliament, at which it was decreed that the King's Admiral, William Spalding, should permit none but merchants and mariners to leave Ireland, that the English colonists should not be allowed to desert the country. It was also decreed to arrest those who sold horses, salt, armour, iron, gold, silver, coin, or other provisions, to any of the Irish, by land or water.

This baby Viceroy, or vice-regal boy, was succeeded, in 1383, by the King's cousin, Philip Courtenay. But he did not arrive till 1385, when he found the Earls of Ormond and Desmond at loggerheads (at the beginning of that old battle which it took centuries to decide), the Irish fighting in the interior, and Spanish and Scotch pirates sweeping the merchandise from the coasts.

What was to be done at this fearful juncture of affairs? The chief nobles and prelates met in Council, and decided that nothing could save the country but the presence of the King, Richard II. It was therefore determined to send the Archbishop of Dublin and the Bishop of Ossory to London, to press this matter on the King and his Council.

The appeal was unsuccessful, but the King consented to nominate his favourite minion, Robert de Vere, ninth Earl of Oxford (the only son of Sir Thomas de Vere and Maud, the daughter of the Viceroy, Sir Raoul D'Ufford) as Chief Ruler of Ireland.

The English Parliament, who were only too glad to remove this prime favourite from Court, granted him a debt of thirty marks, due as the ransom of Charles de Blois, taken prisoner in Bretagne. They also allowed him the pay for five hundred men-at-arms, and a thousand archers. He was created Marquis of Dublin and Duke of Ireland, and invested with most despotic power in Irish affairs. In March, 1386, Royal orders were sent out to impress ships to convey him and his retinue to Waterford; but when the time for his departure came, either he or his master had changed his mind, so Sir John Stanley was sent to Ireland as his Deputy. The King had accompanied his favourite to Wales, and what less could the favourite do than to accompany the King back to England? But the English nobles hated him, and conspired, with the Duke of Gloucester, one of the King's uncles, to drive him into exile. De Vere raised an army in Wales, and marched against the nobles, but was signally defeated, and had to flee for his life. He died five years after this, at Louvain, of a wound from a wild boar, received while hunting. His remains were embalmed and brought to England, enclosed in a cypress coffin. Richard opened the coffin with his own hands, and fondly gazed upon the dead face of his friend. He then attired the corpse in rich robes, with rings and chains of gold, and interred it at Colne Priory, in Essex. It was thus Richard loved De Vere.*

In the year of Grace, 1388, Ireland was constituted a penal settlement for Englishmen, convicted of having violated the constitution of their country. Five Judges who had certified in Council, at Nottingham, that the King was above all law, and could annul all acts which he deemed prejudicial to himself, were condemned to exile for life, in Ireland; Sir Robert Belknap, Chief Justice of the King's Bench, was sent to Drogheda; Sir Roger Fulthorpe and William Burgh, Justices of the same Court, to Dublin; Sir John Carey, Baron of the Exchequer, and John Locton, King's Sergeant-at-Law, to Waterford; and Friar Thomas Rushok, Bishop of Chichester, who advised these Judges to an illegal decision, was "*banished to Cork!*"

It is true that these noble convicts were allowed two servants each, and from twenty to thirty pounds a year, to defray the expenses of their altered position; but they were not allowed to travel more than two leagues from the localities to which they were banished. The Bishop of Chichester, who disposed of one of his mitres, for £333, was permitted to carry only forty marks of the sum with him, together with a bed, a

* *De Vere.*—Maud, the Duke of Ireland's mother, and the daughter of the Viceroy D'Ufford, by the Countess of Ulster, was, in her old age, imprisoned for her devotion to Richard II. She asserted that he had not been put to death, but was still alive, in Scotland, waiting his opportunity to arise and regain his throne. She also distributed gold and silver tokens, such as Richard was accustomed to present to his most favoured friends, with a white hart under a tree, with golden coronet and chain.

cloak, and a prayer-book. He might receive gifts towards his support, to the amount of forty marks, but no more. This bishop died, and was buried in Cork; and a prior of that city, named John Grey, received money from the King's private purse to provide a marble coffin. It was thus the Bishop's extreme loyalty was punished and rewarded. Belknap, Holt, and Burgh were allowed, after a time, to return to England, and to practise, without impeachment.

The affairs of the colony were administered from 1387 to 1394, by the following persons:—

A.D. 1387-9, Alexander Balscot, Bishop of Ossory, who was also Lord Chancellor. Balscot was reprimanded for using the seal of De Vere, in public instruments, and for advancing or using De Vere's banners and pennons, in resisting Irish rebels, after attainder had been issued against the Duke of Ireland. We conclude the Bishop acted in this way with the sanction of the King. He was ordered, for the future, to use the Royal colours. He was also commanded to summon the nobles and commons, and before their eyes to have the Duke's ensigns torn and defaced, and his seal broken up.

Richard White, Prior of the Hospitallers of Kilmainham, appears to have been united with Balscot in the administration.

A.D. 1389. Sir John Stanley, who had been Deputy to De Vere, undertook the government of the colony, on his own account, for three years. During his administration, the burgesses of Galway, jealous of the preference shown by the Irish Government to Cork and Limerick, tolled their great bell, and handed over the keys of their city to William Burke, the King's enemy, and aided him in resisting the Royal officers.

James Butler, Earl of Ormond, became Viceroy in 1391. He was formerly known as Ormond of Gowran, where he had a castle; but from 1391, he took up his residence at Kilkenny, where the Butlers have continued to reside up to the present day. The Kilkenny property was purchased by this James Butler, from the heirs of Sir Hugh de Spenser, Earl of Gloucester, and Isabel, his wife, daughter of Gilbert de Clare. The property originally belonged to the princes of Ossory.

Thomas Plantagenet, Duke of Gloucester, the King's uncle, was nominated Viceroy in 1393, but as entire confidence was not placed in him, Richard resolved to visit Ireland himself.

CHAPTER XLVII.

RICHARD II. VISITS IRELAND—ART MAC MURROUGH, KING OF LEINSTER, OPPOSES RICHARD'S PROGRESS — ART MAC MURROUGH SWEARS ALLEGIANCE—RICHARD'S ROYAL ENTERTAINMENTS IN DUBLIN.

A.D. 1394-1395. THE young King of England, Richard II., landed at Waterford, in Ireland, on the 2nd of October, 1394. He was then in his twenty-eighth year. He is described as of the middle height, with fair hair, and a round and ruddy, but somewhat effeminate face.

His expedition to Ireland had been delayed for a year, on account of the death of his Queen, Anne of Bohemia. "It appears," says Froissart, "that the King felt her loss very severely, venting his anguish on the Palace of Sheen, where she died, and causing it to be razed to the ground." He states further, "The King ordered extraordinary preparations for the funeral; nothing was ever seen like it before. There was no talk of the King marrying again, for he would not hear of it; nevertheless, not very long afterwards, he married Isabel, daughter of Charles VI. of France."

Richard was accompanied to Ireland by the Duke of Gloucester, and other noblemen. In his army were four thousand squires, or men-at-arms, and thirty thousand archers, a larger army than some historians have assigned to Edward III., at the battle of Crecy.

He landed at Waterford, in what Art Mac Murrough, an illegitimate descendant of Diarmaid Mac Murrough, esteemed his territories or kingdom. According to the Irish, or Brehon law of succession, the first Diarmaid had no authority whatever of making over Leinster, or any portion of it, on his only legitimate child, Eva, or her husband Strongbow. Illegitimacy was no bar to succession amongst Irish chieftains. Donnell or Donald Cavanagh, or Kavanagh—for these Celtic names are variously spelt—the illegitimate son of Diarmaid, and the friend of Strongbow, to whom he was as true as Jonathan to David, (and under somewhat similar circumstances,) had, if we are correct, a true title to the throne of Leinster. The chieftaincy, generally, devolved on the next of kin, if he had the necessary personal qualifications, and possessed capacity and valour.

This Art Mac Murrough, who comes out to bar the pass against Richard II., appears to have been every inch, by descent, mental and moral qualifications, and personal appearance, a true-bred and true-born Irish King. Some old Irish writers say "he held in his fair hand the sovereignty and the charters of the province of Leinster. At his approach the whole of Leinster trembled." The old annalists say "he was replete with hospitality, knowledge, and chivalry; the prosperous and kingly enricher of churches and monasteries, with his alms and offerings."

This Art Mac Murrough had fair grounds of dispute with the English rulers of Ireland. He had married an English wife, Eliza le Veele, Baroness of the Norragh, who was entitled to estates in the county Kildare, in the province of Leinster, of which her husband, Art Mac Murrough was the hereditary prince; so that both wife and husband had a double claim; she, by a descent from

Norman conquerors, and by alliance with the Irish prince of the country, and he, by Irish Brehon law, and English alliance. But the Crown took possession of the estates, on the ground of her having forfeited them by marrying one of the principal enemies of the King of England.

If Art Mac Murrough had not been an enemy before, this was provocation enough, to make him one. Knowing, or suspecting, that Richard would be likely to visit Ross, in his march from Waterford to Dublin, he hastened and took that town, which he "ravished," in true Irish style, carrying away cattle, gold, silver, and hostages from the chief inhabitants.

The rapid movements of the Irish, and their style of warfare, quite baffled and disconcerted both Richard and his English troops. The Earl of Ormond, who understood more of the Irish mode of warfare than any of the pure English, made an attempt against Offaly, the territory of O'Conor, and failed. The Earl Marshal tried his prentice hand at a predatory excursion—a mode of warfare peculiarly Irish—and lost far more than he gained. So Richard hastened on, as well as he could, helter-skelter, to the capital, from which he wrote to his Privy Council in England, saying he had made many journeys, and had passed through the country of the famous Irish rebel Makemurgh [Mac Murrough], and that he now required money for the payment of his army, and for his housekeeping in Dublin.

And, to do Richard justice, he kept open house there. If we can credit the account of Robert Ireleffe, the entertainments given by Henry II., in 1172, in his wattled palace, near the city of Dublin, were inferior to those of King Richard. Robert Ireleffe says that ten thousand persons were daily fed and entertained at the Royal table, in Dublin. The varieties of dishes were amazing, some castellated and painted, some blazing with wild-fire. There were three hundred cooks in the kitchen. There was also great " preciousness " of gold and silver vessels in the pantry; and great perfection of new and curious music in the grand dining hall; some, perhaps, the production of Froissart, who had made Richard a present of a handsomely bound volume of songs and music. Truly King Richard was more at home in entertaining his friends than in fighting his enemies. Enfin, qui y a-t-il au monde de plus utile qu'un cuisinier? Un cuisinier qui a inventé un plat nouveau, a plus fait pour le bonheur de l'humanité, que celui qui a découvert un planète.* Richard must have held with Napoleon the Great, who—though no gourmand himself—came to the conclusion that the "belly governs the world."

But Richard and his counsellors resolved to try the effect of religion, as well as of dainty and rich dishes, upon the Irish; so he lays aside his banners, quartered with leopards, and substitutes the golden cross, with the motto *In hoc signo vinces* instead; for which the Irish, to do them justice, always had a reverence. It was with a banner of this kind that Lord Mowbray, the Earl of Nottingham, and other English nobles went forth to meet the Irish Chieftain, Art Mac Murrough, who issued from a wood mounted on a black horse, and rode into the open field of Ballygarry.

* " To conclude, who in this world is more useful than a good cook ? A cook who has invented a new dish, has done more for the happiness of mankind, than the astronomer who has discovered a new planet."

The terms of peace having been read by John Molton, a priest of Lincoln, and interpreted into Irish, by Edmond Vale, a Prior of the Hospitallers of Kilmainham, Mac Murrough came forward, and laying aside his girdle, sword, and cap, placed his hands between those of Nottingham, and received the kiss of peace, and vowed allegiance, on condition that his wife's property should be restored, that he should be paid an annual income, for keeping the peace, and that he should receive other territories instead of those which he had made over to Mowbray, the nominal lord of Carlow.

King Richard proceeded, in person, to Drogheda, where he gave the kiss of peace to "Le grand Onel," as the Anglo-Norman Knights called him; then to O'Brien of Thomond; then to O'Conor of Connaught. In this way, with three royal kisses, he conquered these three Irish Kings, of whom he afterwards made three English knights.

We can imagine these three Irish monarchs, the night before their inauguration, attired in rich silk, and fur, from the royal wardrobes, holding their vigils, in the old cathedral of Christchurch, Dublin; now and then looking askance at the tomb of Strongbow, and anon mingling curses with their prayers, against the souls and bodies of the whole fraternity of Anglo-Norman and English adventurers.

Knowing the power of the religious element upon the Irish mind, and the ability of churchmen in extracting their fees, the King, with some degree of foresight, stipulated, that the penalty for the infringement of the solemn treaty of peace, just made, should be paid in hard cash, into the papal treasury, agents for which were then collecting in Ireland.

The English Privy Council were a little annoyed, that the Irish rebels were received into grace and favour, without paying fines; but still, on the whole, they approved of the King's proceedings, and expressed their admiration of his courage and discretion.

We shall see, by and by, that no good whatever resulted from this visit of Richard to Ireland. Hume, the English historian, in utter ignorance of the state of Ireland, at this period, says, " Some insurrections of the Irish obliged the King to make an expedition into that country, *which he reduced to obedience;* and he recovered, in some degree, by this enterprise, his character of courage, which had suffered a little, by the inactivity of his reign."

Froissart, with far better appreciation of the real state of affairs, says, that the submission of the three most potent of the Irish Kings "was considered a very great acquisition, and the accomplishment of the object of the armament; for during the time of King Edward's reign, of happy memory, he had never had such success [with Ireland] as King Richard." But he proceeds to say, *" The honour was great, but the advantage small,* for with such savages nothing can be done," in the way of lasting peace. Irish chieftains would be bound by no treaty or compact (no matter how sacred the mode of its ratification) for one hour longer than it suited their interests or convenience.

CHAPTER XLVIII.

ROGER MORTIMER, VICEROY — RICHARD II. VISITS IRELAND A SECOND TIME — THE PICTURE OF AN IRISH CHIEFTAIN — RICHARD II. LOSES HIS THRONE.

A.D. 1395-1399. IN quitting Ireland, as Richard did, after a residence of nine months, which was principally engaged in feasting the Irish chieftains and other nobles, the Viceroyship was committed to the hands of Roger Mortimer, who was then twenty-one years old. He had married Eleanora, the daughter of the Duke of Surrey, the King's half brother. This Roger Mortimer, as we have seen, had been Viceroy before, when a mere boy, from 1382 to 1383.

It is a wise and necessary policy—of which even barbarous and half civilised nations see the necessity—to place *men*, and not children, to rule in troublous and revolutionary times. What sane captain would think of placing a child at the helm of a ship, during rough seas and boisterous weather? But this was the way in which England too frequently acted towards Ireland.

This Roger was next in succession to the English Crown. Indeed, his claims had been acknowledged by the English Parliament, in 1385. He was the eldest son of Philippa, and the only son of Lionel, Duke of Clarence, who was the third son of Edward III. He was also the proper representative of the great houses of Marshal, De Lacy, De Burgh, De Broase, and De Joinville.

Roger was constituted Lieutenant of Ulster, Connaught, and Meath, where his great estates lay; while Sir William Scrope, or Le Scrop, was appointed chamberlain and justiciary, for Leinster, Munster, and Louth. Walsingham once said that "Human nature could not produce a more cruel or more wicked man than William Scrope." He could not have been quite so bad as this; for we are told that his wife wrought a complete change or reformation in him, by simply threatening to leave him, if he did not change his ways. "I will no longer," said she, "emperil my soul's salvation, by remaining with you, unless you swear a solemn oath, that you will discontinue all your evil practices." Scrope swore, as he was directed, and kept his oath. Nay, more, from that time forward, he, who had been a miser and a cheat, kept "a plentiful house," was very charitable, "remitted great fines," and procured many pardons, where lives and lands were in jeopardy; so that after his conversion, his name was never uttered, without the blessings and prayers of those whom he had formerly defrauded and oppressed. But in the end, he was beheaded, by Henry IV.—For nothing very good, we conclude.

His chief, Roger Mortimer, directed his thoughts to Irish military affairs, and made war on the O'Byrnes and O'Tooles. In 1898, to gratify some foolish freak, he marched into Carlow, in the dress and accoutrements of an Irish chieftain, and fell at the head of his soldiers, who were routed with great slaughter.

His dead body was carried off by the enemy, but was afterwards recovered by his mother, Philippa, Duchess of Clarence, who sent chalices to two of the churches in the district. We conclude that the body was restored by the intervention of the Irish clergy.

It was principally to revenge the death of this foolhardy young man, that Richard resolved on making a second expedition to Ireland, which in the end, resulted in the loss of his crown and life.

Men of all arms, to the number of 30,000, were mustered at Milford; where horses, cows, calves, salted meat, bread, and water were shipped for the expedition to Ireland. They cast anchor in the harbour of Waterford, on the 1st of June. After six days' rest they marched to Kilkenny, where they waited fourteen days, for Edward Plantaganet, Duke of Albemarle, Constable of England, upon whom the Earldom of Cork had been conferred. On the 23rd of June Richard marched against Mac Murrough, King of Leinster, who had rejected all his overtures of peace and friendship; at which we cannot be surprised, when we remember that the English monarch had violated his compact, and had granted the barony of Norragh, which belonged to Mac Murrough's wife, to the Duke of Surrey.

We are told, by a French gentleman, who accompanied King Richard to Ireland, that "Mac Murrough's uncle, with divers others, bare-legged and unshod, with halters about their necks, humbly submitted themselves to the King; falling prostrate at his feet, craving mercy; whom the King freely pardoned, conditionally, that he and his companions should take an oath, from that time forward, to continue true and loyal subjects." They were willing to take any number of oaths the King pleased.

A message was then sent to the rebellious nephew, Mac Murrough, to make a like submission, with the same sort of hempen collar about his neck; who replied, that "for all the gold in the world, he would not submit; but would continue to war and damage the King, in all that he might."

The Frenchman, whose account of the transactions we are quoting, says he was encouraged to make this bold reply, from the knowledge that the King's army wanted victuals; and he well knew that money could not supply the want. The necessity was such, that for the space of eleven days, the soldiers lived upon what they could find in a wasted country, of which the Irish enemy had made a clean sweep of food. The very war horses were faint and starved, and dying from exposure to rain and wind. A biscuit a day, between five men, was considered a good allowance. Knights, esquires, and gentlemen, were all subjected to the same hard fare. "Pastime and mirth were banished from the army, and the camp was full of heaviness."

In the height of this extremity, three ships laden with provisions, made their appearance on the coast, when some of the hungry troopers, greedy for food, waded into the sea, above the bridles of their horses, in order to seize it; and in the scramble, hard blows were given, and returned, and some of the provisions spoiled by the salt water.

The day after this affair of the provision ships, the King's army recommenced its march to Dublin, accompanied by the wild and vindictive screams and hootings of the Irish, from the neighbouring woods and morasses, into which no English soldier would dare to follow them.

But, by and by, news was brought to the English camp that Mac Murrough desired an interview with King Richard. The news brought joy to the bosom of every English soldier. The Earl of Gloucester, attended by 200 lances and 1,000 arches, was appointed to meet Mac

Murrough; who "descended from a mountain; not far from the sea, riding a horse without a saddle, which cost him 400 cows ;* attended by the multitudes of the Irish. The horse was fair, and in his descent from the hill, ran as swift as any stag, hare, or the swiftest beast that I have ever seen. In his right hand he [Art Mac Murrough] bare a great long dart, which he cast from him with much dexterity. He was tall of stature, well composed [*i. e.*, put together], strong, and active ; his countenance fierce and cruel."

His men stayed behind him, at the wood's side, while he dismounted and met the Earl, at a little ford. " Much speech passed between him and the Earl; but the words were not words of peace." The Irish King would agree to no terms but those which had been formerly arranged, and shamefully violated by the English monarch. Richard was greatly enraged, on receiving the Earl of Gloucester's report of the interview, or parley, and swore, by St. Edward, that he would not leave Ireland until he had Mac Murrough in his hands, dead or alive.

King Richard and his army arrived at Dublin the day after this interview, footsore and weary ; but there, in that "good town, the best in the realm, seated on the sea, and rich in merchandise, they found plenty of victuals to relieve the army, horse and foot, (consisting of about 30,000 or thereabout,) and the prices of the same did not much increase."

* *Four hundred cows.*—" In that country they barter by exchange, horses for beasts, or one commodity for another, and not for ready money."—*The Story of King Richard the Second. His last being in Ireland.* Dublin ed., by Walter Harris, 1770.

But in the midst of their feasting and plenty, Richard did not forget Mac Murrough, and the way in which he had bearded him and his Deputy, among the Wicklow mountains. He therefore divided his army into three parts, in order to hunt him up, or run him down, in the woods. But Richard did not understand this kind of warfare. "In my opinion," says the French writer, whom we have been quoting, "it was impossible to be effected, *while the leaves were on the trees;* but after that time, when the trees were bare, then to burn the wood, would be the best means to do service upon him."

Poor, weak-minded King Richard was not afforded the opportunity of doing upon Mac Murrough the contemplated "service," for, before the leaves had fallen from the trees, the crown had fallen from his own brow. The Duke of Albemarle had just arrived in Dublin, with reinforcements. "He was more beloved of the King (his cousin) than any of his blood; and by his advice the King was, for the most part, directed; therefore, poor Richard was all joy and gladness at his coming, and dallied with him, in Dublin, for six weeks, without receiving news from England," "which, undoubtedly," as the French writer says, "in my opinion, was a presage that God was displeased with the King."

The news came at last, and bad news it proved. "A small barque, the messenger of ill-news, arrived in the port of Dublin, with the intelligence that Henry, Duke of Lancaster, had risen in arms against his cousin, the King; that he had slain the Lord Treasurer, and had been countenanced and supported by the Archbishop of Canterbury, who was publishing a bull of plenary indulgence, offering a reward in Paradise to all who would assist the Duke to dethrone King Richard. "And, sir," said the messenger to the King, "this bull of the Pope, and the Archbishop's discourse, do so work on the hearts of the giddy people, that they follow Henry of Lancaster, who doth purpose to take your goods, castles, and lands, and to depose you; and all men, old and young, poor and rich, submit themselves to him."

The King, sorrowful and pensive, assembled a Council, to decide on the measures to be taken in the emergency. It was the opinion of the majority that the King should return to England at once; that his presence and prompt action would put down the rebellion; but there was a Hushai in the Council of Richard, as well as in that of Absalom, who recommended delay and procrastination. "The Duke of Albemarle, who possessed the King's heart, withstood the Council—whereof many suspicions of his faith arose. 'Sir,' said he, 'make no such haste for your departure; we must first provide shipping to transport your army. Here we have but one hundred sail of all sorts. You will do much better, to send the Earl of Salisbury, before you, to make head against the Duke of Lancaster. Yourself will do well to march to Waterford, at which port we shall assemble sufficient shipping, to transport your whole army; and then, there is no doubt, your presence will be able to break and dissolve the Duke.'"

Richard adopted the counsel of this false friend, and, as a consequence, lost his crown and kingdom; which passed into the hands of the Duke of Lancaster, who became Henry IV. of England. The previous conduct of King Richard to his cousin, Henry of Lancaster, which provoked this rebellion, is a portion of English, not Irish history. Herein we have the seed, or ground, from which the Wars of the Roses, between the Houses of York and Lancaster, sprung.

Froissart tells us, that when the "Londoners" heard that Richard had set out, on this second and fatal expedition to Ireland, they said, "Well, Richard of Bordeaux [where he was born] has taken the road to Bristol and Ireland. It will be his destruction. Never will he return thence with joy."

Considering the state of affairs in England, and the number of enemies he had gathered round his throne, it was madness for him to leave England, at the time he did. The people, who see the shadow of coming events more clearly than Kings or statesmen, were not mistaken, in this prediction, of Richard's downfall.

CHAPTER XLIX.

THE REIGN OF HENRY IV., DUKE OF LANCASTER.

A.D. 1400-1413. ALEXANDER BALSCOT, Bishop of Ossory, was Lord Deputy or Viceroy when Henry IV. seized the English throne. He held the position but two months, when he was succeeded by Sir John Stanley, who was appointed for three years.

It was during Stanley's term of office that Mac Murrough assured his wife that he would never make peace till her lands had been restored. "He is now," the Council writes to Henry, at "open war, gone to aid the Earl of Desmond, to suppress the Earl of Ormond, after which he will return, with all the powers he can lead, to destroy the country."

But this was not all; the O'Niell had mustered a great host, to ravage the land, unless the Irish Government gave up his son, cousin, and other hostages, then confined in Dublin Castle. "The Irish," says the despatch, "have become strong and haughty, and the border English are unable to make successful attacks upon them; so the loyal subjects are destroyed, harassed, and the settlement in peril of final destruction."

Henry, under these circumstances, resolves to appoint his son, Thomas, a boy who had not attained his twelfth year, as Viceroy. This child's play at Irish king-making occurred in 1401. This boy had been appointed, on his father's coronation, Lord High Steward of England.

Prince Thomas landed at Dalkey, near Dublin, on the 13th of November, 1402. Soon after his arrival, the Dublin Council laid before the King the great inconvenience and danger which the slow payments from England entailed on his son. " With heavy hearts we testify to your Highness, that our Lord, your son, is so destitute of money, *that he has not a penny in the world*, nor can borrow a single penny, because all his jewels and plate, that he can spare, of that which he *must* keep, are pledged, and lie in pawn. All his soldiers are departed from him, and the people of his household are on the point of leaving." Thomas Cranley, Archbishop of Dublin, one of the Council, had paid "his very all" in order to keep things going.

This impoverished state of affairs prevailed till November, 1404, when Prince Thomas left Ireland, placing the administration in the hands of Sir Stephen Scrope, who had been faithful to poor King Richard, to the last, for which he was tried in a court of chivalry, and honourably acquitted, and afterwards employed by Henry IV.

Sir Stephen Scrope died at Castle-Dermot, of the plague, in 1408, leaving a buxom widow, named Millie, or Millicent, behind him, who the next year married the immortal Sir John Falstaff, then serving in Ireland. Sir John Falstaff was a Norfolk gentleman, or esquire. Millie was the daughter of Robert Lord Tiptoft. There is no allusion to Falstaff's wife, or Scrope's widow, in Shakspear's play of *Henry IV.* If Falstaff went to

Ireland to "flesh his maiden sword," he could have been no poltroon, for there was hard fighting to be done there at that time. We find in the Patent Roll of Ireland, in the 3rd year of Henry IV., A.D. 1402, *a royal grant of two forfeited horses*, to Sir John Falstaff. Was it his friend, Prince "Hal," who used his influence with the King, or Sir Stephen Scrope, to procure his boon companion these two garrons? Perhaps the matter was arranged by "Millie." A horse must have been a godsend to a fat bachelor like Falstaff. "If I travel but four foot [without a horse] I break my wind." "Give me my horse, you rogues, give me my horse, I pray thee, good Prince Hal, help me to my horse."

Prince Thomas, Prince Hal's brother, assumed the office of Chief Governor, a second time, in 1406; and though still a mere lad, appears to have made a "stiff" or "hard bargain" with the King, his father, in money matters. His salary was to be £7,000 a year; but if it should fall one month in arrear, after the date of the quarterly payment, he was to be at liberty to withdraw from the service. Should the King, or Prince Thomas's elder brother, the Prince of Wales, visit Ireland, Prince Thomas was still to be chief ruler, and in receipt of his viceregal salary. If the King should resolve to deprive him of the Irish Government, or give it to the Prince of Wales, he, Prince Thomas, should get six months' notice.

Prince Thomas went to Kilkenny, where he held a Parliament, and where the burghers of the town presented him with a butt of wine. Shortly after he went out to make war on the Irish, near Kilmainham, where he was severely wounded, and had a narrow escape of being slain.

He returned to England, in 1410, having appointed Thomas Butler, son of James, third Earl of Ormond, and Prior of the Hospital of Kilmainham, to succeed him in the Viceroyship.

Ormond held the office of Viceroy, or Deputy Viceroy, till 1413, when he was succeeded by Sir John Stanley, who had succeeded Bishop Balscot in 1400.

Sir John Stanley bore the character of a very cruel man, among the Irish; and what was worse than all, he plundered the hereditary bard Niall, the son of the famous Aed O'Higgin, the two of whom "satirised him to death." Lest the reader should have the slightest doubt of the miraculous power of Irish satire, we give the following statement of the fact from the *Annals of the Four Masters:*—

"Age of Christ 1414, John Stanley, the Deputy of the King of England, arrived in Ireland; a man that gave neither mercy nor protection to clergy, laity, or men of science; but subjected as many as he came upon, to cold, hardship, and famine. It was he who plundered Niall, son of Hugh Higgin. The O'Higgin, with Niall, then satirised John Stanley, who lived after this satire but five weeks, for he died of the virulence of the lampoons. This was the second poetical miracle performed by this Niall O'Higgin."

We regret to say that the satire or lampoon of which Sir John Stanley died, is not extant.

An *aoir*, or *aeir*, is a poem in which the victim is not only lampooned, but cursed and imprecated.

Irish poets, or rhymers, possessed great power in this way, from time immemorial. Once upon a time the great and distinguished Seanchan, with his troop of subordinate ollamhs, paid a visit to Guaire, King of Connaught. The cross old man being displeased with the fare at court, refused the rations provided for him. After a three days' fast, his wife persuaded him to try an egg. By some neglect of the servants, the mice had sucked it. The rhymer was so exasperated that he vowed to satirise the mice, but upon reflection, determined to lampoon the cats.

Irish poets were fond of this sort of thing, but they did not confine it to the cats; they more frequently satirised men, and very often great men. We read in the *Book of Ballymote* (fol. 77, p. 2, col. b.) of a poet named Athairne, of Binn-Edair (now Howth), satirising the men of Leinster, for having killed his only son. "He continued for a full year to satirise the Leinstermen, and bring fatalities upon them, so that neither corn, grass, nor foliage grew for them, that year."

The impression was abroad at an early time, that poets could satirise people to death. The wife of Caier, King of Connaught, conceived a criminal passion for the poet Neidhe, and offered him a ball of silver; but he, like a second Joseph, rejected her advances, till she offered him the kingdom. "How can that be, seeing the King is living," said Neidhe.—"It will be easy enough," replied the Queen, "for you are a poet, and can *rhyme him to death*, or bring a blemish on his cheek. A man with blemish cannot enjoy the kingdom." The poet went to work, and composed an *aeir*. The King went to the well next morning, to wash his face, and drawing his hand across his cheek *felt three great boils*.

If Irish poets could satirise Irish kings and Irish

deputies after this fashion, we are not surprised to find the English Government making laws and regulations against them.

We read in the *Four Masters*, under date 1576, of Sir Henry Sidney, "suppressing the custom of keeping poets and literary men."

But poets and satirists laugh at penal laws. The famous Florence Mac Carthy, who knew this as well as any man in Ireland, wrote a letter (which is still preserved in the State Paper Office), in which he pretty broadly recommends the Government to employ the poets, for he knew they were a class of men who might be tempted to direct their Greek fire against each other, and their own chieftains.

"The two sorts of people of the greatest ability and authority to persuade the Irish gentlemen, are the priests and the rhymers. The priests may not be trusted to do service to the Queen,* while of the rhymers, only some may, if employed by those gentlemen whose followers they are by lineal descent."

Mac Carthy then goes on to say (and we blush, for Florence's sake, to quote his words), "*I mean to employ one of special trust and sufficiency.*" It is supposed that he here refers to the famous Irish poet, Aenghus O'Daly, who wrote the fearful lampoon on the poverty, meanness, and want of hospitality of Irish chieftains, for which he paid the penalty of his life. He was stabbed to the heart, in the house of O'Meagher, chief of Ikerrin, in the county of Limerick.

* *Do service to the Queen.*—Considering the kind of service required, this must be viewed as a compliment to "the priests."

The terrific satire for which he met this fearful death, is entitled *The Tribes of Ireland*. It has been translated from the Irish, and annotated by Dr. O'Donovan.

The poet O'Daly, who represents himself as taking a tour through Ireland, commences with Connaught, in this style:—

"These Roddys are niggards and schemers,
They are vendors of stories (odd dreamers),—
Who talk of St. Kallin's miraculous powers,
And how he continually showers wealth on their tribe.
They are worse, in good sooth, than I care to describe,
Moreover, if you sit at their table,
You'll soon think the Barmecide's banquet no fable! *

"I called on them once on Shrove Tuesday, at night,
But the devil a pancake, flour, oatmeal, or brancake,
In parlour or kitchen saluted my sight.
I walked off. I'd have starved ere I'd pray to
One imp of the gang, for a single potatoe.†"

"All the Jennings‡ feed hogs, and *are* hogs, too, I think,
Such deaf and blind mopers! Such ditch-water topers!
That is, when they *can* have ditch-water to drink!
They have cumbered the land since the time of
Magh-Guaire's hot battle, which poets do rhyme of.

* *Barmecide's banquet.*—See the story of the barber's sixth brother in the *Arabian Nights Entertainment*, Halifax Edition of 1851. "Come on," said the Barmecide, "let us have something to eat; then he called to his servants, and ordered them to bring in some victuals, but no servant appeared; yet he pretended that meat was on the table, and invited my brother to sit down and partake of the feast!—p. 261."
—*Dr. O'Donovan.*

† *Single Potatoe.*—There is no mention of potatoes in the original. In Shakspeare's time potatoes were a luxury. The poet Mangan, who had a horror of potatoes, is not very happy in his translation here.—*Ibid.*

‡ *Jennings*, a very respectable County of Galway family—a branch of the Burkes.—*Ibid.*

> "In the house of the black-headed Gilduff* I passed
> A whole day, without meeting one bit fit for eating.
> Heaven bless them!—they do teach a sinner to fast!
> I never yet saw, or read of in story,
> A niggardlier mansion than Gort-in-shy-gory."

The poet leaves Connaught for Leinster, of which he thus writes:—

> "Escaping from Connaught I came into Leinster,
> Where I met neither Esquire, dame, chieftain, nor spinster,
> To give me a bit, till I came to the house of O'Byrne,†
> Where I got some roast meat; but cannot tell whether
>   'Twas goat's flesh or leather;
> But for drink I plumbed vainly jug, pitcher, and churn,
> And a tallish tin tankard, with horn nose.
> *What* swash they do tipple is more than myself knows.

> "The Iregaine‡ broad lands, which of old had their share,
> Of our conflicts of peril, lie weed-grown and sterile;
> Of cheese, bread and butter, their farm-steads are bare;
> And, as to a smack of flesh-meat, you
> Might offer them £10, ere one pound would greet you.

> "O'Conor § brags much of his cattle; their milk,
> Ne'ertheless, is enough to half poison that ilk;
> They are poor, skinny, hunger-starved stots, the same cattle,
> When they walk you can hear their dry bones creak and rattle.

* *Gilduff*—*i. e.*, the house of O'Shaughnessy of Gort [Inshy-gory], in the County of Galway.—*Dr. O'Donovan.*

† *O'Byrne*—*i. e.*, of Newrath, or Glenmalure, in the County of Wicklow.—*Dr. O'Donovan.*

‡ *Iregaine*—*i. e.* the barony of Tinahinch in the Queen's County, the country of the O'Dunnes.—*Dr. O'Donovan.*

§ *O'Conor*—*i. e.*, Calvagh O'Conor Faly. The translation is wide of Aenghus's meaning here. Take the following:—
> "A handful of meal in a trough in his house!
> Lord save them from hunger, 'twould starve a good mouse!
> The minstrels, the harp-strings, do rattle and flitter,
> With noise like the sow's singing bass to her litter."—*Dr. O'Donovan.*

"The sooty-faced swine-herds of Granard* I hate,
They are shabby and seedy in garb, and though greedy
As cormorants over the pot and the plate,
Yet, O Heavens! only think, in their utter
Abasement they really eat bread without butter!"

Let us now turn our face, with our itinerant poet, to Ulster:—

"I'd travel the island of Banba all over,
From the sea to the centre,—before I would enter;
That niggard Mac Mahon†—his damnable door!
He'll give you the ghost of a dinner,
That leaves you, by Jing, rather hungrier and thinner!

"Should you visit that hungriest town in the land,
Famed for nothing but no bread, which men call Clontobred,‡
You had best, my gay spark, make your will beforehand;
Far from getting an oaten or wheaten
Cake in it to eat, you yourself may be eaten.§

"My curse on Drumsnaghta,‖ that beggarly hole,
Without meat-stall or fish-shop,—priest, vicar, or bishop!
I saw in their temple—and oh! my sick soul!
A profound Irish feeling of shame stirs
Thy depths at the thought, playing hookey, two gamesters."

The poet after launching his satires, or lampoons, right and left, amongst the tribes of Ulster, turns to his own

* *Granard*, in the County of Longford.—*Dr. O'Donovan.*

† *Mac Mahon*—*i. e.*, chief of Oriel or County of Monaghan.—*Ibid.*

‡ *Clontobrid*, a Herenach church in the County of Monaghan.—*Ibid.*

§ *You yourself may be eaten.*—The translator goes too far here, for Aenghus makes no allusion to eating the living. He merely says that the cake was so thin, small, and light, that the fly might carry it off under her wing.—*Ibid.*

‖ *Drumsnaghta*, now Drumsnat, near Monaghan.—*Ibid.*

clan, that of the O'Dalys, of which he speaks with becoming caution:—

" By me the Clan-Daly* shall never be snubbed,
I say nothing about them, for were I to flout them,
The world would not save me from getting well drubbed,
While with *them* at my beck (or my back) I
Might drub the world well without fear of one black eye!"

The poet turns from Ulster to Munster, on which he is exceedingly severe:—

" One day, feeling footsore and faintish, I made,
By tardy approaches, my way to the Roches;†
It relieved me, at least, to creep into the shade;
I got bread, but my landlady shut her
Old rat-haunted cupboard at once on the butter!

" Dunboy‡ of the crab-apple verjuicy wine,
Which every fool praises—in silver set phrases,—
Is just such a dog-hole as badgers might dine
In for want of a better. No peasant
In Munster would say he thought hell more unpleasant.

" Three reasons there were why I lately withdrew
In a hurry from Bantry: its want of a pantry
Was one; and the dirt of its people was two;
Good heavens! how they daub and bespatter
Their duds! I forget the third reason. No matter.

" Mac Dermod of Muskerry,§ *you* have a way,
Which at least I must term odd. You gave me, Mac Dermod,
One hot summer's noon, half a wine-glass of whey! ‖
Before I could reach Ballincollick ¶
I swallowed six bushels of dust through your frolic!

* *Clan-Daly—i. e.*, the O'Donnells of Tirconnell.—*Dr. O'Donovan.*
† *The Roches—i. e.*, the Roches of Fermoy, in the County of Cork. *Ibid.*
‡ *Dunboy—i. e.*, O'Sullivan Beare's chief fortress in Bantry Bay.—*Ibid.*
§ *Mac Dermod of Muskerry—i. e.*, Mac Carthy of Muskerry, who had his chief residence at Blarney.—*Ibid.*
‖ *Whey.*—The poet is not very happy here. It should be,—
  " You gave me Mac Dermod,
  With a good deal of blarney, one wine-glass of whey!"—*Ibid.*
¶ *Ballincollick,* now Ballincollig, at this time the seat of William Barrett.—*Ibid.*

"The Mac Auliffes* I loathe, for I never could yet
Take to humbug and humdrums, slow coaches and dumb drums.
They're a lazy, yet saucy, and cock-nosish set;
They sleep upon beds of green heather,
And eat all that falls in their way—lamb or leather.

"Last Easter I spent with Mac Donough,† a stiff
Kind of person, yet silly—so gloomy and chilly
His whole house appeared that it *did* seem as if
Easter Sunday, that holy and high day,
Had fallen, by some fatal mistake, on Good Friday.

"The ragged O'Keeffe of Claragh !‡ he shivers and shakes,
The sad ragamuffin! He has'nt got stuff in
His carcase to battle with agues and aches;
But I spare him, he's drooping, the luckless
Poor devil. The cloakless are always the pluckless.

"Poor little Red Robin, the snow hides the ground,
And a worm, or a grub, is scarce to be found;
Still don't visit the O'Keeffe;§ rather brave the hard weather,
He'd soon bring your breast and your backbone together!"

The last house visited in Munster, in the county Tipperary—where the poet rhymed or satirised himself to death—was that of O'Meagher; and it is worthy of notice, that O'Meagher was the only chieftain whom he did not satirise :

"Last, O'Meagher, for yourself, last, tho' certes not least,
You're a prince, and are partial to mirth and the feast.
Huge cauldrons, vast fires, with fat sheep, calves and cows, and
Harp-music distinguish your house 'mid a thousand."

* *Mac Auliffes* of Castle Mac Auliff, County of Cork. This clan inhabited perhaps the wildest and poorest territory in all Ireland.—*Dr. O'Donovan.*

† *Mac Donough*—i. e., Mac Carthy of Duhallow, at this time a powerful Irish chieftain.—*Ibid.*

‡ *O'Keeffe of Claragh*, near Millstreet, County of Cork. He was a minor branch of the O'Keeffe family.—*Ibid.*

§ *The O'Keeffe*—i. e., the O'Keeffe of Dromagh, County of Cork or chief of the family, at this time a fifth-rate chieftain in Munster. —*Ibid.*

The versified paraphrase of these lampoons by James Clarence Mangan are not always correct translations of the original. The literal translation of what O'Daly said or wrote in the house of O'Meagher was as follows:—

> " A large fire in the House of O'Meagher,
> Men, and meat, beside it ;
> A large cauldron of fermented wine grapes,
> *Under which O'Meagher's cow calves.*"

It is probable that O'Meagher's servant understood the last line as containing a sneer, and that it excited his wrath to plunge a sharp knife into the poet's neck.

"Many are the bitter satires I have written," said the poet, "on the nobles and clans of Munster; but none ever requited me with a blow till the O'Meagher gave me my death wound. I perish, smitten down by a chieftain whom I eulogised; this increases my lamentation and woe."

If it be true that this Aenghus O'Daly accepted the pay of Sir George Carew, or any other Irish governor, to satirise and lampoon his country, in this general way, after having partaken of its hospitality, he most certainly deserved punishment. He received, in the end, something more terrible than satire, from a Tipperary man, an "O'Meagher of the Sword," or Irish Skein.

These Irish poets were a hot-blooded race, and adepts at the knife and the hatchet, as well as the lampoon. We discover from the *Annals of Ireland* for 1213, that an ancestor of this Aenghus O'Daly, who was also a poet—for professions at this time were hereditary amongst the Irish—slew a servant of the O'Donnell, for insulting him. O'Donnell, who was pleased to look upon the manslaughter, or murder, as a serious offence against himself, if not against the Commonwealth, was enraged, and endeavoured to seize O'Daly, who composed a poem, in which he expresses the utmost astonishment, that anything so trifling as the murder of a churl should produce a bad feeling between him and O'Donnell :—

> " A trifling difference—you see,
> Your shepherd had affronted me ;
> I raised my axe, and killed the clown.
> Oh God ! and can this cause a frown ?"

But it did; so the poet had to make his escape to Scotland, where he composed another poem, which smoothed the raven-down of darkness on the chieftain's brow. The poem opened—

> " O'Donnell, kind of hand."

The poet obtained peace for his panegyric. "O'Donnell received him into friendship, and gave him lands and possessions, as was pleasing to him."

It appears from a state paper, written many years after the death of Sir John Stanley, who had been rhymed or lampooned off the face of the earth, by the Irish bard Niall, the son of O'Higgin, that this Viceroy had injured and defrauded, not only the pure Celts, but also the English colonists. The state paper is addressed to Henry V., and reads thus :—

"Monsieur John de Stanley, whom God assoil, your lieutenant, of your land of Ireland, in your time, and in the time of the King, your father, and your predecessor, King Richard, paid little or nothing of his debts to your lieges, but committed divers extortions and oppressions, from time to time, against the form of your laws, and to the great injury of your land. For which, may it please your most gracious Lordship to compel the heirs of the said John de Stanley, who was greatly enriched by the goods of your land, to come hither, and make payment of his debts, and amend the defaults done by him, as shall appear best to your Highness."

Whether or not his Highness, in compassion for Sir John Stanley's soul, gave command that his debts should be paid, does not appear.

CHAPTER L.

DURING THE REIGN OF HENRY V.—ARCHBISHOP CRANLEY—PRIOR BUTLER—
SIR JOHN TALBOT-THE EARL OF ORMOND—A PROPOSAL FOR A CRUSADE
AGAINST THE IRISH ENEMY.

A.D. 1414-1422. ON the death of Sir John Stanley, which occurred the 18th of January, 1414, the Council elected Thomas Cranley, the English Archbishop of Dublin, as Viceroy. Cranley was " greatly praised for his liberality ;" he was "a good almsman," "a great clerk," "a doctor"—of divinity, of course, being an archbishop,—"an excellent preacher "—which was not a necessary qualification of an archbishop,—"a great builder;" "of tall stature ; beautiful ; of sanguine complexion ; courteous."

Being, at this time, nearly eighty years of age, he did not go out with Prior Butler,* and Patrick Barrett, Bishop of Ferns, on military, or predatory excursions against the "Irish enemy;" but did what was more becoming his spiritual functions—convened the clergy together, at Castle-Dermot, to pray for success on the arms of the English ; a practice which is esteemed

* *Prior Butler.*—This Prior Butler, of Kilmainham, near Dublin, was of the Ormond family. He was styled " Prior *Bacoaugh*," or the " Lame Prior." But notwithstanding his priorship, and his lameness, he was a great soldier. He served with Henry V. of England, in the French wars, and took part at the siege of Rouen. None were more praised than he, and his Irish troops. It is said, by some, that he died in Normandy, in 1419; but there is another account, that he was poisoned by a jealous woman, after he had returned to England.

orthodox, and becoming, in an archbishop of the 19th century. But the prayers of this good old man were not answered, for the forces of the Prior and the Bishop, were routed by O'Conor, of Offaly, and Mac Geoghegan, "who carried off many hostages and slew various nobles."

Archbishop Cranley's ecclesiastical mode of defence, against the Irish enemy—namely, prayer—was not much esteemed in those warlike days. The Irish colonists brought charges against him, and he had to appeal to the chivalrous English monarch, Henry V., the conqueror of Agincourt. His appeal took the form of a Latin epistle, or poem, of 106 verses; but Henry, who had more faith in heavy battalions than in prayer or Providence, concluded that the old churchman had mistaken his vocation, in accepting the office of chief ruler of Ireland, and therefore appointed Sir John Talbot, a real soldier, in his stead.

Sir John Talbot landed at Dalkey, on the 10th of November, 1414, and on the 30th of the same month, his commission was read in the Cathedral of Holy Trinity, Dublin, in the presence of Archishop Cranley, and the whole Council.

Sir John Talbot carried the war into Leix, O'Moore's country, which he devastated with fire and sword; and struck such terror into the hearts of other Irish chieftains, that some of them submitted themselves, voluntarily, and amongst the number, Morice, a notorious traitor and rebel. But, as Sir John Davies says of Talbot, "he had power to make them seek the 'King's peace,' but not to reduce them to the obedience of subjects."

The English colonists, who were at first delighted with such a warlike Viceroy, soon found that his victories were far more expensive than the peaceful tactics of Archbishop Cranley; they, therefore, entreated the King "graciously to provide Talbot a sufficient payment, so that his soldiers might be able to pay for their victuals, and other things, which they took of his faithful and poor lieges, for the safety of his land, aforesaid." The poor lieges having the choice of being plundered by their enemies or friends, choose the former.

After a time they speak out more fully, and accuse Talbot of excessive extortions and oppressions, on both ecclesiastics and laymen, whose property he had taken, without payment. He gave protection to neither saint nor sanctuary; and with the doom of Sir John Stanley (who had been rhymed to death) before his eyes, he "injured and defrauded the poets of Erin."

It was during Sir John Talbot's administration that the famous Irish chieftain, "Art Cavanagh Mac Murrough, King of Leinster, died, A.D. 1417;" "a man who defended his province against the English and Irish, from the age of sixteen to his 60th year—a man distinguished for hospitality, knowledge, and feats of arms." The reader will remember Froissart's description of him, descending from a mountain near the sea, mounted on a horse without a saddle, to meet Richard's ambassador, the Earl of Gloucester, who came to propose terms of peace. Mac Murrough was on his guard. On a former occasion he had been invited to a banquet by English lords, who came armed with the intention of murdering him; when his minstrel, or harper, discovering the plot, put him on his guard by striking up and singing the *Rosg-catha*, a war song. An Irish annalist says, "He was one of the greatest heroes the world ever saw. Had I the tongues of men and angels I would never be able to relate his merits."

Talbot was recalled from the Irish Chief-Governorship, in 1419, and his brother Richard (who had been appointed Archbishop of Dublin, instead of Thomas Cranley) became Viceroy in his stead.

He was succeeded, in the April of 1420, by James, fourth Earl of Ormond, who had just returned from Normandy. This Earl made war on O'Moore, near Athy ; and if we can believe what chroniclers say, the sun stood still above the Red Moor, "*almost lodging in the west, and miraculously standing in his epicycle, for the space of three hours.*"

Things had arrived at such a pass, that, at a Parliament, convened by Ormond, there was an address to the King, that he would be graciously pleased to write to the Holy Father, the Pope, to publish "*a crusade against Irish enemies*, for the relief and salvation of the land, and the perpetual destruction of those enemies, by the aid of God." This, in the Land of Saints ! It would appear, from state papers, that the Irish, whom the English colonists imagined they were divinely commissioned to destroy, were worse than the Canaanites or Saracens. There were not only fightings with "the enemy," or wild Irish without, but contentions in high places, and charges of complicity, with O'Conor of Offaly. Sir John Talbot arraigned the Viceroy, the Earl of Ormond, and his brother, the Prior of Kilmainham, for treason, for encouraging O'Conor to levy black mail on behalf of his wife, and to ride roughshod through Kildare, despoiling, slaying, and destroying liege subjects, and burning up the country. But the Crown, seeing the scandal likely to arise from such charges, directed that the proceedings should be quashed.

CHAPTER LI.

THE ENGLISH COUNCIL IN IRELAND AGREE TO PAY TRIBUTE, OR BLACK MAIL, TO IRISH CHIEFTAINS—EDMUND MORTIMER—NOBLE CONDUCT OF HENRY V.—SIR JOHN TALBOT—SIR JOHN GREY—SIR JOHN SUTTON—ANONYMOUS LETTERS—THE BRAVE PRIOR OF KILMAINHAM CHALLENGES THE EARL OF ORMOND.

A.D. 1422-1446. IN the year 1422, when Henry VI. succeeded to the throne of England, James, the fourth Earl of Ormond, was Irish Viceroy. If Irish affairs were neglected during the reigns of warlike English monarchs like Edward I., Edward III., Henry IV., and Henry V., what could we expect during the infancy and minority of the young prince Henry VI., and during the "Wars of the Roses," which desolated the whole of England? It may appear to some a wonder that Ireland did not take advantage of the opportunity to throw off the English yoke altogether. The simple explanation is, that the Irish had too much fighting amongst themselves, to unite in any project for the general welfare of the country.

O'Neill, of Ulster, made a raid into Meath, and routed the English troops, slaying their commander, and carrying away both hostages and spoil. The Viceroy, Ormond, feeling his inability to resist such incursions by the sword, proposed to his Council, the payment of tribute to the most powerful of the Irish chieftains, to which the Council agreed, granting Sir William Burke, who was now more Irish than the Irish themselves, £40, and his brother £20.

Edmund Mortimer was appointed Viceroy in 1423, the year after Henry V. died. This Mortimer was considered the proper and true heir to the English Crown, which had been unjustly seized by Henry of Lancaster. Mortimer was descended from Philippa, only daughter of the Duke of Clarence, second son of Edward III. He had a better right to the Crown than Henry IV., who had plucked it from the brow of Richard II. Both Richard II. and the English Parliament had acknowledged the claims of Mortimer. The wars of the Roses resulted from the usurpation of Henry IV. of Lancaster. The result of these wars was to place Edward IV., the son of the Duke of York, a descendant of Anne Mortimer, sister to the last Earl of March, on the English throne.

It was most fortunate for Edmund Mortimer that he had no ambition, and that he had qualities which gained the heart of the young warlike prince, afterwards Henry V., for Henry IV. had committed the care of young Mortimer, when quite a boy, to his son, which looked somewhat like placing a high-bred "Charles" in the cage of a young lion. But the young lion took to the young dog.

But young Edmund had over-zealous friends, Lady Spenser amongst the number, who had the boy stolen from the guardianship of the Prince of Wales; but he was soon retaken in the Chiltham Woods. The following year, Owen Glengower, the uncle of Edmund, and of his younger brother, Roger Mortimer, managed, by means of false keys, to gain access to Windsor Castle, from which he carried off both his nephews; but they were subsequently recovered. A similar plot to carry off young Mortimer, and proclaim him King, was discovered in 1416, as Henry V. was about to sail to France, for which Edmund's brother-in-law, the Earl of Cambridge, Sir Thomas Grey, of Heton, and Lord Scrope, of Masham, were beheaded. It is marvellous that the heroic Henry V. did not remove the innocent head, or cause, of all these plottings against his new throne. How different the conduct of Edward IV., shortly after he had assumed the throne!

A London tradesman, who kept a shop at the sign of the "Crown," remarked, in a joking way, to a customer that he would "make his son heir to the *Crown*." Edward, hearing what he considered a taunt at his assumption of the Crown of England, had the jocose tradesman arrested and executed.

Edmund Mortimer, who, as we have stated, was fortunate enough to have no ambition for a crown, served under Henry V. in Normandy; and in 1418 and 1423, was appointed Irish Viceroy, during the minority of Henry VI.

Mortimer appointed Edward Dantsey, Bishop of Meath, as his Deputy. The commission was duly executed, by letters patent, at Castle Ludlow; but when Dantsey produced his commission to the previous Deputy Governor, Richard Talbot, Archbishop of Dublin, and Chancellor to the Privy Council—which he did, at the Convent of Drogheda—Talbot refused to recognise its legality, expressing doubts as to the power of a Viceroy to make a Deputy, under his private seal. A writ was then issued from Westminster, to which Talbot, on the advice of some Irish judges demurred; but in the

end, the knotty point was overcome, by the arrival of
the Viceroy himself, and the consequent extinction of
the Deputy that was, or that would have been. It was
a contest between two stars, to see which of them should
give light to the Emerald Isle, when the sun arose, and
extinguished them both.

Edmund Mortimer arrived in Ireland in 1424, and
was very well received, both by the English and Irish,
as he was a sort of un-crowned king. He had even succeeded in making amicable terms with many of the
native chieftains, who were in possession of the immense
territories, which he claimed, as Earl of Ulster; when he
was seized by the plague, and died in the January of
1425. Like his father and grandfather he ended his
days in Ireland, in the early bloom of manhood, when
holding the office of Viceroy.

As he, and his brother, Roger, died without issue, the
earldom of Ulster, and the lordship of Connaught and
Meath, devolved on their nephew, Richard Plantagenet,
Duke of York, son of their sister, Anne Mortimer,
Countess of Cambridge; who made over her claims on
the Crown of England, to her son, Richard. She was
the grandmother of Edward IV., of the House of York,
or the White Rose. This Richard fell in the battle of
Wakefield, in 1460, when fighting against Margaret,
the wife of Henry VI., of the House of Lancaster, or
the Red Rose. But more of him hereafter.

On the death of Edmund Mortimer, in 1425, Sir
John Talbot became Viceroy. Being an energetic
soldier, he came down upon a number of Irish chieftains,
whom he caught like rats in a trap, in the Castle of

Trim,* where they had expected to meet Edmund
Mortimer. Amongst the number were Prince Owen
O'Neill, and Calvach O'Conor, of Offaly. He compelled the latter to liberate a number of Englishmen,
and amongst the number, the Marshal of the English
army in Ireland. He also obliged him to forego the
"black rent," which he levied on the King's subjects in
Meath. Donagh, Chief of the O'Byrnes, covenanted at
the same time, "for a consideration," to protect Sir John
Talbot's tenants in Wexford, and to allow his brother,
Richard, the Archbishop of Dublin, to collect his rents
and fees amongst the mountains of Wicklow.

Sir John Talbot left Ireland in 1425, before he had
been a year in office; but during that time, he had
managed to feather his nest, and that of his two brothers,
with lands in the counties Dublin and Meath.

He was succeeded by the Earl of Ormond, in 1425.
Ormond entered into a compact with O'Neill, who had
been captured at Trim Castle. O'Neill consented to
acknowledge himself liegeman of the King of England.
He also agreed to aid the Duke of York, nephew of
Edmund Mortimer, in guarding his territories, in Ulster,
from which O'Neill promised he would exact no black
rent. He also promised to forego all claims on John
Swayne, the Primate of Armagh, and his successors—
whatever those claims may have been†—probably im-

* *Trim Castle.*—Edmund Mortimer obtained from his cousin,
Henry V., in 1415, a confirmation of his ancestral rights and privileges in Meath, and, amongst other things, authority to hold something
like a royal court in Trim Castle. Here the northern chieftains had
assembled, to do him honour, when they were entrapped by Sir John
Talbot.

† *Whatever these claims may have been.*—John Mey, the successor of
John Swayne, in the Primacy, obtained admission to the archdiocese,

munity from eric, or blood money, and all other kind of taxes, or levies,—and not to molest him or any of his clergy.

The English bishops, at this time, though Roman Catholic, were not in favour with Irish chieftains. At this we shall not be surprised, if we bear in mind, that they were greater adepts in the use of the sword of State, and the weapons of the God of War, than in "the use of the sword of the Spirit."

The Earl of Ormond was succeeded in office of Viceroy, by Sir John Grey, who landed at Howth, the 31st of July, 1427, and was sworn in the next day, at the Castle of Swords, near Dublin. He retired from office the next year, and was succeeded by Sir John Sutton. A Parliament was assembled, at Dublin, in 1429, during Sutton's administration, which took notice of certain anonymous communications, sent from Ireland, to England, reflecting on the conduct of certain persons in authority, in the Irish Government. Sutton laid a copy of these anonymous letters before a Council, assembled in Drogheda, in April, 1429. After they had been read aloud, Richard Talbot, Archbishop of Dublin, demanded of the members individually, whether they had hand, act, or part in their composition, or transmission; or whether they were cognizant of them. After each and all had denied all knowledge of them, the same questions were put, by the Viceroy, to the Archbishop himself, who returned the same answer, "Not guilty, upon my honour."

on the condition of rendering to O'Neill six yards of good cloth; and three yards of the same material, for his wife's tunic. These gifts were in recognition of O'Neill's regal authority. One feels disposed, from their character, to conclude, his Majesty, O'Neill, was "out at the elbows."

But notwithstanding your plighted honour, Master Richard, we have our doubts respecting your Grace. The paper complained of certain noble persons, having refused to march with the former Viceroy, Sir John Gray, against the Irish enemy. Two years after, this warlike archbishop was commanded to appear before the King and Council, to answer for the tumultuous and oppressive proceedings of his armed followers, and was compelled, under a penalty of five hundred pounds, to release John Butler, brother of the Earl of Ormond, whom he had captured, and held in durance vile.

Sir Thomas Strange was appointed Sutton's Deputy, in 1429; and in 1431, Sir John Stanley (grandson of the Sir John Stanley who had been rhymed to death, by an Irish poet) became Viceroy.

In 1431 the supplies had been so reduced, by the Wars of the Roses, that Sir John Stanley had to apply to England, in person, for money, or provisions, of some kind, to meet his current expenses. He carried with him a paper, drawn up by the Council, in Dublin, which tells a miserable tale of the state of things within the pale, the boundaries of which were decreasing year by year; the Irish enemy continuing to encroach from the north, west, and south; "so that there was not left within the pale, or in the counties of Dublin, Meath, Louth, and Kildare, a surface of scarcely thirty miles in length, and twenty miles in breadth, as a man may ride, or go, to answer the King's writ." "Within these nine years there were in the county of Catherlagh [Carlow] a hundred and forty-eight castles and piles defensible, well-vaulted, embattled, and inhabited, that are now destroyed, and under the subjection of the said enemies."

While England was fighting the battles of the Roses, Ireland was fighting the battles of the Shamrocks. To be idle in Ireland, during so much fighting in England, would have been deemed a national disgrace.

In 1438 the Irish Chief Governorship was committed to Sir Leon Welles; who left Ireland, after a short residence, appointing his brother William, as his Deputy. Thomas Fitzgerald, Prior of Kilmainham, who does not seem to have approved of any deputy, save his friend, Richard Talbot, Archbishop of Dublin, laid an ambush at Kilcock, for William Welles, caught him, and immured him in the jail of the Fitzgeralds. There was a weak attempt to bring the brave Prior "to book;" but what did he care for writs, or prosecutions? He, and his accomplices, were directed to appear in Court, on a fixed day. He appeared—although not on the day fixed— and produced a royal pardon; made his bow, and rode off boldy, to his residence at Kilmainham; like a man who would " do it again," if the opportunity presented itself.

His next attack was made upon the conduct and administration of the Earl of Ormond, who had been appointed Deputy in the place of William, the brother of Sir Leon Welles. The accusation, which was got up by Archbishop Talbot, went so far as to make a charge of treason against the Earl of Ormond. The accusers and accused appeared in person, before Henry VI. The Talbot party were represented by the Prior of Kilmainham, who offered to maintain the truth of his statements, by single combat. The old Earl accepted the challenge, and a day was fixed for the fight. They were to meet in Smithfield, the usual place for such encounters. The constable of the Tower, who was his keeper and trainer, permitted the Earl, "for his breathing"—which, we conclude, was short and asthmatical—" and ease against the day of battle, to go as far as forty miles from London."

The Prior of Kilmainham, who was placed in the custody of the English Treasurer, Giles Thorndon, was furnished with money, attendants, and armour, at the royal cost, and was instructed in certain points of sword exercise, by Philip Trehere, a fishmonger, and a professional swordsman.

The day appointed for this extraordinary duel, between an earl and a prior, at length arrived; the lists were prepared, the field in readiness, and the Londoners in a high state of excitement and expectation, when a number of sober churchmen stepped in, and marred their sport, by representing to the King, the scandal of such a contest; who prohibited the combat.

The case was carried from the Court of Mars, at Smithfield, to Westminster, where the charges against the Earl of Ormond were fully investigated, and pronounced false, and to have originated in envy and malice. The Earl's enemy, Richard Talbot, Archbishop of Dublin, who was then Lord Deputy, was commanded by the King, to issue writs and make proclamation, like Haman, in the case of Mordecai, of the Royal decision in favour of the Earl of Ormond. And soon after, his trusty friend, the Prior of Kilmainham, was dismissed from office, by the Visitor-General of Hospitallers, for avarice and dilapidations of the house. His successor, Fitzgerald, discovered, that after his deposition, he had broken open the box containing the Royal seal, which he carried off, and affixed to a number of illegal grants. He was wise in his generation, like the unjust steward.

CHAPTER LII.

SIR JOHN TALBOT—THE ANTI-IRISH STATUTES OF THE PARLIAMENT OF
TRIM—DEATH OF SIR JOHN TALBOT.

A.D. 1446-1449. IN 1446, the famous old soldier, Sir John Talbot, the brother of the Archbishop, who had succeeded Edmund Mortimer, in 1425, was re-appointed Viceroy, and discharged the duties of his difficult and arduous post, with all his old fire and former vigour. In 1447 a grant was made to him of the Earldom of Waterford and the Barony of Dungarvan, with their castles, lordships, and royal rights, and the wreck of the sea from Youghal to Waterford; but before he could possess these estates, he had to conquer them, to catch his hare before he made his hare soup; and the Powers, Walshes, Grants, and D'Altons, at one time "English subjects," now "Irish enemies," were by no means easy to catch, or to cook.

He called a Parliament, in the great castle of Trim, where, in 1425, he had bagged a number of Irish chieftains; but this was a game that could not be played twice,*

* *Played twice.*—The *Annals of Ulster*, under date A.D. 1447, say, "Felim, son of Philip O'Reilly, worthy materies of a King of Briefney, was taken prisoner, at Ath-Truim [Trim], by Furnival, the Deputy of the King of England. At that time Ath-Truim was visited by a great plague, of which Felim died. This Furnival was a son of curses, for his venom, and a devil for his evils; and the learned say of him that there came not from the time of Herod, by whom Christ was crucified, any one so wicked in evil deeds."—*Annals of Ulster*, A.D. 1447.

Furnival, as the reader is aware, is one of the titles of the Talbot or Shrewsbury family. We should like to know on what authority the learned compilers of the *Annals of Ulster* assert, *that Christ was crucified by Herod.*

by the same man; so he set himself to enact new laws, or re-enact old statutes. One was that "Englishmen should not use a beard upon the upper lip; that the said lip should be shaved, once, at least, in every two weeks. By another enactment, the sons of labourers, or tillers of ground, should, under penalty of fine and imprisonment, follow the avocation of their parents. This looks something like the institution of castes, such as prevail in India. We are aware that among the Irish, the higher professions, such as that of poet, brehon, or judge, and physician, were hereditary, as they were amongst the Egyptians; but we are not aware that this state of things extended to farm labourers, or tillers of the ground.

Another enactment of this Parliament, held at the Castle of Trim, forbade the use of gilt bridles, harness, or peytrells, or gilt chains, which crossed the chests of war-horses,—"No man shall be so hardy, henceforth, as to use any gilt bridles, peytrells, or other gilt harness, except knights and prelates of holy church; and if any be found with such bridle, peytrell, or other gilt harness, from the 1st of next May, it may be lawful for any man that will, to take the said man, his horse, and harness, to hold or possess the same, as his own goods."

Sir John Talbot served for many years in the wars of France, where he made a name, with which mothers hushed noisy children to silence. "Hush, the Talbot is coming!" At the advanced age of eighty, he landed at Bordeaux, to aid the nobles of Guienne, against the King of France. He was killed by a shot, in an attempt to relieve the fortress of Chatillon. He seems to have courted danger, for he was mounted on a white horse,

with a coat of red velvet. His eldest son, John, who
had been Chancellor of Ireland, fell in attempting to
rescue his father. His herald, an old and faithful
servant, was asked if he should know his master, if he
saw him. "To which," writes De Courcy, "he replied
joyfully, deeming him to be still alive." Thereupon he
was taken to the place, where the bloody and disfigured
corpse lay. "Look," they said, "and see if that is your
master." The poor fellow changed colour. He then
knelt down beside the body, put a finger into the dead
man's mouth, and felt for the presence, or absence, of
some particular tooth; he then kissed him, and exclaimed,
"My lord and master, my lord and master, is it you!
I pray God, pardon your sins. I have been your officer
of arms forty years, or more; it is time I gave you
back your trust"—taking off his coat of mail, and laying it at the feet of the corpse.

Sir John Talbot had resigned the office of Irish
Viceroy in 1447, when his brother, Richard, the Archbishop of Dublin, who was almost as great a warrior as
himself, was appointed Chief Magistrate.

CHAPTER LIII.

RICHARD PLANTAGENET, DUKE OF YORK, AND HIS WIFE, THE ROSE OF RABY—LAWS ENACTED AGAINST THE MARCHERS—DISORGANISED STATE OF SOCIETY—LOW EXCHEQUER—RISING IN ENGLAND UNDER JACK CADE—THE EARL OF ORMOND—BATTLE OF ST. ALBANS—ASSERTION OF IRISH INDEPENDENCE OF ENGLAND-DEATH OF THE DUKE OF YORK, AND HIS SON EDMUND, EARL OF ULSTER—CRUELTY OF LORD CLIFFORD.

A.D. 1449-1461. ON the 5th of July, 1449, Richard Plantagenet, Duke of York, Earl of March and Ulster, and Lord of Connaught and Meath, became Viceroy. It is supposed that this appointment was arranged by Margaret, the Queen of Henry VI. (he was a mere cipher in her hands), in order to take the regency of the English territories in France, out of the Duke's hands, and place them in those of his rival, the Duke of Somerset.

This Richard Plantagenet, Duke of York, was the head of the Yorkist, or White Rose party. He was descended from Lionel, the third son of Edward III., and is supposed to have had a better title to the English throne than Henry VI., the grandson of Henry IV., of Lancaster, who violently seized it from Richard II.

The Duke landed at Howth, accompanied by his wife, Cecilia, the daughter of Ralph Neville, Earl of Westmoreland, and Baron of Raby. The Duchess of York, on account of her great beauty, was styled "The Rose of Raby." She was distinguished, not only for her beauty and high capacity, but also for the circumstance of her having been the mother of two kings, Edward IV. and Richard III., and we may also add of George, Duke of Clarence,* born in Dublin Castle; and, if historians be correct, drowned, in the Tower of London, in a butt of Malmsey, at his own particular request.

The Duke convened a Parliament in Dublin, in October, 1449, in which it was enacted that the "Marchers," or those who dwelt on the borders, for the protection of those within the pale, should keep no more horse or foot soldiers than they could, themselves, honestly maintain. Those borderers were in the habit of exacting *coigne* or "night-suppers," and of distressing the poor farmers, by numerous and unjust exactions; who felt that it did not signify much to them whether they were robbed or plundered by their friends, from the Marches, or the Irish enemy, from the interior. The statute for putting down this state of things goes on to say, "The chief captains of said Marchers lead and lodge upon one husbandman a hundred men, horse and foot, on one night. The captains bring their wives, pages, and sons, with a following of Irish enemies and English rebels," who eat up and spy out the land. The tenant, or husbandman, "who will not be at their truce," or who refuses to entertain them, they burn, rob, spoil, and kill; and for the most part the land was in this way wasted and destroyed.

Such a state of things could only be met by extreme measures, so it was declared by this Parliament, that it was lawful for every liege or loyal man, to take or kill

* *George, Duke of Clarence.*—The Earls of Desmond and Ormond were sponsors at his baptism, in Dublin Castle. He was born October 21st, 1449.

any of those notorious robbers, found plundering, by night or by day, and that every man that killed or took any such, should, for each one of them, have a penny a head from each ploughland, and a farthing a head from each cottage, within the barony "where the manslaughter was done." The sheriff of the county was to levy the money, within a month after the manslaughter, and "deliver it to him who made the homiside."

This fearfully disordered state of society, in which the dwellers within the pale were directed to protect themselves, by homicide, resulted, for the most part, or principally, from the bankrupt condition of the Irish treasury; there was no money to pay regular troops, to keep the Irish chieftains in check, or even to guard the pale, which was every year becoming more and more circumscribed. The Duke wrote, at this time, to his brother-in-law, the Earl of Salisbury, informing him that the chieftain Mac Geoghegan, with three or four Irish captains, had burned down his large town of Rathmore, in the county Meath, and that they were then assembled in the woods, waiting their opportunity "to hurt and grievance the King's subjects;" he therefore entreats the Earl to hasten his payments, according to his letters of warrant, to the treasurer; that he may "wage men in sufficient number to resist the malice of their enemies." He goes on to say, "Necessity will compel me to go to England, and to live there upon my poor livelihood, for I had lever be dead than any inconvenience shall fall thereunto, in my default; for it shall never be chronicled, nor remain in scripture, by the Grace of God, that Ireland was lost by my negligence." The Duke afterwards declared, in the English Parliament, that in France, Normandy, and Ireland, "for lack of payment of his wages, he had been compelled to sell his substance, borrow from his friends, and pledge his plate and jewels."

The Duke returned to England, unexpectedly, in September, 1450; but we are not disposed to think that this sudden movement was altogether the result of his pecuniary necessities in Ireland. The mind of the people of England, at this time, was like a trembling Irish bog. It had nothing stable to rest on. Henry VI. was no more than a puppet in the hands of a clever French woman, Queen Margaret; Englishmen complained that both the honour of England and English territories in France had been compromised and lost; that it was hard enough to submit to the rule of a monarch without capacity or power, whose title to the throne was legitimate, but more difficult to bow to the rule of one whose right to reign was so generally questioned.

Such a state of public feeling could not fail to breed or produce commotion and rebellion. The claims of the House of York, or Mortimer, were often spoken of, but the Duke was away in Ireland; the time had come, but the man had not presented himself; when suddenly there arose a claimant to the English throne among the insurgent commons of Kent, an Anglo-Irishman, who called himself John Mortimer. It was generally believed that his real name was *Jack Cade*, and by this name he is best known in English history; but his followers gave him the title of "Sir John Amend-all," and sometimes *John Mend-all*.

He came to put things to rights, and he seemed to

have the necessary pluck to do so, along with the proper daring and dash of a successful adventurer. He bore the honourable title, "The Captain of Kent." Some assert he was a physician, named John Aylmer, who had married a squire's daughter. An English chronicler says, he was "a young man of goodly stature, gaily attired in scarlet, and of pregnant wit." Hume calls him "a man of low condition, a native of Ireland, who had been obliged to fly to France, for crimes." Thousands flocked to his standard, on his assumption of the royal name of Mortimer; whom he addressed, on the abuses of government, inflaming their minds to demand immediate redress.

The Court, fully sensible of their danger, sent out a force against him, under the command of Sir Humphrey Stafford, who was defeated and slain near Sevenoaks. After this success, Cade advanced toward London, and encamped, with his followers, on Blackheath. Although elated with victory, he preserved the appearance of moderation, and sent to the Court, or Council, a list of grievances; and promised that when these were redressed, and Lord Say, the Treasurer, and Cromer, the Sheriff of Kent, were punished, they would lay down their arms. The Council, not deeming it wise or prudent to venture on harsh measures against men whose complaints appeared both reasonable and true, having carried the King, for safety, to Kenilworth, opened the gates of the City of London, to Cade and his followers. John Cade, in armour, over a gown of blue velvet, with gilt helmet and spurs, and naked sword in hand, rode through the city. Fabian, an alderman, who was present, says, "As Cade came to London Stone, he struck it with his sword, and said, 'Now is Mortimer Lord of this City.'"

He led his followers into the fields, during night, and did his utmost to keep them from plunder and violence, but without effect. They insisted on having the lives of Lord Say, and Sheriff Cromer, whom they had in their hands, and had their will. They then broke into private houses, and perpetrated numerous acts of violence, till Lord Scales, the Governor of the Tower of London, went out against them, with a sufficient force, and routed them with great slaughter. One thousand marks were offered for the taking of Cade, " quick or dead." He was killed by one Iden, a gentleman of Sussex. There can be no doubt that John Cade was the forerunner of Richard, Duke of York, for the English crown; and that he, to some extent, prepared and smoothed his way; but there is no true ground for asserting, as some of the Lancasterian party asserted, that Cade was instigated by persons in high places, to act the part he did. He was the creature of circumstances, the natural and almost involuntary production of the times and the state of public feeling in the country. It would be impossible for a Wat Tyler, a Jack Cade, or a Lambert Simnel, to arise in the present day. But we are not so sure that Lambert Simnel was not what he represented himself to be.

The Duke of York, as we have said, returned, unexpectedly, from Ireland, to England, in the September of 1450, appointing Sir James Butler, eldest son of the Earl of Ormond, as his Deputy. This James Ormond is styled by English chroniclers, "The Lord Butler." He served under old Sir John Talbot, and the Duke of York, in France; to the latter of whom, in the civil wars of England, he became a dire enemy.

In 1452 he succeeded his father, as Earl of Ormond. He bore also the title of Earl of Wiltshire. The old Earl of Ormond had often held office in Ireland, and had often taken the field in Ireland, at the head of his followers; and is described as the "best captain of the English, in Ireland, for many ages." He was not, as his enemies asserted, unwieldy and unlusty to labour; for six weeks before his death he performed marvels of bravery on the O'Mulryans of Limerick, the O'Dempseys of Leix, and the O'Conors of Offaly, sacking fortresses, burning castles, and taking preys. It is mentioned as a portentous fact, that the year before his death, the river Liffey, which flows through Dublin, dried up. If it had occurred the year he died, it would have been still more remarkable. He was best known as "The White Earl."

In 1453, the new or fifth Earl of Ormond and Earl of Wilts, became Viceroy, and appointed as his Deputy, John Mey, Archbishop of Armagh. There were great contentions in Kildare and Meath, between the Ormonds or Butlers, and the Fitzgeralds; and the Archbishop was totally powerless in putting them down; so that the Mayor of Dublin was asked to lend a hand to the Fitzgeralds, which he did, willingly, as Dublin depended, for much of its supplies, on Kildare, which belonged to the Fitzgeralds.

The Duke of York, whose presence and following in England hung like a dark cloud, charged with dangerous elements, around the throne of Henry VI. of Lancaster, was again nominated Viceroy; but feeling the time for action had come, and the importance of his presence in England, he appointed Edmund Fitz-Eustace as his Deputy.

The next year he defeated the Lancasterians, at the

battle of St. Albans, captured Henry VI., and was declared Protector of England and Lieutenant of Ireland. On this occasion he appointed Thomas Fitzgerald, Earl of Kildare, and natural enemy of the house of Ormond, as his Deputy, who held the office from 1455 to 1459.

The Yorkists slew, at the battle of St. Albans, about 5,000 Lancasterians, among whom were the Duke of Somerset, the Earl of Northumberland, the Earl of Stafford, eldest son of the Duke of Buckingham, Lord Clifford, and many other persons of noble descent. This, as Hume says, was the " first blood spilt in that fatal quarrel, which lasted thirty years, was signalised by twelve pitched battles, and is computed to have cost the lives of eighty princes of the blood, and almost entirely to have annihilated the ancient nobility of England."

The Duke of York, having been unsuccessful in the next battle, through the treachery of Sir Andrew Trollope, fled to Ireland, where he was warmly received, as was another Duke of York, in a later period of English history. He was formally acknowledged by the Irish Parliament, as Viceroy, or chief ruler.

Encouraged by the presence of a Viceroy, or Chief Governor, who was generally acknowledged in England, as well as in Ireland, to possess a better title to the Crown than the weak-minded Henry VI., the Parliament of Ireland took the bold step of announcing its legislative independence. In further vindication of its rights, it declared that, according to ancient prescription, the King's subjects in Ireland were not bound to answer any writs, except those under the great seal of Ireland; and that any one attempting to enforce an English decree, in

Ireland, should suffer forfeiture of all his Irish property, and be fined 1,000 marks. It was also ordained that any appeal of treason in Ireland, should be determined in the court of the Marshal of Ireland; and that no pardon or commutation of sentence in England, could avail in such case. Another statute of this Parliament decreed that while the Duke of York, as Lord Lieutenant, resided in Ireland, any man who directly, or indirectly, sought to compass his destruction, or death, or to provoke rebellion, or disobedience towards him, should stand as attainted of high treason against the person of the King.

The Anglo-Irish were proud of their new Viceroy, "whose hearts he had exceeding tied unto him;" so that when the Earl of Ormond and Wilts, his late Deputy (who was now altogether bound up with the Lancasterian party), sent over one William Overy with a writ for his apprehension for treason, and open rebellion against the King, the Irish seized the messenger, and had him hanged, drawn, and quartered.

The Butlers, the Earl of Ormond's party, did their best to sow discord in the Irish camp, but failed, for the Earls of Kildare and Desmond (the hereditary foes of the Butlers), with the Barnwells, Prestons, and other Anglo-Irish persons of distinction, gathered round him, and even enlisted some of the native chieftains in favour of the White Rose of York.

The severities practised by the Earl of Ormond and Lord Scales in England, where, for a time, they had everything their own way, was such, that the people of Kent invited the Earl of Warwick, and Edward, the Duke of York's son, afterwards Edward IV. of England, to come over from Calais and help them. A ballad was set up, on the gates of Canterbury, declaring that England, under the administration of Queen Margaret and her cruel advisers, had become "The Kingdom of Satan," and praying the "Gracious Lord Jesu, most benign," to send home from Ireland, the "True Blood, Richard, Duke of York," whose trials the writer compared to those of the patriarch Job.

Warwick and young Edward sent over "Little Falconbridge, a knight of great reverence," to test the men of Kent, and see of what metal they were composed. The reply being favourable, they landed at Sandwich, with fifteen hundred men. Large numbers of southerners flocked to their standard, together with the Archbishop of Canterbury, the Papal Legate, and several prelates.

Having defeated the Royal army at Northampton, captured the King, and entered London in triumph, they sent swift couriers and flying posts to Ireland for the Duke of York. He obeyed the summons, without losing an hour, and arrived in London, which he entered with a naked sword borne before him, and took up his lodgings in the King's chamber, the doors of which he broke open; therefore, as the chronicler says, "the common people babbled that he should be king, and that King Henry should no longer reign."

But the fickle fortune of war had otherwise decided. One month had not passed, before he found himself unexpectedly beleaguered by the Queen's army, in his Castle of Sandal, near Wakefield. The Queen's army numbered from eighteen to twenty thousand men; notwithstanding the Duke resolved to leave his stronghold and go forth, with a mere handful of followers, to meet them. Sir David Hall, the Duke's old servant and chief counsellor, prayed him to tarry within the walls till his son Edward (afterwards Edward IV.) came up with his Marchmen and Welsh soldiers.

"Ah, Davy, Davy, hast thou loved me so long, and now wouldst thou have me dishonoured," was his reply. "Thou never sawest me within a fortress, when I was regent in Normandy; and when the Dauphin himself came with all his forces to rescize me; and shall it now be said that a woman has made a dastard of me. Therefore advance my banner in the name of God and St. George, for surely I will fight them, though I fight alone."

His forces issued forth and descended the hill, where they were completely surrounded. Two-thirds of the Yorkist soldiers lay dead on the field. The Duke himself fell, fighting valiantly, with Sir Davy Hall and many other trusty friends by his side.

The Duke's son, Edmund, Earl of Ulster, a lad of sixteen, "a fair gentleman of maidenlike person," was carried from the field by his tutor, a priest named Robert Apsall. They were encountered before they could make good their escape, by Lord Clifford, a Lancasterian. The boy, quite dismayed, fell down on his knees, imploring mercy.

"Save him," said the chaplain, "he is a prince's son, and may, peradventure, do you good hereafter."

"By God's blood," exclaimed Clifford, looking at him, "thy father slew mine, and so will I thee, and all thy kin," striking him to the heart with his dagger.

"Go now," he said, turning to the chaplain, "and tell his mother and brother what I have done and said."

He afterwards had the lad's head struck off, encircled

with a paper crown, and sent as a present to Queen Margaret—" Beauteous Margaret," as Shakspeare styles her in his Henry VI.—" at which there was much joy and rejoicing."

The father's head, along with that of the Earl of Warwick, were set up on poles over the gate of York. When Edward IV. came to the throne, he had his father's head, and that of the Duke of Warwick, removed, and the heads of four Lancasterian leaders placed there in their stead.

The Earl of Ormond and Wilts, the great enemy of the Duke of York, was taken prisoner at Towton, and beheaded at Newcastle. As he left no legitimate offspring, the title of the Earl of Wiltshire became extinct. An act of attainder was passed the same year against his brothers, John and Thomas Butler, who were the adherents of the Red Rose or Lancasterian party.

CHAPTER LIV.

EDWARD IV.—THE EARL OF DESMOND BEHEADED BY TIPTOFT—TIPTOFT BEHEADED BY THE EARL OF OXFORD—TIPTOFT'S CHARACTER—RIVAL VICEROYS—THE KING'S DEATH.

A.D. 1461-1481. ON the accession of Edward IV., the son of the Duke of York, to the English throne, the large, but nominal estates of the Earldom of Ulster, the Lordship of Connaught, and the Liberty of Meath, became vested in the Crown. Edward sent O'Neill, the real prince and ruler of Ulster, a collar of gold, bearing upon it the arms of the House of York; but O'Neill, notwithstanding that he wore the Englishman's collar, made the Anglo-Norman settlers, on his border, pay him sixty pounds a year of "black rent," or mail. Meath and Kildare paid to O'Conor of Offaly, forty pounds each; Kilkenny and Tipperary, to O'Carroll, a like sum; Limerick, to O'Brien, forty pounds; Cork, to Mac Carthy, forty pounds; and Wexford to Mac Murrough, the King of Leinster, eighty pounds; paid in hard cash, out of the English Exchequer, in Dublin.

Here we have the price, or terms, of the very existence of the English in Ireland. If they were not driven out, it was because Irish chieftains considered it for their interest that they should remain. Forty, sixty, or eighty pieces in gold, had an attraction for the chief of a wild Irish clan, in those days.

In leaving Ireland for England, for the last time, in 1461, the Duke appointed Thomas, seventh Earl of

Kildare, as his Deputy. He was re-appointed Deputy Governor, by Edward IV., when his brother the Duke of Clarence was appointed Lieutenant. In 1462 Clarence nominated Sir Roland Fitz-Eustace, who was succeeded, the same year, by William Sherwood, Bishop of Meath.

Thomas Fitz-Gerald, eighth Earl of Desmond, and son of the Usurper, James, the seventh Earl, was nominated Deputy, the same year, in the place of the Bishop of Meath. He is described as an affable, eloquent, and hospitable man; and, as kind and munificent to the poets and antiquaries of the Irish race. The famous collegiate church of Youghal was endowed by this noble earl.

A difference having arisen between him and the former Deputy, Sherwood, Bishop of Meath, the affair was referred to the King, of whom Desmond had been esteemed the friend and confidant. Edward being satisfied, or apparently satisfied, with Desmond's representations, backed by the Irish Parliament, who certified that the Earl had jeopardised his "life for the King's father, the Duke of York, and had ever been the King's true and faithful liegeman, sent him back to Ireland, re-established in his position, as Deputy Governor, with many tokens of royal favour.

But royal tokens are not always the best evidences of loyal friendship. If the general account of the transaction is to be believed, this Earl had had too much of Edward's confidence, who appears to have been a treacherous friend. It is stated that he and his brother-in-law favoured the projects of the Earl of Warwick, the "King-maker," who was so opposed to the King's marriage with Elizabeth Grey; and that the Earl of Desmond, in the confidence of friendship, recommended

Edward to divorce his queen. It is said by Leland and Cox that this nobleman lost his head for calling the Queen of Edward IV. a "tailor's wife," or widow. But his fault was far more serious than this. " This Lord Thomas, Earl of Desmond,* was greatly beloved by Edward IV., who appointed him to the government of Ireland. Before the two friends parted (on the Earl's leaving England to assume the office of Irish Deputy), King Edward asked him, and entreated him to say whether he saw aught amiss in his conduct, or in the administration of the offices of his kingdom. The Earl assured him he knew of nothing but his unwise marriage with the beautiful widow of Woodville, Lady Elizabeth, whom the King had clandestinely espoused; wherefore, I think, said the Earl to his Majesty, you would do well in divorcing the present Queen, and forming a new alliance with some powerful princess." This advice, which the King took in good part, afterwards cost this Earl Thomas his head. For during some bitter altercation with his Queen, the King said to her:—" Had I hearkened to my cousin Desmond's advice, I should have humbled thy proud spirit."

" What advice ?" said she.

" It matters not now," said he.

" But it does matter, and I must know it : dare that

* Dowling states that this Thomas, whom the Four Masters laud as " the most illustrious of his tribe, for his comeliness, stature, hospitality, chivalry, humanity, bounteousness in bestowing jewels and riches on the laity, clergy, and poets," was not Earl of Desmond, because his father (Garrett, the son of James) was still living. " Vide pedegrew Desmondie quod non fuit comes, patum tum nevebat, et cetera." Usurping his father's title, and going to Tredaff, he [*i. e.*, his father] " gave him his curse, and said, ' Thou shalt have an ill end.' "—*See Annals of Ireland (O'Donovan's),* A.D. 1468.

Irish rebel interfere, and make mischief between man and wife, and they, too, his rightful sovereigns! What was it?"

She pressed him so hard, that he told her all, for he deemed his friend, Desmond, who was then the Deputy of Ireland, safe from her hands. But in the course of time, she obtained his removal, and had my Lord of Worcester—a friend of her own—appointed in his place; who, on his arrival, arraigned the Earls of Desmond and Kildare of "alliance, fosterage, et alterage avecq les Irois enemies du Roy comme en donnant a eux chevaulx et harneis et armors et supportant eux envers les foilax sujects du Roy."

Finding him guilty of treason, on all these counts, they brought the order for beheading him to the King, who refused to sign it; but the Queen, who hated Desmond as bitterly as Herodias did John the Baptist—and with far better reason—obtained the signet by stealth, and placed it, with her own fair hand on the paper, and sent it to Worcester, who instantly acted on it, as he laid claim to some of the Earl's estates. Desmond's brother, and his five sons—when they heard of the Earl's death—all rose in rebellion.

When Edward IV. was made acquainted with the treachery, he became so enraged with the Queen, that she had to leave the court, and fly to a place of safety. Worcester was shortly after beheaded himself. Kildare boldly repaired to Edward, who received him kindly, and had his attainder reversed.

Seventeen years after this wicked execution of the Earl of Desmond, Richard III. wrote—and it is pleasant to hear a word of manly indignation against the unjust shedding of blood, from such a quarter—that the Earl had been "extortiously slain and murdered, by colour of the laws, within Ireland, by certain persons, then having the Government and rule there, against all manhood, reason, and conscience."

But, on the other hand, it must be borne in mind that the adoption of Desmond's advice, of divorcing the Queen, would have bastardised her offspring, and would have probably saved Richard III. the trouble and great scandal of disposing of the two young princes in another way. It is not at all improbable that the Earl of Desmond may have been egged on, to recommend the divorce, by Richard III. himself.

Tiptoft, Earl of Worcester, who had been appointed to fill the place of Viceroy, was esteemed the most learned English nobleman of his day. He had studied at Balliol College, Oxford, had visited Jerusalem, and had delivered a Latin oration in Rome, which brought tears to the eyes of Pope Pius II.

Sir Richard Fitz-Eustace, the Treasurer, and the father-in-law of the Earl of Kildare, was arraigned before Worcester for having incited the Earl of Desmond to assume the Kingship of Ireland. Fitz-Eustace solemnly denied the charge, and Sir John Gilbert, by whom it was made, withdrew before the day of trial, and joined O'Conor, "the enemy of the King of England."

The treacherous execution of the Earl of Desmond raised a host of enemies about the path of the new Deputy, Worcester, with which he was quite unable to contend. The murdered "Earl's sons, being of tender age," his kinsman, Gerald, unfurled his banners and marched, with his English and Irish retainers into Leinster, sweeping the English territories of the pale, with fire and sword. The Irish Parliament passed an act attainting Gerald of treason, but this was all they could do.

The great Earl of Ormond,* in describing the effect of the murder of the Earl on the Irish mind, says, "They have such a cankered malicious rebellion, rooted in them, evyr sithens the putting to excution of one Thomas, Erle of Desmond, at Drogheda, that they ben as far separated from the knowledge of any duty of allegiance, that a subject oght to owe his prince, as a Turke is to believe Christianity. Thei blaspheme the King, and have their ears and eies open every day, gaping to have assistance in this open rebellion, out of Spain."

The Earl of Worcester retired from Ireland in 1468, when his post of Deputy was bestowed upon the Earl of Kildare.

That "false, fleeting, perjured Duke of Clarence" (as he was styled by some), to whom Kildare was Deputy, had never put his foot into the country. But Edward suspected that he and his brother-in-law, Warwick, the King-Maker, intended to establish themselves in Ireland, and perhaps constitute Ireland an independent and separate kingdom. And Warwick, with his standard of

* *The Great Earl of Ormond.*—The Butlers, who had been the ablest and most active opponents of the Duke of York and Edward IV., were restored to royal favour. Edward said Sir John Butler (at one time known as "that great rebel, John of Ormond, Knight") "was the goodliest knight he ever beheld, and the finest gentleman in Christendom; and that if good breeding, nurture, and liberal qualities were lost in the world, they might be all found in the Earl of Ormond."

the "White bear and ragged staff," was just the man to do it.

Edward, sensible of the danger, made a proclamation in York, the 23rd of March, 1470, in which he stated that he had "utterly discharged his brother Clarence from the Viceroyalty of Ireland, for the great and heinous offence he had committed." A thousand pounds in hand, or an annuity of a hundred a year for life, was offered to any one who should capture the Duke of Clarence or his father-in-law, the Earl of Warwick.

When Warwick and Clarence united to drive the King out of the country, and to replace Henry VI. upon the throne (which throne he occupied for a few short months), Tiptoft, Earl of Worcester, was apprehended by the Red Rose, or Lancasterian party, as he lay concealed among the branches of a tree in Havering forest. He was beheaded on Tower Hill, by the sentence of the Earl of Oxford, whose father had been executed on the same spot, by the command of Worcester, whose cruelty was such as to gain him the name of the "Butcher of England." Caxton, the printer, in his edition of Worcester's English version of *Tullius, his Book of Friendship*, published eleven years after the Viceroy's death, says he knew none like him among the lords of the temporality, in science and moral virtue. He speaks of him as "flowering in virtue and cunning;" or, as we should say, in virtue and wit. "Oh good Lord!" he continues, "what great loss was that noble and virtuous and well-disposed lord! What worship he had at Rome, in the presence of our Holy Father, the Pope, and in all other places, till his death; at which death every man might learn to die!"

Could it have been from Tiptoft or Caxton that Addison got the idea of teaching his friend, or the world, how a Christian ought to die?

"I hope, and doubt not," continues the printer, who was a good Catholic, "that God received his soul into his everlasting bliss."

The Four Masters, under date A.D. 1470, give the following account of his death:—"The Earl of Warwick and the Duke of Clarence, cut into quarters, the wreck of the maledictions of the men of Ireland" (or in other words, "the body of the man who had been accursed by the people of Ireland")—"namely, the Saxon Justiciary, by whom the Earl had been destroyed. It was in revenge of Thomas [the eighth Earl of Desmond, whom Tiptoft had beheaded at Drogheda] that this ignominious punishment had been inflicted on him; and the Earl of Kildare was then appointed Lord Justice."

The Four Masters make a mistake in saying that Kildare was then appointed Lord Justice, or chief ruler. Thomas, Earl of Kildare, succeeded the Earl of Worcester, in 1468, as Deputy to the Duke of Clarence, and he continued to hold the position of chief ruler, from 1468 to 1475, when he was superseded by William Sherwood, Bishop of Meath, the declared enemy of the Geraldines; who is supposed to have favoured the compassing of the death of Thomas, Earl of Desmond. The friends of the Earls of Kildare and Desmond brought various charges against him, which his friends in the Irish Parliament recommended him to go to England and meet, in the presence of the King, and his brother Clarence, the Irish Viceroy. The Bishop declined, saying he was so occupied in the field, with hostings, that is, going out at the head of armed soldiers, that he could not quit the camp. But in the end he consented to go, when he was well backed up by his friends, in the Irish Parliament, who loved a warlike or fighting bishop, in their heart of hearts; and who testified, that, to the best of his power, he had defended and governed the King's liege subjects; praying that his Highness would thank him for his services, and give no credence to any charges which might be brought against him.

Thomas, Earl of Kildare, the Bishop's rival for the Viceroyship, died in 1477, and was succeeded by his son, Gerald, whom the Irish Council elected as Irish Governor; but the King nominated Henry, Lord Grey. But in 1478, when the Duke of Clarence was attainted of treason, and put to death, John de la Pole, Duke of Suffolk, was nominated Lieutenant of Ireland.

De la Pole's appointment was cancelled soon after it had been made, in favour of Edward's infant son, George; on which occasion Henry, Lord Grey, was appointed Deputy to the young Prince; but to this appointment of a Deputy, a strong party in the Irish Government took exception. Kildare, who had been elected by the Council, refused to recognise Grey's commission.

Grey landed in Ireland in 1478, attended by a body of 300 archers, and men-at-arms; but James Keating, Prior of Kilmainham, another warlike churchman, being constable of Dublin Castle, refused to admit the new English Deputy; and having garrisoned the fortress, and broken down the draw-bridge, he defied him, his archers, and men-at-arms.

Kildare, as Deputy, summoned a Parliament at Naas,

which sustained his pretensions, and voted him a subsidy; and Grey, as Deputy, held a Parliament at Trim, which voted that the ordinances made at Naas should be cancelled.

What was to be done in this great emergency? Why, the King, who in the hour of difficulty or danger could do a dashing and bold thing, ordered a new great seal to be made, and commanded that they should "damn, annul, and suspend" the old great seal. So Thomas Archbold, Master of the Irish Mint, was directed to engrave a new seal, as near as he could, to the pattern of the old, with the difference of a rose in every part.

It is hard to say when or how the quarrel between the two Deputies would have ended, when the young Prince George, who was the Viceroy or Lieutenant, died, and with him fell his Deputy, Grey.

Edward conferred the Viceroyship on his second son, Richard, Duke of York, giving him Robert Preston, Viscount of Gormanstown, in Ireland, as his Deputy. But a year had not passed before Preston was withdrawn, and his trusty and well-beloved cousin, the eighth Earl of Kildare, appointed or re-appointed in his stead.

After the death of Edward IV., in 1481, Kildare continued in office as Deputy to the young Prince, Richard, who, with his brother Edward V., is supposed to have been murdered in the Tower of London.

CHAPTER LV.

RICHARD III.—HIS IRISH POLICY—HIS PRIVATE AGENTS, LACY AND BARRETT.

A.D. 1483-1485. RICHARD III., understanding there was "grete doubte and ambiguyte" among the Irish, respecting the day that his reign commenced, wrote to "signifie that by the sufferaunce of oure blessed Creatour; that we entered into oure just title, taking upon us oure dignitie royall and supreme governaunce of this our royme, the xxvi day of Juyn, in the yere of oure Lord mccclxxxiii. And after that we woll that ye doo make all writing and records among you."

The doubt respecting the commencement of King Richard's reign, resulted from the public not knowing the exact time his nephews, young King Edward VI., and his brother, Richard, had been put to death in the Tower. There was mystery and dark design in every thing that Richard III. did; so that it can scarcely be said that his picture, drawn by Shakspear, is a caricature, or misrepresentation—with one exception, that Richard was no hunchback.* We learn from Sir Horace Walpole's *Inquiry into the Person and Age of the Long-lived Countess of Desmond*, that she danced with Richard, when Duke of Gloucester, and always affirmed that he was the handsomest man in the room. This *judicium* in

* *No hunchback.*—Hume says, "This Prince was of small stature, humpbacked, and had a harsh and disagreeable countenance; so that his body was, in every particular, no less deformed than his mind."—*Hume's History of England*, vol. 3, p. 281.

refutation of the *spretæ injuria formæ* of the calumniated prince, has been handed down, by oral tradition; but it had no effect in removing the unsightly protuberance from King Richard's shoulders. Neither Garrick nor Keane dared to touch that protuberance.

Richard's character, for design, cunning, and ability, are clearly manifest in his administration of Irish affairs.

He appointed his only son, Edward, who was eleven years old, as Viceroy. This was a matter of course, adopted by most of his predecessors, in order to keep the Deputy, who was the real governor, in check.

Before nominating the Deputy, he sent over a confidential messenger, named William Lacy, with private letters and secret instructions, telling Master William to be sure to regulate his words and conduct according to those he should speak to.

Before William Lacy opened anything to the Council, he was to "practice to have speech with" and learn the disposition of Gerald Earl of Kildare; as a great deal depended on the way in which the Earl might receive the offer of Deputy; or the terms he might make, in accepting it. Richard knew it would be impossible to pass him by.

Master William Lacy sees the Earl (who had his own private suspicions, of Richard); he tells him of the "special favour and tenderness" of the King towards him, not only on account of his good fame, and noble disposition, but likewise in consideration of his great services to his father, the late Duke of York; and asks him if he will accept the post of Deputy Viceroy, to his son Edward, for one year; the continuation of the appointment to depend on the royal pleasure. If the Earl agreed to accept the appointment, on these terms, he was to repair to England, at once, and arrange with the King about the future government.

Kildare had no objection to accept the office of Deputy, but not for one year, but for nine or ten, with a salary of £1,000 per annum; and if the King would throw in the manor of Leixlip, about nine miles from Dublin, and the custody of the Castle of Wicklow, it would smooth the way for a final arrangement. As for going to London, to see the King, who was in the habit of receiving his guests in the Tower, that was a more serious affair than governing Ireland. At any rate, before going there, he should have the King's bond, counter-signed and sealed by the principal English nobles, guaranteeing his safe return.

Richard agreed to the Earl of Kildare's terms, for accepting the office of Deputy, but marvelled that he should desire any promises, seals, or writing of any of his lords, insuring his safe return from England. The King's own honour should be esteemed a tower of strength. And so no doubt it would have been, if the Earl had never heard of any other *Tower*.

Matters had advanced so far, when Richard's only son, Prince Edward, the Viceroy, died, and the office was conferred on John de la Pole, the King's nephew; the Earl of Kildare still occupying the post of Deputy, or active ruler.

Richard, at this time, sent over another secret agent to Ireland, one Thomas Barrett, of Somerset, monk, who had been appointed to a bishoprick in Connaught. Barrett had received a passport, which directed all Government officers to receive, and entertain him, and his servants, well, and courteously. This must have been against the grain of those who held Barrett as a royal spy.

The object of Barrett's mission was, no doubt, to collect all the information he could respecting Irish affairs, generally, and report to his master. As a churchman, he would gain access where others would be denied admittance, and scent or spy out treason, in holes and corners, where no one suspected its existence.

Barrett informed Kildare that the special and singular cause of his mission was to incite him, by all possible means, to bring the earldom of Ulster into the King's power. Barrett showed Kildare the King's instructions, which were, of course, manufactured for the occasion. " No man," says these instructions, " can do more than his cousin, Kildare, seeing that the great O'Neill hath married the Earl's sister," which great O'Neill, on account of that marriage, the King would accept to favour, as his brother Edward had done, giving him his "livery," or collar of gold, with its white boar and circlet of roses and suns.

Bishop Barrett, having done his best to win the great O'Neill, by the influence of his brother-in-law, the Earl of Kildare, directed his steps to the south and west, with letters to Lords Barry and Roche, to John and Piers Power, to Nangle, Bermingham, and to his namesake Barrett, the most Irish of all the English in Munster; and last, but not least, to James, the ninth Earl of Desmond, the son of Thomas, who had been beheaded by Tiptoft, the Earl of Worcester, at Drogheda; which Thomas, Earl of Desmond, had jeopardised himself for the King's father, at " divers seasons of great necessity." The King had "inward compassion" for the unjust execution of the Earl's father; but then the King's own relatives and friends, even his own dear brother, Clarence—and he might have added, his two sweet nephews—were subjected to the like unjust treatment; so that he must not take the death of a father too much to heart.

This James, Earl of Desmond, was at this time but twenty-five years of age, and unmarried; so Bishop Barrett conveyed to him the royal desire that he would not throw himself away, by marrying an Irish woman; that he himself intended to provide for him in such wise, and of such noble blood, as should redound to the weal and honour of himself, and of all his friends and kinsmen. The King also recommended that he should renounce the wearing and usage of the Irish array, and adopt English apparel, after the fashion of the gowns, doublets, hose, and bonnets, which he sent him. The royal parcel contained a long gown of cloth of gold, lined with satin and damask; two doublets, one of velvet, and another of crimson satin; three shirts and kerchiefs, three stomachers, three pair of hose, one of scarlet, one of violet, and the third black; three bonnets, two hats, and two tippets of velvet. Think of these, surmounted with the collar of gold, with the white bear and roses and suns, styled the "King's livery;" and what dog in Munster, in his "bra brass collar," with his master's name inscribed thereon, could hold up his head or tail more proudly than this ninth Earl of Desmond?

In what manner or mood he received these presents—which were not altogether unusual—we cannot say; but as touching his marriage with some English lady of noble blood, young James of Desmond preferred to choose for himself, and married an O'Brien.

> "Those Geraldines, those Geraldines, not long our air they breathed,
> Not long they fed on venison, in Irish waters seathed,
> Not often had their children been by Irish mothers nursed,
> When from their full and genial hearts an Irish feeling burst.
> The English monarch strove in vain, by law and force and bribe,
> To win from Irish thoughts and ways, this *more* than Irish tribe,
> For still they clung to fosterage, to brehon, cloke, and bard;
> What king dare say to Geraldine, your Irish wife discard?"

It is thought that Thomas, the sixth earl, lost the earldom, for marrying an Irish maiden beneath his rank. The poet Moore has immortalised the memory of this earl and his beautiful bride, in the sonnet commencing—

> "You who call it dishonour to bow to this flame."

This young nobleman, hunting on the banks of the Feal, near the town of Listowel, strayed from his companions and lost his way; and, being benighted, took shelter in the house of Mac Cormac, one of his dependents. Mac Cormac had a fair daughter, of whom the young Earl became suddenly enamoured. He wooed and won her heart, and married her; but his alliance with the humble maiden excited the brutal pride of his followers, who regarded the indulgence of his honourable love as an unpardonable offence; they, therefore, deserted his person and pennon, and selected his uncle as leader and chief. He, with a broken heart, fled, with his beautiful bride, to Rouen, in France, where he died. It is to the honour of the heroic and chivalrous Henry V. of England, who was then in France, that he expressed his admiration of the young Earl's character, conduct, and choice, by attending, as chief mourner, at his grave.

CHAPTER LVI.

THE GREAT EARL OF KILDARE—LAMBERT SYMNEL CROWNED IN DUBLIN—GERALD, THE SON OF THE GREAT EARL—SILKEN THOMAS—THE LAST EARL OF DESMOND.

A.D. 1485-1509. SIX months after Henry VII. came to the throne, John de la Pole, nephew of King Richard, and Lieutenant of Ireland, was superseded in his office, by Jasper of Hatfield, Duke of Bedford, who commanded the left wing of Henry's army at Bosworth field; but Gerald, Earl of Kildare, continued to hold the position of Deputy, or Irish Governor.

Henry was aware that the feeling and good wishes of the Geraldines, and of the Irish colonists were with the House of York; but he felt convinced that Ireland could not be governed without, or in opposition to, the great Irish Earl, Gerald of Kildare, who was not only strong in his possessions and following, but also in his family connexions or alliances with the principal Irish chieftains. His eldest daughter, Eleanor, had married Mac Carthy Reagh, the principal Irish chieftain of Cork; his sister Alice was the wife of Con O'Neill, of Ulster; another sister, Eustacia, had married Mac William Burke, Lord of Clanrickarde, in Connaught, while Oliver, the Earl's son, had married Meadbh, the daughter of O'Conor of Offaly. Then there were the Fitz-Geralds of Munster, another powerful branch of the same great family, with the Earls of Desmond at its head.

What could the King do under such circumstances? The only house which had hitherto curbed the power and ambition of the Fitz-Geralds was the House of Ormond, but Thomas Butler, Earl of Ormond, had taken up his abode in England, and was one of Henry's Privy Council, and his cousin, Sir Piers Butler, who represented the Earl of Ormond in Ireland, had married Margaret, the sister of the Earl of Kildare.

To attempt to displace, or make war on such an Anglo-Irish chieftain, would have been to make war on the Irish themselves, both Norman and Celt, with whom this great earl was such a favourite. And that he possessed most of the qualities and qualifications to win the hearts of a warlike and half-civilised nation, we shall show before we conclude this chapter.

The cautious Henry did not only not dare to dismiss the Earl from his post of Deputy Viceroy, but was compelled to wink at his overt acts of treason against the royal person, in supporting a dangerous claimant to the Crown, and taking part in a sham coronation in Dublin.

Henry had not been seated on the English throne two years, before a report got bruited abroad that Richard, the son of the late Duke of Clarence, was alive, and would one day come forward and assert his undoubted rights.

Such prophecies not unfrequently lead to their own fulfilment. The rumour spread in Ireland, where the grandson of the good Viceroy, the Duke of York, could not fail to be welcomed, and where the white rose was always the favourite. Nor was it forgotten that the Duke of Clarence was born in Dublin.

When the rumour had got well abroad, and the Irish

colonists were on the tip-toe of expectation, "a learned Oxford cleric" arrived in Ireland, with a lad of noble appearance and bearing. There was an evident mystery about both, and private conferences were held with persons of position and authority, when it came to be generally understood, or believed, that the real and true heir of the English throne was in Dublin. "How like the old duke." "And his grandmother, God rest her soul, the Rose of Raby," were the exclamations of some of the old Dublin folk, who remembered their favourite Viceroy, the Duke of York.

The Viceroy, and other noblemen, who were personally acquainted with the Duke of Clarence and his family, examined the boy, and put a number of searching questions to him, respecting his former life, and private and domestic affairs; which he answered with great accuracy, and without hesitation; so that Kildare and his brother, Sir Thomas Fitz-Gerald, the Chancellor, and other chief persons who met the lad, felt quite sure he was what he represented himself—Richard, Earl of Warwick, the son of the late Duke of Clarence.

Having satisfied themselves on this point, the boy was committed to the care of Sir Thomas Fitz-Gerald, the Lord Deputy's brother, who carried him to his castle, and treated him as a royal personage.

He arrived in Dublin in May, 1487, and on Whit-Sunday, the 24th of the same month, he was anointed and crowned in the same city. The ceremony was performed in the presence of the Deputy, Kildare, John de la Pole, Earl of Lincoln, nephew of Richard III., and in the presence of Baron Lovell, of Northamptonshire, and in the presence of the Archbishop of Dublin, and of the Prior of Kilmainham, and of the Chancellor, Judges, Privy Councillors, and principal Irish nobles, who performed fealty and did homage to him, as King of England and Lord of Ireland. His claims were also explained and set forth in a sermon, delivered on the occasion, by the Bishop of Meath.

There can be no doubt that these noblemen firmly believed that the handsome lad, who had won all hearts, was really the son of the Duke of Clarence. Even the King's friends, who retained their allegiance intact, had to confess that he was "surely an honourable boy to look upon, and did not shame his royal robes."

Kildare, who was too great and honourable a man to practise such a deceit, or support a mere adventurer to the English throne, assumed the high and dangerous responsibility of accepting the office of Regent and Protector to the Royal Pretender. He convened a Parliament, which issued proclamations and writs, and other documents, in the name of the young King, Richard IV., as he was styled. Coin was issued from the Irish Mint, bearing his image. The spiritual peers voted a subsidy, in order to procure a decision, or bull, from Rome, in his favour. It was positively dangerous to breathe even a suspicion of his legitimacy, or royal descent. Archbishop Ottaviano, who opposed the subsidy, would have been killed for so doing, by John de la Pole, if the Earl of Kildare had not interfered to save his life.

But those men gave a still more striking proof of their conviction that the boy brought over to Ireland was what he was represented. Sir Thomas Fitz-Gerald resigned his post as Chancellor, and levied an army, in which he was joined by Lincoln, Lovel, Plunkett, Swart, and many others, in order to place the noble-looking boy upon the English throne. They landed in Lancashire, on the 4th June, 1487, and proceeded thence to Yorkshire; but the proclamation of a new claimant to the English throne was not received with the same credence in England that it had gained in Ireland, so that the Yorkshiremen fought shy of the affair.

King Henry, who had received early intimation of the proposed landing, had scouts, stationed along the western coast. He came up with the Irish party, which was under the command of De la Pole, Earl of Lincoln, at the village of Stoke, about a mile from Newark-on-Trent. The force under the command of De la Pole was greatly out-numbered by the royal army. Nothwithstanding his disparity in numbers, Lincoln marched down the hill, and fell, with tremendous power and spirit, upon Henry's army. The Irish soldiers fought boldly, and stuck to it valiantly, although unprovided with armour, against the arrows of the English archers. The battle raged for three hours, with hand to hand close fighting, and it was not until Lincoln, Swart, Fitz-Gerald, Plunkett, and 4,000 of their followers, lay stretched on the field, that Henry could claim the victory.

It was firmly believed, in London, that Henry had been defeated; so fully believed, that the Lieutenant of the Tower offered the Earl of Surrey (who was confined there for fighting against Henry at Bosworth-field), his liberty.

The young "Pretender," in whose interests this bloody battle was fought, and his attendant Simond, the learned priest of Oxford, were captured. The latter was immured for life, in fetters, in a dark dungeon; and the former, whom Henry's adherents asserted was the son of Thomas Symnel, was incarcerated in the Tower of London, where it was said he had been confined previous to this attempt on the English throne; and from which he had escaped, by the aid of the learned priest of Oxford.

The common report is, that Henry held the lad in such contempt, that he made him a turnspit, in the royal kitchen, and subsequently, a master of the royal falcons. But Henry was too astute and suspicious a prince, to leave so dangerous a claimant to his throne, at liberty; a lad for whom the Irish nation, with its nobles, rose in arms, as one man, compelling him to fight the battle of Bosworth-field over again, or a worse battle than Bosworth-field.

When the King and his Council first heard that the Irish had taken up a boy, who was said to be the son of the Duke of Clarence, and had proclaimed him as king, they brought forward a sham claimant, a half idiotic youth, as the Irish impostor; who was paraded through the streets of London, to the great amusement of the people. It is probable that this lad, named Lambert Symnel, became a turnspit, and master of the falcons; and that the true heir was returned to the Tower, from which he had escaped.

Francis Lovel, Baron of Northamptonshire, who had been living at the Court of the Dowager Duchess of Burgundy, (the daughter of the Duke of York), was supposed to have escaped, after the battle of Stoke, and to have been drowned in the river Trent; but there is another and more reliable statement, that he secreted himself in a vault at Minster-Lovel. This impression gains authority from the fact, that the skeleton of a man, seated at a table, with book, paper, and pens before him, was discovered about two hundred years ago, in the vaults of that old Minster.

But what punishment was inflicted on the head and front of this bold attempt to place the noble-looking boy, or pretended son of Clarence, on the throne of Henry VII? None that we know of. It was the King's policy to let the treason storm blow by, after securing the person of the lad, styled Lambert Symnel. The King was put to "the pin of his collar" to rule England, and had no time to take up arms, to hunt down that great Irish lion, the Earl of Kildare. Henry, writing to the citizens of Waterford, in October, 1487, says that "the Earl of Kildare, with the support of the people of Dublin, still adhered to their seditious opinions." It was more than opinions with the Earl and the people of Dublin. They crowned a rival king, in Dublin; and took up arms and entered England to make war against Henry, whom they solemnly declared they would not have to reign over them. The English Council was as much afraid of "riling" the great Irish lion, as the King himself, for in a Parliament, convened in November, 1487, they attainted the *English* nobles and gentlemen, who fought against the King at Stoke, but adopted no such measures with respect to the Irish nobles, who organised and boldly carried out the rebellious movement.

Instead of pains and penalties, friendly negotiations were commenced with the Earl and his party; and Sir Richard Edgecombe, a member of the Privy Council, was sent over, and directed to enter into communication with the Anglo-Irish leaders; and to deliver royal pardons to all who cared to obtain them, or were willing to become faithful and obedient subjects for the future.

The independence and sang-froid with which the Anglo-Irish nobles received the English Commissioner, and his pardons, was amusingly displayed by what occurred at Kinsale. He arrived in that harbour, after a four days' sail, and sent word to De Courcy, the thirteenth baron of Kinsale, to repair to him on board. De Courcy replied, that if he expected his homage, he must come ashore to receive it, as he " possessed no authority, under his commission, till he had set foot in Ireland."

Sir Richard Edgecombe sailed from Kinsale to Waterford, where he was loyally received; and from Waterford to Dublin, at which port he was informed that the Lord Deputy, the Earl of Kildare, " *had gone on a pilgrimage* " —probably to St. Patrick's Purgatory—and would be absent from Dublin for four or five days. If rebellions against the authority of the King of England, were placed by him in the category of sins, for which he had to atone, four or five days would never have sufficed for his shriving.

To pass the time, Sir Richard went to Malahide, where he got "good cheer from Sir Peter Talbot and his lady," and then returned to Dublin, where he took up his abode in a Dominican friary; where he was "put to great costs and charges."

But after five days, the Earl of Kildare returned, with 200 horsemen, and sent messengers to conduct the Commissioner to Thomas Court; and in the great chamber of that vice-regal palace, surrounded by Anglo-Irish lords, and with all the majesty of an Irish king, he received and welcomed him.

Sir Richard delivered his letters, and asked for a private audience. The question for decision was, would the Earl and his party become *bona-fide* "English subjects." The Earl asked for five days to consider the matter, and in the meantime invited Sir Richard to his Castle, at Maynooth, where he had "great cheer," without being put to "great costs," as he had been at the Dominican Friary.

At the expiration of the five days, Sir Richard got impatient and irritated at the Earl's feigned and unreasonable delays, and told him right plainly and sharply of his unfitting behaviour.

In the end the Earl and his party agreed to become "English subjects," and to give good sureties for their good faith; but they refused to sign the bond, produced by Sir Richard, and requested him to desist from demanding it.

To this Sir Richard replied " with short answers, and right fierce and angry words;" when Kildare and the Council plainly told him, "We will not sign your bond; rather than do so, we will become Irish, every one of us."

Sir Richard, feeling it was no use to press the bond any further, and that he must accept the best security for the Earl's future loyal conduct he could procure, cogitated "through the night on as sure an oath as he could," which oath was to be made on the Host; and lest a fraud should be practised, he had the Host consecrated by his own chaplain.

The Lords of the Council, having assembled in the King's Chamber, in the Monastery of Thomas Court, Sir Richard, on behalf of the King, received the homage of Kildare, and placed the collar of the King's livery about his neck. When this portion of the proceeding was over, they retired to the chapel, where the Earl was shriven and absolved from the curse he had incurred, in opposing the King of England, contrary to the Pope's bull. The priest at the altar then held out the Host, which he had divided into three parts, and Kildare, extending his right hand over the parts, repeated his solemn oath of allegiance to Henry, concluding with the words, "So help me this Holy Sacrament, in form of bread, here present, to my salvation, or damnation."

There is no good evidence, that, after this, the Earl was guilty of disloyalty; although he was invited in May, 1492, to support the pretensions of Perkin Warbeck, who called himself Richard, Duke of York, the second son of Edward IV., who is supposed to have been put to death, in the Tower of London, at the direction of his uncle, Richard III.

Warbeck landed in Cork, where he was received and countenanced by the Mayor, John Walters, and the principal citizens. He wrote to the Earl of Kildare and the Earl of Desmond, to aid him in dethroning Henry; but before he could receive replies, left for Paris, to which he had been invited by Charles VIII. He was warmly and affectionately welcomed to Flanders, by the Duchess of Burgundy, who acknowledged him as her nephew, assigning him a guard of thirty persons, in scarlet and blue livery. He sailed from Flanders in 1495, with 600 followers, and made a landing on the coast of Kent, where 160 of his people were made prisoners, and afterwards hanged. Not liking his reception in Kent, he resolved to try Cork, a second time, where he met with much kindness, and little aid; so he determined to try Scotland. He there married a daughter of the Earl of Huntley, and persuaded the Scots to invade England; but a "treacherous peace" having been concluded between England and Scotland, he resolved, for a third time, to visit his Irish friends.

He arrived in Cork in July, 1497, where he was joined by the Earl of Desmond, and the Duke of Lincoln, who commenced the siege of Waterford; which made a successful resistance, beating back the assailants; for which spirited conduct, they received, with other honours, the motto for their city arms, *Intacta manet Waterfordia*. Henry, like a wise king, reserved his more substantial favours for his enemies. The Earl of Desmond, who provided both men and arms for the siege, was not only pardoned, but received a grant of the customs of Limerick, and other, the King's hereditaments, in the ports, city, and towns of Cork, Kinsale, Baltimore, and Youghal.

John Walters, Mayor of Cork, was treated somewhat differently. He was tried at Westminster, found guilty of treason, and hanged at Tyburn, with his friend and protégé, Master Perkin Warbeck. Their heads were set up on London Bridge.

The Earl of Kildare, who was suspected of aiding Perkin Warbeck, was superseded as Deputy. He went to England to defend himself against this, and various other charges of disloyalty and violence, and was kindly received by the King. When accused of burning the Cathedral of Cashel, he confessed the fact, observing, "By ——, I would never have done it, if it had not been told me the Archbishop was within;" at which reply the King laughed right merrily. The King could not but enjoy this stroke of grim Irish humour, inasmuch, as the Archbishop of Cashel had joined the confederation in support of Warbeck.

When asked, previous to his trial, to select his own counsel, and told by the King he should have whatever good fellow he chose, he replied, without hesitation, "Then marry, I can see no better man in England than your highness."

"A wiser man might have made a worse choice," was Henry's reply.

When some one objected against him, that all Ireland could not rule this Earl, the King remarked, "Then, in good faith, this Earl shall rule all Ireland."

The Earl returned from England, in 1496, to take charge of the Irish Government. He convened a Parment in 1498, the first held under Poyning's law; which decided, that all proposed laws, or "bills," as we now style them, should be submitted to the King and Council, before they became law.

The first act of this Parliament was the passing of a "bill" to annul the attainder against the Earl himself, for high treason.

In 1503 he was summoned to England, where the King expressed his entire approval of his Irish administration. I believe it was on this occasion he was created a Knight of the Garter.

There was no change made in the Irish Government, on the accession of Henry VIII. to the English throne, in 1509. Gerald, the old Earl of Kildare, who had been Lord Deputy to Prince Henry, retained his office, when the Prince became King.

He made a warlike expedition to Munster, in 1510, against the Mac Carthys, in which he was assisted by James, son of the Earl of Desmond. He took the Castle of Kanturk, in Duhallow, and the Castle of Palace,

situated among the Lakes of Killarney. The Castle of
Palace, otherwise Caislean na Cartha, was the principal
residence of Mac Carthy Mor, or More, which signifies
"great." It stood on an eminence, to the north of the
Lower Lake of Killarney, near the entrance to the Gap
of Dunloe. The Mac Carthy More must have had a
taste for the sublime and beautiful. We may also add,
for the tragic and horrible, for the field, in front of his
castle, still called *Park-an croh*, or the "Gallow's-field,"
was the place where Mac Carthy dispensed *justice*. This
castle was destroyed in 1837, by a road jobber, who
wanted the stones. Oh, shade of Mac Carthy More!

The old Earl, after visiting Killarney, directed his
footsteps to Limerick, where he was joined by Hugh
Roe O'Donnell; so they resolved to cross the Shannon,
and visit their old friend Turlough O'Brien, who collected a large army to give the Lord Deputy a warm
welcome. The armies encamped so near each other, the
first night, that the men's voices were distinctly heard
from the opposite camps. Whether the Deputy, or his
friend, O'Donnell, heard anything which led them to
conclude they would meet a warmer welcome than they
desired, we cannot say; but of this there can be no
doubt, that the next morning they packed up their traps
and marched off; but not before they had been eased of
some of the *impedimenta* of war, by O'Brien, who "took
large spoil and slew several of the English," among
whom we meet the name of Barnwell, of Cricktown, of
Meath, and a baron of Kent.

The Lord Deputy crossed the Shannon again, in 1512,
and took the Castles of Roscommon and Cavetown, and
then visited the Curlieu mountains, where he met and

renewed his treaty with his friend, O'Donnell, who had just returned after a pilgrimage to Rome.

The old Earl's last campaign was to O'Carroll's country, where he commenced the siege of the Castle of O'Banan's-leap; but failing to take it, he retired to Athy, where he died, full of years and warlike honour. It is supposed that the immediate cause of his death was an old wound, he had received in O'Moore's country. He was interred in Christ Church, Dublin, and his son, Gerald or Garrett Oge, reigned in his stead.

Stanihurst describes the Earl of Kildare as "a mighty man of stature, full of honour and courage; open and plain, hardly able to rule himself, when moved by anger; not so sharp as short, being easily displeased and sooner appeased. Being in a rage with some of his servants, one of his horsemen offered Master Boice, a favourite squire, a horse, if he would pluck a hair from the Earl's beard. "Done," said Boice, walking up to the Earl, who was "parching in the head of his choler," may it please your good lordship, one of your horsemen has promised me a choice horse, if I snip one hair from your beard." "Well," quoth the Earl, foregoing his anger, "I agree thereto; but if thou pluck more than one, I promise thee to bring my fist to thy ear."

The noble old Earl was succeeded by his son Gerald, as Irish Deputy. He commenced his reign, or rule, by making fierce war upon some of the Irish chieftains. O'Moore of Leix, who defied his authority, was driven, for protection, to the covert of his woods. O'Reilly, of Cavan, he slew, after rasing his castle to the ground. Shaun O'Toole he also slew, sending his head as a present to the Mayor of Dublin; as some compensation to the inhabitants of that city for the raid made upon them, by the O'Byrnes and O'Tooles, in Cullenswood, on that ever memorable Black Monday. He marched from Wicklow to Clonmel, which he took by surprise, and returned from his rapid expedition, laden with trophies and spoil.

The next year he marched into Ulster, storming the castles of Dungannon and Dundrum, leaving his mark in fire and blood behind him.

Such a course of prosperous conquest could not fail to produce many enemies, and amongst the number, Cardinal Wolsey, who caused the Earl to be summoned to England, to answer certain charges touching his loyalty.

Thomas Howard, Earl of Surrey, was appointed Lord Deputy, during the absence of Earl Gerald. Surrey was the son of the Earl who won the great battle of Flodden Field.

On the son of the hero of Flodden, devolved the unknightly office, or duty, of collecting materials of accusation from the servants and followers of the Earl of Kildare, against their lord. The accusations were of disloyalty; but most of them were of a very indefinite character. The principal charge was that of having written to O'Carroll, telling him to "keep good peace to the English in Ireland, until an English Deputy came there. But when an English Deputy come, then do thy best to make war upon the English." As this letter, if such ever existed, was not forthcoming, it was proposed by Wolsey that William Delahide, the Earl's secretary, should be sent to the Tower, and tortured, to make him confess having written it. But against such a proceeding Surrey, himself, indignantly protested.

The Earl, while in England, waiting his trial, seems to

have been unaware of the machinations of Wolsey, Surrey, and Henry VIII. against him; for he was well received at Court, and was one of the royal train of distinguished noblemen, who accompanied Henry, when he met the King of France, on the "Field of the Cloth of Gold." He was even allowed and encouraged, when in England, to pay his addresses to the Lady Elizabeth Gray, daughter of the Marquis of Dorset, to whom he was afterwards married.

The evidence proving insufficient, the Earl returned to Ireland, and Lord Deputy Surrey, who went there to prepare materials for the accusation, withdrew. Kildare was restored, after a short time, to his office of Deputy.

But Wolsey is prepared with a new accusation. He accuses the Earl of conniving, with his kinsman, the Earl of Desmond, in promoting a French invasion of Ireland. On this charge he is committed to the Tower of London. But the Earl of Surrey, now Duke of Norfolk, and the Marquis of Dorset, his father-in-law, and several other persons of high position, whose hearts the Earl has managed to win, become security for his future faith and allegiance. So he is released; and, after an absence of two or three years, returns to Ireland, where he is received with great rejoicing. There is a procession, headed by the Mayor of Dublin and the principal citizens, who meet their conquering hero on the Green of Mary's Abbey.

But there are new charges of disloyalty in the wind. He is again wanted in London, and receives a royal summons to go there. "Men think here," says the Earl of Ossory, writing to Cromwell, who proved even a more dangerous enemy to Gerald than Wolsey, "that all the parchment and wax in England, will not bring Kildare hither again."

Ossory was mistaken; Gerald of Kildare, who was unacquainted with the deep and treacherous character of Henry VIII., obeyed the summons, and, after some delay, was clapped into the Tower, where it was reported he was beheaded; but this was not the case.

His son, "Silken Thomas,"* hears the report, and marches upon Dublin, appears before the Council, and publicly renounces his allegiance to the English monarch, delivering up the sword and robes of state, which he held as his father's Deputy.

Cromer, the Lord Chancellor, implored the young man, with tears in his eyes, to revoke what he had done, and to retain the sword of state.

At that moment the Irish bard, or rhymer of the family rose, and entreated the youth, who was scarcely twenty-one, to revenge his father's death.

The rhymer's words struck a cord, which vibrated through the heart and soul, of Silken Thomas and his hundred and forty horsemen. So, casting aside the sword of state, "which weighed nothing in his estimation against his father's blood," he rushed, with his followers from the Council Chamber.

As the rising of this young man was without forethought or arrangement, and as the first act of revenge of his wild horsemen was the murder of Archbishop Allen, the hereditary enemy of the Earl of Kildare, the

---

* *Silken Thomas.*—He was called "Silken Thomas," and the "Silken Lord," from the material and richness of his clothing, caparisons, banners, &c.

enterprise turned out a most signal failure, the bare report of which killed his father, Gerald. After numerous defeats and misfortunes, the foolish youth delivered himself up to Sir Leonard Gray, the new Viceroy, who shipped him off to London. He was sent as prisoner to the Tower, where—if we are to believe his own letters—he was shamefully neglected. "I never had ony money since I came to prison, but 'a nobull,' and have neither hosyn, doublet, shoys, nor shirt; and should have none still, but that pore [fellow] prysoners, of their gentlyness, hath somehow given me hosyn, shoys, and old shyrtes." He speaks of himself as "barefote and barelegyd, divers times, whan it hath not been very warm."

Think of the tenderly reared and richly attired Silken Thomas, Earl of Kildare, the very beau-ideal, or, more correctly, Beau Brummel, of Irish Anglo-Norman knights, "barefote and barelegyd," accepting a pair of old trowsers, shoes, or a shirt, of a kind fellow-prisoner! Who was the Lieutenant of the Tower at this time?

We find there were "words of comfort spoken to Lord Thomas, to induce him to yield himself up, more especially as regarded his life." In other words, his life, *at least*, was promised him, by Lord Leonard Gray. Henry, writing to the Deputy, says, "The doying whereof"—that is the apprehension of the Earl—"we accept thankfully; yet, if he had been apprehended, after such sorte as was convenable to his deservyinges, the same had been much more thankful and better to our contentacion."—*Henry VIII. to Skeffyngton, S. P.*, cvi.

Perhaps the promise of the Lord Deputy, that the Earl's life should be spared, caused Henry to have him neglected, hoping to dispose of his prisoner in this way. But the royal malice could not brook the long delay,.so the noble young Earl was sent from the Tower, to Tyburn, where he was hanged, with five of his uncles.

The object of this *coup de main*, was to dispose of the whole house of Kildare, by one fell swoop ; to cut down, or root up, the family tree, or, more correctly, to lop off the Kildare branch of the great Geraldine tree. But two younger brothers of Silken Thomas, sons of the late Earl, by Elizabeth Gray, daughter of the Marquis of Dorset, yet remained, the elder of whom was Gerald, between twelve and thirteen years of age, and the younger, Edward. These two boys were the *spes gregis*, the hope of the flock. Around them Irish Anglo-Norman knights and numerous Irish chieftains clustered, like bees around a new queen, with lances in rest and skeins as sharp and polished as the stings of wasps. The younger of the boys was privately and mysteriously conveyed to his mother, who was then at Beaumanoir; but of the elder, his brave aunt, Lady Eleanor, the sister of the late Earl, and the widow of Mac Carthy Reagh, took charge, while residing at Kilbrittan Castle, county Cork.

But Lady Eleanor was, just at this time, about to marry the great Irish chieftain, O'Donnell, "being partly moved thereto" by the hope of securing a strong arm to defend her out-lawed nephew, whose only offence was his claim to his father's title and inheritance. Brabason, writing to Aylmer, says, "The late Erle of Kildare's sister is gone to be married to Manus O'Donnell. With whom is gone young Gerrot, Delahide [his father's secretary], and others, which I like not. I was never in despair of Ireland till now."

Lady Eleanor left Kilbrittan Castle in the month of June, 1538, accompanied by the young Earl and her own son, Mac Carthy Reagh, who was first cousin to the Earl. They passed through Thomond and Galway, on their way to O'Donnell's country, and were escorted from Galway, to the end of her journey, by Ulick de Burgh, afterwards created Earl of Clanricarde.

A lady riding pillion-wise, and safely, from one end of Ireland to the other, accompanied by two boys, one of whom was out-lawed, was significant of Irish sympathy with the Earls of Kildare. The Earl of Desmond, or O'Brien of Thomond, or O'Conor of Connaught, or De Burgh of Galway, might have made a handsome sum of the boy's head, but they spurned it. Henry was savage with his Deputy, for allowing the prey to escape; but it was not his fault.

The travellers were met, at the end of their journey, at O'Donnell's mansion, by O'Neill, who entered into a close compact with O'Donnell and O'Conor, for the future protection of young Gerald, who was appointed a guard of "twenty-four horsemen, well armed and apparelled, to wait upon him, at his pleasure." From this young shoot sprang the present top branch of the great Geraldine tree.

Formerly, and for centuries, this great Geraldine tree had two top branches, the Kildare and the Desmond branches. One of these is still green and fruitful; but the other was lopped off, in the days of Queen Elizabeth.

It is a sad story, or picture, with which to conclude this volume of "HISTORICAL PORTRAITS," but I suppose I must tell it.

Sir William Pelham, Irish Viceroy in 1582, writes to the Queen:—"The Earl [of Desmond], without rest anywhere, fleeth from place to place, and maketh mediation for peace by the Countess, who, yesterday, I licensed to have speech of with me here, whose abondance of tears bewrayed sufficientlie the miserable state both of herself, her husband, and their followers." Again:— "The Earl is unhowsed of all goods, and must noe tread the woods and bogs, which he will do, as unwieldily as any man in the world, of his age. He shrowded himself in glyns and swamps, and in the winter of 1582, kept a cold Christmas, in Kilgueg Woods."

On the 4th of January, 1583, his hiding-place was discovered. He was now stricken down with palsy and ague. The hovel in which he and his lady slept, was surrounded. He narrowly escaped in his shirt, and both he and she remained, all night, under the bank of the neighbouring river, up to their chins in water.

Lurking in wild desert places, and feeding on horse-flesh and carrion, the famishing Earl sent a party of kern to seize on some cattle in the neighbourhood. The plunderers stripped the wife and children of the owner, who, obtaining the assistance of some soldiers from Castlemain Fort, went in pursuit.

After a weary chase, the military refused to proceed any further; but on being promised two beeves of the prey, they went forward. "The track was followed, by daylight, to Balliore, and by the moonshine to Glenaginty, under Sliavloghra, where the chasers climbed the hill, above the glinne, to spy whether they might see onie fire in the wood, or hear onie stir; and when they got to the top, they saw a fire beneath them. One stole down, and saw a cabin, with a number of men asleep. As day dawned, the whole party descended, and entered the cabin, with a great cry. Those within rushed out, leaving an infirm old man behind." One of the soldiers, Kelly, struck at him, and almost severed his hand from his body. He again raised his sword, to despatch him, when the old man cried out,. "*I am the Earl of Desmond: spare my life.*" He was carried off alive, on the backs of his captors; but the men being weary, and fearing a rescue, held a council, at which they resolved to despatch him. Having laid him on the ground, and held him there, Kelly cut his head from his body, for which there was ten thousand pounds reward.

The head was taken to the Black Earl of Ormond, the Earl of Desmond's son-in-law, who had it pickled, placed in a pipkin, and forwarded as a "dainty dish" to the Queen. It was afterwards impaled on London Bridge.

The Earl's vast estates, in the counties of Cork, Waterford, and Limerick, were divided out amongst English "Undertakers," and adventurers. Sir Walter Raleigh got 12,000 acres, including the town of Youghal. The Poet Spenser got 3,000 acres, with Kilcoleman Castle, where he wrote his *Faerie Queene*, and other poems. He was afterwards "burnt out," by the Irish, and fled to England. Ben Jonson says, "he died, for lake of bred," in King Street, London, refusing 20 pieces sent to him by Lord Essex, saying, he was "sorry he had no time to spend them."

THE NAMES OF SUBSCRIBERS.

THE MOST NOBLE THE MARQUIS OF KILDARE, M.R.I.A.

Alexander, Rt. Rev. Dr., Bishop of Derry.
Arran, Rt. Hon. Earl, K.P.
Avonmore, Right Hon. Viscount, Belle-Isle, Tipperary.
Attenborough, Robert, London, W.
Bailey, Daniel, London, W.
Bandon, Right Hon. the Earl of, Castle Bernard, Bandon.
Barrington, Hon. and Rev. I. R., Herts.
Barron, Sir H. Winston, Bart., D.L., Barron Court, Waterford.
Barry, A. H. Smith, D.L., M.P., Foaty, Queenstown, Cork.
Batty, Rev. W. Edmund, Fulham.
Batty, Rev. George Staunton, Fulham.
Barlow, Captain John, Director of Government Prisons, Dublin Castle.
Becher, Lady, Ballygiblin, Mallow, co. Cork.
Bernard, Colonel, The Hon. Henry Boyle, J.P., Coolmain Castle, co. Cork.
Bernard, Mrs. C., London, W.
Berry, Parsons, M.R.C.S.E., Mallow.
Blackburne, E. L., F.S A., London.
Bleakley, Rev. John, Vicar of Ballymodan, Bandon.
Boothby, Captain, York.
Boyle, Edmund M., Rock Wood, Torquay, Devon.
Brent, John, F.A.S., D.L., Canterbury.
Burgoyne, Field-Marshal Sir John Fox, Bart., G.C.B., D.C.L., F.R.S., Bayswater, W.
Burney, George, Millwall, London, E.
Caparn, Rev. Wm. John, Vicarage, Isle of Dogs.
Carbery, Right Hon. Lord, Castle Freke, co. Cork (2 copies).
Cardigan, Countess of, Dean Park, Wandsford (2 copies).
Carew, W. H. Pole, D.L. Antony, Torpoint, Devonport.
Carew, Lt.-Colonel, R.M., Cahir Abbey House, Cahir.
Carew, Robert T., J.P., D.L., Ballinamona Park, Waterford.
Carey, Richard, Munster Bank, Skibbereen, co. Cork.
Chamen, R. T., London, W.
Chichester, Right Hon. the Earl of, L.L. (4 copies).
Clarendon, Right Hon. the Earl of, Grove Park, Watford.
Clive, Charles Meysey, D.L., Eaton Place, South, S.W.
Coey, Sir Edward, D.L., Belfast.
Cotter, Sir James, Bart., J.P., Hawthorn, Mallow.
Cotton, Charles, Cork.
Courtown, Rt. Hon. Earl of, D.L., Courtown House, Gorey, co. Wexford.
Cox, Miss, Alexandra Villas, Midleton Park, Queenstown.
Coxhead, Mrs., Russell Square (2 copies).
Croker, T. F. Dillon, F.S.A., Brompton.
Crosbie, Major, D.L., Ballyheigue Castle, Tralee
Darnley, Right Hon. the Earl, D.L., Cobham Hall.
Darnley, Countess, Cobham Hall.
Dawson, George K. S. Massy, D.L., Ballinacourte, near Tipperary.
Deasy, Right Hon. Rickard, Baron of the Exchequer, Blackrock, Dublin.
De la Poer, Edmund, D.L., M.P., Gurteen, co. Waterford.
Desart, Right Hon. Earl of, D.L., Desart House, Kilkenny.
Delacour, Rev. R. W., Killowen, Bandon.

Downing, M'Carthy, M.P., J.P., Prospect House, Skibbereen.
Drew, Rev. P. W., Heathfield Towers, Rector of Youghal.
Drewe, E. S., D.L., The Grange, Honiton, Devonshire.
Dunscombe, N., J.P., King Willliamstown House, co. Cork.
Dunstan, Ross, The Hollow, Yorkshire.
Eastlake, Lady, Fitzroy Square, W.
Esmonde, Sir John, Bart., M.P., D.L., Gorey, Wexford.
Fermoy, Right Hon. Lord, Cus. Rot., co. and city of Cork.
Fitzgerald, Rt. Rev. Dr., Bishop of Killaloe.
Fitzgerald, Rev. F. A. H., Weybread Vicarage. Harleston, Norfolk.
Fitzgerald, Major, Arabella Row, Grosvenor Place, S.W.
Fitzgerald, Charles L., D.L., Turlough Park, Castlebar.
Fitzgerald, M. E., S.I.C., Roundstone, co. Galway.
Fitzgerald, Rev. Augustine, The Glebe, Portadown, co. Armagh.
Fitzgerald, Peter, Knight of Kerry, D.L., Glanleam, Valentia, co. Kerry.
Fitzgerald, T. D., R.M., Bandon.
Fitzgerald, Robert, J.P., Levally, Rathdowney, Queen's County.
Fitzpatrick, J. W., J.P., Kilmacud Manor, co. Dublin.
Fortescue, Right Hon. Chichester, M.P., London.
Fortescue, Hon. D. F., M.P., High Sheriff, County Waterford, and Mayfair, London.
Foot, H. B., J.P., Carrigacunna Castle, Killavullen, near Mallow.
Frith, Wm. Powell, R.A., Bayswater.
Gardiner, R. M., Com. General, London.
Gibson, William, Merrion Square, Dublin.
Gibson, Captain William, Rockforest, Roscrea.
Gibson, Rev. Charles E., Bayshill Lawn, Cheltenham.
Gibson, Edward, Barrister-at-law, Fitzwilliam Square, Dublin.
Gibson, James, Q.C., Mountjoy Square, Dublin.
Gibson, John E., Barrister-at-Law, Merrion Square, Dublin.
Gibson, Charles Bernard, Junior, Kansas, U.S.A.
Gibson, Miss, Laurel Court, Minster Precincts, Peterborough.
Gillman, Major Bennett W., J.P., The Retreat, Clonakilty.
Godson, Rev. Arthur R., Gordon Square.
Grace, Captain Sheffield, 68th Regiment.
Granard, Rt. Hon. Earl of, K.P., Castle Forbes, co. Longford.
Grant, Miss, Inveraven Bank, Perth.
Grant, Alexander, Monkstown, co. Cork.
Haines, Charles C., Mallow.
Halifax, Rt. Hon. Viscount, G.C.B., Garowby House, Yorkshire.
Hall, Mrs. S. C., London.
Hamilton, George, Eastwell Park, Kent.
Hanhart, Michael, London, W.
Hartington, Right Hon. the Marquis of, M.P., P.C.
Hay, Peter, Governor of Gov. Prison, Spike Island.
Hayman, Rev. Samuel, Rector of Doneraile, co. Cork.
Hungerford, The Misses, The Island, Clonakilty.
Hungerford, T. W., J.P., Willow Hill, Carrigaline, co. Cork.
Hungerford, William, The Square, Clonakilty.
Hungerford, Winspear Toye, Farleigh Place, St. Luke's, Cork.
Heal, J. Harris, London, W.
Jebb, The Lady Amelia, West Brompton (2 copies).
Jebb, Captain Gladwyn, Yorkshire.
Joyce, John, Governor, County Gaol, Cork.
Justice, Walter, Gordon Square (3 copies)
Justice, Thomas H., M.D., Mallow.
Justice, William T., Manchester.
Justice, Miss, Mount Justice, co. Cork.
Justice, John B. C., J.P., Woodside, Cork
Keane, Most Rev. William, D.D., Bishop of Cloyne.

Kearney, Rev. T. N., LL.D., Kilbrittain (2 copies).
Kearney, Patrick J., D.L., Miltown House, Clonmellon, co. Meath.
Kelly, Charles, Parsonstown, King's County.
Kelly, J. H., M.D., Spike Island, Queenstown.
Kelly, Edmund M., Barrister-at-Law, Blackrock, co. Dublin.
Lambkin, Robert, J.P., Cork.
Larcom, Sir Thomas, Bart., M.R.I.A., K.C.B.
Lawler, Denis Shine, J.P., Killarney.
Leader, Benjamin, J.P., Stake Hill, Boherbue, co. Cork.
Leinster, His Grace the Duke of, P.C.
Lentaigne, John, D.L., M.R.I.A., Inspector-General of Prisons, Dublin Castle.
Lichfield, Right Hon. the Earl of, L.L. (6 copies).
Listowel, The Countess Dowager, Convamore, Mallow.
Lynn, Frank W., F.R.G.S., London.
Lytton, Right Hon. Lord Bulwer, P.C., D.C.L., D.L.
Lloyd, The Lady Anne, Strancally Castle, co. Waterford.
Macnamara, F. E., Munster Bank, Cork.
Martley, Francis Blackburne, Dublin.
M'Carthy, Rev. John P. P., Mallow.
M'Carthy, John George, Cork.
M'Carthy, F. D., J.P., Glen Curragh, Skibbereen.
M'Carthy, John, D.L., Rathduane, Millstreet, co. Cork.
M'Carthy, F. J., R.M., Castleview, Kilmallock.
M'Carthy, G. E., J.P., Skibbereen, co. Cork.
M'Carthy, F. B. S. T., Compass Hill, Kinsale.
Mahony, Richard, D.L., Dromore, Kenmare, co. Kerry.
Maguire, Edward, D.L., Jamestown, Golden Ball, co. Dublin.
M'Donnell, Robert, M.D., F.R.C.S., Dublin.
Mathew, James Charles, Q.C., Cornwall Gardens, Queen's Gate, W.
Meredith, Mrs., London.
Midleton, Right Hon. the Viscount, D L.
Miles, Mrs., Firbeck Hall, Yorkshire (2 copies).
Montford, Miss Mary, Glasnevin.
Moriarty, Right Rev. Dr., Bishop of Kerry.
Moriarty, John, Mallow.
Murphy, George Stormont, London.
Murphy, Nicholas D., M.P., Cork.
Murphy, John N., D.L., Clifton, Cork.
Napier, Rt. Hon. Sir Joseph, Bart., Merrion Square, Dublin.
Norman, Rev. Edward, Willowbrook, Millstreet, co. Cork.
Neligan, Miss D., London.
Norreys, Sir Denham Jephson, Bart., D.L., The Castle, Mallow.
Newman, Mrs., Sen., Dromore House, Mallow.
O'Conor Don, The, D L., M.P., Balanagare, Frenchpark, co. Roscommon.
O'Connor, J. E., National Bank, Castle-Island, Kerry.
O'Connor, James, National Bank, Tralee.
O'Brien, E. W., D.L., Foynes, Limerick.
O'Donovan, The, J.P., Lissard, Skibbereen, co. Cork.
O'Ferrall, Right Hon. R. More, D.L., Ballyna, Enfield, co. Meath.
O'Hagan, Right Hon. Lord, Lord High Chancellor of Ireland.
O'Neill, Hon. Edward, M.P., D.L., Shane's Castle, Co. Antrim.
Orpen, Hungerford, J.P., Killaba Castle, Killarney.
Orpen, Sir Richard J. T., Great George's Street, Dublin.
O'Sullivan, J. E., J.P., Skeaf House, Timoleague, co. Cork.
O'Shee, Nicholas Power, D.L., Gardenmorris, co. Kilkenny.
Paccaud, Louis S., Napa City, Napa co., California.
Peachey, Frederick, The Chestnuts, Clapham.
Pelham, Lord, M.P., Stanmer Park, Lewes (6 copies).
Perrier, Mrs., Kensington.

Perry, Rev. Frederick, Fitzroy Street, London, W.
Pim, Jonathan, M.P., Monkstown, co. Dublin.
Power, Captain, J.P., Affane. Cappoquin, co. Waterford.
Pownall, Henry, D.L., Russell Square.
Pownall, Very Rev. Dean, Vicar of Hoxton.
Powerscourt, Right Hon. Viscount, Powerscourt Castle, co. Wicklow.
Prescott, Rev. Peter, Bow Road, London, E.
Proctor, John, London.
Putland, Charles, D. L., Bray Head, co. Wicklow.
Putland, Mrs., Bray-Head, co. Wicklow.
Q. * * * * *
Qusin, Richard, M.D., F.R.C.P., London.
Ranelagh, The Rt Hon. The Viscount, D.L., New Burlington Street, W.
Reade, Philip, J.P., The Woodparks, Scariff, co. Clare.
Riversdale, W. Alcock Stawell, Lisnegar, co. Cork.
Roch, George, Woodbine Hill, Youghal.
Ronayne, Joseph P., C.E., Rinn-Ronein, Queenstown.
Richmond, His Grace the Duke of, K.G.
Ryan, Bishop, Right Rev., D.D., Bradford.
Stuart De Decies, Right Hon. Lord, L L., Waterford.
Sadleir, Rev. F. Ralph, D.D., Cambridge Terrace, Hyde Park.
Schofield, James, Keppel Street, Russell Square.
Scully, Vincent, Q.C., Merrion Square, Dublin (2 copies).
Sealy, Winthrop, B., J.P., Gortnahorna House, Bandon.
Sealy, William, Burren House, co. Cork.
Sealy, Ludlow, Burren House, co. Cork.
Seymour, W. D., J.P., Queenstown.
Sheehan, Francis, Munster Bank, Dungarvan.
Sheil, Sir John, K.C.B., F.R.G S., Eaton Place, S.W. (The late)
Shelley, Lady, Dowager, Maresfield Lodge, East Cowes.
Sheppard, Colonel, Woodbine Hill, Youghal.
Sherson, A. Nowell, Thurloe Square, S.W.
Shirley, Evelyn P., D.L., Lough Fea, Carrickmacross, co. Monaghan.
Smith, Abel, M.P., Woodhall, Herts.
S. I. L.
Stamer, Miss Mary, Glasnevin.
Stawell, Colonel Alcock, Kilbrittain Castle, Bandon (2 copies).
Stawell, Mrs. Colonel Alcock. Kilbrittain Castle, Bandon (2 copies).
Stebbing. Rev. H., D.D., F.R.S., St. James' Parsonage, Hampstead Road.
Stokes, Wm., M.D., M.R.I.A., Dublin.
Sweeny, James, Monkstown, co. Dublin.
Tarrant, Charles, C.E., County Surveyor, Waterford.
Tighe, Rt. Hon. Wm. F. F., L. & C. R., P.C., Woodstock Park, Innistiogue, co. Kilkenny.
Thackwell, Lady, Aghada Hall, Cork Harbour.
Thomas, Enoch, London, W.
Trench, Wm. Stuart, J.P., Essex Castle, Carrickmacross, co. Monaghan.
Tobin, Sir Thomas, F.R.S., F.S.A., D.L., Ballincollig, co. Cork.
Townshend, the Most Hon. the Marquis, Raynham Hall.
Van Dissel. Mdlle., Laurel Court, Minster Precincts, Peterborough.
Vane, Right Hon. Earl, Holderness House, Park Lane (2 copies)
Verney, Sir Harry, Bart., M.P., K.C.H., D.L., Claydon House, Bucks.
Waterford, Louisa, Marchioness of, Ford Castle, Northumberland.
Walters, Rev. T., Boyton Vicarage, Launceston.
Watkins, Richard. Canal Iron Works, Millwall.
Wellington, His Grace the Duke of, K.G.
White, Miss. Cornwall Terrace, Regent's Park.
Wilson, E. D., Barrister-at-Law, 13, Gray's Inn Square, London
Wyatt-Edgell, Rev. E., F.S.S., Grosvenor Street, Grosvenor Square.

39 PATERNOSTER ROW, E.C.
LONDON: *January* 1871.

GENERAL LIST OF WORKS

PUBLISHED BY

Messrs. LONGMANS, GREEN, READER, and DYER.

ARTS, MANUFACTURES, &c.	12	INDEX	21—24
ASTRONOMY, METEOROLOGY, POPULAR GEOGRAPHY, &c.	7	MISCELLANEOUS WORKS and POPULAR METAPHYSICS	6
BIOGRAPHICAL WORKS	3	NATURAL HISTORY & POPULAR SCIENCE	8
CHEMISTRY, MEDICINE, SURGERY, and the ALLIED SCIENCES	9	PERIODICAL PUBLICATIONS	20
		POETRY and THE DRAMA	18
COMMERCE, NAVIGATION, and MERCANTILE AFFAIRS	19	RELIGIOUS and MORAL WORKS	14
		RURAL SPORTS, &c.	19
CRITICISM, PHILOLOGY, &c.	4	TRAVELS, VOYAGES, &c.	16
FINE ARTS and ILLUSTRATED EDITIONS	11	WORKS of FICTION	17
HISTORY, POLITICS, and HISTORICAL MEMOIRS	1	WORKS of UTILITY and GENERAL INFORMATION	20

History, Politics, Historical Memoirs, &c.

The History of England from the fall of Wolsey to the Defeat of the Spanish Armada. By JAMES ANTHONY FROUDE, M.A.

CABINET EDITION, 12 vols. cr. 8vo. £3 12s.
LIBRARY EDITION, 12 vols. 8vo. £8 18s.

The History of England from the Accession of James II. By Lord MACAULAY.

LIBRARY EDITION, 5 vols. 8vo. £4.
CABINET EDITION, 8 vols. post 8vo. 48s.
PEOPLE'S EDITION, 4 vols. crown 8vo. 16s.

Lord Macaulay's Works. Complete and uniform Library Edition. Edited by his Sister, Lady TREVELYAN. 8 vols. 8vo. with Portrait, price £5 5s. cloth, or £8 8s. bound in tree-calf by Rivière.

An Essay on the History of the English Government and Constitution, from the Reign of Henry VII. to the Present Time. By JOHN EARL RUSSELL. Fourth Edition, revised. Crown 8vo. 6s.

Selections from Speeches of Earl Russell, 1817 to 1841, and from Despatches, 1859 to 1865; with Introductions. 2 vols. 8vo. 28s.

Varieties of Vice-Regal Life. By Major-General Sir WILLIAM DENISON, K.C.B. late Governor-General of the Australian Colonies, and Governor of Madras. With Two Maps. 2 vols. 8vo. 28s.

On Parliamentary Government in England: its Origin, Development, and Practical Operation. By ALPHEUS TODD, Librarian of the Legislative Assembly of Canada. 2 vols. 8vo. price £1 17s.

The Constitutional History of England since the Accession of George III. 1760—1860. By Sir THOMAS ERSKINE MAY, K.C.B. Second Edit. 2 vols. 8vo. 33s.

A Historical Account of the Neu- trality of Great Britain during the American Civil War. By MONTAGUE BERNARD, M.A. Royal 8vo. price 16s.

The History of England, from the Earliest Times to the Year 1866. By C. D. YONGE, Regius Professor of Modern History in the Queen's University, Belfast. New Edition. Crown 8vo. 7s. 6d.

A History of Wales, derived from Authentic Sources. By JANE WILLIAMS, Ysgafell, Author of a Memoir of the Rev. Thomas Price, and Editor of his Literary Remains. 8vo. 14s.

A

Lectures on the History of England, from the Earliest Times to the Death of King Edward II. By WILLIAM LONGMAN. With Maps and Illustrations. 8vo. 15s.

The History of the Life and Times of Edward the Third. By WILLIAM LONGMAN. With 9 Maps, 8 Plates, and 16 Woodcuts. 2 vols. 8vo. 28s.

History of Civilization in England and France, Spain and Scotland. By HENRY THOMAS BUCKLE. New Edition of the entire work, with a complete INDEX. 3 vols. crown 8vo. 24s.

Realities of Irish Life. By W. STEUART TRENCH, Land Agent in Ireland to the Marquess of Lansdowne, the Marquess of Bath, and Lord Digby. Fifth Edition. Crown 8vo. 6s.

The Student's Manual of the History of Ireland. By M. F. CUSACK, Authoress of the 'Illustrated History of Ireland, from the Earliest Period to the Year of Catholic Emancipation.' Crown 8vo. price 6s.

A Student's Manual of the History of India, from the Earliest Period to the Present. By Colonel MEADOWS TAYLOR, M.R.A.S. M.R.I.A. Crown 8vo. with Maps, 7s. 6d.

The History of India, from the Earliest Period to the close of Lord Dalhousie's Administration. By JOHN CLARK MARSHMAN. 3 vols. crown 8vo. 22s. 6d.

Indian Polity: a View of the System of Administration in India. By Lieut.-Col. GEORGE CHESNEY. Second Edition, revised, with Map. 8vo. 21s.

Home Politics: being a Consideration of the Causes of the Growth of Trade in relation to Labour, Pauperism, and Emigration. By DANIEL GRANT. 8vo. 7s.

Democracy in America. By ALEXIS DE TOCQUEVILLE. Translated by HENRY REEVE. 2 vols. 8vo. 21s.

Waterloo Lectures: a Study of the Campaign of 1815. By Colonel CHARLES C. CHESNEY, R.E. late Professor of Military Art and History in the Staff College. Second Edition. 8vo. with Map, 10s. 6d.

The Military Resources of Prussia and France, and Recent Changes in the Art of War. By Lieut.-Col. CHESNEY, R.E. and HENRY REEVE, D.C.L. Crown 8vo. 7s. 6d.

The Overthrow of the Germanic Confederation by Prussia in 1866. By Sir A. MALET, Bart. K.B.C. late H.B.M. Envoy and Minister at Frankfort. With 5 Maps. 8vo. 18s.

The Oxford Reformers—John Colet, Erasmus, and Thomas More; being a History of their Fellow-Work. By FREDERIC SEEBOHM. Second Edition. 8vo. 14s.

History of the Reformation in Europe in the Time of Calvin. By J. H. MERLE D'AUBIGNÉ, D.D. VOLS. I. and II. 8vo. 28s. VOL. III. 12s. VOL. IV. price 16s. and VOL. V. price 16s.

Chapters from French History; St. Louis, Joan of Arc, Henri IV. with Sketches of the Intermediate Periods. By J. H. GURNEY, M.A. New Edition. Fcp. 8vo. 6s. 6d.

The History of Greece. By C. THIRLWALL, D.D. Lord Bishop of St. David's. 8 vols. fcp. 28s.

The Tale of the Great Persian War, from the Histories of Herodotus. By GEORGE W. COX, M.A. late Scholar of Trin. Coll. Oxon. Fcp. 3s. 6d.

Greek History from Themistocles to Alexander, in a Series of Lives from Plutarch. Revised and arranged by A. H. CLOUGH. Fcp. with 44 Woodcuts, 6s.

Critical History of the Language and Literature of Ancient Greece. By WILLIAM MURE, of Caldwell. 5 vols. 8vo. £3 9s.

History of the Literature of Ancient Greece. By Professor K. O. MÜLLER. Translated by LEWIS and DONALDSON. 3 vols. 8vo. 21s.

The History of Rome. By WILHELM IHNE. Translated and revised by the Author. VOLS. I. and II. 8vo. [Just ready.

History of the City of Rome from its Foundation to the Sixteenth Century of the Christian Era. By THOMAS H. DYER, LL.D. 8vo. with 2 Maps, 15s.

History of the Romans under the Empire. By Very Rev. CHARLES MERIVALE, D.C.L. Dean of Ely. 8 vols. post 8vo. price 48s.

The Fall of the Roman Republic; a Short History of the Last Century of the Commonwealth. By the same Author. 12mo. 7s. 6d.

Historical and Chronological Encyclopædia; comprising Chronological Notices of all the Great Events of Universal History, including Treaties, Alliances, Wars, Battles, &c.; Incidents in the Lives of Eminent Men, Scientific and Geographical Discoveries, Mechanical Inventions, and Social, Domestic, and Economical Improvements. By the late B. B. WOODWARD, B.A. and W. L. R. CATES. 1 vol. 8vo.
[In the press.

History of European Morals from Augustus to Charlemagne. By W. E. H. LECKY, M.A. 2 vols. 8vo. price 28s.

History of the Rise and Influence of the Spirit of Rationalism in Europe. By the same Author. Cabinet Edition (the Fourth). 2 vols. crown 8vo. price 16s.

God in History; or, the Progress of Man's Faith in the Moral Order of the World. By the late Baron BUNSEN. Translated from the German by SUSANNA WINKWORTH; with a Preface by Dean STANLEY 3 vols. 8vo. 42s.

Socrates and the Socratic Schools. Translated from the German of Dr. E. ZELLER, with the Author's approval, by the Rev. OSWALD J. REICHEL, B.C.L. and M.A. Crown 8vo. 8s. 6d.

The Stoics, Epicureans, and Sceptics. Translated from the German of Dr. E. ZELLER, with the Author's approval, by OSWALD J. REICHEL, B.C.L. and M.A. Crown 8vo. 14s.

The History of Philosophy, from Thales to Comte. By GEORGE HENRY LEWES. Third Edition, rewritten and enlarged. 2 vols. 8vo. 30s.

The Mythology of the Aryan Nations. By GEORGE W. COX, M.A. late Scholar of Trinity College, Oxford. 2 vols. 8vo. price 28s.

The English Reformation. By F. C. MASSINGBERD, M.A. Chancellor of Lincoln. 4th Edition, revised. Fcp. 7s. 6d.

Maunder's Historical Treasury; comprising a General Introductory Outline of Universal History, and a Series of Separate Histories. Fcp. 6s.

Critical and Historical Essays contributed to the *Edinburgh Review* by the Right Hon. Lord MACAULAY:—

CABINET EDITION, 4 vols. 24s.
LIBRARY EDITION, 3 vols. 8vo. 36s.
PEOPLE'S EDITION, 2 vols. crown 8vo. 8s.
STUDENT'S EDITION, crown 8vo. 6s.

History of the Early Church, from the First Preaching of the Gospel to the Council of Nicæa, A.D. 325. By the Author of 'Amy Herbert.' New Edition. Fcp. 4s. 6d.

Sketch of the History of the Church of England to the Revolution of 1688. By the Right Rev. T. V. SHORT, D.D. Lord Bishop of St. Asaph. Eighth Edition. Crown 8vo. 7s. 6d.

History of the Christian Church, from the Ascension of Christ to the Conversion of Constantine. By E. BURTON, D.D late Regius Prof. of Divinity in the University of Oxford. Fcp. 3s. 6d.

Biographical Works.

The Life of Isambard Kingdom Brunel, Civil Engineer. By ISAMBARD BRUNEL, B.C.L. of Lincoln's Inn, Chancellor of the Diocese of Ely. With Portrait, Plates, and Woodcuts. 8vo. 21s.

The Life and Letters of the Rev. Sydney Smith. Edited by his Daughter, Lady HOLLAND, and Mrs. AUSTIN. New Edition, complete in One Volume. Crown 8vo. price 6s.

A Memoir of G. E. L. Cotton, D.D. late Lord Bishop of Calcutta; with Selections from his Journals and Letters. Edited by Mrs. COTTON. With Portrait. 8vo. *[Just ready.*

Some Memorials of R. D. Hamp- den, Bishop of Hereford. Edited by his Daughter, HENRIETTA HAMPDEN. With Portrait. 8vo. *[Just ready.*

The Life and Travels of George Whitefield, M.A. of Pembroke College, Oxford, Chaplain to the Countess of Huntingdon. By J. P. GLEDSTONE. Post 8vo.
[Just ready.

Memoir of Pope Sixtus the Fifth. By Baron HÜBNER. Translated from the Original in French, with the Author's sanction, by HUBERT E. H. JERNINGHAM. 2 vols. 8vo. *[In the press.*

The Life and Letters of Faraday.
By Dr. BENCE JONES, Secretary of the Royal Institution. Second Edition, with Portrait and Woodcuts. 2 vols. 8vo. 28s.

Faraday as a Discoverer. By JOHN TYNDALL, LL.D. F.R.S. Professor of Natural Philosophy in the Royal Institution. New and Cheaper Edition, with Two Portraits. Fcp. 8vo. 3s. 6d.

Lives of the Lord Chancellors and Keepers of the Great Seal of Ireland, from the Earliest Times to the Reign of Queen Victoria. By J. R. O'FLANAGAN, M.R.I.A. Barrister. 2 vols. 8vo. 36s.

Dictionary of General Biography; containing Concise Memoirs and Notices of the most Eminent Persons of all Countries, from the Earliest Ages to the Present Time. Edited by WILLIAM L. R. CATES. 8vo. price 21s.

Memoirs of Baron Bunsen, drawn chiefly from Family Papers by his Widow, FRANCES Baroness BUNSEN. Second Edition, abridged; with 2 Portraits and 4 Woodcuts. 2 vols. post 8vo. 21s.

The Letters of the Right Hon. Sir George Cornewall Lewis to various Friends. Edited by his Brother, the Rev. Canon Sir G. F. LEWIS, Bart. 8vo. with Portrait, 14s.

Life of the Duke of Wellington. By the Rev. G. R. GLEIG, M.A. Popular Edition, carefully revised; with copious Additions. Crown 8vo. with Portrait, 5s.

Father Mathew: a Biography. By JOHN FRANCIS MAGUIRE, M.P. Popular Edition, with Portrait. Crown 8vo. 3s. 6d.

History of my Religious Opinions. By J. H. NEWMAN, D.D. Being the Substance of Apologia pro Vitâ Suâ. Post 8vo. price 6s.

Letters and Life of Francis Bacon, including all his Occasional Works. Collected and edited, with a Commentary, by J. SPEDDING. VOLS. I. & II. 8vo. 24s. VOLS. III. & IV. 24s. VOL. V. 12s.

Felix Mendelssohn's Letters from Italy and Switzerland, and Letters from 1833 to 1847, translated by Lady WALLACE. With Portrait. 2 vols. crown 8vo. 5s. each.

Memoirs of Sir Henry Havelock, K.C.B. By JOHN CLARK MARSHMAN. People's Edition, with Portrait. Crown 8vo. price 3s. 6d.

Essays in Ecclesiastical Biography. By the Right Hon. Sir J. STEPHEN, LL.D. Cabinet Edition. Crown 8vo. 7s. 6d.

The Earls of Granard: a Memoir of the Noble Family of Forbes. Written by Admiral the Hon. JOHN FORBES, and Edited by GEORGE ARTHUR HASTINGS, present Earl of Granard, K.P. 8vo. 10s.

Vicissitudes of Families. By Sir J. BERNARD BURKE, C.B. Ulster King of Arms. New Edition, remodelled and enlarged. 2 vols. crown 8vo. 21s.

Lives of the Tudor Princesses, including Lady Jane Grey and her Sisters. By AGNES STRICKLAND. Post 8vo. with Portrait, &c. 12s. 6d.

Lives of the Queens of England. By AGNES STRICKLAND. Library Edition, newly revised; with Portraits of every Queen, Autographs, and Vignettes. 8 vols. post 8vo. 7s. 6d. each.

Maunder's Biographical Treasury. Thirteenth Edition, reconstructed and partly re-written, with above 1,000 additional Memoirs, by W. L. R. CATES. Fcp. 6s.

Criticism, Philosophy, Polity, &c.

The Subjection of Women. By JOHN STUART MILL. New Edition. Post 8vo. 5s.

On Representative Government. By JOHN STUART MILL. Third Edition. 8vo. 9s. crown 8vo. 2s.

On Liberty. By the same Author. Fourth Edition. Post 8vo. 7s. 6d. Crown 8vo. 1s. 4d.

Principles of Political Economy. By the same. Sixth Edition. 2 vols. 8vo. 30s. or in 1 vol. crown 8vo. 5s.

Utilitarianism. By the same. 3d Edit. 8vo. 5s.

Dissertations and Discussions. By the same Author. Second Edition. 3 vols. 8vo. 36s.

Examination of Sir W. Hamilton's Philosophy, and of the principal Philosophical Questions discussed in his Writings. By the same. Third Edition. 8vo. 16s.

Inaugural Address delivered to the University of St. Andrews. By JOHN STUART MILL. 8vo. 5s. Crown 8vo. 1s.

Analysis of the Phenomena of the Human Mind. By JAMES MILL. A New Edition, with Notes, Illustrative and Critical, by ALEXANDER BAIN, ANDREW FINDLATER, and GEORGE GROTE. Edited, with additional Notes, by JOHN STUART MILL. 2 vols. 8vo. price 28s.

The Elements of Political Economy. By HENRY DUNNING MACLEOD, M.A. Barrister-at-Law. 8vo. 16s.

A Dictionary of Political Economy; Biographical, Bibliographical, Historical, and Practical. By the same Author. VOL. I. royal 8vo. 30s.

Lord Bacon's Works, collected and edited by R. L. ELLIS, M.A. J. SPEDDING, M.A. and D. D. HEATH. New and Cheaper Edition. 7 vols. 8vo. price £3 13s. 6d.

A System of Logic, Ratiocinative and Inductive. By JOHN STUART MILL. Seventh Edition. 2 vols. 8vo. 25s.

Analysis of Mr. Mill's System of Logic. By W. STEBBING, M.A. New Edition. 12mo. 3s. 6d.

The Institutes of Justinian; with English Introduction, Translation, and Notes. By T. C. SANDARS, M.A. Barrister-at-Law. New Edition. 8vo. 15s.

The Ethics of Aristotle; with Essays and Notes. By Sir A. GRANT, Bart. M.A. LL.D. Second Edition, revised and completed. 2 vols. 8vo. price 28s.

The Nicomachean Ethics of Aristotle. Newly translated into English. By R. WILLIAMS, B.A. Fellow and late Lecturer Merton College, Oxford. 8vo. 12s.

Bacon's Essays, with Annotations. By R. WHATELY, D.D. late Archbishop of Dublin. Sixth Edition. 8vo. 10s. 6d.

Elements of Logic. By R. WHATELY, D.D. late Archbishop of Dublin. New Edition. 8vo. 10s. 6d. crown 8vo. 4s. 6d.

Elements of Rhetoric. By the same Author. New Edition. 8vo. 10s. 6d. Crown 8vo. 4s. 6d.

English Synonymes. By E. JANE WHATELY. Edited by Archbishop WHATELY. 5th Edition. Fcp. 3s.

An Outline of the Necessary Laws of Thought: a Treatise on Pure and Applied Logic. By the Most Rev. W. THOMSON, D.D. Archbishop of York. Ninth Thousand. Crown 8vo. 5s. 6d.

The Election of Representatives, Parliamentary and Municipal; a Treatise. By THOMAS HARE, Barrister-at-Law. Third Edition, with Additions. Crown 8vo. 6s.

Speeches of the Right Hon. Lord MACAULAY, corrected by Himself. People's Edition, crown 8vo. 3s. 6d.

Lord Macaulay's Speeches on Parliamentary Reform in 1831 and 1832. 16mo. price ONE SHILLING.

Walker's Pronouncing Dictionary of the English Language. Thoroughly revised Editions, by B. H. SMART. 8vo. 12s. 16mo. 6s.

A Dictionary of the English Language. By R. G. LATHAM, M.A. M.D. F.R.S. Founded on the Dictionary of Dr. S. JOHNSON, as edited by the Rev. H. J. TODD, with numerous Emendations and Additions. 4 vols. 4to. price £7.

Thesaurus of English Words and Phrases, classified and arranged so as to facilitate the expression of Ideas, and assist in Literary Composition. By P. M. ROGET, M.D. New Edition. Crown 8vo. 10s. 6d.

The Debater; a Series of Complete Debates, Outlines of Debates, and Questions for Discussion. By F. ROWTON. Fcp. 6s.

Lectures on the Science of Language, delivered at the Royal Institution. By MAX MÜLLER, M.A. &c. Foreign Member of the French Institute. 2 vols. 8vo. price 30s.

Chapters on Language. By F. W. FARRAR, M.A. F.R.S. late Fellow of Trin. Coll. Cambridge. Crown 8vo. 8s. 6d.

A Book about Words. By G. F. GRAHAM. Fcp. 8vo. 3s. 6d.

Southey's Doctor, complete in One Volume, edited by the Rev. J. W. WARTER, B.D. Square crown 8vo. 12s. 6d.

Historical and Critical Commentary on the Old Testament; with a New Translation. By M. M. KALISCH, Ph.D. Vol. I. *Genesis*, 8vo. 18s. or adapted for the General Reader, 12s. Vol. II. *Exodus*, 15s. or adapted for the General Reader, 12s. Vol III. *Leviticus*, Part I. 15s. or adapted for the General Reader, 8s.

A Hebrew Grammar, with Exercises. By the same. Part I. *Outlines with Exercises*, 8vo. 12s. 6d. KEY, 5s. Part II. *Exceptional Forms and Constructions*, 12s. 6d.

Manual of English Literature, Historical and Critical : with a Chapter on English Metres. By THOMAS ARNOLD, M.A. Second Edition. Crown 8vo. 7s. 6d.

A Latin-English Dictionary. By J. T. WHITE, D.D. of Corpus Christi College, and J. E. RIDDLE, M.A. of St. Edmund Hall, Oxford. Third Edition, revised. 2 vols. 4to. pp. 2,128, price 42s.

White's College Latin-English Dictionary (Intermediate Size), abridged from the Parent Work for the use of University Students. Medium 8vo. pp. 1,048, price 18s.

White's Junior Student's Complete Latin-English and English-Latin Dictionary. Revised Edition. Square 12mo. pp. 1,058, price 12s.

Separately { ENGLISH-LATIN, 5s. 6d.
{ LATIN-ENGLISH, 7s. 6d.

An English-Greek Lexicon, containing all the Greek Words used by Writers of good authority. By C. D. YONGE, B.A. New Edition. 4to. 21s.

Mr. Yonge's New Lexicon, English and Greek, abridged from his larger work (as above). Square 12mo. 8s. 6d.

The Mastery of Languages; or, the Art of Speaking Foreign Tongues Idiomatically. By THOMAS PRENDERGAST, late of the Civil Service at Madras. Second Edition. 8vo. 6s.

A Greek-English Lexicon. Compiled by H. G. LIDDELL, D.D. Dean of Christ Church, and R. SCOTT, D.D. Dean of Rochester. Sixth Edition. Crown 4to. price 36s.

A Lexicon, Greek and English, abridged for Schools from LIDDELL and SCOTT's *Greek-English Lexicon*. Twelfth Edition. Square 12mo. 7s. 6d.

A Practical Dictionary of the French and English Languages. By Professor LÉON CONTANSEAU, many years French Examiner for Military and Civil Appointments, &c. New Edition, carefully revised. Post 8vo. 10s. 6d.

Contanseau's Pocket Dictionary, French and English, abridged from the Practical Dictionary, by the Author. New Edition. 18mo. price 3s. 6d.

A Sanskrit-English Dictionary. The Sanskrit words printed both in the original Devanagari and in Roman letters ; with References to the Best Editions of Sanskrit Authors, and with Etymologies and comparisons of Cognate Words chiefly in Greek, Latin, Gothic, and Anglo-Saxon. Compiled by T. BENFEY. 8vo. 52s. 6d.

New Practical Dictionary of the German Language; German-English, and English-German. By the Rev. W. L. BLACKLEY, M.A. and Dr. CARL MARTIN FRIEDLÄNDER. Post 8vo. 7s. 6d.

Staff College Essays. By Lieutenant EVELYN BARING, Royal Artillery. 8vo. with Two Maps, 8s. 6d.

Miscellaneous Works and *Popular Metaphysics.*

The Essays and Contributions of A. K. H. B. Author of 'The Recreations of a Country Parson.' Uniform Editions :—

Recreations of a Country Parson. FIRST and SECOND SERIES, 3s. 6d. each.

The Commonplace Philosopher in Town and Country. Crown 8vo. 3s. 6d.

Leisure Hours in Town; Essays Consolatory, Æsthetical, Moral, Social, and Domestic. Crown 8vo. 3s. 6d.

The Autumn Holidays of a Country Parson. Crown 8vo. 3s. 6d.

The Graver Thoughts of a Country Parson. FIRST and SECOND SERIES, crown 8vo. 3s. 6d. each.

Critical Essays of a Country Parson, selected from Essays contributed to *Fraser's Magazine*. Crown 8vo. 3s. 6d.

Sunday Afternoons at the Parish Church of a Scottish University City. Crown 8vo. 3s. 6d.

Lessons of Middle Age, with some Account of various Cities and Men. Crown 8vo. 3s. 6d.

Counsel and Comfort Spoken from a City Pulpit. Crown 8vo. 3s. 6d.

Changed Aspects of Unchanged Truths ; Memorials of St. Andrews Sundays. Crown 8vo. 3s. 6d.

Present-Day Thoughts; Memorials of St. Andrews Sundays. Crown 8vo. 3s. 6d.

Short Studies on Great Subjects.
By JAMES ANTHONY FROUDE, M.A. late
Fellow of Exeter College, Oxford. Third
Edition. 8vo. 12s.

**Lord Macaulay's Miscellaneous
Writings:—**
LIBRARY EDITION, 2 vols. 8vo. Portrait, 21s.
PEOPLE'S EDITION, 1 vol. crown 8vo. 4s. 6d.

The Rev. Sydney Smith's Mis
cellaneous Works; including his Contributions to the *Edinburgh Review.* 1 vol.
crown 8vo. 6s.

The Wit and Wisdom of the Rev.
SYDNEY SMITH: a Selection of the most
memorable Passages in his Writings and
Conversation. Crown 8vo. 3s. 6d.

The Silver Store. Collected from
Mediæval Christian and Jewish Mines. By
the Rev. S. BARING-GOULD, M.A. Crown
8vo. 3s. 6d.

Traces of History in the Names
of Places; with a Vocabulary of the Roots
out of which Names of Places in England
and Wales are formed. By FLAVELL
EDMUNDS. Crown 8vo. 7s. 6d.

The Eclipse of Faith; or, a Visit to a
Religious Sceptic. By HENRY ROGERS.
Twelfth Edition. Fcp. 5s.

Defence of the Eclipse of Faith, by its
Author. Third Edition. Fcp. 3s. 6d.

Selections from the Correspondence
of R. E. H. Greyson. By the same Author.
Third Edition. Crown 8vo. 7s. 6d.

Families of Speech, Four Lectures
delivered at the Royal Institution of Great
Britain. By the Rev. F. W. FARRAR,
M.A. F.R.S. Post 8vo. with 2 Maps, 5s. 6d.

Chips from a German Workshop;
being Essays on the Science of Religion,
and on Mythology, Traditions, and Customs.
By MAX MÜLLER, M.A. &c. Foreign
Member of the French Institute. 3 vols.
8vo. £2.

Word Gossip; a Series of Familiar
Essays on Words and their Peculiarities.
By the Rev. W. L. BLACKLEY, M.A. Fcp.
8vo. 5s.

An Introduction to Mental Phi
losophy, on the Inductive Method. By
J. D. MORELL, M.A. LL.D. 8vo. 12s.

Elements of Psychology, containing the
Analysis of the Intellectual Powers. By
the same Author. Post 8vo. 7s. 6d.

The Secret of Hegel: being the
Hegelian System in Origin, Principle, Form,
and Matter. By JAMES HUTCHISON STIR
LING. 2 vols. 8vo. 28s.

Sir William Hamilton; being the Philosophy of Perception: an Analysis. By the
same Author. 8vo. 5s.

The Senses and the Intellect.
By ALEXANDER BAIN, LL.D. Prof. of Logic
in the Univ. of Aberdeen. Third Edition.
8vo. 15s.

The Emotions and the Will, by the
same Author. Second Edition. 8vo. 15s.

On the Study of Character, including
an Estimate of Phrenology. By the same
Author. 8vo. 9s.

Mental and Moral Science: a
Compendium of Psychology and Ethics.
By the same Author. Second Edition.
Crown 8vo. 10s. 6d.

Strong and Free; or, First Steps
towards Social Science. By the Author of
'My Life and What shall I do with it?'
8vo. 10s. 6d.

The Philosophy of Necessity; or,
Natural Law as applicable to Mental, Moral.
and Social Science. By CHARLES BRAY.
Second Edition. 8vo. 9s.

The Education of the Feelings and
Affections. By the same Author. Third
Edition. 8vo. 3s. 6d.

On Force, its Mental and Moral Corre
lates. By the same Author. 8vo. 5s.

Time and Space; a Metaphysical
Essay. By SHADWORTH H. HODGSON.
(This work covers the whole ground of
Speculative Philosophy.) 8vo. price 16s.

The Theory of Practice; an Ethical Inquiry. By the same Author. (This work,
in conjunction with the foregoing, completes
a system of Philosophy.) 2 vols. 8vo.
price 24s.

A Treatise on Human Nature;
being an Attempt to Introduce the Experimental Method of Reasoning into Moral
Subjects. By DAVID HUME. Edited, with
Notes, &c. by T. H. GREEN, Fellow, and
T. H. GROSE, late Scholar, of Balliol College, Oxford. [*In the press.*

Essays Moral, Political, and Li
terary. By DAVID HUME. By the same
Editors. [*In the press.*

_{*} The above will form a new edition of
DAVID HUME'S *Philosophical Works,* complete in Four Volumes, but to be had in Two
separate Sections as announced.

Astronomy, Meteorology, Popular Geography, &c.

Outlines of Astronomy. By Sir J. F. W. HERSCHEL, Bart. M.A. New Edition, revised; with Plates and Woodcuts. 8vo. 18s.

Other Worlds than Ours; the Plurality of Worlds Studied under the Light of Recent Scientific Researches. By R. A. PROCTOR, B.A. F.R.A.S. Second Edition, revised and enlarged; with 14 Illustrations. Crown 8vo. 10s. 6d.

The Sun; Ruler, Light, Fire, and Life of the Planetary System. By the same Author. With 10 Plates (7 coloured) and 107 Woodcuts. Crown 8vo. price 14s.

Saturn and its System. By the same Author. 8vo. with 14 Plates, 14s.

The Handbook of the Stars. By the same Author. Square fcp. 8vo. with 3 Maps, price 5s.

Celestial Objects for Common Telescopes. By T. W. WEBB, M.A. F.R.A.S. Second Edition, revised and enlarged, with Map of the Moon and Woodcuts. 16mo. price 7s. 6d.

Navigation and Nautical Astronomy (Practical, Theoretical, Scientific) for the use of Students and Practical Men. By J. MERRIFIELD, F.R.A.S. and H. EVERS. 8vo. 14s.

A General Dictionary of Geography, Descriptive, Physical, Statistical, and Historical ; forming a complete Gazetteer of the World. By A. KEITH JOHNSTON, F.R.S.E. New Edition. 8vo. price 31s. 6d.

M'Culloch's Dictionary, Geographical, Statistical, and Historical, of the various Countries, Places, and principal Natural Objects in the World. Revised Edition, with the Statistical Information throughout brought up to the latest returns By FREDERICK MARTIN. 4 vols. 8vo. with coloured Maps, £4 4s.

A Manual of Geography, Physical, Industrial, and Political. By W. HUGHES, F.R.G.S. Prof. of Geog. in King's Coll. and in Queen's Coll. Lond. With 6 Maps. Fcp. 7s. 6d.

The States of the River Plate: their Industries and Commerce, Sheep Farming, Sheep Breeding, Cattle Feeding, and Meat Preserving; the Employment of Capital, Land and Stock and their Values, Labour and its Remuneration. By WILFRID LATHAM, Buenos Ayres. Second Edition. 8vo. 12s.

Maunder's Treasury of Geography, Physical, Historical, Descriptive, and Political. Edited by W. HUGHES, F.R.G.S. With 7 Maps and 16 Plates. Fcp. 6s.

Natural History and Popular Science.

Ganot's Elementary Treatise on Physics, Experimental and Applied, for the use of Colleges and Schools. Translated and Edited with the Author's sanction by E. ATKINSON, Ph.D. F.C.S. New Edition, revised and enlarged; with a Coloured Plate and 620 Woodcuts. Post 8vo. 15s.

The Elements of Physics or Natural Philosophy. By NEIL ARNOTT, M.D. F.R.S. Physician-Extraordinary to the Queen. Sixth Edition, re-written and completed. 2 Parts, 8vo. 21s.

The Forces of the Universe. By GEORGE BERWICK, M.D. Post 8vo. 5s.

Dove's Law of Storms, considered in connexion with the ordinary Movements of the Atmosphere. Translated by R. H. SCOTT, M.A. T.C.D. 8vo. 10s. 6d.

Sound: a Course of Eight Lectures delivered at the Royal Institution of Great Britain. By Professor JOHN TYNDALL, LL.D. F.R.S. New Edition, with Portrait and Woodcuts. Crown 8vo. 9s.

Heat a Mode of Motion. By Professor JOHN TYNDALL, LL.D. F.R.S. Fourth Edition. Crown 8vo. with Woodcuts, price 10s. 6d.

Researches on Diamagnetism and Magne-Crystallic Action; including the Question of Diamagnetic Polarity. By Professor TYNDALL. With 6 Plates and many Woodcuts. 8vo. 14s.

Notes of a Course of Nine Lectures on Light, delivered at the Royal Institution, A.D. 1869. By Professor TYNDALL. Crown 8vo. 1s. sewed, or 1s. 6d. cloth.

NEW WORKS PUBLISHED BY LONGMANS AND CO.

Notes of a Course of Seven Lectures on Electrical Phenomena and Theories, delivered at the Royal Institution, A.D. 1870. By Professor TYNDALL. Crown 8vo. 1s. sewed, or 1s. 6d. cloth.

Professor Tyndall's Essays on the Use and Limit of the Imagination in Science. Being the Second Edition, with Additions, of a Discourse on the Scientific Use of the Imagination. 8vo. 3s.

Light: its Influence on Life and Health. By FORBES WINSLOW, M.D. D.C.L. Oxon. (Hon.) Fcp. 8vo. 6s.

A Treatise on Electricity, in Theory and Practice. By A. DE LA RIVE, Prof. in the Academy of Geneva. Translated by C. V. WALKER, F.R.S. 3 vols. 8vo. with Woodcuts, £3 13s.

The Correlation of Physical Forces. By W. R. GROVE, Q.C. V.P.R.S. Fifth Edition, revised, and Augmented by a Discourse on Continuity. 8vo. 10s. 6d. The *Discourse*, separately, price 2s. 6d.

The Beginning: its When and its How. By MUNGO PONTON, F.R.S.E. Post 8vo. with very numerous Illustrations.

Manual of Geology. By S. HAUGHTON, M.D. F.R.S. Fellow of Trin. Coll. and Prof. of Geol. in the Univ. of Dublin. Second Edition, with 66 Woodcuts. Fcp. 7s. 6d.

Van Der Hoeven's Handbook of ZOOLOGY. Translated from the Second Dutch Edition by the Rev. W. CLARK, M.D. F.R.S. 2 vols. 8vo. with 24 Plates of Figures, 60s.

Professor Owen's Lectures on the Comparative Anatomy and Physiology of the Invertebrate Animals. Second Edition, with 235 Woodcuts. 8vo. 21s.

The Comparative Anatomy and Physiology of the Vertebrate Animals. By RICHARD OWEN, F.R.S. D.C.L. With 1,472 Woodcuts. 3 vols. 8vo. £3 13s. 6d.

The Origin of Civilisation and the Primitive Condition of Man; Mental and Social Condition of Savages. By Sir JOHN LUBBOCK, Bart. M.P. F.R.S. Second Edition, revised, with 25 Woodcuts. 8vo. price 16s.

The Primitive Inhabitants of Scandinavia. Containing a Description of the Implements, Dwellings, Tombs, and Mode of Living of the Savages in the North of Europe during the Stone Age. By SVEN NILSSON. 8vo. Plates and Woodcuts, 18s.

Homes without Hands: a Description of the Habitations of Animals, classed according to their Principle of Construction. By Rev. J. G. WOOD, M.A. F.L.S. With about 140 Vignettes on Wood. 8vo. 21s.

Bible Animals; being a Description of Every Living Creature mentioned in the Scriptures, from the Ape to the Coral. By the Rev. J. G. WOOD, M.A. F.L.S. With about 100 Vignettes on Wood. 8vo. 21s.

The Harmonies of Nature and Unity of Creation. By Dr. G. HARTWIG. 8vo. with numerous Illustrations, 18s.

The Sea and its Living Wonders. By the same Author. Third Edition, enlarged. 8vo. with many Illustrations, 21s.

The Tropical World. By the same Author. With 8 Chromoxylographs and 172 Woodcuts. 8vo. 21s.

The Polar World: a Popular Description of Man and Nature in the Arctic and Antarctic Regions of the Globe. By the same Author. With 8 Chromoxylographs, 3 Maps, and 85 Woodcuts. 8vo. 21s.

A Familiar History of Birds. By E. STANLEY, D.D. late Lord Bishop of Norwich. Fcp. with Woodcuts, 3s. 6d.

Kirby and Spence's Introduction to Entomology, or Elements of the Natural History of Insects. Crown 8vo. 5s.

Maunder's Treasury of Natural History, or Popular Dictionary of Zoology. Revised and corrected by T. S. COBBOLD, M.D. Fcp. with 900 Woodcuts, 6s.

The Elements of Botany for Families and Schools. Tenth Edition, revised by THOMAS MOORE, F.L.S. Fcp. with 154 Woodcuts, 2s. 6d.

The Treasury of Botany, or Popular Dictionary of the Vegetable Kingdom; with which is incorporated a Glossary of Botanical Terms. Edited by J. LINDLEY, F.R.S. and T. MOORE, F.L.S. assisted by eminent Contributors. Pp. 1,274, with 274 Woodcuts and 20 Steel Plates. TWO PARTS, fcp. 8vo. 12s.

The British Flora; comprising the Phænogamous or Flowering Plants and the Ferns. By Sir W. J. HOOKER, K.H. and G. A. WALKER-ARNOTT, LL.D. 12mo. with 12 Plates, 14s.

The Rose Amateur's Guide. By THOMAS RIVERS. New Edition. Fcp. 4s.

Loudon's Encyclopædia of Plants; comprising the Specific Character, Description, Culture, History, &c. of all the Plants found in Great Britain. With upwards of 12,000 Woodcuts. 8vo. 42s.

Maunder's Scientific and Literary Treasury; a Popular Encyclopædia of Science, Literature, and Art. New Edition, thoroughly revised and in great part rewritten, with above 1,000 new articles, by J. Y. JOHNSON, Corr. M.Z.S. Fcp. 6s.

A Dictionary of Science, Literature, and Art. Fourth Edition, re-edited by the late W. T. BRANDE (the Author) and GEORGE W. COX, M.A. 3 vols. medium 8vo. price 63s. cloth.

Chemistry, Medicine, Surgery, and the Allied Sciences.

A Dictionary of Chemistry and the Allied Branches of other Sciences. By HENRY WATTS, F.C.S. assisted by eminent Scientific and Practical Chemists. 5 vols. medium 8vo. price £7 3s.

Elements of Chemistry, Theoretical and Practical. By WILLIAM A. MILLER, M.D. LL.D. Professor of Chemistry, King's College, London. Fourth Edition. 3 vols. 8vo. £3.
PART I. CHEMICAL PHYSICS, 15s.
PART II. INORGANIC CHEMISTRY, 21s.
PART III. ORGANIC CHEMISTRY, 24s.

A Manual of Chemistry, Descriptive and Theoretical. By WILLIAM ODLING, M.B. F.R.S. PART I. 8vo. 9s. PART II. nearly ready.

A Course of Practical Chemistry, for the use of Medical Students. By W. ODLING, M.B. F.R.S. New Edition, with 70 new Woodcuts. Crown 8vo. 7s. 6d.

Outlines of Chemistry; or, Brief Notes of Chemical Facts. By the same Author. Crown 8vo. 7s. 6d.

Lectures on Animal Chemistry Delivered at the Royal College of Physicians in 1865. By the same Author. Crown 8vo. 4s. 6d.

Lectures on the Chemical Changes of Carbon, delivered at the Royal Institution of Great Britain. By the same Author. Crown 8vo. 4s. 6d.

Chemical Notes for the Lecture Room. By THOMAS WOOD, F.C.S. 2 vols. crown 8vo. I. on Heat, &c. price 3s. 6d. II. on the Metals, price 5s.

A Treatise on Medical Electricity, Theoretical and Practical; and its Use in the Treatment of Paralysis, Neuralgia, and other Diseases. By JULIUS ALTHAUS, M.D. &c. Second Edition, revised and partly re-written; with Plate and 62 Woodcuts. Post 8vo. price 15s.

The Diagnosis, Pathology, and Treatment of Diseases of Women; including the Diagnosis of Pregnancy. By GRAILY HEWITT, M.D. &c. President of the Obstetrical Society of London. Second Edition, enlarged; with 116 Woodcuts. 8vo. 24s.

Lectures on the Diseases of Infancy and Childhood. By CHARLES WEST, M.D. &c. Fifth Edition. 8vo. 16s.

On the Surgical Treatment of Children's Diseases. By T. HOLMES, M.A. &c. late Surgeon to the Hospital for Sick Children. Second Edition, with 9 Plates and 112 Woodcuts. 8vo. 21s.

A System of Surgery, Theoretical and Practical, in Treatises by Various Authors. Edited by T. HOLMES, M.A. &c. Surgeon and Lecturer on Surgery at St. George's Hospital, and Surgeon-in-Chief to the Metropolitan Police. Second Edition, thoroughly revised, with numerous Illustrations. 5 vols. 8vo. £5 5s.

Lectures on the Principles and Practice of Physic. By Sir THOMAS WATSON, Bart. M.D. Physician-in-Ordinary to the Queen. New Edition in the press.

Lectures on Surgical Pathology. By JAMES PAGET, F.R.S. Third Edition, revised and re edited by the Author and Professor W. TURNER, M.B. 8vo. with 131 Woodcuts, 21s.

Cooper's Dictionary of Practical Surgery and Encyclopædia of Surgical Science. New Edition, brought down to the present time. By S. A. LANE, Surgeon to St. Mary's Hospital, &c. assisted by various Eminent Surgeons. VOL. II. 8vo. completing the work. [*Early in* 1871.

On Chronic Bronchitis, especially as connected with Gout, Emphysema, and Diseases of the Heart. By E. HEADLAM GREENHOW, M.D. F.R.C.P. &c. 8vo. 7s. 6d.

The Climate of the South of France as Suited to Invalids; with Notices of Mediterranean and other Winter Stations. By C. T. WILLIAMS, M.A. M.D. Oxon. Assistant-Physician to the Hospital for Consumption at Brompton. Second Edition. Crown 8vo. 6s.

Pulmonary Consumption; its Nature, Treatment, and Duration exemplified by an Analysis of One Thousand Cases selected from upwards of Twenty Thousand. By C. J. B. WILLIAMS, M.D. F.R.S. Consulting Physician to the Hospital for Consumption at Brompton; and C. T. WILLIAMS, M.A. M.D. Oxon.
[*Nearly ready.*

Clinical Lectures on Diseases of the Liver, Jaundice, and Abdominal Dropsy. By C. MURCHISON, M.D. Physician and Lecturer on the Practice of Medicine, Middlesex Hospital. Post 8vo. with 25 Woodcuts, 10s. 6d.

Anatomy, Descriptive and Surgical. By HENRY GRAY, F.R.S. With about 410 Woodcuts from Dissections. Fifth Edition, by T. HOLMES, M.A. Cantab. With a New Introduction by the Editor. Royal 8vo. 28s.

Clinical Notes on Diseases of the Larynx, investigated and treated with the assistance of the Laryngoscope. By W. MARCET, M.D. F.R.S. Crown 8vo. with 5 Lithographs, 6s.

The House I Live in; or, Popular Illustrations of the Structure and Functions of the Human Body. Edited by T. G. GIRTIN. New Edition, with 25 Woodcuts. 16mo. price 2s. 6d.

Outlines of Physiology, Human and Comparative. By JOHN MARSHALL, F.R.C.S. Professor of Surgery in University College, London, and Surgeon to the University College Hospital. 2 vols. crown 8vo. with 122 Woodcuts, 32s.

Physiological Anatomy and Physiology of Man. By the late R. B. TODD, M.D. F.R.S. and W. BOWMAN, F.R.S. of King's College. With numerous Illustrations. VOL. II. 8vo. 25s.

VOL. I. New Edition by Dr. LIONEL S. BEALE, F.R.S. in course of publication; PART I. with 8 Plates, 7s. 6d.

Copland's Dictionary of Practical Medicine, abridged from the larger work, and throughout brought down to the present state of Medical Science. 8vo. 36s.

A Manual of Materia Medica and Therapeutics, abridged from Dr. PEREIRA'S *Elements* by F. J. FARRE, M.D. assisted by R. BENTLEY, M.R.C.S. and by R. WARINGTON, F.R.S. 1 vol. 8vo. with 90 Woodcuts, 21s.

Thomson's Conspectus of the British Pharmacopœia. Twenty-fifth Edition, corrected by E. LLOYD BIRKETT, M.D. 18mo. 6s.

Essays on Physiological Subjects. By GILBERT W. CHILD, M.A. F.L.S. F.C.S. Second Edition. Crown 8vo. with Woodcuts, 7s. 6d.

The Fine Arts, and *Illustrated Editions.*

In Fairyland; Pictures from the Elf-World. By RICHARD DOYLE. With a Poem by W. ALLINGHAM. With Sixteen Plates, containing Thirty-six Designs printed in Colours. Folio, 31s. 6d.

Life of John Gibson, R.A. Sculptor. Edited by Lady EASTLAKE. 8vo. 10s. 6d.

Materials for a History of Oil Painting. By Sir CHARLES LOCKE EASTLAKE, sometime President of the Royal Academy. 2 vols. 8vo. 30s.

Albert Durer, his Life and Works; including Autobiographical Papers and Complete Catalogues. By WILLIAM B. SCOTT. With Six Etchings by the Author and other Illustrations. 8vo. 16s.

Half-Hour Lectures on the History and Practice of the Fine and Ornamental Arts. By. W. B. SCOTT. Second Edition. Crown 8vo. with 50 Woodcut Illustrations, 8s. 6d.

The Lord's Prayer Illustrated by F. R. PICKERSGILL, R.A. and HENRY ALFORD, D.D. Dean of Canterbury. Imp. 4to. 21s.

The Chorale Book for England: the Hymns Translated by Miss C. WINKWORTH; the Tunes arranged by Prof. W. S. BENNETT and OTTO GOLDSCHMIDT. Fcp. 4to. 12s. 6d.

Six Lectures on Harmony. Delivered at the Royal Institution of Great Britain. By G. A. MACFARREN. 8vo. 10s. 6d.

Lyra Germanica, the Christian Year. Translated by CATHERINE WINKWORTH; with 125 Illustrations on Wood drawn by J. LEIGHTON, F.S.A. Quarto, 21s.

Lyra Germanica. the Christian Life. Translated by CATHERINE WINKWORTH; with about 200 Woodcut Illustrations by J. LEIGHTON, F.S.A. and other Artists. Quarto, 21s.

The New Testament, illustrated with Wood Engravings after the Early Masters, chiefly of the Italian School. Crown 4to. 63s. cloth, gilt top ; or £5 5s. morocco.

The Life of Man Symbolised by the Months of the Year in their Seasons and Phases. Text selected by RICHARD PIGOT. 25 Illustrations on Wood from Original Designs by JOHN LEIGHTON, F.S.A. Quarto, 42s.

Cats' and Farlie's Moral Emblems; with Aphorisms, Adages, and Proverbs of all Nations: comprising 121 Illustrations on Wood by J. LEIGHTON, F.S.A. with an appropriate Text by R. PIGOT. Imperial 8vo. 31s. 6d.

Shakspeare's Midsummer Night's Dream, illustrated with 24 Silhouettes or Shadow Pictures by P. KONEWKA, engraved on Wood by A. VOGEL. Folio, 31s. 6d.

Sacred and Legendary Art. By Mrs. JAMESON. 6 vols. square crown 8vo. price £5 15s. 6d.

Legends of the Saints and Martyrs. Fifth Edition, with 19 Etchings and 187 Woodcuts. 2 vols. price 31s. 6d.

Legends of the Monastic Orders. Third Edition, with 11 Etchings and 88 Woodcuts. 1 vol. price 21s.

Legends of the Madonna. Third Edition, with 27 Etchings and 165 Woodcuts. 1 vol. price 21s.

The History of Our Lord, with that of His Types and Precursors. Completed by Lady EASTLAKE. Revised Edition, with 13 Etchings and 281 Woodcuts. 2 vols. price 42s.

The Useful Arts, Manufactures, &c.

Gwilt's Encyclopædia of Architecture, with above 1,600 Woodcuts. Fifth Edition, with Alterations and considerable Additions, by WYATT PAPWORTH. 8vo. 52s. 6d.

A Manual of Architecture: being a Concise History and Explanation of the principal Styles of European Architecture, Ancient, Mediæval, and Renaissance; with their Chief Variations and a Glossary of Technical Terms. By THOMAS MITCHELL. With 150 Woodcuts. Crown 8vo. 10s. 6d.

Italian Sculptors: being a History of Sculpture in Northern, Southern, and Eastern Italy. By C. C. PERKINS. With 30 Etchings and 13 Wood Engravings. Imperial 8vo. 42s.

Tuscan Sculptors, their Lives, Works, and Times. By the same Author. With 45 Etchings and 28 Woodcuts from Original Drawings and Photographs. 2 vols. imperial 8vo. 63s.

Hints on Household Taste in Furniture, Upholstery, and other Details. By CHARLES L. EASTLAKE, Architect. Second Edition, with about 90 Illustrations. Square crown 8vo. 18s.

The Engineer's Handbook; explaining the principles which should guide the young Engineer in the Construction of Machinery. By C. S. LOWNDES. Post 8vo. 5s.

Lathes and Turning, Simple, Mechanical, and Ornamental. By W. HENRY NORTHCOTT. With about 240 Illustrations on Steel and Wood. 8vo. 18s.

Principles of Mechanism, designed for the use of Students in the Universities, and for Engineering Students generally. By R. WILLIS, M.A. F.R.S. &c. Jacksonian Professor in the Univ. of Cambridge. Second Edition, enlarged; with 374 Woodcuts. 8vo. 18s.

Handbook of Practical Telegraphy, published with the sanction of the Chairman and Directors of the Electric and International Telegraph Company, and adopted by the Department of Telegraphs for India. By R. S. CULLEY. Third Edition. 8vo. 12s. 6d.

Ure's Dictionary of Arts, Manufactures, and Mines. Sixth Edition, re-written and greatly enlarged by ROBERT HUNT, F.R.S. assisted by numerous Contributors. With 2,000 Woodcuts. 3 vols. medium 8vo. £4 14s. 6d.

Treatise on Mills and Millwork. By Sir W. FAIRBAIRN, Bart. With 18 Plates and 322 Woodcuts. 2 vols. 8vo. 32s.

Useful Information for Engineers. By the same Author. FIRST, SECOND, and THIRD SERIES, with many Plates and Woodcuts. 3 vols. crown 8vo. 10s. 6d. each.

The Application of Cast and Wrought Iron to Building Purposes. By the same Author. Fourth Edition, with 6 Plates and 118 Woodcuts. 8vo. 16s.

Iron Ship Building, its History and Progress, as comprised in a Series of Experimental Researches. By W. FAIRBAIRN, Bart. F.R.S. With 4 Plates and 130 Woodcuts, 8vo. 18s.

Encyclopædia of Civil Engineering, Historical, Theoretical, and Practical. By E. CRESY, C.E. With above 3,000 Woodcuts. 8vo. 42s.

A Treatise on the Steam Engine, in its various Applications to Mines, Mills, Steam Navigation, Railways, and Agriculture. By J. BOURNE, C.E. New Edition; with Portrait, 37 Plates, and 546 Woodcuts. 4to. 42s.

Catechism of the Steam Engine, in its various Applications to Mines, Mills, Steam Navigation, Railways, and Agriculture. By JOHN BOURNE, C.E. New Edition, with 89 Woodcuts. Fcp. 6s.

Recent Improvements in the Steam-Engine. By JOHN BOURNE, C.E. being a SUPPLEMENT to his 'Catechism of the Steam-Engine.' New Edition, including many New Examples, with 124 Woodcuts. Fcp. 8vo. 6s.

Bourne's Examples of Modern Steam, Air, and Gas Engines of the most Approved Types, as employed for Pumping, for Driving Machinery, for Locomotion, and for Agriculture, minutely and practically described. In course of publication, to be completed in Twenty-four Parts, price 2s. 6d. each, forming One Volume, with about 50 Plates and 400 Woodcuts.

A Treatise on the Screw Propeller, Screw Vessels, and Screw Engines, as adapted for purposes of Peace and War. By JOHN BOURNE, C.E. Third Edition, with 54 Plates and 287 Woodcuts. Quarto, 63s.

Handbook of the Steam Engine. By JOHN BOURNE, C.E. forming a KEY to the Author's Catechism of the Steam Engine. With 67 Woodcuts. Fcp. 9s.

A History of the Machine-Wrought Hosiery and Lace Manufactures. By WILLIAM FELKIN, F.L.S. F.S.S. With several Illustrations. Royal 8vo. 21s.

Mitchell's Manual of Practical Assaying. Third Edition for the most part re-written, with all the recent Discoveries incorporated. By W. CROOKES, F.R.S. With 188 Woodcuts. 8vo. 28s.

Reimann's Handbook of Aniline and its Derivatives; a Treatise on the Manufacture of Aniline and Aniline Colours. Revised and edited by WILLIAM CROOKES, F.R.S. 8vo. with 5 Woodcuts, 10s. 6d.

On the Manufacture of Beet-Root Sugar in England and Ireland. By WILLIAM CROOKES, F.R.S. With 11 Woodcuts. 8vo. 8s. 6d.

Practical Treatise on Metallurgy, adapted from the last German Edition of Professor KERL's *Metallurgy* by W. CROOKES, F.R.S. &c. and E. RÖHRIG, Ph.D. M.E. 3 vols. 8vo. with 625 Woodcuts, price £4 19s.

The Art of Perfumery; the History and Theory of Odours, and the Methods of Extracting the Aromas of Plants. By Dr. PIESSE, F.C.S. Third Edition, with 53 Woodcuts. Crown 8vo. 10s. 6d.

Chemical, Natural, and Physical Magic, for Juveniles during the Holidays. By the same Author. With 38 Woodcuts. Fcp. 6s.

Loudon's Encyclopædia of Agri-culture: comprising the Laying-out, Improvement, and Management of Landed Property, and the Cultivation and Economy of the Productions of Agriculture. With 1,100 Woodcuts. 8vo. 21s.

Loudon's Encyclopædia of Gardening: comprising the Theory and Practice of Horticulture, Floriculture, Arboriculture, and Landscape Gardening. With 1,000 Woodcuts. 8vo. 21s.

Bayldon's Art of Valuing Rents and Tillages, and Claims of Tenants upon Quitting Farms, both at Michaelmas and Lady-Day. Eighth Edition, revised by J. C. MORTON. 8vo. 10s. 6d.

Religious and *Moral Works*.

An Exposition of the 39 Articles, Historical and Doctrinal. By E. HAROLD BROWNE, D.D. Lord Bishop of Ely. Eighth Edition. 8vo. 16s.

Examination-Questions on Bishop Browne's Exposition of the Articles. By the Rev. J. GORLE, M.A. Fcp. 3s. 6d.

The Life and Epistles of St. Paul. By the Rev. W. J. CONYBEARE, M.A. and the Very Rev. J. S. HOWSON, D.D. Dean of Chester.

LIBRARY EDITION, with all the Original Illustrations, Maps, Landscapes on Steel, Woodcuts, &c. 2 vols. 4to. 48s.

INTERMEDIATE EDITION, with a Selection of Maps, Plates, and Woodcuts. 2 vols. square crown 8vo. 31s. 6d.

STUDENT'S EDITION, revised and condensed, with 46 Illustrations and Maps. 1 vol. crown 8vo. 9s.

The Voyage and Shipwreck of St. Paul; with Dissertations on the Ships and Navigation of the Ancients. By JAMES SMITH, F.R.S. Crown 8vo. Charts, 10s. 6d.

Evidence of the Truth of the Christian Religion derived from the Literal Fulfilment of Prophecy. By ALEXANDER KEITH, D.D. 37th Edition, with numerous Plates, in square 8vo. 12s. 6d.; also the 39th Edition, in post 8vo. with 5 Plates, 6s.

The History and Destiny of the World and of the Church, according to Scripture. By the same Author. Square 8vo. with 40 Illustrations, 10s.

The History and Literature of the Israelites, according to the Old Testament and the Apocrypha. By C. DE ROTHSCHILD and A. DE ROTHSCHILD. With 2 Maps. 2 vols. post 8vo. price 12s. 6d.
VOL. I. *The Historical Books,* 7s. 6d.
VOL. II. *The Prophetic and Poetical Writings,* price 5s.

Ewald's History of Israel to the Death of Moses. Translated from the German. Edited, with a Preface and an Appendix, by RUSSELL MARTINEAU, M.A. Second Edition. 2 vols. 8vo. 24s.

History of the Karaite Jews. By WILLIAM HARRIS RULE, D.D. Post 8vo. price 7s. 6d.

The Life of Margaret Mary Hallahan, better known in the religious world by the name of Mother Margaret. By her RELIGIOUS CHILDREN. Second Edition. 8vo. with Portrait, 10s.

The See of Rome in the Middle Ages. By the Rev. OSWALD J. REICHEL, B.C.L. and M.A. 8vo. 18s.

The Evidence for the Papacy as derived from the Holy Scriptures and from Primitive Antiquity. By the Hon. COLIN LINDSAY. 8vo. 12s. 6d.

The Pontificate of Pius the Ninth; being the Third Edition, enlarged and continued, of 'Rome and its Ruler.' By J. F. MAGUIRE, M.P. Post 8vo. Portrait, price 12s. 6d.

Ignatius Loyola and the Early Jesuits. By STEWART ROSE. New Edition, in the press.

An Introduction to the Study of the New Testament, Critical, Exegetical, and Theological. By the Rev. S. DAVIDSON, D.D. LL.D. 2 vols. 8vo. 30s.

A Critical and Grammatical Commentary on St. Paul's Epistles. By C. J. ELLICOTT, D.D. Lord Bishop of Gloucester and Bristol. 8vo.
Galatians, Fourth Edition, 8s. 6d.
Ephesians, Fourth Edition, 8s. 6d.
Pastoral Epistles, Fourth Edition, 10s. 6d.
Philippians, Colossians, and Philemon, Third Edition, 10s. 6d.
Thessalonians, Third Edition, 7s. 6d.

Historical Lectures on the Life of Our Lord Jesus Christ: being the Hulsean Lectures for 1859. By C. J. ELLICOTT, D.D. Lord Bishop of Gloucester and Bristol. Fifth Edition. 8vo. 12s.

The Greek Testament; with Notes, Grammatical and Exegetical. By the Rev. W. WEBSTER, M.A. and the Rev. W. F. WILKINSON, M.A. 2 vols. 8vo. £2 4s.

Horne's Introduction to the Critical Study and Knowledge of the Holy Scriptures. Twelfth Edition; with 4 Maps and 22 Woodcuts and Facsimiles. 4 vols. 8vo. 42s.
Compendious Introduction to the Study of the Bible. Edited by the Rev. JOHN AYRE, M.A. With Maps, &c. Post 8vo. 6s.

The Treasury of Bible Knowledge; being a Dictionary of the Books, Persons, Places, Events, and other Matters of which mention is made in Holy Scripture. By Rev. J. AYRE, M.A. With Maps, 15 Plates, and numerous Woodcuts. Fcp. 6s.

Every-day Scripture Difficulties explained and illustrated. By J. E. PRESCOTT, M.A. VOL. I. *Matthew* and *Mark;* VOL. II. *Luke* and *John.* 2 vols. 8vo. price 9s. each.

The Pentateuch and Book of Joshua Critically Examined. By the Right Rev. J. W. COLENSO, D.D. Lord Bishop of Natal. Crown 8vo. price 6s.

The Four Cardinal Virtues (Fortitude, Justice, Prudence, Temperance) in relation to the Public and Private Life of Catholics: Six Sermons for the Day. With Preface, Appendices, &c. By the Rev. ORBY SHIPLEY, M.A. Crown 8vo. with Frontispiece, 7s. 6d.

The Formation of Christendom. By T. W. ALLIES. PARTS I. and II. 8vo. price 12s. each.

Four Discourses of Chrysostom, chiefly on the parable of the Rich Man and Lazarus. Translated by F. ALLEN, B.A. Crown 8vo. 3s. 6d.

Christendom's Divisions; a Philosophical Sketch of the Divisions of the Christian Family in East and West. By EDMUND S. FFOULKES. Post 8vo. 7s. 6d.

Christendom's Divisions, PART II. *Greeks and Latins.* By the same Author. Post 8vo. 15s.

The Hidden Wisdom of Christ and the Key of Knowledge; or, History of the Apocrypha. By ERNEST DE BUNSEN. 2 vols. 8vo. 28s.

The Keys of St. Peter; or, the House of Rechab, connected with the History of Symbolism and Idolatry. By the same Author. 8vo. 14s.

The Power of the Soul over the Body. By GEO. MOORE, M.D. M.R.C.P.L. &c. Sixth Edition. Crown 8vo. 8s. 6d.

The Types of Genesis briefly considered as Revealing the Development of Human Nature. By ANDREW JUKES. Second Edition. Crown 8vo. 7s. 6d.

The Second Death and the Restitution of All Things, with some Preliminary Remarks on the Nature and Inspiration of Holy Scripture. By the same Author. Second Edition. Crown 8vo. 3s. 6d.

Thoughts for the Age. BY ELIZABETH M. SEWELL, Author of 'Amy Herbert.' New Edition. Fcp. 8vo. price 5s.

Passing Thoughts on Religion. By the same Author. Fcp. 5s.

Self-examination before Confirmation. By the same Author. 32mo. 1s. 6d.

Thoughts for the Holy Week, for Young Persons. By the same Author. New Edition. Fcp. 8vo. 2s.

Readings for a Month Preparatory to Confirmation from Writers of the Early and English Church. By the same. Fcp. 4s.

Readings for Every Day in Lent, compiled from the Writings of Bishop JEREMY TAYLOR. By the same Author. Fcp. 5s.

Preparation for the Holy Communion; the Devotions chiefly from the works of JEREMY TAYLOR. By the same. 32mo. 3s.

Principles of Education drawn from Nature and Revelation, and Applied to Female Education in the Upper Classes. By the same Author. 2 vols. fcp. 12s. 6d.

Bishop Jeremy Taylor's Entire Works: with Life by BISHOP HEBER. Revised and corrected by the Rev. C. P. EDEN. 10 vols. £5 5s.

England and Christendom. By ARCHBISHOP MANNING, D.D. Post 8vo. price 10s. 6d.

The Wife's Manual; or, Prayers, Thoughts, and Songs on Several Occasions of a Matron's Life. By the Rev. W. CALVERT, M.A. Crown 8vo. 10s. 6d.

Singers and Songs of the Church: being Biographical Sketches of the Hymn-Writers in all the principal Collections; with Notes on their Psalms and Hymns. By JOSIAH MILLER, M.A. Second Edition, enlarged. Post 8vo. 10s. 6d.

'Spiritual Songs' for the Sundays and Holidays throughout the Year. By J. S. B. MONSELL, LL.D. Vicar of Egham and Rural Dean. Fourth Edition, Sixth Thousand. Fcp. price 4s. 6d.

The Beatitudes. By the same Author. Third Edition, revised. Fcp. 3s. 6d.

His Presence not his Memory, 1855. By the same Author, in memory of his SON. Sixth Edition. 16mo. 1s.

Lyra Germanica, translated from the German by Miss C. WINKWORTH. FIRST SERIES, the *Christian Year*, Hymns for the Sundays and Chief Festivals of the Church; SECOND SERIES, the *Christian Life.* Fcp. 8vo. price 3s. 6d. each SERIES.

Lyra Eucharistica; Hymns and Verses on the Holy Communion, Ancient and Modern: with other Poems. Edited by the Rev. ORBY SHIPLEY, M.A. Second Edition. Fcp. 5s.

Shipley's Lyra Messianica. Fcp. 5s.

Shipley's Lyra Mystica. Fcp. 5s.

Endeavours after the Christian Life: Discourses. By JAMES MARTINEAU. Fourth Edition, carefully revised. Post 8vo. 7s. 6d.

Invocation of Saints and Angels; for the use of Members of the English Church. Edited by the Rev. ORBY SHIPLEY, M.A. 24mo. 3s. 6d.

Travels, Voyages, &c.

The Playground of Europe. By LESLIE STEPHEN, late President of the Alpine Club. Post 8vo. with Frontispiece. [*Just ready.*

Westward by Rail: the New Route to the East. By W. F. RAE. Post 8vo. with Map, price 10s. 6d.

Travels in the Central Caucasus and Bashan, including Visits to Ararat and Tabreez and Ascents of Kazbek and Elbruz. By DOUGLAS W. FRESHFIELD. Square crown 8vo. with Maps, &c., 18s.

Cadore or Titian's Country. By JOSIAH GILBERT, one of the Authors of the 'Dolomite Mountains.' With Map, Facsimile, and 40 Illustrations. Imp.8vo.31s.6d.

Zigzagging amongst Dolomites; with more than 300 Illustrations by the Author. By the Author of 'How we Spent the Summer.' Oblong 4to. price 15s.

The Dolomite Mountains. Excursions through Tyrol, Carinthia, Carniola, and Friuli. By J. GILBERT and G. C. CHURCHILL, F.R.G.S. With numerous Illustrations. Square crown 8vo. 21s.

Pilgrimages in the Pyrenees and Landes. By DENYS SHYNE LAWLOR. Crown 8vo. with Frontispiece and Vignette, price 15s.

How we Spent the Summer; or, a Voyage en Zigzag in Switzerland and Tyrol with some Members of the ALPINE CLUB. Third Edition, re-drawn. In oblong 4to. with about 300 Illustrations, 15s.

Pictures in Tyrol and Elsewhere. From a Family Sketch-Book. By the same Author. Second Edition. 4to. with many Illustrations, 21s.

Beaten Tracks; or, Pen and Pencil Sketches in Italy. By the same Author. With 42 Plates of Sketches. 8vo. 16s.

The Alpine Club Map of the Chain of Mont Blanc, from an actual Survey in 1863—1864. By A. ADAMS-REILLY, F.R.G.S. M.A.C. In Chromolithography on extra stout drawing paper 28in. × 17in. price 10s. or mounted on canvas in a folding case, 12s. 6d.

England to Delhi; a Narrative of Indian Travel. By JOHN MATHESON, Glasgow. With Map and 82 Woodcut Illustrations. 4to. 31s. 6d.

History of Discovery in our Australasian Colonies, Australia, Tasmania, and New Zealand, from the Earliest Date to the Present Day. By WILLIAM HOWITT. 2 vols. 8vo. with 3 Maps, 20s.

The Capital of the Tycoon; a Narrative of a 3 Years' Residence in Japan. By Sir RUTHERFORD ALCOCK, K.C.B. 2 vols. 8vo. with numerous Illustrations, 42s.

Guide to the Pyrenees, for the use of Mountaineers. By CHARLES PACKE. Second Edition, with Maps, &c. and Appendix. Crown 8vo. 7s. 6d.

The Alpine Guide. By JOHN BALL, M.R.I.A. late President of the Alpine Club. Post 8vo. with Maps and other Illustrations.
Guide to the **Eastern Alps,** price 10s. 6d.
Guide to the **Western Alps,** including Mont Blanc, Monte Rosa, Zermatt, &c. price 6s. 6d.
Guide to the **Central Alps,** including all the Oberland District, price 7s. 6d.
Introduction on Alpine Travelling in general, and on the Geology of the Alps, price 1s. Either of the Three Volumes or Parts of the *Alpine Guide* may be had with this INTRODUCTION prefixed, price 1s. extra.

Roma Sotterranea; or, an Account of the Roman Catacombs, especially of the Cemetery of San Callisto. Compiled from the Works of Commendatore G. B. DE ROSSI, by the Rev. J. S. NORTHCOTE, D.D. and the Rev. W. B. BROWNLOW. With Plans and numerous other Illustrations. 8vo. 31s. 6d.

Memorials of London and London Life in the 13th, 14th, and 15th Centuries; being a Series of Extracts, Local, Social, and Political, from the Archives of the City of London, A.D. 1276-1419. Selected, translated, and edited by H. T. RILEY, M.A. Royal 8vo. 21s.

Commentaries on the History, Constitution, and Chartered Franchises of the City of London. By GEORGE NORTON, formerly one of the Common Pleaders of the City of London. Third Edition. 8vo. 14s.

The Northern Heights of London; or, Historical Associations of Hampstead, Highgate, Muswell Hill, Hornsey, and Islington. By WILLIAM HOWITT. With about 40 Woodcuts. Square crown 8vo. 21s.

The Rural Life of England. By the same Author. With Woodcuts by Bewick and Williams. Medium, 8vo. 12s. 6d.

Visits to Remarkable Places:
Old Halls, Battle-Fields, and Scenes illustrative of striking Passages in English History and Poetry. By the same Author. 2 vols. square crown 8vo. with Wood Engravings, 25s.

Narrative of the Euphrates Expedition carried on by Order of the British Government during the years 1835, 1836, and 1837. By General F. R. CHESNEY, F.R.S. With 2 Maps, 45 Plates, and 16 Woodcuts. 8vo. 24s.

Works of Fiction.

Lothair. By the Right Hon. B. DISRAELI, Cabinet Edition (the Eighth), complete in One Volume, with a Portrait of the Author, and a new General Preface. Crown 8vo. price 6s.—By the same Author, Cabinet Editions, revised, uniform with the above:—

CONINGSBY, 6s.	ALROY; IXION; the
SYBIL, 6s.	INFERNAL MAR-
TANCRED, 6s.	RIAGE; and PO-
VENETIA, 6s.	PANILLA. Price 6s.
HENRIETTA TEMPLE, 6s.	YOUNG DUKE and COUNT ALARCOS, 6s.
CONTARINI FLEMING and RISE OF ISKANDER, 6s.	VIVIAN GREY, 6s.

The Modern Novelist's Library.
Each Work, in crown 8vo. complete in a Single Volume:—

MELVILLE'S GLADIATORS, 2s. boards; 2s. 6d. cloth.
———— GOOD FOR NOTHING, 2s. boards; 2s. 6d. cloth.
———— HOLMBY HOUSE, 2s. boards; 2s. 6d. cloth.
———— INTERPRETER, 2s. boards; 2s. 6d. cloth.
———— QUEEN'S MARIES, 2s. boards; 2s. 6d. cloth.
TROLLOPE'S WARDEN, 1s. 6d. boards; 2s. cloth.
———— BARCHESTER TOWERS, 2s. boards; 2s. 6d. cloth.
BRAMLEY-MOORE'S SIX SISTERS OF THE VALLEYS, 2s. boards; 2s. 6d. cloth.

Stories and Tales by the Author of 'Amy Herbert,' uniform Edition :—

AMY HERBERT, 2s. 6d.	KATHARINE ASHTON, 3s. 6d.
GERTRUDE, 2s. 6d.	MARGARET PERCIVAL, 5s.
EARL'S DAUGHTER, 2s. 6d.	LANETON PARSONAGE, 4s. 6d.
EXPERIENCE OF LIFE, 2s. 6d.	URSULA, 4s. 6d.
CLEVE HALL, 3s. 6d.	
IVORS, 3s. 6d.	

A Glimpse of the World. Fcp. 7s. 6d.
Journal of a Home Life. Post 8vo. 9s. 6d.
After Life; a Sequel to the 'Journal of a Home Life.' Post 8vo. 10s. 6d.

A Visit to my Discontented Cousin. Reprinted, with some Additions, from *Fraser's Magazine.* Crown 8vo. price 7s. 6d.

Ierne; a Tale. By W. STEUART TRENCH, Author of 'Realities of Irish Life.' 2 vols post 8vo. [*Just ready.*

Three Weddings. By the Author of 'Dorothy,' &c. Fcp. 8vo. 5s.

The Giant; a Witch's Story for English Boys. Edited by ELIZABETH M. SEWELL, Author of 'Amy Herbert,' &c. Fcp. 8vo. price 5s.

Uncle Peter's Fairy Tale for the XIXth Century. By the same Author and Editor. Fcp. 8vo. 7s. 6d.

Vikram and the Vampire; or, Tales of Hindu Devilry. Adapted by RICHARD F. BURTON, F.R.G.S. &c. With 33 Illustrations. Crown 8vo. 9s.

Becker's Gallus; or, Roman Scenes of the Time of Augustus. Post 8vo. 7s. 6d.

Becker's Charicles: Illustrative of Private Life of the Ancient Greeks. Post 8vo. 7s. 6d.

Tales of Ancient Greece. By GEORGE W. COX, M.A. late Scholar of Trin. Coll. Oxford. Being a collective Edition of the Author's Classical Series and Tales, complete in One Volume. Crown 8vo. 6s. 6d.

Cabinet Edition of Novels and Tales by G. J. WHYTE MELVILLE:—

THE GLADIATORS, 5s.	HOLMBY HOUSE, 5s.
DIGBY GRAND, 5s.	GOOD FOR NOTHING, 6s.
KATE COVENTRY, 5s.	QUEEN'S MARIES, 6s.
GENERAL BOUNCE, 5s.	THE INTERPRETER, 5s.

Our Children's Story. By One of their Gossips. By the Author of 'Voyage en Zigzag,' &c. Small 4to. with Sixty Illustrations by the Author, price 10s. 6d.

Wonderful Stories from Norway, Sweden, and Iceland. Adapted and arranged by JULIA GODDARD. With an Introductory Essay by the Rev. G. W. COX, M.A. and Six Illustrations. Square post 8vo. 6s.

c

Poetry and The Drama.

Thomas Moore's Poetical Works, the only Editions containing the Author's last Copyright Additions:—
Shamrock Edition, price 3s. 6d.
Ruby Edition, with Portrait, 6s.
Cabinet Edition, 10 vols. fcp. 8vo. 35s.
People's Edition, Portrait, &c. 10s. 6d.
Library Edition, Portrait & Vignette, 14s.

Moore's Lalla Rookh, Tenniel's Edition, with 68 Wood Engravings from Original Drawings and other Illustrations. Fcp. 4to. 21s.

Moore's Irish Melodies, Maclise's Edition, with 161 Steel Plates from Original Drawings. Super-royal 8vo. 31s. 6d.

Miniature Edition of Moore's Irish Melodies, with Maclise's Illustrations (as above), reduced in Lithography. Imp. 16mo. 10s. 6d.

Southey's Poetical Works, with the Author's last Corrections and copyright Additions. Library Edition. Medium 8vo. with Portrait and Vignette, 14s.

Lays of Ancient Rome; with *Ivry* and the *Armada*. By the Right Hon. LORD MACAULAY. 16mo. 4s. 6d.

Lord Macaulay's Lays of Ancient Rome. With 90 Illustrations on Wood, Original and from the Antique, from Drawings by G. SCHARF. Fcp. 4to. 21s.

Miniature Edition of Lord Macaulay's Lays of Ancient Rome, with Scharf's Illustrations (as above) reduced in Lithography. Imp. 16mo. 10s. 6d.

Goldsmith's Poetical Works, Illustrated with Wood Engravings from Designs by Members of the ETCHING CLUB. Imp. 16mo. 7s. 6d.

Poems of Bygone Years. Edited by the Author of 'Amy Herbert.' Fcp. 8vo. 5s.

Poems, Descriptive and Lyrical. By THOMAS COX. New Edition. Fcp. 8vo. price 5s.

'Show moral propriety, mental culture, and no slight acquaintance with the technicalities of song.'
ATHENÆUM.

Madrigals, Songs, and Sonnets. By JOHN ARTHUR BLAIKIE and EDMUND WILLIAM GOSSE. Fcp. 8vo. price 5s.

Poems. By JEAN INGELOW. Fifteenth Edition. Fcp. 8vo. 5s.

Poems by Jean Ingelow. With nearly 100 Illustrations by Eminent Artists, engraved on Wood by DALZIEL Brothers. Fcp. 4to. 21s.

Mopsa the Fairy. By JEAN INGELOW. With Eight Illustrations engraved on Wood. Fcp. 8vo. 6s.

A Story of Doom, and other Poems. By JEAN INGELOW. Third Edition. Fcp. price 5s.

Glaphyra, and other Poems. By FRANCIS REYNOLDS, Author of 'Alice Rushton.' 16mo. 5s.

Bowdler's Family Shakspeare, cheaper Genuine Edition, complete in 1 vol. large type, with 36 Woodcut Illustrations, price 14s. or in 6 pocket vols. 3s. 6d. each.

Arundines Cami. Collegit atque edidit H. DRURY, M.A. Editio Sexta, curavit H. J. HODGSON, M.A. Crown 8vo. price 7s. 6d.

Horatii Opera, Pocket Edition, with carefully corrected Text, Marginal References, and Introduction. Edited by the Rev. J. E. YONGE, M.A. Square 18mo. 4s. 6d.

Horatii Opera, Library Edition, with Copious English Notes, Marginal References and Various Readings. Edited by the Rev. J. E. YONGE, M.A. 8vo. 21s.

The Æneid of Virgil Translated into English Verse. By JOHN CONINGTON, M.A. Corpus Professor of Latin in the University of Oxford. New Edition. Crown 8vo. 9s.

The Story of Sir Richard Whittington, Thrice Lord Mayor of London, A.D. 1397, 1406-7, and 1419. Written in Verse and Illustrated by E. CARR. With Eleven Plates. Royal 4to. 21s.

Hunting Songs and Miscellaneous Verses. By R. E. EGERTON WARBURTON. Second Edition. Fcp. 8vo. 5s.

Works by Edward Yardley:—
FANTASTIC STORIES, fcp. 3s. 6d.
MELUSINE AND OTHER POEMS, fcp. 5s.
HORACE'S ODES TRANSLATED INTO ENGLISH VERSE, crown 8vo. 6s.
SUPPLEMENTARY STORIES AND POEMS, fcp. 3s. 6d.

Rural Sports, &c.

Encyclopædia of Rural Sports; a Complete Account, Historical, Practical, and Descriptive, of Hunting, Shooting, Fishing, Racing, &c. By D. P. BLAINE. With above 600 Woodcuts (20 from Designs by JOHN LEECH). 8vo. 21s.

The Dead Shot, or Sportsman's Complete Guide; a Treatise on the Use of the Gun, Dog-breaking, Pigeon-shooting, &c. By MARKSMAN. Fcp. with Plates, 5s.

A Book on Angling: being a Complete Treatise on the Art of Angling in every branch, including full Illustrated Lists of Salmon Flies. By FRANCIS FRANCIS. Second Edition, with Portrait and 15 other Plates, plain and coloured. Post 8vo. 15s.

Wilcocks's Sea-Fisherman: comprising the Chief Methods of Hook and Line Fishing in the British and other Seas, a glance at Nets, and remarks on Boats and Boating. Second Edition, enlarged, with 80 Woodcuts. Post 8vo. 12s. 6d.

The Fly-Fisher's Entomology. By ALFRED RONALDS. With coloured Representations of the Natural and Artificial Insect. Sixth Edition, with 20 coloured Plates. 8vo. 14s.

The Book of the Roach. By GREVILLE FENNELL, of 'The Field.' Fcp. 8vo. price 2s. 6d.

Blaine's Veterinary Art: a Treatise on the Anatomy, Physiology, and Curative Treatment of the Diseases of the Horse, Neat Cattle, and Sheep. Seventh Edition, revised and enlarged by C. STEEL. 8vo. with Plates and Woodcuts, 18s.

Horses and Stables. By Colonel F. FITZWYGRAM, XV. the King's Hussars. Pp. 624; with 24 Plates of Illustrations, containing very numerous Figures engraved on Wood. 8vo. 15s.

Youatt on the Horse. Revised and enlarged by W. WATSON, M.R.C.V.S. 8vo. with numerous Woodcuts, 12s. 6d.

Youatt on the Dog. (By the same Author.) 8vo. with numerous Woodcuts, 6s.

The Horse's Foot, and how to keep it Sound. By W. MILES, Esq. Ninth Edition, with Illustrations. Imp. 8vo. 12s. 6d.

A Plain Treatise on Horse-shoeing. By the same Author. Sixth Edition, post 8vo. with Illustrations, 2s. 6d.

Stables and Stable Fittings. By the same. Imp. 8vo. with 13 Plates, 15s.

Remarks on Horses' Teeth, addressed to Purchasers. By the same. Post 8vo. 1s. 6d.

Robbins's Cavalry Catechism; or, Instructions on Cavalry Exercise and Field Movements, Brigade Movements, Out-post Duty, Cavalry supporting Artillery, Artillery attached to Cavalry. 12mo. 5s.

The Dog in Health and Disease. By STONEHENGE. With 70 Wood Engravings. New Edition. Square crown 8vo. 10s. 6d.

The Greyhound. By the same Author. Revised Edition, with 24 Portraits of Greyhounds. Square crown 8vo. 10s. 6d.

The Ox, his Diseases and their Treatment; with an Essay on Parturition in the Cow. By J. R. DOBSON, M.R.C.V.S. Crown 8vo. with Illustrations, 7s. 6d.

Commerce, Navigation, and Mercantile Affairs.

The Elements of Banking. By HENRY DUNNING MACLEOD, M.A. of Trinity College, Cambridge, and of the Inner Temple, Barrister-at-Law. Post 8vo.
[*Nearly ready.*

The Law of Nations Considered as Independent Political Communities. By Sir TRAVERS TWISS, D.C.L. 2 vols. 8vo. 30s. or separately, PART I. *Peace,* 12s. PART II. *War,* 18s.

The Theory and Practice of Banking. By HENRY DUNNING MACLEOD, M.A. Barrister-at-Law. Second Edition. entirely remodelled. 2 vols. 8vo. 30s.

M'Culloch's Dictionary, Practical, Theoretical, and Historical, of Commerce and Commercial Navigation. New Edition, revised throughout and corrected to the Present Time; with a Biographical Notice of the Author. Edited by H. G. REID, Secretary to Mr. M'Culloch for many years. 8vo. price 63s. cloth.

Works of Utility and General Information.

Modern Cookery for Private Families, reduced to a System of Easy Practice in a Series of carefully-tested Receipts. By ELIZA ACTON. Newly revised and enlarged; with 8 Plates, Figures, and 150 Woodcuts. Fcp. 6s.

A Practical Treatise on Brewing; with Formulæ for Public Brewers, and Instructions for Private Families. By W. BLACK. Fifth Edition. 8vo. 10s. 6d.

Chess Openings. By F. W. LONGMAN, Balliol College, Oxford. Fcp. 8vo. 2s. 6d.

The Cabinet Lawyer; a Popular Digest of the Laws of England, Civil, Criminal, and Constitutional. 25th Edition; with Supplements of the Acts of the Parliamentary Session of 1870. Fcp. 10s. 6d.

The Philosophy of Health; or, an Exposition of the Physiological and Sanitary Conditions conducive to Human Longevity and Happiness. By SOUTHWOOD SMITH, M.D. Eleventh Edition, revised and enlarged; with 113 Woodcuts. 8vo. 7s. 6d.

Maunder's Treasury of Knowledge and Library of Reference: comprising an English Dictionary and Grammar, Universal Gazetteer, Classical Dictionary, Chronology, Law Dictionary, Synopsis of the Peerage, Useful Tables, &c. Fcp. 6s.

Hints to Mothers on the Management of their Health during the Period of Pregnancy and in the Lying-in Room. By T. BULL, M.D. Fcp. 5s.

The Maternal Management of Children in Health and Disease. By THOMAS BULL, M.D. Fcp. 5s.

How to Nurse Sick Children; containing Directions which may be found of service to all who have charge of the Young. By CHARLES WEST, M.D. Second Edition. Fcp. 8vo. 1s. 6d.

Notes on Hospitals. By FLORENCE NIGHTINGALE. Third Edition, enlarged; with 13 Plans. Post 4to. 18s.

Pewtner's Comprehensive Specifier; a Guide to the Practical Specification of every kind of Building-Artificer's Work: with Forms of Building Conditions and Agreements, an Appendix, Foot-Notes, and Index. Edited by W. YOUNG, Architect. Crown 8vo. 6s.

Tidd Pratt's Law relating to Benefit Building Societies; with Practical Observations on the Act and all the Cases decided thereon, also a Form of Rules and Forms of Mortgages. Fcp. 3s. 6d.

Collieries and Colliers: a Handbook of the Law and Leading Cases relating thereto. By J. C. FOWLER, of the Inner Temple, Barrister, Stipendiary Magistrate. Second Edition. Fcp. 8vo. 7s. 6d.

Willich's Popular Tables for Ascertaining the Value of Lifehold, Leasehold, and Church Property, Renewal Fines, &c.; the Public Funds; Annual Average Price and Interest on Consols from 1731 to 1867; Chemical, Geographical, Astronomical, Trigonometrical Tables, &c. Post 8vo. 10s.

Coulthart's Decimal Interest Tables at Twenty-four Different Rates not exceeding Five per Cent. Calculated for the use of Bankers. To which are added Commission Tables at One-eighth and One-fourth per Cent. 8vo. 15s.

Periodical Publications.

The Edinburgh Review, or Critical Journal, published Quarterly in January, April, July, and October. 8vo. price 6s. each Number.

Notes on Books: An Analysis of the Works published during each Quarter by Messrs. LONGMANS & Co. The object is to enable Bookbuyers to obtain such information regarding the various works as is usually afforded by tables of contents and explanatory prefaces. 4to. Quarterly. *Gratis.*

Fraser's Magazine. Edited by JAMES ANTHONY FROUDE, M.A. New Series, published on the 1st of each Month. 8vo. price 2s. 6d. each Number.

The Alpine Journal: A Record of Mountain Adventure and Scientific Observation. By Members of the Alpine Club. Edited by LESLIE STEPHEN. Published Quarterly, May 31, Aug. 31, Nov. 30, Feb. 28. 8vo. price 1s. 6d. each No.

INDEX.

ACTON's Modern Cookery	20
ALCOCK's Residence in Japan	16
ALLIES on Formation of Christendom	14
ALLEN's Discourses of Chrysostom	14
Alpine Guide (The)	16
—— Journal	20
ALTHAUS on Medical Electricity	10
ARNOLD's Manual of English Literature	6
ARNOTT's Elements of Physics	8
Arundines Cami	18
Autumn Holidays of a Country Parson	6
AYRE's Treasury of Bible Knowledge	14
BACON's Essays by WHATELY	5
—— Life and Letters, by SPEDDING	4
—— Works	5
BAIN's Mental and Moral Science	7
—— on the Emotions and Will	7
—— on the Senses and Intellect	7
—— on the Study of Character	7
BALL's Guide to the Central Alps	16
—— Guide to the Western Alps	16
—— Guide to the Eastern Alps	16
BARING's Staff College Essays	6
BAYLDON's Rents and Tillages	13
Beaten Tracks	16
BECKER's *Charicles* and *Gallus*	17
BENFEY's Sanskrit-English Dictionary	6
BERNARD on British Neutrality	1
BERWICK's Forces of the Universe	8
BLACK's Treatise on Brewing	20
BLACKLEY's Word-Gossip	7
—— German-English Dictionary	6
BLACKIE and GOSSE's Poems	18
BLAINE's Rural Sports	19
—— Veterinary Art	19
BOURNE on Screw Propeller	13
—— 's Catechism of the Steam Engine	13
—— Examples of Modern Engines	13
—— Handbook of Steam Engine	13
—— Treatise on the Steam Engine	13
—— Improvements in the same	13
BOWDLER's Family SHAKSPEARE	18
BRAMLEY-MOORE's Six Sisters of the Valley	17
BRANDE's Dictionary of Science, Literature, and Art	10
BRAY's (C.) Education of the Feelings	7
—— Philosophy of Necessity	7
—— On Force	7
BROWNE's Exposition of the 39 Articles	13
BRUNEL's Life of BRUNEL	3
BUCKLE's History of Civilisation	2
BULL's Hints to Mothers	20
—— Maternal Management of Children	20
BUNSEN's God in History	3
—— Memoirs	4

BUNSEN (E. De) on Apocrypha	15
—— 's Keys of St. Peter	15
BURKE's Vicissitudes of Families	4
BURTON's Christian Church	3
—— Vikram and the Vampire	17
Cabinet Lawyer	20
CALVERT's Wife's Manual	15
CARR's Sir R. WHITTINGTON	18
CATES's Biographical Dictionary	4
CATS and FARLIE's Moral Emblems	12
Changed Aspects of Unchanged Truths	6
CHESNEY's Euphrates Expedition	17
—— Indian Polity	2
—— Waterloo Campaign	2
CHESNEY's and REEVE's Military Essays	2
CHILD's Physiological Essays	11
Chorale Book for England	11
CLOUGH's Lives from Plutarch	2
COLENSO (Bishop) on Pentateuch and Book of Joshua	14
Commonplace Philosopher in Town and Country	6
CONINGTON's Translation of Virgil's Æneid	18
CONTANSEAU's Two French Dictionaries	6
CONYBEARE and HOWSON's Life and Epistles of St. Paul	13
COOPER's Surgical Dictionary	10
COPLAND's Dictionary of Practical Medicine	11
COTTON's (Bishop) Life	3
COULTHART's Decimal Interest Tables	20
Counsel and Comfort from a City Pulpit	6
Cox's (G. W.) Aryan Mythology	3
—— Tale of the Great Persian War	2
—— Tales of Ancient Greece	17
Cox's (T.) Poems	18
CRESY's Encyclopædia of Civil Engineering	13
Critical Essays of a Country Parson	6
CROOKES on Beet-Root Sugar	13
CULLEY's Handbook of Telegraphy	12
CUSACK's Student's History of Ireland	2
D'AUBIGNÉ's History of the Reformation in the time of CALVIN	2
DAVIDSON's Introduction to New Testament	14
Dead Shot (The), by MARKSMAN	19
DE LA RIVE's Treatise on Electricity	8
DENISON's Vice-Regal Life	1
DE TOCQUEVILLE's Democracy in America	2
DISRAELI's Lothair	17
—— Novels and Tales	17
DOBSON on the Ox	19
DOVE's Law of Storms	8
DOYLE's Fairyland	11
DYER's City of Rome	2

NEW WORKS PUBLISHED BY LONGMANS AND CO.

EASTLAKE'S Hints on Household Taste 12
———— History of Oil Painting 11
———— Life of Gibson 11
Edinburgh Review 20
EDMUNDS'S Names of Places 7
Elements of Botany 9
ELLICOTT'S Commentary on Ephesians 14
———— Lectures on Life of Christ 14
———— Commentary on Galatians 14
———————————— Pastoral Epist. 14
———————————— Philippians,&c. 14
———————————— Thessalonians 14
EWALD'S History of Israel 14

FAIRBAIRN'S Application of Cast and Wrought Iron to Building 12
———— Information for Engineers 12
———— Treatise on Mills and Millwork 12
———— Iron Shipbuilding 12
FARADAY'S Life and Letters 4
FARRAR'S Chapters on Language 5
———— Families of Speech 7
FELKIN on Hosiery & Lace Manufactures.. 13
FENNEL'S Book of the Roach 19
FFOULKES'S Christendom's Divisions 15
FITZWYGRAM on Horses and Stables 19
FORBES'S Earls of Granard 4
FOWLER'S Collieries and Colliers 20
FRANCIS'S Fishing Book 19
FRASER'S Magazine....................... 20
FRESHFIELD'S Travels in the Caucasus 16
FROUDE's History of England 1
———— Short Studies 7

GANOT'S Elementary Physics 8
GIANT (The) 17
GILBERT'S Cadore 16
———— and CHURCHILL'S Dolomites 16
GIRTIN'S House I Live In 11
GLEDSTONE'S Life of WHITEFIELD 3
GODDARD'S Wonderful Stories 17
GOLDSMITH'S Poems, Illustrated 18
GOULD's Silver Store 7
GRAHAM'S Book About Words 5
GRANT'S Ethics of Aristotle................ 5
———— Home Politics.................... 2
Graver Thoughts of a Country Parson...... 6
Gray's Anatomy............................ 11
GREENHOW on Bronchitis 10
GROVE on Correlation of Physical Forces .. 9
GURNEY'S Chapters of French History 2
GWILT's Encyclopædia of Architecture 12

HAMPDEN's (Bishop) Memorials 3
Hare on Election of Representatives 5
HARTWIG's Harmonies of Nature.......... 9
———— Polar World 9
———— Sea and its Living Wonders.... 9
———— Tropical World................. 9
HAUGHTON'S Manual of Geology 9
HERSCHEL'S Outlines of Astronomy........ 8
HEWITT on the Diseases of Women 10
HODGSON'S Time and Space................ 7
———— Theory of Practice 7
HOLMES'S Surgical Treatment of Children.. 10

HOLMES's System of Surgery 10
HOOKER and WALKER-ARNOTT'S British Flora................................... 9
HORNE'S Introduction to the Scriptures .. 14
———— Compendium of the Scriptures .. 14
How we Spent the Summer............... 16
HOWITT'S Australian Discovery............ 16
———— Northern Heights of London.... 16
———— Rural Life of England 16
———— Visits to Remarkable Places 17
HÜBNER'S Pope Sixtus 3
HUGHES'S Manual of Geography 8
HUME'S Essays 7
———— Treatise on Human Nature........ 7

IHNE's History of Rome 2
INGELOW'S Poems 18
———— Story of Doom 18
———— Mopsa 18

JAMESON'S Legends of Saints and Martyrs.. 12
———— Legends of the Madonna 12
———— Legends of the Monastic Orders 12
———— Legends of the Saviour........ 12
JOHNSTON'S Geographical Dictionary 8
JUKES on Second Death 15
———— on Types of Genesis 15

KALISCH'S Commentary on the Bible...... 5
———— Hebrew Grammar............... 5
KEITH on Destiny of the World............. 14
———— Fulfilment of Prophecy.......... 14
KERL's Metallurgy, by CROOKES and RÖHRIG 13
KIRBY and SPENCE'S Entomology.......... 9

LATHAM's English Dictionary.............. 5
———— River Plate..................... 8
LAWLOR's Pilgrimages in the Pyrenees 16
LECKY'S History of European Morals 3
———— Rationalism..................... 3
Leisure Hours in Town.................... 6
Lessons of Middle Age 6
LEWES's Biographical History of Philosophy 3
LEWIS's Letters 4
LIDDELL and SCOTT'S Greek-English Lexicon 6
———— Abridged ditto 6
Life of Man Symbolised.................... 12
———— Margaret M. Hallahan........... 14
LINDLEY and MOORE'S Treasury of Botany 9
LINDSAY's Evidence for the Papacy........ 14
LONGMAN's Edward the Third 2
———— Lectures on History of England 2
———— Chess Openings................ 20
Lord's Prayer Illustrated 11
LOUDON's Encyclopædia of Agriculture 13
———— Gardening 13
———— Plants 9
LOWNDES's Engineer's Handbook........... 12
LUBBOCK's Origin of Civilisation 9
Lyra Eucharistica 15
—— Germanica 11, 15
—— Messianica 15

NEW WORKS PUBLISHED BY LONGMANS AND CO.   23

Lyra Mystica 15
MACAULAY's (Lord) Essays 3
—————— History of England .. 1
—————— Lays of Ancient Rome 18
—————— Miscellaneous Writings 7
—————— Speeches 5
—————— Works 1
MACFARREN's Lectures on Harmony 11
MACLEOD's Elements of Political Economy 5
—————— Dictionary of Political Economy 5
—————— Elements of Banking.......... 19
—————— Theory and Practice of Banking 19
McCULLOCH's Dictionary of Commerce 19
—————— Geographical Dictionary 8
MAGUIRE's Life of Father Mathew 4
—————— PIUS IX...................... 14
MALET's Overthrow of Germanic Confederation 2
MANNING's England and Christendom 15
MARCET on the Larynx 11
MARSHALL's Physiology 11
MARSHMAN's History of India 2
—————— Life of Havelock 4
MARTINEAU's Endeavours after the Christian Life 15
MASSINGBERD's History of the Reformation 3
MATHESON's England to Delhi 16
MAUNDER's Biographical Treasury 4
—————— Geographical Treasury 8
—————— Historical Treasury 3
—————— Scientific and Literary Treasury 10
—————— Treasury of Knowledge........ 20
—————— Treasury of Natural History .. 9
MAY's Constitutional History of England.. 1
MELVILLE's Digby Grand.................. 17
—————— General Bounce 17
—————— Gladiators 17
—————— Good for Nothing 17
—————— Holmby House................. 17
—————— Interpreter 17
—————— Kate Coventry................ 17
—————— Queen's Maries 17
MENDELSSOHN's Letters 4
MERIVALE's Fall of the Roman Republic .. 2
—————— Romans under the Empire 2
MERRIFIELD and EVERS's Navigation 8
MILES on Horse's Foot and Horse Shoeing. 19
—————— on Horses' Teeth and Stables 19
MILL (J.) on the Mind 5
MILL (J. S.) on Liberty 4
—————— Subjection of Women 4
—————— on Representative Government 4
—————— on Utilitarianism 4
——'s Dissertations and Discussions 4
—————— Political Economy 4
MILL's System of Logic................. 5
—————— Hamilton's Philosophy 4
—————— Inaugural Address at St. Andrew's. 4
MILLER's Elements of Chemistry 10
—————— Hymn Writers 15
MITCHELL's Manual of Architecture 12
—————— Manual of Assaying 13
MONSELL's Beatitudes 15
—————— His Presence not his Memory.. 15
—————— 'Spiritual Songs' 15
MOORE's Irish Melodies.................. 18
—————— Lalla Rookh 18
—————— Journal and Correspondence 3
—————— Poetical Works............... 18
—————— (Dr. G.) Power of the Soul over the Body 15

MORELL's Elements of Psychology 7
MORELL's Mental Philosophy 7
MÜLLER's (Max) Chips from a German Workshop 7
—————— Lectures on the Science of Language............................... 5
—————— (K. O.) Literature of Ancient Greece 2
MURCHISON on Liver Complaints 11
MURE's Language and Literature of Greece 2

New Testament Illustrated with Wood Engravings from the Old Masters 12
NEWMAN's History of his Religious Opinions 4
NIGHTINGALE's Notes on Hospitals 20
NILSSON's Scandinavia 9
NORTHCOTE's Sanctuary of the Madonna.. 14
NORTHCOTT on Lathes and Turning 12
NORTON's City of London 16
Notes on Books............................ 20

ODLING's Animal Chemistry 10
—————— Course of Practical Chemistry .. 10
—————— Manual of Chemistry............ 10
—————— Lectures on Carbon 10
—————— Outlines of Chemistry 10
O'FLANAGAN's Irish Chancellors 4
Our Children's Story 17
OWEN's Comparative Anatomy and Physiology of Vertebrate Animals 9
—————— Lectures on the Invertebrata...... 9

PACKE's Guide to the Pyrenees 16
PAGET's Lectures on Surgical Pathology .. 10
PEREIRA's Manual of Materia Medica...... 11
PERKINS's Italian and Tuscan Sculptors .. 12
PEWTNER's Comprehensive Specifier 20
Pictures in Tyrol 16
PIESSE's Art of Perfumery 13
—— Chemical, Natural, and Physical Magic 13
PONTON's Beginning 9
PRATT's Law of Building Societies 20
PRENDERGAST's Mastery of Languages 6
PRESCOTT's Scripture Difficulties........ 14
Present-Day Thoughts, by A. K. H. B. 6
PROCTOR's Handbook of the Stars 8
—————— Saturn 8
—————— Other Worlds than Ours 8
—————— Sun.......................... 8

RAE's Westward by Rail 16
Recreations of a Country Parson 6
REICHEL's See of Rome................... 14
REILLY's Map of Mont Blanc.............. 16
REIMANN on Aniline Dyes 13
REYNOLDS's Glaphyra 18
RILEY's Memorials of London 16
RIVERS's Rose Amateur's Guide 9
ROBBINS's Cavalry Catechism 19
ROGERS's Correspondence of Greyson 7
—————— Eclipse of Faith 7
—————— Defence of Faith 7
ROGET's Thesaurus of English Words and Phrases 5
Roma Sotterranea 16

RONALDS's Fly-Fisher's Entomology 19
ROSE's Loyola 14
ROTHSCHILD's Israelites 14
ROWTON's Debater 5
RULE's Karaite Jews 14
RUSSELL on Government and Constitution 1
———'s (Earl) Speeches and Despatches 1

SANDARS's Justinian's Institutes 5
SCOTT's Lectures on the Fine Arts 11
——— Albert Durer 11
SEEBOHM's Oxford Reformers of 1498 2
SEWELL's After Life 17
——— Glimpse of the World 17
——— History of the Early Church 8
——— Journal of a Home Life 17
——— Passing Thoughts on Religion .. 15
——— Poems of Bygone Years 18
——— Preparation for Communion ... 15
——— Principles of Education 15
——— Readings for Confirmation 15
——— Readings for Lent 15
——— Examination for Confirmation .. 15
——— Stories and Tales 17
——— Thoughts for the Age 15
——— Thoughts for the Holy Week 15
SHAKSPEARE's Midsummer Night's Dream,
illustrated with Silhouettes 12
SHIPLEY's Four Cardinal Virtues 14
——— Invocation of Saints 15
SHORT's Church History 3
Smart's WALKER's English Dictionaries .. 5
SMITH's (SOUTHWOOD) Philosophy of Health 20
——— (J.) Paul's Voyage and Shipwreck 14
——— (SYDNEY) Life and Letters 3
——— Miscellaneous Works .. 7
——— Wit and Wisdom 7
SOUTHEY's Doctor 5
——— Poetical Works 18
STANLEY's History of British Birds 9
STEBBING's Analysis of MILL's Logic 5
STEPHEN's Ecclesiastical Biography 4
——— Playground of Europe 16
STIRLING's Secret of Hegel 7
——— Sir WILLIAM HAMILTON 7
STONEHENGE on the Dog 19
——— on the Greyhound 19
STRICKLAND's Tudor Princesses 4
——— Queens of England 4
Strong and Free 7
Sunday Afternoons at the Parish Church of
a Scottish University City 6

TAYLOR's History of India 2
——— (Jeremy) Works, edited by EDEN 15
THIRLWALL's History of Greece 2
THOMSON's Conspectus 11
——— Laws of Thought 5
Three Weddings 17

TODD (A.) on Parliamentary Government .. 1
——— and BOWMAN's Anatomy and Physiology of Man 11
TRENCH's Ierne 17
——— Realities of Irish Life 2
TROLLOPE's Barchester Towers 17
——— Warden 17
TWISS's Law of Nations 19
TYNDALL's Diamagnetism 8
——— Faraday as a Discoverer 4
——— Lectures on Electricity 9
——— Lectures on Light 8
——— Lectures on Sound 8
——— Heat a Mode of Motion 8
——— Essays on the Imagination in
Science 9
Uncle PETER's Fairy Tale 18
URE's Dictionary of Arts, Manufactures, and
Mines 12

VAN DER HOEVEN's Handbook of Zoology.. 9
Visit to my Discontented Cousin 17

WARBURTON's Hunting Songs 18
WATSON's Principles and Practice of Physic 10
WATTS's Dictionary of Chemistry 10
WEBB's Objects for Common Telescopes.... 8
WEBSTER & WILKINSON's Greek Testament 14
WELLINGTON's Life, by GLEIG 4
WEST on Children's Diseases 10
——— on Nursing Children 20
WHATELY's English Synonymes 5
——— Logic 5
——— Rhetoric 5
WHITE and RIDDLE's Latin Dictionaries .. 6
WILCOCKS's Sea Fisherman 19
WILLIAMS's Aristotle's Ethics 5
——— History of Wales 1
WILLIAMS on Climate of South of France.. 10
——— Consumption 11
WILLICH's Popular Tables 20
WILLIS's Principles of Mechanism 12
WINSLOW on Light 8
WOOD's (J. G.) Bible Animals 9
——— Homes without Hands 9
——— (T.) Chemical Notes 10
WOODWARD and CATES's Encyclopædia .. 3

YARDLEY's Poetical Works 18
YONGE's History of England 1
——— English-Greek Lexicons 6
——— Two Editions of Horace 18
YOUATT on the Dog 19
——— on the Horse 19

ZELLER's Socrates 3
——— Stoics, Epicureans, and Sceptics.. 3
Zigzagging amongst Dolomites 16

www.ingramcontent.com/pod-product-compliance
Lightning Source LLC
Chambersburg PA
CBHW022146300426
44115CB00006B/370